FAILURE OF CONTRACTS

# Failure of Contracts

## *Contractual, Restitutionary and Proprietary Consequences*

Edited by
FRANCIS D. ROSE
*Professor of Commercial and Common Law,
University of Buckingham*

• HART •
PUBLISHING
OXFORD
1997

Hart Publishing
Oxford
UK

Distribution in North America
by Northwestern University Press
625 Colfax Street
Evanston, Illinois
60208, USA



Hart Publishing is a specialist legal publisher based in Oxford, England.
To order further copies of this book or to request a list of other publications please write to:

Hart Publishing, 19 Whitehouse Road, Oxford, OX1 4PA
Telephone: +44 (0)1865 434459 or Fax: (0)1865 794882
e-mail: hartpub@janep.demon.co.uk

Payment may be made by cheque payable to 'Hart Publishing' or by credit card.

British Library Cataloguing in Publication Data
Data Available
ISBN 1–901362–04–3

Typeset in 10pt Sabon
by SetAll, Abingdon
Printed in Great Britain on acid-free paper
byBiddles Ltd.,
Guildford and King's Lynn

# Contents

# *Preface*

The economic and practical context of the Law of Contract is such that it will always be an active and important area of the law. This is even more so when there is change in related areas of the law and in their relationship with it. A number of such developments made it particularly timely for a conference exploring this activity in the Law of Contract and related areas, particularly the Law of Restitution. The conference was held in Cambridge in September 1996 and attracted a large international gathering of scholars. After each speaker delivered his or her paper, a commentator was invited to deliver a response. The responses themselves proved to be valuable complements to the main papers and most of them are therefore also included here. For this collection, the authors of the main papers and the responses have taken into account the valuable and wide ranging discussions stimulated by them. Readers of this volume are therefore indebted to a large number of people, not only the authors of the essays appearing here but also the chairmen of the individual sessions and all those who contributed to the ensuing discussions.

The papers in this collection range over a number of different themes. It is not intended to form a comprehensive treatise dealing systematically with all matters concerning the failure of contracts. What it does aim to do is to highlight, in different ways, different writers' perspectives on a range of key issues of contemporary interest. It begins with a central concern of contract failure: the appropriateness of the primary remedy, damages, to compensate a disappointed plaintiff, in particular the capacity of the rules on damages to accommodate plaintiffs according to whether they are in business or are consumers. The common lawyer will not be surprised that it is not just the remedies, principles and policies of the law that matter, but the facts to which they must be applied and the way in which the facts and the law are dealt with.

No matter how central they are traditionally regarded as being, satisfaction of expectations and compensation are increasingly seen as ranking with a number of options which may be available in a case of contract failure. Equity supplements the law with the possibility of specific enforcement, perhaps more likely after a recent decision of the Court of Appeal. More prominent is the possibility of reversing unjust enrichment, with a restitutionary remedy. Consideration of the different possible remedial responses to contract failure and their purposes in turn require reassessment of the aims and effects of contracts themselves, and in particular of the defendant's ability to buy his freedom to pursue more profitable opportunities elsewhere.

A significant body of recent cases has been concerned with the contractual capacity of public authorities and the effects of invalid contracts. They have raised very difficult questions, in one case requiring the litigants, together with the parties in a host of similar cases, to wait nearly a year—ironically, since the basic issue was about interest—while the House of Lords grappled with the possible solutions, their Lordships ultimately delivering a varied response. Interest is habitually sought and awarded in practice, but the underlying rules receive little attention, the issue being effectively assigned to the vagaries of statute law. The attempt to exploit the limited scope for compound interest has given rise to wide-ranging debate about equitable proprietary rights in cases of contract failure, a matter of deep concern to insolvency lawyers and raising fundamental issues in the law of trusts.

Invalidity is also a possible consequence of the competition rules of the Treaty of Rome, inviting investigation of the circumstances in which restitution is available in situations affected by the law of the European Communities, an area largely unexplored prior to the 1996 volume of the *Restitution Law Review*. It is by now trite to observe that European Community law cannot be ignored by English lawyers and that it does not simply raise discrete issues but affects the operation and evolution of the domestic law of Member States of the European Union.

Likewise, the development of the Union calls for better knowledge and understanding by members of the different domestic laws of other Member States. It is a concern of everyone interested in international trade and/or wanting a deeper understanding of different possible responses to problems common to different jurisdictions and a better appreciation of the influences on European Community Law and eventually one's own domestic law. Particular attention from the viewpoints of German and French law is given in this collection to comparative treatments of termination of contracts, the failure and renegotiation of long-term contracts and competition between the law of contract and of delict/tort. Further treatment of the tension and/or overlap between these two major divisions of the law emphasises the curious situation that, in England and Scotland, the United Kingdom contains two adjacent but traditionally different jurisdictions which have tended to coexist with little cross-fertilisation—indeed, at the time of writing the House of Lords' next task within the area of contract and restitution is a case on the conflict of laws between England and Scotland. As is noted, the temporary export of an English Roman lawyer has contributed to reinvigorating study of the Law of Restitution in Scotland, a particular contribution being made in the drafting by a Scottish Law Commissioner, in a personal capacity, of a code on the law of unjust(ified) enrichment. Its appearance coincides with the eventual publication of an abandoned proposal for a contract code for the English and Scottish Law Commissions and the recent contract codes produced by UNIDROIT and the European Contract Commission. Whatever the future of such exercises, codification is firmly back on the agenda.

Codification highlights a particular difficulty with categorising the law, thrown up by the resistance of facts to fitting neatly within a single classification, so exposing possible tension between different policies underlying different categories. One possible solution is a principle of subsidiarity, most obviously giving primacy to contract. But identifying such a possibility is simply to begin an enquiry into its scope, the different ways in which it operates in different jurisdictions and, ultimately, its desirability for one's own jurisdiction.

Indeed, a continuing undertaking of recent years has been how to reconcile liberating one area of law from domination by another with regulating their co-existence. One danger is to attempt the exercise without proper appreciation of the prior development of the law, to attempt to rebuild in ignorance of how the current structure of the law came about and what it truly is. The task is important and needs to be carried out properly. But it is not an end in itself. For the law does and must evolve; and, so far as possible, should do so in a rational and principled way. It will never be completely neat and tidy, but it is important that there is progress towards coherence, in the light of an informed and comprehensive debate, to which this collection seeks to provide a contribution.

The conference at which the papers in this book were delivered coincided with the retirement of Guenter Treitel from the Vinerian Chair of English Law in the University of Oxford. Tribute to his outstanding contribution to the English Law of Contract has been paid elsewhere: in *Consensus ad Idem (Essays on the Law of Contract in Honour of Guenter Treitel)*. It is in the nature of Festschrifts that they tend to be prepared in secret, so with the risk of overlooking details of the long and rich career which they are designed to celebrate. It is therefore fortunate that compilation of the current collection has provided the opportunity to complete the Bibliography of Professor Treitel's work so far, which first appeared in *Consensus ad Idem*. Much more than that, it is also a happy opportunity to note the mark of distinction conferred by the award of a Knighthood in the latest New Year's Honours List. With our gratitude for his enormous contribution to the understanding and development of the Law of Contract, our warmest congratulations go to Sir Guenter for such a richly deserved honour.

Francis Rose
May Day 1997

# *Table of Cases*

**New Zealand**



**United Kingdom**

**United States**



**Miscellaneous**

# *List of Contributors*

**Editor:**

Francis Rose
*Professor of Commercial and Common Law, University of Buckingham*

**Contributors:**

Malcolm Clarke
*Reader in Commercial Contract Law, St John's College, Cambridge*

Gerhard Dannemann
*Fellow of Worcester College, Oxford; DAAD Lecturer in German Law and Deputy Director, Centre for the Advanced Study of European and Comparative Law, University of Oxford*

Brice Dickson
*Professor of Law, University of Ulster*

Steve Hedley
*Fellow of Christ's College, Cambridge; Lecturer in Law, University of Cambridge*

Alison Jones
*Lecturer in Law, King's College, London*

Christian Lapoyade Deschamps
*Professor of Law, Université Montesquieu, Bordeaux IV*

Hector L. MacQueen
*Professor of Private Law, University of Edinburgh*

Richard Nolan
*Fellow of St. John's College, Cambridge; Lecturer in Law, University of Cambridge*

Janet O'Sullivan
*Fellow of Selwyn College, Cambridge; Lecturer in Law, University of Cambridge*

Edwin Peel
*Fellow of Keble College, Oxford*

Geoffrey Samuel
*Professor of Law, University of Kent at Canterbury*

Erich Schanze
*Professor of Law, Institute for Comparative Law, Philipps-Universität Marburg*

Eltjo Schrage
*Professor of Law, Free University of Amsterdam*

John Stevens
*Lecturer in Law, University of Birmingham*

Robert Stevens
*Fellow of Lady Margaret Hall, Oxford*

Felicity Toube
*Barrister, 3–4 South Square, Gray's Inn, London*

Janet Ulph
*Senior Lecturer in Law, Nottingham Trent University*

Peter Watts
*Associate Professor of Law, University of Auckland*

Sarah Worthington
*Lecturer in Law, Birckbeck College, London*

# 1

# *Loss and Gain at Greater Depth: The Implications of the* Ruxley *Decision*

JANET O'SULLIVAN

## 1. INTRODUCTION

Even the most committed exponent of classical contract doctrine must by now acknowledge that consumer contracts cannot be governed by precisely the same rules and principles as, say, contracts for the sale of cargoes of grain. In recent years, the legislature has dealt with specific problems of consumer transactions, regulating, for example, employment and consumer credit contracts, exclusion clauses and, now, unfair terms, whilst the courts have developed principles to tackle problems of small print, unconscionable bargains, disappointment, mental distress and even, in the domestic context, the strictures of privity.

However, when it comes to the cornerstone of contract doctrine, the compensation of unfulfilled expectations[1] on breach, there has been a general reluctance to abandon principles derived from, and fitting only, the paradigm commercial case of the sale of fungible goods with a ready market. Despite academic work[2] pointing out that, unlike businesses, consumers generally contract for goods and services for the pleasure or utility they confer, the courts have, on the whole, failed to develop consistent principles to respect the non-pecuniary expectation or "consumer surplus" which each of us derives from our jobs, our possessions, our leisure and, most of all, our homes. As is often the way, this vital issue was finally addressed following a small county court dispute, on this occasion about the depth of a swimming pool. This paper aims to consider the implications of that decision, *Ruxley Electronics and Construction Ltd* v. *Forsyth*,[3] primarily in its context of domestic building

[1] As Friedmann points out in "The Performance Interest in Contract Damages" (1995) 111 LQR 628, references to contractual "expectations" and the "expectation interest" are inaccurate and would be better replaced by the "performance interest", but the familiar terminology will be retained throughout.

[2] Particularly the seminal article by Harris, Ogus and Phillips "Contract Remedies and the Consumer Surplus" (1979) 95 *LQR* 581.

[3] [1994] 1 WLR 650, CA; *rvrsd* [1996] AC 344, HL.

work, but also with regard to its wider significance for non-commercial transactions.

## 2. THE FACTS AND JUDGMENTS

### *The Facts in Outline*

Stephen Forsyth commissioned Ruxley Electronics, a company controlled by a Mr Hall, to build a pool in his garden. The total price for the pool and its enclosure (detailed in a separate agreement) was just over £70,000. The contract originally specified that the pool was to have a maximum depth of 6 feet 6 inches, but the depth specification was increased some time later, at Forsyth's request, to 7 feet 6 inches, apparently because Forsyth was a tall man and wished to feel confident that he would not hit his head when diving. When the pool was completed, Forsyth discovered that it had a maximum depth of 6 feet 6 inches and that it was only 6 feet deep at the crucial entry point for dives, some distance from the end of the pool. Forsyth relied on this breach of specification, together with other alleged defects, to resist paying the balance of the contract price. Ruxley sued for their money and Forsyth counterclaimed for damages.

Judge Diamond QC tried the action. He found that there was a breach of the depth specification, although the pool as constructed was perfectly safe to dive into. He also found that the two conventional methods of assessing damages for defective building work led to dramatically different figures. The cost of cure was a staggering £21,650, since the only practical way of increasing the depth of the pool to conform to the specification would be to remove the existing pool, excavate further and construct a new pool. On the other hand, there was *no* difference in market value between the pool as built and the pool as it should have been built.[4] According to the official handbook of diving, the minimum safe depth for dives from the side of a pool is 5 feet, and therefore the average pool owner (of average height) would be indifferent between a pool of 6 feet and one of 7 feet. In addition, it is worth noting that there was no allegation that Ruxley had saved any money by building the pool too shallow.

The judge refused to award the cost of cure, explaining,

> "not only am I not satisfied that Mr. Forsyth intends to build a new pool at a cost of £21,650, but in addition it seems to me that this cost would be wholly disproportionate to the disadvantage of having a pool whose maximum depth is 6 feet as opposed to 7 feet 6 inches. In those circumstances I find that it would be unreasonable for Mr. Forsyth to carry out this work at such a cost".[5]

[4] The judge expressed surprise at this evidence, since the pool as built was not suitable for the addition of a diving board, as a deeper pool would have been.

[5] The first instance judgment is not reported; this passage is quoted by Staughton LJ at [1994] 1 WLR 650, 655.

However, he did not simply turn to the other conventional measure and send Forsyth away with the difference in market value, namely absolutely nothing. He recognised that Forsyth had lost something of value from the breach, as a swimming pool is designed to provide "pleasurable amenity", and awarded £2,500 as general damages for "loss of amenity brought about by the shortfall in the depth of water".[6]

### *The Court of Appeal Decision*

The majority of the Court of Appeal (Dillon LJ dissenting) allowed Forsyth's appeal, awarding him the cost of cure. The court applied a literal reading of the compensatory aim that contract damages should place a victim of a breach of contract, as far as money can, in the same position as if the contract had been performed,[7] which, they reasoned, only the cost of cure could achieve. They dismissed the judge's conclusion that it would be unreasonable to rebuild the pool, arguing that reasonableness is a matter of mitigation only: a plaintiff cannot claim the cost of cure where there is "some cheaper alternative that will make good his loss"; but, if there is no alternative course which will provide what he requires, then "he is entitled to the cost of repairs or reinstatement even if that is very expensive".[8]

Moreover, they held that the judge erred by placing emphasis on the genuineness of Forsyth's intention to rebuild, on the basis that it is generally no concern of a defendant what a plaintiff does with his damages. For this reason, Forsyth's proferred undertaking to rebuild the pool was dismissed as unnecessary and he was awarded the full cost of cure without condition.

### *The House of Lords' Decision*

The House of Lords unanimously allowed the contractor's appeal, restoring the judgment of the trial judge. Their Lordships emphasised that, contrary to the Court of Appeal's view, there is a substantial body of case law from England, the Commonwealth and the USA establishing that the cost of cure will not be awarded where it would be "unreasonable for the plaintiff to insist on reinstatement, as where, for example, the expense of the work involved would be out of all proportion to the benefit to be obtained".[9]

Numerous authorities were cited in support, including the important House of Lords' case *East Ham Corporation* v. *Bernard Sunley & Sons Ltd*,[10] in which Lord Cohen said, "There is no doubt that wherever it is reasonable for the employer to insist upon reinstatement the courts will treat the cost of

[6] [1994] 1 WLR 650, 654.
[7] *Robinson* v. *Harman* (1848) 1 Ex 850.
[8] [1994] 1 WLR 650, 659.
[9] [1995] 1 WLR 118, 135; [1996[ AC 344, 369.
[10] [1966] AC 406.

reinstatement as the measure of damage."[11] This was approved in *Darlington Borough Council* v. *Wiltshier Northern Ltd.*[12] by Steyn LJ, who said,

> "in the case of a building contract, the prima facie rule is the cost of cure, i.e. the cost of remedying the defect . . . But where the cost of remedying the defects involves expense out of all proportion to the benefit which could accrue from it, the court is entitled to adopt the alternative measure of the difference of the value of the works."[13]

The same principle was applied in the famous case from the New York Court of Appeals, *Jacob & Youngs* v. *Kent*,[14] in which the owner had specified for plumbing using pipes of "Reading manufacture", but the builder had mistakenly installed equivalent pipes made by a different manufacturer. Cardozo J expressed the view that a plaintiff, "is entitled to the money which will permit him to complete, unless the cost of completion is grossly and unfairly out of proportion to the good to be attained".[15]

So far as Forsyth's intention was concerned, the judge had refused to believe Forsyth's evidence that he intended to rebuild the pool, and this was relied on as another factor indicating the unreasonableness of the cost of cure. Lord Lloyd said, "if, as the judge found, Mr. Forsyth had no intention of rebuilding the pool, he has lost nothing except the difference in value, if any."[16] Moreover, Forsyth's proffered undertaking to rebuild the pool did not make any difference. It could not make the unreasonable reasonable and would not, "be allowed to create a loss, which does not exist, in order to punish the defendants [*sic.*] for their breach of contract".[17]

However, the rejection of the cost of cure did not mean that the difference in market value was the only other alternative. With differing degrees of enthusiasm, the House acknowledged that Forsyth had lost something from the breach—the depth of specification, reflecting his personal preference, had not been fulfilled. Lord Mustill stressed that it would be unacceptable if a defaulting builder could escape unscathed merely by showing that, to the mind of the average onlooker or the average potential buyer, the results which he has produced seem just as good as those which he promised. As Oliver J observed in *Radford* v. *De Froberville*,[18] it is for the plaintiff to judge what performance he requires in exchange for the price and the court should honour that choice.

Their Lordships therefore restored the trial judge's middle-ground award of £2,500 damages for loss of amenity, rejecting Forsyth's tactical argument that

11 [1966] AC 406 at 434.
12 [1995] 1 WLR 68.
13 *Ibid.* at 79.
14 (1921) 129 NE 889.
15 *Ibid.* at 891.
16 [1996] AC 344, 373.
17 *Ibid.* at 373.
18 [1977] 1 WLR 1262.

this was unprecedented and only the cost of cure was permissible. There was "no need to remedy the injustice of awarding too little, by unjustly awarding far too much".[19]

### 3. THE PRESENTATION OF FACTS BY APPELLATE COURTS

Before dealing with the main implications of the decision, I will mention briefly one aspect which I consider noteworthy, although in one sense it does not have any substantive significance for our consideration of failed contracts. However, it is an example of an irritatingly common trend which might be termed the "selective presentation" of the facts of a dispute by an appellate court, particularly unhelpful in a largely uncodified area such as the law of obligations.[20]

It is one of the most extraordinary features of the Court of Appeal and House of Lords' judgments in *Ruxley* that the same dispute is presented in two drastically different ways, slanted in accordance with the result reached, of added significance since leave to appeal was refused by the Court of Appeal. In that court, Forsyth was presented as the long-suffering, innocent victim of cowboy builders, as highlights from the judgement of Staughton LJ reveal[21]:

> "The progress of the works was anything but smooth. When the pool was first completed by subcontractors whom Ruxley had engaged, a crack appeared across the bottom of it . . . Eventually Mr. Hall agreed that the existing pool would be renewed and replaced . . . Various defects were asserted by Mr. Forsyth . . . Some but not all were remedied . . . Then Mr. Forsyth, who had not previously spent a great deal of time at the house, discovered that the maximum depth of water in the pool was not 7 feet 6 inches . . . the maximum depth, where it was most needed, was only 6 feet."

> "The contract . . . as originally written, had been amended following a conversation between Mr. Forsyth and Mr. Hall. Mr. Forsyth had asked for an increase in the maximum depth to 7 feet 6 inches, saying that he was a big man and would feel safer when diving and more comfortable with the greater depth of water."

In marked contrast, the House of Lords presented Forsyth as a pedantic, demanding client, trying to find technical breaches of contract to avoid paying for good work carried out by honest contractors. Extracts from Lord Lloyd's speech give the flavour[22]:

[19] [1996] AC 344, 361.

[20] e.g. compare also the presentation of the facts of *Banque Bruxelles Lambert SA* v. *Eagle Star Insurance Co Ltd* [1995] QB 375 by Phillips J and by the Court of Appeal.

[21] [1994] 1 WLR 650, 652–4.

[22] [1996] AC 344, 361–3.

"The depth of the pool was to be 6 feet 6 inches at the deep end.

Subsequently Mr. Forsyth wanted the depth increased to 7 feet 6 inches . . . Mr. Hall agreed to increase the depth without extra charge . . .

Work started in 1987 . . . But the subcontractor did not do the job properly . . . Mr. Hall agreed to remove the existing pool and replace it free of charge. He also agreed to reimburse the professional charges which Mr. Forsyth had incurred . . .

In . . . 1988 the plaintiffs submitted their invoice. But Mr. Forsyth insisted on a reduction of £10,000 to compensate him for the disturbance which he had suffered during the rebuilding of the pool. Mr. Hall reluctantly agreed. Still Mr. Forsyth did not settle the plaintiffs' invoice . . .

Then on 19 January 1990 the plaintiffs commenced these proceedings . . .

The trial commenced . . . on 14 May 1993. On 16 May Mr. Forsyth dismissed his solicitors and counsel. On 17 May he amended his counterclaim to raise for the first time the question of the depth of the pool . . .

His two main arguments, neither of which had been pleaded prior to the third day of the trial, were, first that the contract was an entire contract, and that as the swimming pool had never been completed, he owed nothing, and indeed was entitled to recover back instalments which he had already paid.

His second argument was that he was entitled to recover the cost of rebuilding the pool . . ."

The difference in tone between the two versions of events is so striking as to be almost humorous, but it reveals a serious issue. Anyone, practitioner or academic, seeking to understand and extract principles from appellate decisions can only do so sensibly within the factual matrix of the particular dispute. In *Ruxley* this is very difficult to locate, particularly as the first instance judgment has never been reported (and is not even available on Lexis).

It would be immensely helpful if the record of the tribunal which hears the evidence were abstracted at the beginning of every reported appellate decision, as well as the appellate court's summary of the facts. It is natural for an appellate court to emphasise those facts which are material to their decision on the law, and to play down those they consider irrelevant, but the two versions of events presented in *Ruxley* go dangerously beyond a difference of emphasis. This makes for uncertainty and undermines the authority of the case, for it enables critics of either court's judgment to pick out material points omitted by that court, but stressed and relied on by the other. For example, the Court of Appeal did not mention the £10,000 price reduction already extracted by Forsyth for "disturbance", whereas the House of Lords omitted the reason why Forsyth had asked for the increased depth specification, namely that he was a tall man and was nervous about diving into a shallow pool, clearly of significance in valuing his unfulfilled expectation and his "loss of amenity".

## 4. THE COST OF CURE

I approached *Ruxley* feeling instinctively that Forsyth should get the full cost of cure, however disproportionate or unreasonable this seemed. Far better that, I thought, than to render all promises bought for their utility value entirely worthless and such expectations unprotected on breach. By leaving Forsyth with the difference in market value, the law would be acknowledging that there is no point contracting to fulfil a personal preference unless that preference is shared by the market, a prospect far less acceptable than the occasional windfall to someone like Forsyth.

This reaction was based on the view prevalent before *Ruxley* that the only alternative to awarding the cost of cure was to award the difference in market value and that the cost of cure was the best, albeit crude, method of recognising and respecting the plaintiff's expectation.

However, *Ruxley* has raised the welcome prospect of isolating and compensating the unfulfilled personal preference in a more sophisticated manner, without resort to the full cost of cure. So I am *almost* ready to abandon my instinctive view and to conclude that it is possible to show appropriate respect for the expectations of perverse plaintiffs without resorting to the inefficiency and overcompensation inherent in awarding the full cost of cure. By concentrating on the extreme examples—the hideous folly, the brand of pipes or bricks which differ from specification but are otherwise suitable—I have almost been convinced by the House of Lords' common sense[23] appeal to "reasonableness" and "proportion".

Almost, but not quite. *Ruxley* is itself an extreme case and, particularly as the House of Lords presented the facts, Forsyth's appeal for the full cost of cure had very little merit.[24] Yet we are concerned, not with the merits of the result in *Ruxley*, but with its implications. I remain uneasy that a principle formulated after focusing almost exclusively on extraordinary cases, on perverse plaintiffs, may have unwelcome consequences for the vast majority of disputes, the commonplace cases of shoddy work, minor defects or deviations from specification. I am not sure that the House of Lords' solution is the best way to identify and isolate the "extreme cases" for which the cost of cure is not appropriate.

[23] *Ibid.* at 354.

[24] e.g. the pool as built complied with the original depth specification and the increase to 7 feet 6 inches appears to have been agreed after the conclusion of the contract, without consideration.

### *Intention*

Before *Ruxley*, there was some doubt about the principles that determined when the cost of cure would be awarded,[25] but it was generally thought that a plaintiff would be entitled to the cost of cure, even where it greatly exceeded the difference in value, if he had already carried out the works of reinstatement or demonstrated an intention to do so.[26] This approach was open to criticism, on the basis that a plaintiff will rarely be able or willing to carry out the work before trial, until he has the damages to spend on the job, whilst requiring evidence of future intention is pretty meaningless and runs contrary to the normal principle that it is of no concern to the court or the defendant what a plaintiff does with his damages.

It now seems that a genuine intention to rebuild is not a sufficient condition for cost of cure damages, but instead is merely another factor helping to demonstrate the true economic value of the plaintiff's loss and thus the reasonableness of the cost of cure measure, complementing or competing with the court's view of whether the cost of cure is disproportionate.

Of course, the two will often coincide, as many plaintiffs will share the judge's reluctance to countenance spending a large amount of money to obtain a small benefit. However, where the plaintiff does intend to reinstate, the new emphasis seems likely to reduce his chances of obtaining the cost of cure. Even if the judge believes the plaintiff's evidence (and very often he will not, precisely because it is difficult to imagine any "reasonable person" spending a lot of money for a small benefit), he will still be free to conclude that the cost of cure is disproportionate and thus unreasonable.

In future, there may be little point giving evidence of intention to rebuild, however genuine that intention is. In addition, it is unclear how the courts will treat the exceptional plaintiff who has actually carried out the reinstatement prior to trial—can this course of action now be condemned as unreasonable too?[27]

### *Reasonableness*

It is now clear that the cost of cure will not be awarded where it is "unreasonable" to reinstate, of which one example is where the cost of cure is "wholly disproportionate" to the effects of the breach. There are other examples of such unreasonableness. The most obvious are situations in which the plaintiff wanted the contractual performance solely to make a profit, so that the difference in value would fully compensate him; for example the absentee

[25] Contrast Burrows, *Remedies for Torts and Breach of Contract*, 2nd edn (London, 1994), 148–52, with Treitel, *The Law of Contract*, 9th edn (London, 1995), 852–5.

[26] Burrows, *supra* n 25, pp 148–50.

[27] For example, what would have been the position if Forsyth had rebuilt the pool to the specified depth after the Court of Appeal's judgment, but before the appeal to the House of Lords?

investment owner of property who commissions building work solely to improve the market value of the property. There the plaintiff's sole interest in performance is financial and thus mitigation would require that his damages are confined to the difference in market value (and any consequential loss of profit).[28]

There will also be cases where the plaintiff's interest in performance is not solely financial when the contract is made, but where, through altered circumstances, it is by the time of the trial. An example given in *Ruxley* illustrates the point. If Forsyth had died and his executors had continued the action before selling the property, they would not have been able to recover the cost of cure.[29] Other examples include situations where the property is destroyed by some intervening cause which is independent of the breach, redeveloped or compulsorily purchased before the trial.

I have no problem with such cases. Mitigation requires that a plaintiff cannot demand the cost of cure when he has no, or no continuing, interest in performance other than one which is wholly reflected in the market or exchange value of performance. They are, however, very different from cases where the only objection to the cost of cure is that it is "disproportionate" to the plaintiff's interest in performance.

### *Disproportion*

As the House of Lords demonstrated, there is nothing novel about the disproportion principle in the context of construction contracts, although arguably *Ruxley* has boosted its importance by reducing the weight given to the plaintiff's intention. In addition, an analogous principle seems to be applied elsewhere in the law of obligations.

For example, there is a Canadian nuisance case (better known for its enlightened approach to interference with television reception, contrasted with the English position) in which it was applied. This was *Nor-video Services Ltd* v. *Ontario Hydro*,[30] in which a cable television company sued in nuisance because one of its numerous channels was disrupted by the defendant's hydro-electric plant, so that it was forced to stop supplying that one channel to its subscribers. It would have cost more than $200,000 to restore the lost channel, but the plaintiff had lost no subscribers as a result of

[28] Phillips J relied on this distinction in *Channel Island Ferries Ltd* v. *Cenargo Navigation Ltd, The Rozel* [1994] 2 Lloyds Rep 161, 166, when rejecting an appeal for the cost of curing the "class record" of a commercial ship, distinguishing the Court of Appeal's judgment in *Ruxley* as follows: "it does not apply when the contractual requirement is not an end in itself, but is inserted into a commercial contract because it has financial implications".

[29] [1996] AC 344, 372. This is analogous to *Wigsell* v. *Corporation of the Schools for the Indigent Blind* (1880) 43 LT 218, where executors were denied the cost of building a wall which the defendants had promised to build to enclose a plot purchased from the deceased. Moreover, the executors had not the slightest intention of building a substitute wall, demonstrated by the fact that they had refused what was described in *Radford* v. *De Froberville* [1977] 1 WLR 1262 as "virtually an invitation to proceed for specific performance".

[30] (1978) 84 DLR (3d) 221.

the nuisance and thus maintained the same level of income as if there had been no disruption. The court refused to award the cost of cure, again because Nor-video's desire to reinstate the lost channel was "not a reasonable basis on which to measure damages—not reasonable in the sense that the cost involved in so doing is wholly out of proportion to the value of the signal to the cable business".[31]

The result in *Nor-video* is unproblematic: the plaintiff's interest in the disrupted channel was entirely financial, and this is arguably a better explanation for the unreasonableness of awarding the cost of cure than the notion of disproportion. Moreover, it is a *tort* case; there was no question of the plaintiffs being forced to accept something less satisfactory than they had paid for and no question of ignoring contractual expectations.[32] However, where construction contracts are concerned, the position is different, and it is in that context that I experience some discomfort at the principle.

The word "disproportionate" suggests a mathematical approach, in which one ascertainable figure is compared with another such figure, and where anything higher than a specified percentage difference is rejected as an unacceptable disparity. *Ruxley* gives no meaningful criteria for doing this—there are too many variables.

For example, is the cost of cure to be compared with the difference in market value or with the loss of amenity figure? In *Ruxley* the cost of cure (£21,650) was 8.5 times higher than the loss of amenity award (£2,500) and infinitely more than the difference in market value (nil). The difference in market value is not appropriate, since the principle is needed most where the difference in market value is nil, i.e. precisely where it provides absolutely no assistance. Since the difference will be infinite whatever the size of the cost of cure (£5 or £5m), this renders the cost of cure disproportionate by definition.

It is tolerably clear that the courts in *Ruxley* were making the comparison with the loss of amenity award, but it still does not clarify how much bigger the cost of cure has to be in order to be disproportionate—8.5 times was obviously sufficient, but what about 5 or 1.5 times as much? In addition, as we shall see, the loss of amenity figure was itself no more than an instinctive estimate. Finally, it is not clear which party has the burden of proving "disproportion". With so many variables, it runs the risk of being an instrumental way of justifying the court's prior conclusion that the plaintiff does not deserve the cost of cure[33], and also makes it virtually impossible to advise appropriate settlement terms.

[31] (1978) 84 DLR (3d) 221 at 237.

[32] The latter point applies to some of the other authorities cited by the House of Lords in support of the disproportion principle, such as *C. R. Taylor (Wholesale) Ltd* v. *Hepworth* [1977] 1 WLR 659.

[33] Lord Jauncey used some particularly instrumental language: "If it is unreasonable in a particular case to award the cost of reinstatement, it must be because the loss sustained does not extend to the need to reinstate": [1996] AC 344, 357.

In essence, the principle seems to mean "the cost of cure is very high", which of course is usually because it includes an element of *undoing* the original work. This is unacceptable—it makes the owner's damages depend not on the extent of the defect or the degree of deviation from specification, but on the technical difficulty and thus cost of undoing the breach.

It is likely to have two further, unfortunate implications in the ordinary case of a domestic building contract. First, it conveys the wrong signal to contractors. Assume, for example, a contractor doing domestic building work where, as in *Ruxley*, the employer is not on site supervising his every move. If the contractor monitors the work properly, keeping the employer informed at every stage, he risks spotting mistakes and defects which he will then have to spend money remedying. If, however, he ploughs on with the work, quickly burying any possible defects deeper in the fabric of the construction, he maximises the chances that the cost of curing any such defects will be high and thus rejected as disproportionate. I am not suggesting that there would be no remedy if a builder deceived his employer; rather, that the principle encourages a culture of inefficiency and provides no incentive, indeed a positive disincentive, for builders to monitor work or keep the employer informed.

Secondly, the vagueness of the principle makes the position of an employer complaining of bad workmanship uncertain and risky, and (where the cost of cure is high) enables a contractor to "hold out", offering a low sum which he asserts will adequately compensate the employer for his loss of amenity. As Forsyth's counsel observed after the House of Lords decision, "many an employer may well accept such a sum rather than undergo the uncertainty of litigation".[34]

Such doubts are all very well, but I began by agreeing that there are extreme cases (including *Ruxley*) where the cost of cure is inappropriate. Some principle is certainly needed to describe and isolate those extreme cases, if disproportion is rejected. Two alternative contenders were mentioned in *Ruxley*.

Lord Jauncey expressed the principle slightly differently.[35] He contrasted "a failure to achieve the precise contractual objective" with "the loss which is occasioned by a total failure". In his view, "where the contract breaker has entirely failed to achieve the contractual objective it may not be difficult to conclude that the loss is the cost of achieving that objective", giving the examples of a building that is so defective as to be of no use for its designed purpose and of a folly which collapses after construction. This he contrasts somewhat hesitantly with his view of Forsyth's shallow pool, saying, "however, where the contractual objective has been achieved to a substantial extent, the position may be very different".

I prefer this formulation to the disproportion principle, as it focuses on the result of the breach, not the technical difficulty of remedying it. However, I

[34] Isaac E. Jacob, "Is Near Enough Good Enough?" (1995) 139 *SJ* 676, 677.
[35] [1996] AC 344, 357.

am not sure whether the "contractual objective" is always a helpful concept. It relies on a project having just one, primary, objective, which is rarely realistic. After all, a "contract" is a convenient collection of linked obligations, many of which create discrete expectations. I am reminded of Treitel's criticism of the notion of "entire contracts" when what is needed is the more precise identification of which particular *obligations* within a given contract are entire.[36] Consider *Tito* v. *Waddell (No 2)*[37]—the bulk of the contract was "performed", but the replanting obligation was completely ignored. Was the "contractual objective achieved to a substantial extent" or not? What is the "contractual objective" of a building project involving some demolition work to different parts of a property and then reinstatement of any damage caused?

Another alternative is the American concept of economic waste, as defined by Corbin[38]:

> "In many cases, the structure as it exists, even though it is not exactly in accordance with the contract requirements, is such that it will render substantially all the service that the structure contracted for would have rendered; and reconstruction and completion in accordance with the contract may be possible only at a cost that would be imprudent and unreasonable. The law does not require damages to be measured by a method involving such economic waste."

This is no better, as it seems to encompass far too much. As the High Court of Australia pointed out in *Bellgrove* v. *Eldridge*,[39] it would not permit the cost of cure where the work produced a structure which, though satisfactory as a structure of a particular type, is quite different in character from what was called for by the contract.

On balance, the principle that the cost of cure will not be awarded where it would be "unreasonable" to reinstate is acceptable where it describes a plaintiff whose interest in performance is merely financial, but not where the objection is the "disproportionate" cost of curing the breach. This does not seem to me to be what made *Ruxley* or *Jacob & Youngs* v. *Kent*[40] extreme cases. It is the fact that there was nothing *wrong* with the work; it merely differed from specification. If a home-owner contracts to have his bathroom tiled, he should arguably be entitled to the cost of cure if the work is even slightly shoddy,[41] but not if the builder substituted tiles equivalent in quality but different from those selected. Only in the latter case should he be confined to a "middle-ground" award representing the value of his unfulfilled expectation, yet in both cases the cost of cure will involve the same, considerable, expense of stripping and re-doing the unsatisfactory work.

[36] Treitel, *supra* n 25, pp 700–3.
[37] [1977] Ch 106.
[38] Corbin, *Contracts* (1963), Ch 60, § 1089.
[39] (1954) 90 CLR 613.
[40] *Supra* n 14.
[41] cf. G. W. *Atkins Ltd* v. *Scott* (1991) 7 *Const LJ* 215.

Admittedly, this formulation requires a difficult line to be drawn between "defective" work and work which merely fails to comply with specification. Perhaps the flexibility inherent in the "reasonableness" formulation will suffice to allow the courts to draw this line where appropriate, unconstrained by the unhelpful notion of "disproportion".

## 5. THE MIDDLE-GROUND AWARD

### *The Irrelevance of Market Value*

The most welcome aspect of *Ruxley* is its explicit recognition that not every contractual obligation has as its objective the making of profit and that principles developed to measure commercial expectations may not be appropriate in other contexts. Once this is appreciated, it becomes clear that the "market" or exchange value of performance is only realistic as a measure of loss on breach of contract if either:

(a) mitigation can be readily obtained via a genuine market, such as through the purchase of an acceptable substitute which satisfies the plaintiff's expectation; or
(b) the plaintiff's interest in performance is, or has become, purely financial—a straightforward question of profit.

The vast majority of contractual obligations will fit one or both categories, but many will not. Good examples are promises purchased to secure "one-off" results such as privacy or peace of mind, non-competition or confidentiality. The same applies to many promises purchased for comfort, pleasure or sentiment, such as most contracts for domestic building works, commissioned not to improve the market value of the plaintiff's home, but to make it, in the words of Lord Mustill "more comfortable, more convenient and more conformable to his own particular tastes".[42]

This is not invariably true; sometimes domestic building contracts generate purely financial expectations, a where a non-resident owner commissions works of improvement to increase or preserve the property's investment or letting value, or where an owner commissions work just before putting the property on the market. However, these examples are easily identified and sufficiently unusual that I would like to see a (rebuttable) presumption that the difference in market value is not an appropriate measure of damages for domestic building work.

The merit of this approach becomes clear when the concept of the "market value" of domestic building work is considered. What was the meaning, in *Ruxley*, of the comparison of the market value of the pool as built and the

[42] [1996] AC 344, 360.

pool as it should have been built? The House of Lords dismissed any suggestion that reasonable mitigation would involve moving house to obtain a deeper pool,[43] and it is evident that swimming pools are not commissioned by resident home owners for purely financial reasons; rather, anecdotal evidence suggests that pools often diminish the value of the property. Perhaps for this very reason, the court stressed that they were concerned, not with the value of the property on which the pool was built, but with the value of the "works" themselves. Yet this is even more fictitious, since there is no market in domestic pools separate from the property to which they are attached. If what is meant is that the *price* of commissioning a shallow pool is identical to the price of a deeper pool, then how does that work where the work is defective in some way—how do you calculate the price of a shoddy job?

Overall, measuring the plaintiff's loss using a market that does not exist is arguably the most significant cause of under-compensation for breach of consumer contracts. Unfortunately, this is only partially accepted in *Ruxley*. According to Lord Lloyd, "If the judge had assessed the difference in value in the present case at, say, £5,000, I have little doubt that the Court of Appeal would have taken that figure rather than £21,650".[44]

What is not clear is whether, in that example, the £5,000 would have been awarded *instead of* or *as well as* the £2,500 loss of amenity award. This raises the fundamental question of the nature of the £2,500 award in *Ruxley*, a question on which the House of Lords heard no argument (because of Forsyth's tactical rejection of the award).

### *The Nature of the Loss of Amenity Award*

Only two members of the court made any attempt to explain the basis of the award. Lord Mustill viewed and labelled it as the consumer surplus,[45] in other words the amount by which the particular plaintiff values performance of a particular obligation over and above its market value. He said, "the law must cater for those occasions where the value of the promise to the promisee exceeds the financial enhancement of his position which full performance will secure".[46]

Lord Lloyd on the other hand explained the award as damages for Forsyth's "disappointment".[47] He stressed that the contract was one to provide "pleasurable amenity" and was then able to treat the middle-ground award as another exception to the principle that damages for mental distress or disappointment are not generally awarded for breach of contract,[48] unless the con-

[43] [1996] AC 344, 371.
[44] *Ibid* at 369.
[45] Explicitly acknowledging the article by Harris, Ogus and Phillips, *supra* n 2.
[46] [1996] AC 344, 360.
[47] *Ibid* at 374.
[48] *Addis* v. *Gramophone Co Ltd* [1909] AC 488.

tract (like a holiday contract[49]) has as its object pleasure, peace of mind or freedom from distress.[50]

Unfortunately, these two ways of rationalising the award are not consistent. What if the difference in market value of the pool as built and the pool as it should have been built was something greater than nil—say £1,000. Would the plaintiff be entitled to this £1,000 *and* the £2,500 loss of amenity award?

On Lord Mustill's reasoning, the answer must be yes—the consumer surplus is merely the *excess* over and above the market value of the missing inches, so the plaintiff must have both. However, following Lord Lloyd's reasoning, that would be double recovery. For Lord Lloyd, there is no suggestion that the value of plaintiff's *expectation* is any more than the difference in market value (see above), so that to give the plaintiff £1,000 would put him into the position he would have been in had the contract been properly performed, whereupon he would presumably have suffered no disappointment. Unless you can say that a plaintiff is actually worse off with a defective pool than with no pool at all, which incidentally may well be true with regard to a defective holiday, to give damages for disappointment *and* the difference in value looks like double recovery.

Lord Mustill's rationale is preferable.[51] The reason why the difference in market value undercompensates someone such as Forsyth is because his expectation from performance exceeds that of the market and it is this subjective expectation that the consumer surplus addresses. Damages for mental distress or disappointment are fundamentally different. Harris, Ogus and Phillips caution against muddling the two concepts: "It is important, however, to distinguish 'psychic' costs, such as disappointment, which arise from breach of contract, from the utility value expected from performance".[52]

Mental distress is like death or personal injury—one of the negative results that flow from a breach or a tort to leave you worse off than you were before you started.[53] In contrast, the consumer surplus is part of the expectation—you are not actually worse off, you simply have not become better off to the extent you were promised. This could be described as a "disappointed" or "dashed" expectation, but that is not the sense in which Lord Lloyd used the word and indeed it would apply equally whether or not the contract has anything to do with providing "pleasurable amenity".[54]

49 *Jarvis* v. *Swans Tours Ltd* [1973] QB 233.

50 *Bliss* v. *South East Thames Regional Health Authority* [1987] ICR 700.

51 Arguably one disadvantage is that it retains the concept of market value, to which the consumer surplus is added, rather than attempting a valuation of the plaintiff's expectation in one stage.

52 (1979) 95 *LQR* 581, 596, n 89.

53 See Harris, *Remedies in Contract and Tort* (London, 1988), 95.

54 Lord Lloyd recognised that a disappointment award would not be available for some defects, such as a difference in level between two rooms necessitating a step, but declined to "give a final answer" to whether a middle-ground award should be available in such a case.

It could be argued that labels do not matter, as long as the courts recognise the need for compensation in the right cases. I disagree—the label follows the principle, which itself is vital for the identification of the "right cases" in future. Even within the field of construction contracts, a domestic home-owner may have a preference for a particular sort of heating system, roof tile or floor plan, one which they value even though such specifications make no difference to the objective market value of performance.[55] On breach, there is no "disappointment" and yet there is certainly a consumer surplus.[56] In addition, the *level* of the plaintiff's expectation has no necessary connection with his reaction on breach—his disposition will determine whether he endures the breach with stoicism or suffers distress.

Assuming that Lord Mustill's view prevails, it is still necessary to articulate principles for the identification of instances of a "consumer surplus" and for its proper measurement.

### *Identification*

An obligation to carry out domestic building work is undoubtedly a paradigm example of the generation of a consumer surplus, and it appears (thanks to *Ruxley*) to be the first such example to be explicitly recognised by the English courts.[57] Nonetheless, there does seem to be a strong case for the recognition of the consumer surplus generated by other sorts of consumer transactions. In the normal case (such as the purchase of non-unique goods or services), a sufficiently close substitute can be obtained on an available market, providing a substitute consumer surplus, but there will be other transactions which, like domestic building work, offer no such prospect of market mitigation. Commentators have considered this question in great detail[58] and I will not

[55] Even the employer in *Jacob & Youngs* v. *Kent* might, for example, have suffered from appalling plumbing in a previous home and have received a recommendation from a trusted adviser that Reading pipes were a good brand.

[56] A recent unreported Court of Appeal case, *Freeman* v. *Niroomand* [1996] 9 CL 118, illustrates the point. Mr. Niroomand commissioned a builder to carry out building work at his semi-detached house, namely constructing a porch at the front and an extension to the rear. The dispute involved the porch, which, the contract specified, should mirror the porch on the adjoining house and should be constructed of cavity wall brickwork (to minimise staining from the elements). When the porch was built, it did match the porch next door, but it had not been constructed with cavity walls. As is all too common, the market value of the house was not altered by the addition of the porch, whether or not it complied with the contractual specifications. To cure the breach, the porch either had to be demolished or have its internal dimensions considerably reduced by the addition of an inner layer of brickwork, and for this reason Niroomand gave evidence that he did not wish to reinstate and was not asking for the cost of cure, but for a *Ruxley* "middle ground" award, representing the value of his unfulfilled expectation (avoiding the risk of a weather-stained porch). The Court of Appeal upheld an award of £130, even though there was no "disappointment" in the *Bliss* sense: see *supra* n 50.

[57] Reportedly acknowledged by Lord Mustill in argument—see Jacob, *supra* n 34. The phrase "consumer surplus" appears in one reported case before *Ruxley*, the Lands' Tribunal decision called *Re Kershaw's Application* (1974) 31 P & CR 187, in connection with the modification of a restrictive covenant.

[58] See in particular Harris, Ogus and Phillips, *supra* n 2; Muris, "Cost of Completion or Diminution in Market Value: The Relevance of Subjective Value" (1983) 12 *JLS* 379.

do so here, other than to counter one potential objection to the wider recognition of the consumer surplus, that it will leave defendants at risk from unascertainable, perverse preferences.

This problem will be prevented by the normal principles of remoteness of damage.[59] A plaintiff will only recover if his consumer surplus is the natural and probable response to the promise,[60] or where it is generated by a more unusual preference and this has been brought to the other party's attention at the time of contracting.[61]

### *Quantification*

No explanation is given in the appellate judgments in *Ruxley* as to how the "loss of amenity" figure of £2,500 was obtained and it is difficult to avoid the conclusion that it was plucked randomly from the air. This us unacceptable: principles are vital to aid pre-contract pricing and negotiation, as well as the settlement of disputes. It is not sufficient, as we were reminded in *Ruxley*, that the courts are good at putting figures on intangibles such as pain and suffering or distress.

One option can be rejected immediately. Even though the court should be aiming for the plaintiff's subjective valuation of his expectation, it is not satisfactory to rely entirely on the plaintiff's evidence; there is huge scope for exaggeration and correspondingly little scope for challenge by the defendant.

Recognising this, Harris, Ogus and Phillips would allow the defendant to adduce evidence to show the factors relevant to his expectation of a consumer surplus, within an otherwise objective enquiry, "how would the reasonable man, in the plaintiff's position, have valued the benefit of performance?"[62] This should work well, provided the courts pay more than lip service to Lord Mustill's principle that neither the contractor nor the court has the right to substitute for the employer's individual expectation of performance a criterion derived from what ordinary people would regard as sensible.[63] However, the indications are not promising. Lord Lloyd in *Ruxley* made a point of saying that awards should be low and that Forsyth was lucky to get as much as £2,500.[64] Similar sentiments were expressed in *Freeman* v. *Niroomand*.[65] This is dangerously close to saying—"this breach would not have bothered the reasonable man so you are not going to get much", which is precisely what the award is designed to avoid.

[59] e.g. *Hadley* v. *Baxendale* (1854) 9 Exch 341.

[60] e.g. the value placed by couples on their wedding photographs (see *Diesen* v. *Samson* 1971 SLT 49) or the value placed by home-owners on the comfort and appearance of their homes.

[61] e.g. Forsyth's desire for reassurance about bumping his head on the bottom of the pool.

[62] (1979) 95 *LQR* 581, 585.

[63] [1996] AC 344, 361.

[64] [1996] AC 344, 374.

[65] *Supra* n 56, per Millett LJ, "I am not sure in my own mind that the householder was not fortunate to obtain any damages at all".

We should be seeking the value which *the plaintiff* places on what he has lost. One possibility would be to attempt to award a figure representing what the plaintiff would have accepted to release the defendant from the relevant obligation.[66] However, attempts to quantify this figure tend to be fictitious. As Burrows observes, "even if it is realistic to imagine that the plaintiff would have accepted a price for releasing the defendant, that price cannot be sensibly fixed".[67] The question may be more sophisticated, but it is just as difficult to answer as a straightforward objective question. Specific remedies are the only secure way of protecting the plaintiff's expectation and, where available, do the job very successfully in many instances of the consumer surplus.[68] Without extending the availability of specific performance, there is a related way to ensure, in a case like *Ruxley*, that the plaintiff gets the value *he* places on performance—ironically, the one method which was rejected by both the Court of Appeal and the House of Lords. That is to award the cost of cure, provided the plaintiff gives an undertaking to the defendant to use the damages to cure the breach. This way, in a world with no transaction costs, the parties will bargain, and will settle for such lower figure (in exchange for the release of the undertaking) that represents the value *to the plaintiff* of his expectation.[69] English courts still refuse to acknowledge that judicial remedies might work this way in practice, as their reluctance to award specific performance where it would be difficult to monitor performance reveals.[70] They reject the "undertaking" solution because it would lead to an "economically wasteful" result, but this is only true if the order is executed exactly as drawn. In fact, if the solution is economically wasteful, such as spending £21,650 digging up a serviceable swimming pool, both parties will have an incentive to bargain and minimise the inefficiency.

This solution has two major problems—the transaction costs of negotiating to release the undertaking and risk of the plaintiff "holding out" in the negotiations in an attempt to obtain more than the real value of his expectation.[71]

Yet the transaction costs of another layer of bargaining can be set against the *saving* of costs if no evidence or argument is needed to enable the court to quantify the plaintiff's expectation. In addition, if it became common practice for courts to award the cost of cure coupled with an undertaking, eventually the pre-trial negotiation would take place on this basis, minimising the risk that the plaintiff will accept an unreasonably low award, where the defen-

[66] Applied in *Wrotham Park Estate Co* v. *Parkside Homes* [1974] 1 WLR 798, and more recently in *Jaggard* v. *Sawyer* [1995] 1 WLR 269. See also Sharpe and Waddams, "Damages for Lost Opportunity to Bargain" (1982) 2 *OJLS* 290.

[67] Burrows, *supra* n 25, p 152.

[68] See Harris, Ogus and Phillips (1979) 95 *LQR* 581, 586–9.

[69] *Ibid* at 605 onwards.

[70] Although the recent Court of Appeal decision in *Co-operative Insurance Society Ltd* v. *Argylle Stores (Holdings) Ltd* [1996] 3 WLR 27 indicates a possible softening of judicial attitudes.

[71] Harris, Ogus and Phillips, *supra* n 68, pp 607–8.

dant holds out with such an offer (identified above as a likely result of the *Ruxley* disproportion principle). This might also be seen as the mirror-image of the risk of holding out by the plaintiff associated with the undertaking solution. If all else is equal, at least this way it is the innocent plaintiff who has the opportunity to hold out.

Admittedly this method will not always be appropriate, particularly where the plaintiff (like Mr Niroomand) has indicated that he has no intention of reinstating or where it is, or has become, impossible to reinstate. So it remains important for the courts to solve the difficult problem of quantifying the consumer surplus. Can any assistance be derived from turning the enquiry round and concentrating instead on the defendant's *gains*?

## 6 RESTITUTIONARY SOLUTIONS IN NON-COMMERCIAL CASES?

### *Gain-Based Remedies for Breach of Contract?*

Despite the ongoing academic debate about the possibility of recovering the defendant's gains from a breach of contract,[72] the law reports remain full of assertions, some extremely recent, that contractual remedies have but one aim, to compensate plaintiffs for loss.[73] Unsurprisingly, therefore, the point was not pleaded or argued in *Ruxley*. Indeed, it seems highly likely that the contractors made no appreciable saving from the breach. This point is easily overlooked—commentators urging the acceptance of what I shall, with appropriate hesitation, call "restitutionary damages", have occasionally assumed that the cost of cure will mirror the defendant's saving, so that the debates about the appropriate compensatory measure are unnecessarily convoluted fictions, which would melt away if restitutionary damages were recognised.[74] This assumption is appropriate in cases, such as *Tito* v. *Waddell (No 2)*,[75] in which the defendant has entirely failed to perform a particular obligation, since it will cost the plaintiff precisely as much to do as the defendant has saved by not doing it; but where the breach consists (as it commonly does) of defective work or departure from specification, it will be a matter of coincidence, unrelated to the nub of the plaintiff's complaint, whether or not the defendant has made a gain. So a restitutionary solution will not solve all the compensatory problems highlighted above.

However, I do agree that there should be a place for the disgorgement of gains from breaches of some (but not all) contractual obligations, beyond the

[72] e.g. Jones (1983) 99 *LQR* 443; Farnsworth (1985) 94 *Yale LJ* 1339; Birks [1987] *LMCLQI* 421; *Jackman* (1989) 48 *CLJ* 302; O'Dair [1993] *CLP* 113; Goodhart [1995] *RLR* 3.

[73] e.g. *Surrey County Council* v. *Bredero Homes Ltd* [1993] 1 WLR 1361; *Jaggard* v. *Sawyer* [1995] 1 WLR 269; *Freeman* v. *Mohammed Niroomand*, *supra* n 56, per Millett LJ (even though, ironically, the judge's middle-ground award was explicitly based on the contractor's saving from the breach).

[74] e.g. Birks [1987] *LMCLQ* 421, 431–2.

[75] [1977] Ch 106.

isolated pockets (breaches of fiduciary obligations and those with proprietary implications) of recovery recognised at present and endorsed by the Law Commission.[76] Assume that in future a case occurs, identical in all respects to the facts of *Ruxley*, except that the contractors *do* save money, say £3,000, by building to pool too shallow. Could the employer elect to claim this sum, instead of tackling the difficult tasks of either persuading the court that the cost of cure is appropriate or arguing about the quantum of his consumer surplus?

So far as precedent is concerned, most commentators cite only one relevant authority, an obscure first instance decision from New Zealand.[77] Yet there is House of Lords authority right under our noses containing an *obiter* passage approving just such an award. That authority is *East Ham Corporation* v. *Bernard Sunley & Sons*,[78] described in *Ruxley* as the "leading English authority"[79] on the measure of damages for defective building work. As we have seen, the Lords quoted and relied heavily on Lord Cohen's comments that the cost of cure will be awarded where it is reasonable for the plaintiff to reinstate, as it was on the facts of *East Ham* itself. However, Lord Cohen *also* said,[80] "there are in fact three possible bases for assessing damages, namely (a) the cost of reinstatement; (b) *the difference in cost to the builder of the actual work done and work specified*; or (c) the diminution in value of the work due to the breach".

Admittedly, he viewed the second head as merely another way of measuring the plaintiff's loss, but it is still clear and authoritative recognition of a gain-based award. Extraordinarily, the case has escaped the attention of the Law Commission[81] and every leading commentator on restitution,[82] and was not cited in any of the cases which reject restitutionary damages out of hand.[83]

Moreover, such an award is in my view justifiable on *principle* in a *Ruxley* situation. As I have said, English contractual remedies are geared towards contracts made for profit—the paradigm case being the sale of goods with a ready market. The principles of mitigation and market-based damages lead to full compensation when the contract is solely for profit, and, there, a gain-based remedy is impossible to justify—if your sole expectation was to make money and you have made no less than you expected, then the breach can

[76] Law Commission Consultation Paper "Aggravated, Exemplary and Restitutionary Damages" (*LCCP* No 132, 1993), p 171.

[77] *Samson & Samson Ltd* v. *Proctor* [1975] 1 NZLR 655.

[78] [1966] AC 406.

[79] [1996] AC 344, 368.

[80] [1966] AC 406, 434 (emphasis added), citing *Hudson's Building and Engineering Contracts*, 8th edn (London, 1959).

[81] *Supra* n 76.

[82] Goff and Jones, *The Law of Restitution*, 4th edn (London, 1993); Beatson, *The Use and Abuse of Unjust Enrichment* (Oxford, 1991); Birks, *An Introduction to the Law of Restitution* (London, 1985); Burrows, *The Law of Restitution* (London, 1993).

[83] *Supra* n 73.

truly said to have been efficient.[85] Indeed, commentators have trouble constructing examples of commercial sale contracts which demonstrate the need for gain-based awards.

For example, Sir William Goodhart QC[85] imagines a power company contracting to buy a cargo of oil from the defendant oil company for delivery on 1 February. There is a sudden international crisis and the price of oil shoots up, so the defendant sells the cargo to another purchaser at a much higher price and delivers it on 20 January. But by 1 February the crisis is over and the price of oil falls back to its previous level, so that the plaintiff is able to buy an equivalent cargo for the contract price. Goodhart suggests that a gain-based remedy would not be appropriate in such a case, on the basis that a compensatory award protects the plaintiff's expectation entirely, leaving no justification for any further relief.[86]

I agree, for two further reasons. The first is the credibility of the example: in practice, there would almost certainly be no *breach* in that scenario—if it is easy for the plaintiff to buy oil in the market at the contract price, that is exactly what the defendant would do, thus avoiding any breach and retaining his profit too.[87] Secondly, if the market had continued to rise between 20 January and 1 February, the plaintiff would have been able to demand the difference between the contract price and the then market value, even though that exceeded the defendant's gain, and thus *reciprocity* must surely require like treatment for the plaintiff when the market falls back to the level of the contract price.[88]

On the other hand, where non-commercial obligations are concerned, there is a persistent risk of under-compensation. As I have said, my initial reaction to the facts of *Ruxley* was that the cost of cure is essential otherwise certain obligations become, simply, not worth the paper they are written on, unless acceptable criteria can be devised for the valuation of the consumer surplus. The same concern underlies the need for gain-based awards. For example, the cost of cure/consumer surplus debate does not address all the problems of non-commercial interests, because not every obligation involves a permanent alteration to the plaintiff's property. Arguments about reinstatement have no place when measuring compensation for breach of confidentiality covenants or promises to provide a specified level of resources on a specified occasion. As Farnsworth has pointed out, "it would not help the injured party if courts

[84] I have deliberately omitted the arguments for and against the economic theory of "efficient breach".

[85] [1995] 3 *RLR* 3.

[86] "it is suggested that restitutionary damages should not be available if the plaintiff has in fact been able to obtain satisfactory substitute performance from another source or could have obtained it and has acted unreasonably in failing to do so": *ibid* at 10.

[87] It is not clear why this did not happen in the extraordinary Israeli case of *Adras Ltd* v. *Harlow & Jones GmbH* [1995] RLR 235 (Israel S. Ct.), possibly because the defendant assumed that the plaintiff would do so to mitigate its loss.

[88] Farnsworth (1985) 94 *Yale LJ* 1339, 1374.

were to be more generous in awarding cost to complete since no amount of money can turn back the clock".[89]

I therefore favour a general right to recover gains flowing from breach of any obligation *unless* either the plaintiff's interest in performance is merely to make profit or substitute performance can be readily bought on a genuine market (i.e. excluding those cases where the difference in objective market value provides a meaningful measure of the plaintiff's unfulfilled expectation). I will not expand this general point any further.[90] However, there are some specific justifications for this approach in construction cases. First, breaches of construction contracts, unlike many other breaches, leave the plaintiff with a performance that he can neither reject, retaining or recovering the price,[91] nor dispose of by way of mitigation in order to fulfil his expectation, other than by the unrealistic means of selling the property comprising the defective work and purchasing another.[92] Of course, the cost of cure solves the problem, but this will not always be available, as we have seen. In addition, judicial estimates of the value of the consumer surplus are likely to be problematic, unpredictable and (if *Ruxley* sets the trend) low. Why not give the plaintiff another weapon in his armoury and allow him to claim instead the defendant's saving[93] from the breach?

Secondly, it is peculiarly easy in construction projects for contractors to cut corners, reduce expenditure and thereby maximise profit, for example by the use of inferior materials. One of the critical features of building work is the ease and speed with which such breaches are covered up and incorporated into the fabric of the building. In addition, this feature makes it all the more likely that the cost of cure measure will be very high and therefore rejected, as in *Ruxley*, as disproportionate. What better way for a contractor to maximise his profits than to charge extra for a high-quality specification and then hide away some inferior alternative in the depths of the works?

I accept that a restitutionary solution would be unnecessary if all expectations were fully protected on breach. If and when this utopia is reached, the need for restitutionary damages will melt away, but until then it is a mistake to dismiss this alternative, particularly in the context of domestic building work.

[89] Farnsworth (1985) 94 *Yale LJ* at 1385.

[90] See in particular O'Dair [1993] *CLP* 113.

[91] Described by Farnsworth (1985) 94 *Yale LJ* 1339 as "abuse of contract".

[92] This may be more realistic for an investment owner, but then his expectation, being purely financial, lacks justification for a gain-based award on my approach.

[93] Or arguably the *Wrotham Park* formula "how much the plaintiff would have accepted to release or modify the covenant"—see Farnsworth (1985) 94 *Yale LJ* 1339, 1348. I find this debate problematic and slightly circular, since the modification price which the plaintiff will be prepared to accept will be influenced, *inter alia*, by the recoverability and level of restitutionary awards.

### *A Limited Role for Unjust Enrichment by Subtraction?*[94]

One final thought is inspired by Lord Mustill's comment that it would "unbalance the bargain"[95] if contractors were allowed to keep the contract price, calculated to reflect the obligations they were undertaking,[96] without being required to comply with those obligations, simply because the other party's expectation was not reflected in the market value of performance. If we presume that the contract price reflects and is based on the obligations and specifications which the promisor is undertaking, then on breach there is a loss to the promisee, matched by a corresponding gain to the promisor, since a rational promisee would not have agreed to pay the original contract price in full if he had known in advance that a given obligation or specification would be breached.[97]

Most obviously, this is reflected in the general unease felt at the result in cases such as *City of New Orleans* v. *Firemen's Charitable Association*[98] or *Tito* v. *Waddell* (No 2),[99] where contractual obligations, taken into account when the consideration was negotiated, were then ignored without sanction; but the same reasoning applies to domestic building cases where part of the work is done badly or one of the specifications is ignored. Whether or not the defendant has saved anything from the breach, he has been overpaid. Is there scope for some form of partial failure of consideration remedy in such a case?

I accept that there are enormous obstacles to a conventional restitutionary award. The requirement of a *total* failure of consideration, recently abandoned where only money payments are involved,[100] remains firmly fixed where the failed obligation was to provide goods and services, and is generally justified by the difficulties of apportioning the consideration if a contract has been partially performed.[101] Thus, in a construction case, where the parties had themselves apportioned the consideration to discrete parts of the contract and where the breach consisted of a failure to carry out one of those parts, the Court of Appeal allowed the owner to recover "the amount of the overpayment as money had and received on the basis that the consideration

[94] I am most grateful to Professor Hugh Beale for sending me an advance, up-dated copy of his paper, "Exceptional Measures of Damages—Contract" now Ch 10 of P. Birks (ed.), *Wrongs and Remedies in the Twenty-First Century* (1996) 217.

[95] [1996] AC 344, 360.

[96] Ironically, not true in *Ruxley*: see *supra* n 24.

[97] Admittedly this proves almost too much, because the same is true of every breach of contract, but it will usually be subsumed in an award protecting the plaintiff's expectation, since, to be put into the position he would have been in had the contract been performed, the plaintiff must give credit for the full price.

[98] (1891) 9 So 486.

[99] [1977] Ch 106.

[100] *Goss* v. *Chilcott* [1996] AC 788.

[101] cf. criticism by Goff and Jones, *supra* n 82, p 413, and Burrows *supra* n 82, p 260. The task is surely not beyond the skill of the courts—they are required to do the same under the Law Reform (Frustrated) Contracts Act 1943.

for it had wholly failed".[102] However, this will not be possible where the parties have not made their own apportionment or where the breach consists of doing work badly.

More fundamentally, the requirement that the contract must have been discharged[103] precludes a restitutionary claim where the breach is minor or where the contract has been affirmed or fulfilled. Here the justification is that, while the contract subsists, the plaintiff's action must be on the contract, and that to allow a restitutionary claim in such circumstances would subvert bargains and allow parties to escape losing contracts.[104]

So such theoretical objections prevent a restitutionary action in the straightforward case of defective building work or departure from specification. Yet it seems likely that the courts do not necessarily respect these objections in practice when it comes to valuing the plaintiff's *loss* in an ordinary damages claim; rather they seem to share the feeling that the plaintiff has indeed lost out by paying or agreeing to pay too much.

For example, a case relied on heavily by the House of Lords in *Ruxley* is *G. W. Atkins Ltd* v. *Scott*,[105] in which a home-owner contracted with the plaintiff firm to have three rooms[106] decorated and tiled, for a price of £1,000. The tiling was defective, but not so disastrous as to put off a potential purchaser, so had no effect on the market value of the property. The case was relied on in *Ruxley* because the owner's claim for the cost of cure was rejected as disproportionate and thus unreasonable (it would have cost more than the full contract price to strip and re-do the tiling) and also because he was awarded instead "general damages for bad workmanship". However, the House of Lords failed to mention the basis on which the judge in *Scott* reached the figure for the general damages, approved in the Court of Appeal as follows: "A rough guide to the appropriate amount is to be found in the plaintiff's charge for the tiling work, which could be assessed at £250".[107]

I suspect that first instance tribunals regularly use this approach as the closest approximation to the value of the plaintiff's loss and it is an approach which should be recognised and debated openly. Goff and Jones argue that it is a mistake to disguise a gain to the defendant as a loss, since this tempts the court to decide that there is no loss.[108] But in subtraction cases there *is* a loss, which needs to be quantified somehow. Perhaps the notional overpayment could be viewed as analogous to reliance losses, like pre-contract expenditure,[109] which would not have been incurred if the "defective performance" had been explicitly on offer at the negotiation stage.

[102] *D. O. Ferguson & Associates* v. *Sohl* (1992) 62 Build LR 95.
[103] *Thomas* v. *Brown* (1876) 1 QBD 714.
[104] Burrows, *supra* n 82, pp 250–1.
[105] (1991) 7 Const LJ 215.
[106] Not his roof, as Lord Lloyd said in *Ruxley* [1996] AC 344, 368.
[107] (1991) 7 Const LJ 215 at 221.
[108] Goff and Jones, *supra* n 82, p 416.
[109] e.g. *Anglia Television Ltd* v. *Reed* [1972] 1 QB 60.

The criticism that this method allows the victim to escape from a bad bargain can be answered by saying: are we to condemn as a bad bargain every domestic building contract made to improve the plaintiff's home rather than to enhance its value? The striking thing about *all* the cases I have cited is that even *perfect* performance would not have affected market value. The plaintiff needs to escape, not from a bad bargain, but from the law's inadequate measurement of his expectation. Until the principles governing the consumer surplus are worked out properly, is there any reason why a plaintiff should not, as an alternative, claim that the best estimate of his loss is the extent to which he overpaid for the job?

## 7. CONCLUSION

Consumers who commission building work to their homes are rarely in a position to negotiate the safeguards which are built into standard form building contracts—retentions, stage payments, liquidated damages or defects liability periods—and are forced to rely on judicial remedies to protect their expectations. On balance, and despite some of the details of the judgments, the implications of *Ruxley* should help achieve this most fundamental objective. Any appellate decision which acknowledges, however grudgingly, that consumer expectations are rarely reflected in the exchange or market value of performance, is ultimately to be welcomed.

# 2

# *Loss and Gain at Greater Depth: The Implications of the* Ruxley *Decision—A Comment*

EDWIN PEEL

The facts of *Ruxley Electronics and Construction Ltd* v. *Forsyth*[1] demonstrate once again that, whatever the furtive imagination of the law teacher when seeking to test the boundaries of the law, real life is invariably more accomplished in this regard. In this comment, I shall concentrate almost entirely on the "contractual solutions" put forward as the appropriate remedy for plaintiffs such as Mr Forsyth: first, because Janet O'Sullivan's chapter concentrates on these solutions; secondly, because the arguments in favour of restitutionary damages for breach of contract have been well documented in this collection of papers and elsewhere;[2] thirdly, because there is no evidence that restitutionary damages would have been of any use to Mr Forsyth;[3] and, fourthly, because the clamour for restitutionary damages is based on the perceived inadequacies of compensatory damages. The decision of the House of Lords in *Ruxley* would seem to have gone some way towards redressing some of these inadequacies, perceived or otherwise.

## The Role of the Plaintiff's Intention

It always seemed a slightly curious aspect of the decision of the Court of Appeal to award the cost of reinstatement without requiring any evidence that

1 [1996] AC 344.

2 Waddams in Burrows (ed.), *Essays on the Law of Restitution* (Oxford, Clarendon Press, 1991), Ch. 8; Jones (1983) 99 *LQR* 443; Farnsworth (1985) 94 *Yale LJ* 1339; Birks [1987] *LMCLQ* 421; O'Dair [1993] *CLP* 113; Jackman [1989] *CLJ* 302; Smith (1994) 24 *Can Bus LJ* 121; Goodhart [1995] *RLR* 3; Jaffey [1995] *RLR* 30.

3 There was no suggestion that the defendants had saved any great expense in lopping 9 inches off the deep end, nor that they had made a killing under another contract only by cutting a few corners in this one. This is certainly not to say that the availability of restitutionary damages may not be a sensible development in cases where they are appropriate, but, as demonstrated by the facts in *Ruxley*, they will not always provide a solution to claims based on the defendant's defective performance.

it was the plaintiff's intention so to reinstate.[4] Nor did it seem an entirely convincing explanation that the courts are not usually concerned with what the plaintiff intends to do with his damages.[5] Admittedly, in a "commercial" contract[6] it is only the plaintiff's intention to acquire goods or services *as a means of generating profit*. Once damages are awarded to replace his lost profit, it would be strange to expect the plaintiff to go one step back and acquire the goods or services, or show any intention of doing so.[7] However, in a "consumer" contract,[8] the plaintiff's intention is *to get the goods or services contracted for* and it is this defeated intention which forms a loss for which a claim may be advanced.[9] In such circumstances, it would seem only natural to require evidence of the plaintiff's intention and the best, and only, evidence available may be what the plaintiff plans to do with any damages awarded.[10]

The approach of the Court of Appeal to the role of intention may be seen as one illustration of its failure to accept the full implications of the distinction between commercial contracts and consumer contracts, outlined in Janet O'Sullivan's opening paragraphs. The same could not fairly be said of the House of Lords. When Lord Jauncey observes that intention *is relevant*, but "only to reasonableness and hence to the extent of the loss which has been sustained",[11] he would seem to have in mind both whether the cost of reinstatement would be justified and, if it would not, whether the plaintiff has, at least, satisfied the court that the contract is one which should attract a consumer surplus award.

The one question which remains is whether the House of Lords should have been prepared to go further and always award the cost of reinstatement, provided the plaintiff gives an undertaking to the defendant to use the damages in this way. There are numerous advantages to this solution which are all

[4] [1994] 1 WLR 650, 657 (Staughton LJ), 660 (Mann LJ). Dillon LJ (dissenting) expressed no opinion on the role of intention.

[5] *Ibid.*

[6] i.e. one made purely for financial profit, which would not justify a "consumer surplus" award.

[7] With the exception of *Dean* v. *Ainley* [1987] 1 WLR 1729, where Kerr LJ seems, with respect, to have fallen into the same error (at 1737), the cases relied on by Staughton LJ ([1994] 1 WLR 650, 657) to demonstrate that what the plaintiff does with his damages is not, in general, any concern of the defendant, are all cases where the claim concerns an objectively quantifiable loss which does not depend, for its existence, upon defeat of the plaintiff's intention. See Lord Lloyd in *Ruxley* [1996] AC 344, 373, and Phillips J in *Channel Island Ferries Ltd* v. *Cenargo Navigation Ltd, The Rozel* [1994] 2 Lloyd's Rep 161, 166–7.

[8] i.e. one not made purely for financial profit and which, therefore, may justify a "consumer surplus" award.

[9] Whether the cost of cure or the "consumer surplus".

[10] In this sense, while I agree with Janet O'Sullivan that, normally, requiring evidence of future intention is "pretty meaningless", I am not entirely persuaded by the suggestion that there may be little point in giving evidence of intention in cases like *Ruxley* where the plaintiff is attempting to advance a claim for the cost of cure or the consumer surplus.

[11] [1996] AC 344, 359.

highlighted by Janet O'Sullivan,[12] but the argument which would seem to weigh most heavily against it is the danger of the plaintiff "holding out". If the plaintiff is guaranteed the cost of reinstatement whenever he is prepared to give the necessary undertaking, what is to prevent him from stating that he is willing to do so, right up to the door of the court and until he has obtained a settlement, just short of the cost of reinstatement but well above the real value which he placed on performance, i.e. the consumer surplus?

This problem is acknowledged by Janet O'Sullivan and, perhaps, no more can be said than that, "if all else is equal, at least this way it is the innocent plaintiff who has the opportunity to hold out".[13] But this assumes that the alternative, of limiting the plaintiff to the consumer surplus,[14] would have the effect of enabling the defendant to hold out for an unreasonably low award. This may be true if one follows Lord Lloyd's unhelpful suggestion that consumer surplus awards will generally be modest.[15] However, having explicitly recognised the availability of the consumer surplus, and rejected the option of cost of reinstatement plus undertaking, the courts might reasonably be expected to ensure that awards are made at a level which fairly reflects the extent of the plaintiff's loss and provides an incentive to the defendant contractor to provide full performance.

## The Nature of the Consumer Surplus or Loss of Amenity Award

I find myself unable to agree with Janet O'Sullivan's interpretation of this part of the speech of Lord Lloyd and the suggestion that it differs from that of Lord Mustill in a significant practical way. Ultimately, it seems that both of their Lordships accept that the basis of the award of £2,500 to Mr Forsyth is the loss of amenity or the "consumer surplus". Whereas Lord Mustill does so at a refreshingly explicit and general level,[16] Lord Lloyd prefers to reason by "logical application or adaptation" of previous decisions.[17] The two cases upon which he relies are *Jarvis* v. *Swans Tours Ltd*[18] and *Jackson* v. *Horizon*

[12] Some of which she prefers to treat as the disadvantages of the House of Lords' decision to award only the consumer surplus when there is a disproportion between the difference in value and the cost of cure: see *supra* p. 11.

[13] *Supra* p. 19. It may also seem preferable that, as between the two parties, any "windfall" should accrue to the plaintiff rather than the defendant. But, as in *Ruxley*, the defendant's breach may not always create a windfall and it has been suggested that the problem of unmerited windfalls is better left to the more sensitive responses which may be provided by restitutionary damages: Harris, Ogus and Phillips (1979) 95 *LQR* 581, 593–4.

[14] At least in cases where the cost of reinstatement is unreasonable.

[15] [1996] AC 344, 374. It is submitted that it is only the suggestion that the award should be a modest one, and generally less than the £2,500 which the House of Lords was unable to interfere with in *Ruxley*, which gives credence to some of the claims in the press that the decision of the House of Lords not to award the cost of reinstatement creates a "cowboy builders' charter".

[16] *Ibid* at 360.

[17] *Ibid* at 374.

[18] [1973] QB 233.

*Holidays Ltd.*[19] The potential for misinterpretation of Lord Lloyd's speech stems from his regarding such cases as exceptions to the general rule that, in claims for breach of contract, the plaintiff cannot recover damages for disappointment.[20]

In fairness, that is the way these cases are commonly understood, but the clear recognition of the consumer surplus, based on a distinction between "commercial contracts" and "consumer contracts", confirms that they should now be viewed differently. In their seminal article, when discussing *Jarvis* v. *Swans Tours Ltd*, Harris, Ogus and Phillips stressed the importance of distinguishing "psychic costs", such as disappointment, from the utility value expected from performance, but not provided due to the defendant's breach.[21] The former represent a *diminution* of the plaintiff's pre-contractual level of well-being, whereas the latter represents the failure of the defendant to ensure the *enhancement* of the same. Both may be described in terms of disappointment, but cases such as *Jarvis* v. *Swans Tours Ltd* and *Jackson* v. *Horizon Holidays Ltd* fall clearly within the latter category and, in the light of *Ruxley* v. *Forsyth*, should be viewed as early examples of the consumer surplus.[22] This is not to say that there may not be any genuine exceptions to the rule laid down in *Addis* v. *Gramophone Co Ltd*,[23] but that the rule itself should be understood to apply only to claims of diminution rather than non-enhancement.

Once it is understood that Lord Lloyd only used the terminology of "disappointment" in the loose sense described above, it seems clear that his decision is based, just as much as is Lord Mustill's, on the idea of a consumer surplus. The difference between the two is that, while Lord Mustill was prepared to lay down a general principle which will have to be moulded and refined by future cases, Lord Lloyd, as is fashionable these days, preferred to adopt an incremental approach which leaves for another day questions as to whether further increments may be added. It also follows, if this interpretation is correct, that both of their Lordships would make a consumer surplus award *on top of* an award for an objectively quantifiable difference in value, if supported by the facts.

## The Test of Disproportionality

After *Ruxley*, it seems that a plaintiff will be awarded the cost of curing the defendant's breach when such cost is not "disproportionate". Although, as Janet O'Sullivan notes, it is not entirely clear from the speeches of their

19 [1975] 1 WLR 1468.

20 *Addis* v. *Gramophone Co Ltd* [1909] AC 488.

21 (1979) 95 *LQR* 581, 596 n 89.

22 See Burrows, *Remedies for Torts and Breach of Contract*, 2nd edn (1994), 237, where it is suggested that both cases are probably better understood as examples of the consumer surplus.

23 e.g. *Perry* v. *Sidney Phillips & Son* [1982] 1 WLR 1297; *Watts* v. *Morrow* [1991] 1 WLR 1421.

Lordships which figures are to be compared, it seems that disproportionality must be determined by comparing the cost of reinstatement with the difference in value, *including any consumer surplus award* which the court may be prepared to make.

The one and very obvious drawback with this approach is its uncertainty and, in an attempt to reduce or avoid this, Janet O'Sullivan considers a number of alternatives. The American concept of economic waste would seem to be equally uncertain but two others are worth further consideration. The first is said to be derived from the speech of Lord Jauncey but, again, I find myself at odds with Janet O'Sullivan's interpretation. She suggests that Lord Jauncey expresses the principle of disproportionality differently by contrasting "a failure to achieve the precise contractual objective" with "the loss which is occasioned by a total failure".[24] The difference, it is said, lies in focusing on the result of the breach, not the technical difficulty of remedying it. My own view is that Lord Jauncey does, in fact, have in mind the technical difficulty of remedying the breach and does no more than provide an illustration of when the cost of reinstatement would be disproportionate and unreasonable. If the defendant has simply not performed at all[25] or he has performed, but in a way in which the end product is seriously defective, it will be reasonable for the plaintiff to expect to be paid a sum which will enable him to have the contract performed by another, by building it in the first place or by demolishing the defendant's work and rebuilding. If the defendant has, as in *Ruxley*, performed, but in a way in which the end product only contains minor defects, it will not be reasonable to award damages to undo a great deal of work which is satisfactory, simply to correct that which is not.

Secondly, Janet O'Sullivan attempts to explain why *Ruxley* and cases like *Jacob & Youngs* v. *Kent*[26] are "extreme" cases, where the cost of reinstatement should not be awarded.[27] She suggests that a distinction might be made between cases where the defendant's work is "wrong" or "shoddy" and those where it merely differs from the contract specification. This is very interesting and it is slightly disappointing that it is not considered further. The obvious point to be made is whether such a distinction can be drawn satisfactorily, and one immediately thinks of the facts of *Ruxley*. Is the defendant's breach a mere failure to fulfil the exact specification or "shoddy" work? Janet O'Sullivan considers it to be the former but, if, as she suggests, using perfectly adequate but wrongly matching tiles is shoddy or wrong,[28] should not the same be said of lopping 9 inches off the deep end of a swimming pool?

[24] [1996] AC 344, 357.

[25] e.g. *Radford* v. *De Froberville* [1977] 1 WLR 1262.

[26] (1921) 129 N.E. 889.

[27] Thereby implying that in all other cases it should be.

[28] This does not seem to be a view which would be shared by Lord Jauncey in his consideration of the example of a builder who uses yellow bricks for a lower course, instead of blue, as specified: [1996] AC 344, 358.

An alternative and more limited interpretation of the test of disproportionality may be provided by accepting that, while "commercial" contracts and "consumer" contracts should be treated differently in certain respects, they should, ultimately, be treated the same way. In commercial contracts, the plaintiff will be awarded the cost of reinstatement whenever it is reasonable to insist upon it.[29] It seems tolerably clear that it will only be reasonable to insist on the cost of reinstatement when it is *cheaper* than the difference in value.[30] The same approach could be taken with consumer contracts, save that the difference in value may include an element of consumer surplus, as well as any objectively quantifiable difference.[31] The fact that it is sometimes difficult to assess the difference in value will also support an award of the cost of reinstatement[32] and it is, perhaps, in this context only that any references to "disproportion" in previous "commercial" cases are to be understood.

By recognising the consumer surplus in *Ruxley*, the House of Lords has accepted two inherent and unavoidable uncertainties; namely, which contracts or types of contract qualify for such an award and what is the appropriate level of compensation? It would seem a strange move, therefore, to introduce a third uncertainty in the form of a uniformly applicable test of disproportionality. It may, of course, betray a lack of confidence in the courts' ability to resolve the first two uncertainties. The vagueness of a test of disproportionality, which is amply demonstrated in Janet O'Sullivan's paper, provides maximum flexibility for the courts to award the cost of reinstatement without having to admit that it has no idea what, *exactly*, it should have awarded for the consumer surplus, or whether it should have done so at all. However, it has already been suggested above that the courts should react positively to *Ruxley* and be prepared to fix the level of consumer surplus awards in a way which balances the need to compensate the plaintiff with providing an incentive for the defendant to perform. Limiting the test of disproportionality to asking whether the court is convinced that the plaintiff's claim merits *a* consumer surplus award, which cannot easily be quantified, but would certainly have the effect that the difference in value *exceeds* the cost of reinstatement, might be a useful step in this direction.

[29] *East Ham Corporation* v. *Bernard Sunley & Sons Ltd* [1966] AC 406.

[30] The long-term nature of investment in commercial property and the high return on capital which is normally expected means that, invariably, the cost of reinstatement is the cheaper alternative: *McGregor on Damages*, 15th edn (1988), para. 1091; *East Ham Borough Council* v. *Bernard Sunley & Sons Ltd* [1966] AC 406; *Darlington BC* v. *Wiltshier Northern Ltd* [1995] 1 WLR 68, 79. Where the plaintiff intends to sell the property without remedying the defects, then the difference in value will usually be the appropriate measure: *Rawlings* v. *Rentokil Laboratories* [1972] EGD 744.

[31] This might explain the decision of Judge Norman Richards QC in *Hollebone* v. *Midhurst and Fenhurst Builders Ltd* [1968] 1 Lloyd's Rep 38 to award the cost of reinstatement when it appeared to exceed the difference in value, but only by excluding or failing to put a figure on the consumer surplus which he clearly recognised in the form of the "unique" value which he attached to the plaintiffs' property.

[32] [1996] AC 344, 366, per Lord Lloyd.

**Restitutionary Damages**

As noted earlier, restitutionary damages would have been of no use to Mr Forsyth, but they are rightly considered by Janet O'Sullivan on the hypothesis that the defendant builder had made a saving from his breach of contract.[33] In her opinion, it is difficult to construct an example of a commercial contract[34] which demonstrates the need for a gain-based award,[35] but there is a "persistent" risk of under-compensation for the breach of non-commercial obligations which may be addressed by a restitutionary remedy. For this reason, she supports a general right to recover gains flowing from a breach of contract *unless* the plaintiff's expectations are fully protected by a compensatory award.

As she concedes, this is tacit recognition that, even after the House of Lords' acceptance of the consumer surplus award in *Ruxley*, the courts will not always feel certain that they can do full justice to the plaintiff's expectation. This entitlement of the plaintiff to a "general" right to restitution raises many questions. Exactly how and when would the basis for making a restitutionary award be satisfied? It is one thing to acknowledge that the impetus for a restitutionary award is provided by the inadequacies of compensatory awards, but quite another to make this the trigger for such an award in individual cases. Is the plaintiff to be given the option of suing for either, or is it a matter for the discretion of the court? What if, as in *Ruxley*, the restitutionary remedy is, itself, inadequate? If this compels the court to put a figure on the consumer surplus in some cases, why shouldn't they grasp the nettle and do so in all cases where it would be appropriate?[36] And should the inadequacy of a compensatory award alone be enough? There are those who have suggested that something more may be required, such as the need for a cynical or deliberate breach[37] or the infringement of some proprietary interest.[38]

33 Or created the circumstances in which he was able to make a profit under another contract.

34 i.e. one made purely for financial profit.

35 She cites the case of *Adras Ltd* v. *Harlow & Jones GmbH* (1988) 42(1) PD 221; [1995] *RLR* 235 (English translation) as a good example of this difficulty, though her original assertion that Goodhart ([1995] *RLR* 3, 9–10) supports the decision of the Supreme Court of Israel to award a disgorgement of the defendant's gain must be wrong. Her argument that there is no *breach* in such a case would seem to mirror Goodhart's suggestion that there had been no *wrong* committed which justified a restitutionary remedy. I note that she has now (above p 21) changed her view and joins in Goodhart's *criticism* of the decisions. For an interesting suggestion that any contract should attract a restitutionary remedy where it was part of the bargain that the defendant should forego a gain, see Weinrib, "The Juridical Classification of Obligations" in P. Birks (ed.), *Extending Obligations* (OUP, 1997).

36 If the court decides that there is no consumer surplus, then presumably the plaintiff's expectation will have been fully protected by compensatory damages and there will be no basis, under Janet O'Sullivan's proposal, for a restitutionary remedy.

37 Birks [1987] *LMCLQ* 421.

38 Jackman (1989) 48 *CLJ* 302; Burrows, *The Law of Restitution* (Butterworths, 1993), 403; Law Commission Consultation Paper, "Aggravated, Exemplary and Restitutionary Damages" (LCCP No 132, 1993) p 171.

Since no argument was presented in *Ruxley* on the subject of restitutionary damages it was, perhaps, wise of Janet O'Sullivan not to expand this point further, safe in the knowledge that it is a long way from being laid to rest.

# 3

# *Remedies for Breach of Contract: Specific Enforcement and Restitution*

RICHARD NOLAN*

## 1. INTRODUCTION

This chapter will consider when restitutionary remedies for breach of contract[1] should be available: never, always, or sometimes; and if sometimes, when. It is important to note at the outset that these questions are, in fact, ambiguous as to their import, and may be answered in two, very different, ways. One way of understanding the questions is to see them as asking whether a restitutionary remedy for breach of contract is implicit in, and therefore consistent with, current understanding of just what it is to make a contract and subsequently to commit the wrong of "breaching" the contract; and such questions can be answered by formal legal analysis. However, it is also possible to understand the questions as inviting a re-evaluation of the law of contract, including remedies for breach of contract; and such questions cannot be answered by reference only to legal considerations: moral, political and economic discourse are also relevant in reaching any answer.

This chapter will primarily address the question of restitution for breach of contract in a legal, doctrinal fashion, attempting to ascertain whether such a remedy is appropriate as part of the existing body of contractual doctrine. When doing so, it will not consider contracts whose purpose and effect is to create a relationship between the parties which may properly be described as fiduciary or confidential, so that the restitutionary remedies associated with such relationships can legitimately be invoked, but it will consider other

* The author is grateful for the comments about the paper on which this chapter is based, made by participants in the conference, and especially for the comments of Professor Peter Watts.

[1] All references to "restitutionary remedies for breach of contract", or to "restitution for breach of contract", are references to monetary remedies by which a contract-breaker is compelled to pay the counterparty to the contract profits which the contract-breaker has made through the breach, or a sum equivalent to such profits. The use of the term "restitution" to describe a response to a wrong has been criticised (see, e.g., Smith, "Disgorgement of the Profits of Breach of Contract" (1994) 24 *Can. Bus. LJ* 121) but for present purposes nothing turns on that terminological criticism.

contracts in which equity may intervene.[2] The main conclusion of the chapter is that, unless the law of contract is significantly modified, or developed, restitutionary remedies for breach of contract should be available if, and only if, there has been breach of a contract which both provides for the transfer, or grant, of an interest in property and is, or was, amenable to a decree of specific performance.[3] The chapter will then briefly examine various suggestions for the wider availability of restitutionary remedies for breach of contract, and look at some of the consequences inherent in any such modification or development of the law. However, though legal, doctrinal argument can highlight these consequences, they cannot offer firm conclusions as to whether they are desirable—though such arguments are no less interesting for that.[4]

[2] Indeed, this chapter was prompted by consideration of just such a case, the recent case of *Tang Man Sit* v. *Capacious Investments Ltd* [1996] AC 514, PC.

[3] In this chapter, "a contract amenable to a decree of specific performance", and like expressions, should be taken to mean a contract for the disposition of an interest in property which could be, or, at the time of the breach, could have been, enforced by means of a decree of specific performance, *stricto sensu* (see *Wolverhampton & Walsall Railway Co* v. *London & North Western Railway Co* (1873)L.R. 16 Eq. 433 and the text to n 24 *infra*). Further, references to the availability of specific performance should be taken to mean that a decree of specific performance could have issued in respect of the contract in question, so as to trigger operation of the doctrine of conversion (see *Lysaght* v. *Edwards* (1876) 2 Ch D 499), whether or not the remedy of specific performance is still available at judgment.

[4] In opposing the idea of restitutionary remedies for breach of contract, much has been made of the notion of the "efficient breach of contract" (see generally R.A. Posner, *Economic Analysis of Law*, 4th edn (1992), 93–6) and of the fear that an award of restitution for breach of contract would, quite undesirably, deter parties to a contract from breaching it when it was "efficient" to do so. The theory of efficient breach has, however, been subjected to cogent criticism (see, in particular, Jones, "The Recovery of Benefits Gained from a Breach of Contract" (1983) 99 *LQR* 443; Friedmann, "The Efficient Breach Fallacy" (1989) 18 *J Leg Stud* 1; Macneil, "Efficient Breach of Contract: Circles in the Sky" (1982) 68 *Va LR* 947 and Smith, "Disgorgement of the Profits of Breach of Contract" (1994) 24 *Can Bus LJ* 121). The theory assumes the paramount virtue of economic efficiency, which may be questioned (cf. Birks, "Restitutionary Damages for Breach of Contract: *Snepp* and the Fusion of Law and Equity" [1987] *LMCLQ* 421, 441). Yet, even if its tacit premise is accepted, the theory does not rule out *in limine* a restitutionary response to a breach of contract. A breach of contract would be efficient, in the sense of increasing the general wealth of society, even if the wealth generated by the contracting party in breach were transferred to the other party to the contract through a restitutionary response to the breach (see, e.g., Macneil, "Efficient Breach of Contract: Circles in the Sky" (1982) 68 *Va LR* 947; Smith, "Disgorgement of the Profits of Contract" (1994) 24 *Can Bus LJ* 121, 134). To put the matter in graphic, economic terms, the Pareto frontier, which describes economic efficiency, is a curve, not a point: an efficient breach of a contract may take the parties collectively towards the Pareto frontier, but the fact of an efficient breach gives no guidance as to where on the frontier the parties will find themselves; in other words, it does not say how each of the parties should end up. Furthermore, very little is offered by way of evidence that one particular distribution of wealth is more likely than any other to encourage the overall maximisation of wealth in society. In short, the theory of efficient breach is an argument of economics, which assumes the paramount virtue of economic efficiency, not an incontestable assumption, and does not offer sufficient appropriate evidence, namely empirical economic data, to justify any conclusion that its assumed virtue is best realised in a particular fashion.

Others have argued for a much wider acceptance of restitution for breach of contract (see, e.g., Goff and Jones, *The Law of Restitution*, 4th edn (1993), 416–17; Smith, *supra*, and Sir William Goodhart QC, "Restitutionary Damages for Breach of Contract" [1995] *RLR* 3). Smith offers the positive argument that restitution should always be possible in such circumstances because

It is always useful to be clear about the axioms from which any argument proceeds; and so, although they may seem obvious, it is worth stating the principles from which the following discussion proceeds. Any right and the remedy or remedies for breach of it must form a coherent unity. To say that a person has a legal right is to express both what those bound by the right must do, or abstain from doing (in Austinian terms, "the primary right" of the right-holder in question[5]) and to indicate what consequences will be visited on such people if they breach the obligation incumbent on them (in Austinian terms, "the secondary right" of such person).[6] It is vital to understand that the secondary right is not logically independent of the primary right: this is because the remedy is meant to vindicate the right; a remedy, so far as possible, protects and vindicates a right, and is not a penalty. It follows, therefore, that, should one alter the consequences of breaching a primary right, then by necessary implication the nature of that right is changed. Granted, the law is now formulated in terms of rights, and of the consequent remedies granted in response to infringement of such rights, and, indeed, this structure for legal discourse doubtless has its advantages; but, if it is forgotten that such a structure of discourse is adopted for the sake of convenience in certain contexts, then it may have other, undesirable consequences. First, it may, for example, encourage the inaccurate tendency to discuss remedies as though they are logically wholly severable from the rights they vindicate. Secondly, it may also encourage an unhelpful tendency to think of certain types of right as identical for all purposes of analysis, even when different remedies are available to vindicate some instances, but not others, of a particular type of right.

These matters have some specific consequences for any discussion of restitution for breach of contract. First, restitution for breach of contract is, if anything, a remedy for the wrong of breaching a contract; it is not a cause of

otherwise the law would "allow rights to be expropriated unilaterally": a party to a contract could commit a breach of contract knowing that the price of his breach will be less than the profit he stands to make by the breach. However, this argument is equivocal. First, unless specific enforcement is possible in all cases of a breach of contract, then it will, at least sometimes, be possible to "expropriate" a contractual right—that is, to take it without the consent of the right holder in return for money. The availability of restitution for breach of contract does not alter this fact. What is changed by the availability of restitutionary remedies for breach of contract is the price at which a person's contractual rights can be expropriated, and therefore the likelihood that they will be expropriated: in other words, the degree of protection afforded to a party to a contract is changed, but the nature of the protection is not. Smith's argument therefore rests on a non-legal value judgement as to the appropriate method of pricing the expropriation of contractual rights in a situation of bilateral monopoly: this judgement is that all contractual rights should be priced in the same way when they have been unilaterally expropriated by a counterparty to the contract, and the price for such expropriation, for defeating a party's performance interest in his contract, should include restitution of at least part of the profits made through the breach of contract. That is a perfectly rational and tenable point of view; but it would entail wholesale re-writing of the law of contract, as will be seen in the ensuing text, which is something that should not be undertaken lightly.

[5] Austin, *Lectures on Jurisprudence*, 3rd edn (1869), Lecture XLV, 787 *et seq.*

[6] *Ibid.*

action. So, therefore, it is wrong to talk of a remedy, restitution for breach of contract, without acknowledging its inseparable relation to the substantive performance for which it is a substitute.[7] Secondly, the mere categorisation of a right as "contractual" does not specifically describe the substance of that right, but rather the manner of its genesis, so it is impossible to deduce from that categorisation whether, as a matter of legal, doctrinal analysis, restitution for breach of contract is an appropriate remedy for infringement of a particular contractual right. In order to answer that question, it is necessary to consider what are the legal obligations inherent in making the particular contract, not just the manner in which contractual obligations arise; and, given that the available remedies for infringement of a right illustrate the nature of the right, any such investigation must take account of the remedies currently granted in response to a breach of contract.

This approach stresses that right and remedy form a coherent set: remedy reflects right and *vice versa*. If, as a matter of legal, doctrinal analysis, a remedy is not coherent with the current understanding of a legal entitlement, the approach does not reveal what should be done next: one must be modified, but logic does not dictate which. So, while it is possible to tell by legal analysis whether restitution as a remedy for breach of a contract is consistent with the entitlement, as currently understood, of a person who has the benefit of that contract, nevertheless, if any inconsistency between the two is revealed, non-legal argument must be used to see whether the accepted understanding of an entitlement should preclude grant of the remedy, or grant of the remedy should entail modification of the entitlement.

If any attempt is to be made to see whether restitution for breach of contract is appropriate within the current framework of contract law, it is necessary to describe some pertinent characteristics of that body of law, in particular its remedial aspects. The most important thing to note is that the primary judicial, coercive remedy for breach of contract is an award of damages which is intended to put the plaintiff in as good a position as if the contract had been performed ("expectation damages").[8] This position has been criticised in principle,[9] but its truth as a description of the current state of English law can hardly be in doubt. A plaintiff injured by a breach of contract may also, at his election, claim damages assessed by measure of his reliance on the existence of the contract breached, though such damages can-

[7] "Performance" is here intended to mean acting, or refraining from action, in accordance with the tenor of the primary right. The distinction made here, therefore, is between the action, or restraint from action, to which a right-holder is entitled, and the remedy the right-holder obtains if that action, or restraint from action, does not eventuate, or is not expected to eventuate. By contrast, Friedmann's distinction between "specific remedies" and "substantial remedies" (see Friedmann, "The Performance Interest in Contract Damages" (1995) 111 *LQR* 628) points to a distinction between different types of remedies.

[8] *Robinson* v. *Harman* (1848) 1 Exch. 850, 855, per Parke B, restated more recently in numerous cases including *Tito* v. *Waddell* [1977] Ch 106, 328–34, per Megarry V-C.

[9] See in particular Atiyah, *The Rise and Fall of Freedom of Contract*, and *An Introduction to the Law of Contract*, 4th edn (1989), 30–9, 457–80.

not exceed the expectation damages he might receive:[10] claiming reliance losses is not to be a way in which a plaintiff may escape a bad bargain. Furthermore, damages are a "substitutional remedy":[11] they do not constitute the performance for which the plaintiff had bargained, but they are as near a monetary equivalent as possible to that performance. Some contracts may be remedied by specific remedies, that is by judicial compulsion to perform;[12] nevertheless, the object of such remedies is, like the object of an award of expectation damages, to put the plaintiff in the position contemplated by the contract, but no further forward.

This is but the briefest of outlines of a complex and fascinating area of the law; but even so, it is possible to derive some important conclusions from it. By the means through which it chooses to remedy breaches of contract, English law shows plainly that its aim in enforcing contracts is to vindicate contractual expectations, rather than anything more or less ambitious: a contractual right embodies an expectation of performance, but nothing further, such as the promotion of good faith, or fidelity, in the performance of a contract.

Any discussion of whether a restitutionary remedy for breach of contract is appropriate, and coherent with current contractual doctrine, requires not only a view of the law of contract, but also an understanding of so-called "restitution for wrongs". In cases of "restitution for wrongs" an award is made in favour of a plaintiff by reference to a defendant's gain, not to reverse a flow of wealth from him to the defendant,[13] but rather to strip away profits made by the defendant in consequence, at least in part, of his commission of a wrong against the plaintiff. In such cases, therefore, the legal analysis is that a plaintiff has a right to deny a defendant the freedom to act in a particular way, *and also* a right to remove any incentive the defendant has to act in any the way: the law not only stigmatises a wrong but also stigmatises the defendant's enrichment in consequence of the wrongdoing as itself wrongful. Why it might do so in any given case is a separate question.

It should be noted immediately that one supposed legal justification of the plaintiff's right to a restitutionary remedy for a wrong is, in fact, no justification at all: to say that a restitutionary remedy should be granted for a wrong which involves an invasion of a proprietary right is not a justification. While

[10] *Anglia Television Ltd* v. *Reed* [1972] 1 QB 60; *C.C.C. (London) Films Ltd* v. *Imperial Quadrant Films* [1985] QB 16.

[11] For a discussion of "specific" and "substitutional" remedies, see Friedmann, "The Performance Interest in Contract Damages" (1995) 111 LQR 628.

[12] *Ibid.*

[13] In the context of a breach of contract, for example, the defendant's refusal to perform has not discharged him of liability under the contract and so cannot be described as a flow of wealth from plaintiff to defendant: in other words, the defendant's failure to meet the plaintiff's expectations under the contract cannot be described as a loss of wealth to plaintiff and a corresponding enrichment of the defendant. Any response to the breach measured by the defendant's gain must, therefore, be directed to stripping away the profits made by him through his breach of contract (i.e., a response to, or remedy for, a wrong).

it is true that proprietary rights are normally thought to involve the exclusive right, as against others in the world not holding like rights, to exploit or take advantage of an asset in the manner sanctioned by the right, and while it is true that a restitutionary remedy for a wrong which involves invasion of such a right makes sense, as it restores the integrity of the owner's exclusive rights of exploitation, nevertheless "property" is not a justification for a restitutionary remedy, because "property" depends for its connotation of exclusivity of legal right at least in part upon the very existence of a restitutionary remedy for unlawful acts and omissions adverse to the right-holder, to the "owner".[14] Property cannot be a justification for a restitutionary remedy,though it is consistent with it: a legal concept cannot be justified by a legal remedy, though the two must be consistent with each other.

Rather, the justification for a restitutionary remedy for a wrong must lie in non-legal reasons why the law should sanction certain power relationships. The justification for restitutionary remedies in response to wrongdoing must be sought, for example, in why the law wishes to encourage and protect rights of exclusive exploitation in relation to an asset (i.e. the institution of property) or exclusive rights to certain services (e.g. certain aspects of the duties of fidelity imposed on a fiduciary).

Now restitution for breach of contract does not naturally sit easily with the view, outlined above, of the nature, objects and purpose of the law of contract. An award of restitution for breach of contract is measured by reference to the defendant's gain made in consequence of the breach. Such an award bears no obvious relation whatsoever to the plaintiff's expectations and, therefore, does not seem consistent with current contractual doctrine. In principle, therefore, any award of restitution for breach of contract would appear odd. However, the courts do grant restitutionary remedies for breach of contracts amenable to specific performance. So, for example, in the recent case of *Tang Man Sit* v. *Capacious Investments Ltd*,[15] the plaintiff, Capacious Investments, had contracted with the defendant for the purchase of sixteen houses. A conveyance was not duly executed, and the court ordered specific performance of the contract. Further, the plaintiff was held entitled, at its election, either to compensation for the damage caused by the defendant to properties that should have been conveyed pursuant to the contract, or to an account of the profits earned by the defendant through letting the properties in breach of the contract.[16] Again, in *Lake* v. *Bayliss*[17] the plaintiff was held entitled to the proceeds of sale of land, which the defendant was to sell to him under a con-

[14] This point is but one aspect of the wider argument about the nature, and legitimate use, of the concept of "property" explored by Professor Gray in "Property in Thin Air" [1991] *CLJ* 252.

[15] [1996] AC 514, PC.

[16] The plaintiff was obliged to make an election between these two alternative remedies, and the case was principally concerned with whether this had been done. The requirement of election, though well established in the case law, has been subjected to principled criticism by Birks, "Inconsistency between Compensation and Restitution" (1996) 112 *LQR* 375.

[17] [1974] 1 WLR 1073.

tact enforceable by a decree of specific performance, but which the defendant had instead conveyed to a third party. In view of this case law, it is proposed first to examine whether the availability of specific performance to enforce a contract is a reason to make restitutionary remedies available in response to a breach of that contract, and then to examine whether restitutionary remedies might be granted in response to breach of contract in other circumstances, for example, when other specific remedies for breach of contract are or have been available.[18]

## 2. SPECIFIC REMEDIES AND THE AVAILABILITY OF A RESTITUTIONARY REMEDY FOR BREACH OF CONTRACT

In order to consider whether restitutionary remedies should be available if, and only if, specific performance is available to enforce the contract, it is necessary to highlight certain facts connected with specific performance. These facts raise questions which will then be examined in greater detail.

First, there are some points to be made about specific performance itself. Specific performance is not a restitutionary remedy: it is a specific, as opposed to a substitutional, remedy for breach of contract.[19] One may wonder why the availability of one type of remedy should be relevant to the availability of another, different type of remedy.

Secondly, the rules of law by which the availability of specific performance is governed were developed to delimit the operation of a specific, non-monetary remedy. Are they therefore appropriate to determine the availability of a monetary, substitutional remedy, such as a restitutionary remedy? For example, what of bars to the availability of specific performance, such as severe hardship[20] or uncertainty,[21] which make sense as bars to specific

[18] For the purposes of this point, it does not matter whether damages are regarded as the primary remedy for breach of contract, and specific relief as the exception, or whether a more liberal view is taken of the availability of specific relied (see Treitel, *The Law of Contract*, 9th edn (1995), 923, citing *Tito* v. *Waddell* [1977] Ch. 106, 322, and, more generally, Burrows, *Remedies for Breach of Contract*, 2nd edn (1994), Ch. 3). The point to be made here is simply that specific remedies for breach of contract are not always available, but when they are, the contracting parties' interest in performance of their contract has greater protection than when an award of damages is the only remedy for breach of the contract (see, e.g., *Wilson* v. *Northampton & Banbury Junction Railway Co.* (1874) 9 Ch. App. 279, 284, per Lord Selborne; *Beswick* v. *Beswick* [1968] AC 58, 77, 83, 88 and 102, respectively per Lords Reid, Hodson, Pearce and Upjohn).

[19] For a discussion of "specific" and "substitutional" remedies, see Friedmann, "The Performance Interest in Contract Damages" (1995) 111 *LQR* 628. Specific performance might not, on the most technical of views, be regarded as a *remedy* for *breach* of contract. As Burrows has noted, " 'an action for specific performance is based on the mere existence of the contract, coupled with circumstances which make it equitable to grant a decree' (*Snell's Equity* (29th edn, 1990), 585–6). But in practice, it is a breach of contract, actual or anticipatory, that renders it 'equitable' to grant the decree" (Burrows, *Remedies for Torts and Breach of Contract*, 2nd edn (1994), 335).

[20] *Denne* v. *Light* (1857) 8 De G.M. & G. 774.

[21] *Brace* v. *Wehnert* (1858) Beav. 348.

performance but do not make sense, it is said, as bars to a monetary remedy? This criticism has led several commentators,[22] and at least one judge,[23] to deny that the availability of specific performance is a suitable guide to the availability of a restitutionary remedy for a breach of contract.

Thirdly, specific performance, in the strict sense,[24] is an order that a person perform an executory contract;[25] and specific performance is most commonly decreed in respect of one type of executory contract, a contract for the disposition of an interest in property. The availability of specific performance as a remedy for breach of such a contract has dramatic effects. Equity regards the purchaser under a specifically enforceable contract for the disposition of a legal interest in property as acquiring a corresponding equitable proprietary interest in anticipation of the assurance to him of the legal interest which is the subject of the contract, so that the vendor becomes a trustee for the purchaser.[26] It is these equitable consequences of the availability of specific performance which, as a matter of current legal doctrine, facilitate grant of a restitutionary remedy in respect of a breach of the contract.[27] By contrast, orders directing performance of the obligations embodied in an executed contract are often described as orders directing specific performance, but strictly they are not: such orders constitute a form of specific relief, analogous to specific performance, but they are not instances of specific performance and do not carry the equitable doctrinal consequences of specific performance.[28] Furthermore, other specific remedies for breach of contract, such as injunc-

[22] See, e.g., Friedmann, "Restitution of Benefits Obtained through the Appropriation of Property or the Commission of a Wrong" (1980) 80 *Col L Rev* 504, 514 *et seq*; Jones, "The Recovery of Benefits Gained from a Breach of Contract" (1983) 99 *LQR* 443, 455; Smith, "Disgorgement of the Profits of Breach of Contract" (1994) 24 *Can Bus LJ* 121, 137; Burrows, *Remedies for Torts and Breach of Contract*, 2nd edn (1994), 311, and Sir William Goodhart QC, "Restitutionary Damages for Breach of Contract" [1995] *RLR* 3, 11–12.

[23] *Surrey County Council* v. *Bredero Homes Ltd* [1993] 1 WLR 1361, 1370C, per Steyn LJ.

[24] *Wolverhampton & Walsall Railway Co* v. *London & North Western Railway Co* (1873) LR 16 Eq. 433, 439, per Lord Selborne LC.

[25] An executory contract is one which requires the execution of an instrument, or the doing of an "act in the law", which will put the parties in the position relative to each other which is contemplated by the contract.

[26] This is because "Equity regards as done that which ought to be done": the equity jurisdiction treats the contract, so far as it can, as completed in advance of its formal completion. See *Lysaght* v. *Edwards* (1876) 2 ChD 499, 506–10, per Sir George Jessel MR and, generally, Oakley, *Constructive Trusts*, 2nd edn (1987), Ch. 6, and Megarry and Wade, *The Law of Real Property*, 5th edn (1984), 602–7. By way of note, it has recently been held that the effect of a specifically enforceable contract for the disposition of an equitable proprietary interest can be such as to cause the disposition to occur: *Neville* v. *Wilson* [1996] WLR 460 noted [1996] C.L.J. 436.

[27] The vendor, as a constructive trustee of property which is the subject matter of the contract, must account for such of the profits of the property which he is not expressly or impliedly allowed to retain, and for such profits of his trusteeship. Subject to express agreement to the contrary, the vendor may retain income generated before payment of all sums due to him, but not income generated thereafter, and he must account for all capital benefits: *Cuddon* v. *Tite* (1858) 1 Giff. 395; *Monro* v. *Taylor* (1848) 8 Hare 51.

[28] See, e.g., *Packenham Upper Fruit Co.* v. *Crosby* (1924) 35 *CLR* 386, 394, per Isaacs and Rich JJ and, generally, Meagher, Gummow and Lehane, *Equity: Doctrine & Remedies*, 3rd edn (1992), paras 2001–4.

tions, do not have consequences, equitable or otherwise, which obviously facilitate the grant of restitutionary remedies. So one is driven to ask whether there is a distinction between contracts in respect of which specific performance is available, and other contracts in respect of which specific remedies may be decreed, that justifies such a difference in the availability of restitutionary remedies; and if not, what should be done.

The first set of issues noted in this section bears on the question of whether the availability of specific performance as a remedy for breach of a particular type of contract should be a *sufficient* reason to make available a restitutionary remedy for a breach of that contract, given the views taken so far of the objectives of the law of contract, and the place of remedies in relation to the substantive law. The second and third sets of issues bear on the question whether the availability of specific performance as a remedy for breach of a particular type of contract should be a *necessary* reason to make available a restitutionary remedy for a breach of that contract, again, given the views taken so far of the objectives of the law of contract, and the place of remedies. This, as will be seen, is a more difficult question to answer.

### *Specific Performance: a Sufficient Condition for Restitution?*

Whenever specific performance is available to enforce a contract for the disposition of an interest in property, the purchaser is entitled to acquire particular proprietary rights: he is assured of the acquisition of specific rights, not just of the acquisition of rights or money in lieu. If a vendor tries to defeat the purchaser's rights by breaching the contract and failing to deliver property to the purchaser as promised, then forcing the vendor to pay the purchaser compensatory damages, calculated as at the date of breach, may sufficiently vindicate the purchaser's expectations. However, what if the property subject to the contract has been sold to a third party in breach of contract and at a value greater than the contract price; or what if that property has been exploited profitably by the vendor otherwise than as permitted by the contract?

A restitutionary remedy for breach of contract is justifiable in such situations. The purchaser has an *exclusive* right to the performance promised, and such profits are made by denying the purchaser that to which he is *exclusively* entitled. The purchaser has been wronged by the vendor's failure to deliver in accordance with the contract, but he also is entitled to prevent the vendor from engaging in activity which puts performance of the contract beyond him: the law not only stigmatises a wrong but also stigmatises the vendor's enrichment in consequence of the wrongdoing as itself wrongful, so a restitutionary response to the vendor's actions is appropriate. The very availability of specific performance to remedy a breach of a contract means that the purchaser's rights under such a contract are different from those of a party to a contract which cannot be specifically enforced, different in such a manner that the rights of a purchaser under a contract amenable to specific performance are consonant with the grant to him of a restitutionary remedy for breach of his contract.

It is the intervention of equity, the application of the maxim "Equity regards as done that which ought to be done", which produced these results.[29] Does this matter? There is the technical objection that in cases such as *Tang Man Sit* v. *Capacious Investments Ltd*[30] and *Lake* v. *Bayliss*,[31] where there has been a breach of a specifically enforceable executory contract for the disposition of an interest in property, the restitutionary remedy granted was not "for" a breach of contract, but for a breach of fiduciary duty. Technically, this is true.[32] However, such technicalities should not obscure the reality that the duties arise out of contract, and what determines a breach of those duties is determined in accordance with that contract. But beyond such technical objections, are there other reasons to be concerned that it is the intervention of equity which generates this possibility of a restitutionary remedy for, or in respect of, a breach of contract?

There may be some. If the availability of specific performance is seen as a sufficient, but not as a necessary reason why restitutionary remedies should be available for a breach of contract, then equitable doctrine relating to specifically enforceable executory contracts for the disposition of an interest in property will not in all cases provide the means through which a restitutionary remedy for breach of contract may be granted; so either other existing means will have to be pressed into service to facilitate grant of the remedy, or the courts will have to make a break with current authority.[33] This is a question which must be addressed in the next section. Furthermore, the intervention of equity opens up the possibility of proprietary remedies for, or in respect of, a breach of contract.[34] It is open to question whether or not such remedies are appropriate, but this chapter is concerned with the availability in principle of restitutionary remedies for breach of contract, not their nature, so it will not address that question.

## *Specific Performance: a Necessary Condition for Restitution?*

### An inappropriate guide?

A major objection to using the availability of specific performance as a guide to the grant of restitutionary remedies for breach of contract is that the rules of law by which the availability of specific performance is governed were

[29] See *supra*, n 26.

[30] [1996] AC 514, PC.

[31] [1974] 1 WLR 1073.

[32] For confirmation that the fiduciary duties which arise out of a contract are technically just that—fiduciary, rather than contractual, duties—see *Nelson* v. *Rye* [1996] 1 WLR 1378, 1389–90; noted (1996) 17 *Co Law* 218.

[33] For example, the courts might deploy the equitable remedy of an account of profits, in exercise of the equitable auxiliary jurisdiction, by way of response to a breach of contract.

[34] Consider, for example, the possibilities inherent in *Lake* v. *Bayliss* [1974] 1 WLR 1073.

developed to delimit the operation of a specific, non-substitutional, non-monetary remedy, and that they are therefore unsuitable to determine the availability of a substitutional, monetary remedy for breach of contract, such as a restitutionary remedy.[35] This objection appears quite substantial, but in fact it depends for its validity on certain implicit assumptions as to the availability of restitutionary remedies for breach of contract; and these assumptions are not beyond challenge.

The interests which justify the availability of restitution as a response to a particular breach of contract, and the lack of which explains why it is not available in other cases, are generally seen to be the interests of the victim of the breach, the innocent party,[36] or, at least, the interests of those in a similar position to the victim who need protection from the risk of similar harm.[37] This, for example, is the approach adopted by Friedmann, who advocates that restitution be available as a response to a breach of contract if an affirmative answer can be given to the question:[38]

> "When performance is promised under a contract, is the promisee 'entitled' to it in such a way that if this performance is withheld, appropriated, or otherwise 'taken', the promisee can be regarded as having been deprived of an interest that 'belonged' to him?"

Quite apart from any criticism that this question cannot be answered with any certainty, a criticism accepted by Friedmann himself,[39] it should be noted that the focus of enquiry is entirely located within the interests of the promisee, the victim of the breach. Yet nothing requires such an approach. It is perfectly rational not to ask whether the plaintiff's interest in the performance of a contract, or the need to secure confidence in the courts' ability and willingness to vindicate expectations, mean that a restitutionary remedy should be available in response to the breach, but rather to ask whether the plaintiff's interest in performance, and any institutional needs, sufficiently outweigh any countervailing factors so that the plaintiff should have an *exclusive* right to performance of the contract, which would mean that a restitutionary remedy for breach of the contract would not be inconsistent with the rights of the parties to the contract. The availability of specific performance as a guide to the availability of restitutionary remedies for breach of contract may seem inappropriate if the focus of enquiry is on the plaintiff's interests; but it does not seem so inappropriate once this implicit exclusive focus on the plaintiff's interests is recognised and challenged.

[35] See text to n 20 *supra* for examples of this objection.

[36] See, e.g., Friedmann, "Restitution of Benefits Obtained through the Appropriation of Property or the Commission of a Wrong" (1980) 80 *Col L Rev* 504.

[37] Jackman, "Restitution for Wrongs" [1989] *CLJ* 302, 318–21.

[38] Friedmann, "Restitution of Benefits Obtained through the Appropriation of Property or the Commission of a Wrong" (1980) 80 *Col L Rev* 504, 515.

[39] *Ibid* at 557.

**An incomplete guide?**

There are several other cases in the reports which are not cases concerned with the availability of specific performance, but which, it is argued, are cases where a restitutionary award was made, or should have been made, in response to a breach of contract. If such arguments are valid, then it might be said that the availability of specific performance as a remedy for breach of contract is an incomplete guide to the availability of restitutionary responses to a breach of contract. However, it will be argued that none of the cases considered should in fact be seen as instances of a restitutionary response to a breach of contract, or as cases where a restitutionary remedy should have been ordered. They therefore do not entail the conclusion that the availability of specific performance is an incomplete guide to the availability of restitutionary remedies.

The first case is *Wrotham Park Estate Co Ltd* v. *Parkside Homes Ltd.*[40] In that case, Brightman J refused to order a mandatory injunction that the defendants demolish fourteen houses they had built in breach of a restrictive covenant benefiting the plaintiff's land; he thought that grant of such an injunction was entirely inappropriate for "social and economic reasons", given the shortage of housing then existing. However, he granted the plaintiff damages in lieu of the injunction sought, assessed at five per cent of the defendant's estimated profit from its breach of covenant. This decision has variously been described as "a new development"[41] and "creative",[42] and though subjected to criticism in *Surrey County Council* v. *Bredero Homes Ltd*,[43] it has been properly rescued from that criticism, and applied, in *Jaggard* v. *Sawyer*.[44]

It has been argued[45] that the *Wrotham Park* case cannot be seen as a case of compensation for lost opportunity to bargain, as there is no evidence that the plaintiff would have bargained away its rights. Therefore, it is said, the award made by Brightman J was restitutionary in nature. However, closer examination of the case casts doubt on this conclusion. Brightman J was not willing to grant an injunction which the plaintiff claimed; indeed, no injunction would, following his decision, ever issue to vindicate the plaintiff's rights.[46] Brightman J therefore ordered a money payment in lieu of an injunc-

[40] [1974] 1 WLR 798.

[41] *Surrey County Council* v. *Bredero Homes Ltd* [1993] 1 WLR 1361, 1369G, per Steyn LJ.

[42] Sir William Goodhart QC, "Restitutionary Damages for Breach of Contract" [1995] *RLR* 3, 4.

[43] [1993] 1 WLR 1361, 1367, per Dillon LJ; but *contra* Steyn LJ at 1369–70.

[44] [1995] 1 WLR 269.

[45] See, e.g., Sir William Goodhart QC, "Restitutionary Damages for Breach of Contract" [1995] *RLR* 3, 4–8; Burrows, *Remedies for Torts and Breach of Contract*, *supra* n. 22, at 313 and, judicially, *Surrey County Council* v. *Bredero Homes Ltd* [1993] 1 WLR 1361, 1369, per Steyn LJ.

[46] The defendant was enabled to buy off the plaintiff, but what of successors in title? Successors in title to the defendant would surely be immune from the grant against them of an injunction pursuant to the covenant (see *Surrey County Council* v. *Bredero Homes Ltd* [1993] 1 WLR 1361) and they would not have to pay the plaintiff damages in lieu of an injunction, as the

tion. Now, while it may be true that such an award cannot properly be characterised as damages for lost opportunity to bargain, it does not necessarily follow that the award was restitutionary; rather, the case should be seen as one of compulsory expropriation and compensation of the plaintiff by order of the court in exercise of its discretion.[47] A sum was awarded to the plaintiff in recognition of the fact that its rights were not to be enforced, and consequently were to cease to exist, for a right without any remedy is a nonsense. To summarise, there was continuing infringement by the defendant of a negative stipulation benefiting the plaintiff, and the court was not going to put an end to that infringement, but instead bought the plaintiff off. Indeed, it was recognised a century ago that it was possible to exercise the jurisdiction now conferred by section 50 of the Supreme Court Act 1981 in the manner evidenced by the *Wrotham Park* case, and that such exercise amounts, in substance, if not in form, to the compulsory purchase of rights by order of the court at a price set by the court.[48]

A case very similar to *Wrotham Park* was *Jaggard* v. *Sawyer*.[49] The plaintiff owned the benefit of a restrictive covenant over neighbouring land, and the covenant restricted use of that land to use as a private garden. The defendant built a house on part of his land not bound by the covenant, but constructed an access driveway to the house over other land of his which was subject to the covenant. This constituted a breach of the restrictive covenant by the defendant. The plaintiff sought an injunction to restrain the improper use of the land subject to the covenant. The Court of Appeal, applying *Wrotham Park*,[50] refused an injunction but awarded damages in lieu. In his judgment, Millett LJ argued strenuously that what the court was doing was making a compensatory award. Again, while it may be argued that the award could not constitute damages for lost opportunity to bargain, it does not therefore follow that the award made by the court is restitutionary in nature. Once more, it is a case of compulsory acquisition of a right and compensation in lieu.

plaintiff had been compensated for his loss. Successors in title to the plaintiff would be unable to take advantage of the covenant: it is inconceivable that the court would issue an injunction at the suit of such a successor in title, and likewise inconceivable it would award such a successor in title damages in lieu of an injunction. So what is in issue is indeed a form of compulsory purchase of the plaintiff's transmissible rights, rather than the denial of a remedy to him personally. The mechanics of this form of compulsory purchase are convoluted because it depends in form on the withholding of a remedy, rather than the explicit, complete and final acquisition or abrogation of a right. However, the position would very likely be formalised by discharge or modification of the restrictive covenant over the defendant's land, either through agreement of the parties affect by it or under the Law of Property Act 1925, s 84.

[47] It would be inappropriate to describe as a "restitutionary award" the money paid to someone who has been expropriated by a compulsory purchase order; and, in the same way, it is inappropriate to describe the payment ordered by Brightman J in the *Wrotham Park* case as a "restitutionary award"; see *Jaggard* v. *Sawyer* [1995] 1 WLR 269, 291, per Millett LJ.

[48] *Shelfer* v. *City of London Electric Lighting Co* [1895] 1 Ch. 287, 315–16, per Lindley LJ.

[49] [1995] 1 WLR 269.

[50] [1974] 1 WLR 798.

The next case to be considered, *Surrey County Council* v. *Bredero Homes Ltd*,[51] is a case that has excited much comment.[52] The facts are very similar to those of the *Wrotham Park* case. Houses had been built on a plot in breach of a restrictive covenant between, on the one hand, the vendors of the land in question, Surrey County Council and Mole Valley District Council, and, on the other hand, Bredero, which had purchased and developed the land. The plaintiff vendors claimed damages assessed on the *Wrotham Park* basis. This claim was rejected, both by the High Court and by the Court of Appeal: Surrey and Mole Valley were entitled to compensatory damages but, as they were held to have suffered no loss, they were awarded merely nominal damages. Dillon LJ doubted[53] the decision of Brightman J in the *Wrotham Park* case, though Steyn LJ thought it innovative but entirely justifiable.[54]

Four further points are worthy of note. First, the claim was between the original parties to the covenant in question, unlike the claim in the *Wrotham Park* case. Secondly, the local authorities admitted that they only ever took the restrictive covenant so that they could extract some money from Bredero, in exchange for a release of the covenant, if Bredero wished to develop the land more profitably by building a greater number of houses on it than was permitted by the covenant. Thirdly, the court had no jurisdiction to grant an injunction against Bredero, ordering it to demolish the houses built in breach of covenant, as it had sold them on before the present action was instituted, though a claim for specific equitable relief was made by Bredero in amended pleadings. Fourthly, one of the plaintiffs, Mole Valley, had in fact authorised the construction of the extra houses as a matter of planning law, though it had not waived the covenant. While the acts of a district council discharging its functions as a planning authority will not operate as an effective variation of a contractual right, or as some form of estoppel preventing reliance on such a private right,[55] nevertheless, the actions of Mole Valley can hardly have seemed meritorious to the courts.

In the light of these facts, what is to be made of the case? The local authorities lost an opportunity to bargain away the threat of injunctive enforcement of the covenant. If that situation had come about simply through the default of Bredero, then the local authorities should have recovered compensatory damages for loss of opportunity to bargain: to say, in such circumstances, that the local authorities had suffered no loss, because their land had not been diminished in value, would be to miss the point. However, in the case itself,

[51] [1993] 1 WLR 1361.

[52] Birks, "Profits of Breach of Contract" (1993) 109 LQR 518; Burrows, "No Restitutionary Damages for Breach of Contract" [1993] LMCLQ 453; O'Dair, "Damages for Breach of Contract: A Wrong Turn: [1993] RLR 31.

[53] [1993] 1 WLR 1361, 1366.

[54] *Ibid.* 1369.

[55] For a description of what may constitute a variation of a contractual rights, or an estoppel which prevents reliance on a contractual right, see Treitel, *The Law of Contract*, 9th edn (1995), 94–124.

the local authorities had lost the chance to bargain away the threat of injunctive enforcement of the covenant through their own deliberate delay in bringing proceedings, that is, by waiting to start proceedings until after Bredero had sold all the houses. In such circumstances, it is perfectly plausible to say that the local authorities were the authors of their own loss: they were responsible for their own loss of opportunity.[56] So there was no reason to hold Bredero liable for that loss, and, given that the local authorities could show no other loss, such as loss in the market value of their land, it was quite right that the court refused a loss-based award to the local authorities. Further, it is submitted that the court was right to withhold a restitutionary remedy, as grant of such a remedy would have re-written the bargain between the parties, thereby upsetting, not vindicating, the parties' contractual expectations.

So the courts may well have reached the right result in *Surrey* v. *Bredero*, though the reasoning in the case may be subjected to criticism. The Court of Appeal only considered a compensatory award, in respect of the diminution in value of the plaintiff local authorities' land, and, in the alternative, a restitutionary award; the court did not consider, and dismiss as it might have done, a compensatory award for loss of opportunity to bargain. The approach to loss adopted by the Court of Appeal, focusing as it did on any reduction in the value of the plaintiffs' land, opens the case to criticism that an unjust result was reached; and yet it is possible to deal with that criticism without recourse to restitutionary analysis. Inadequacies in, or in the application of, the law of compensation do not necessarily entail recourse to the law of restitution.

The next case to be considered is *Tito* v. *Waddell (No. 2)*.[57] The facts of that case are well known. Ocean Island (Banana) in the Pacific had been mined for phosphates, and the agreement between the Island land-owners and the British Phosphate Company, which permitted the mining, contained a covenant obliging the British Phosphate Company to restore the island when mining operations there came to an end. This covenant was breached, and the islanders sued. Megarry V-C refused to direct the defendant to perform the covenant.[58] The reason for this refusal was the Vice-Chancellor's view that such specific relief for the breach of covenant would entail expenditure by the defendant wholly disproportionate to any benefit for the plaintiffs, who, incidentally, had been resettled on another island in Fiji during the mining and were not intending to return to and live on Ocean Island. More importantly, Megarry V-C awarded damages for breach of contract calculated by reference to the diminution in value of the islanders' land caused by the British Phosphate Company's breach of contract; he declined to award damages

[56] cf. *Jaggard* v. *Sawyer* [1995] 1 WLR 269, 291G–H, per Millett LJ.

[57] [1977] Ch 106.

[58] What the islanders sought cannot, strictly speaking, be called specific performance: see *Wolverhampton & Walsall Railway Co* v. *London & North Western Railway Co* (1873) LR 16 Eq 433, 439, per Lord Selborne LC.

calculated by reference to the sum that the British Phosphate Company would have had to pay in order to be released from their covenant by the islanders, even though in the *Wrotham Park* case Brightman J had calculated the damages he awarded in that fashion.

There are good reasons to be uneasy about the result of *Tito* v. *Waddell (No. 2)*: the expectations of the islanders were dashed, and yet they received very little[59] from those who dashed their expectations. However, the question remains: is restitution the answer to this problem? One should not assume that, because there is a problem with the case, restitution must be the answer. In *Tito* v. *Waddell (No. 2)*, the only basis for the assessment of loss was diminution in market value of an asset, in this case Ocean Island itself. Such a basis for the assessment of the islanders' loss may seem inadequate, but that may just as well entail a conclusion that there is something awry with the law of compensation as a conclusion that the law of restitution should "come to the rescue". The islanders bargained for a habitable island, not an island more valuable in the market, if indeed there is a "market" in the context. It may seem heretical to suggest that the islanders' loss should be calculated as the expenditure which would be necessary to give them an island as habitable as it was before mining began, rather than an island as saleable as before the mining, but is such a suggestion so implausible?[60] The problem with *Tito* v. *Waddell (No. 2)* is a problem about recognising, ascertaining and monetising loss; restitution is not the obvious, nor the appropriate, solution to such a problem.

So investigation of cases in which specific relief for breach of contract (but not specific performance) has been in issue, albeit belatedly and without hope of success in *Surrey* v. *Bredero*, leads to the conclusion that the cases, in so far as they are justifiable, may be appropriately explained as lying outside the law of restitution and within the law of compensation, and that the deficiencies in the cases which have been highlighted may most appropriately be understood and addressed as deficiencies in the law of compensation for loss. In particular, these cases show that the current law of compensation for

[59] The plaintiffs were awarded compensation assessed at $A 75 per acre, whereas they had claimed $A 73,140 per acre (this being allegedly what was required to restore the land in question on Banaba), and in fact the British Phosphate Commissioners had offered them $A 3,000 per acre to settle the claim before it came to trial.

[60] This proposal to assess loss as the cost of substitute performance raises the issue of damages for the so-called "consumer surplus" addressed by the House of Lords in *Ruxley Electronics & Constructions Ltd* v. *Forsyth* [1996] 1 AC 344. See also Jones, "The Recovery of Benefits Gained from a Breach of Contract" (1983) 99 *LQR* 443 for a discussion of cases in which a claim was made for the sum required to buy equivalent performance. Any requirement indicated in such cases that an undertaking would have to be given as to the use of funds awarded by the court seems odd in principle. Why is it odd, or suspicious, for the plaintiff to show he has suffered non-pecuniary loss, but now to use his damages otherwise than in restoring his position? The requirement of an undertaking may be an indirect way in which the court can ascertain whether the plaintiff is telling the truth when he alleges he has suffered non-pecuniary loss; but it is an imprecise and unprincipled way of doing what the courts have to do day in, day out: deciding whether a person is telling the truth.

breach of contract has problems in recognising, assessing or monetising loss, especially in cases where there is no market value of what the plaintiff has lost through the defendant's breach of contract, and in cases where the plaintiff had a non-pecuniary interest in performance of his contract with the defendant. The rules used to quantify compensation for a breach of contract assume too readily that every plaintiff makes a contract for commercial reasons, and to increase his store of "exchangeable" wealth.[61] However, to award restitution for breach of contract just because it is difficult to quantify loss would be arbitrary in the extreme.

While it is useful to investigate and explain specific cases, it is also desirable to see if there is any general explanation of the courts' reluctance to grant a restitutionary remedy in cases other than those in which specific performance is available to enforce a contract. An explanation may be found in the extent of the restitutionary relief granted in response to a breach of contract.

The two restitutionary remedies which might be granted in response to breach of a contract amenable to specific performance are illustrated respectively by *Lake* v. *Bayliss*[62] and *Tang Man Sit* v. *Capacious Investments*:[63] first, awarding the proceeds of the subject matter of the contract to the party injured by the breach and, secondly, awarding profits made by using the subject matter of the contract to the party injured by the breach.[64] The common feature of both these remedies is that they are measured by reference to the use of property: the use of a particular asset defines their extent. One reason why the courts may be unwilling to grant a restitutionary remedy in respect of a breach of contract which might be remedied by specific relief other than specific performance is the lack of such a limiting factor in those cases. Such a "proprietary nexus", limiting the extent of a restitutionary remedy for breach of a contract amenable to specific performance, can be justified in two different ways, one valid, the other not.

One justification goes as follows. The transfer, to a purchaser under a contract amenable to specific performance, of the value of profits made by the vendor through breaching the contract—giving the purchaser a restitutionary remedy in respect of the breach—does not fulfil the purchaser's expectations,[65] but the benefits transferred to a plaintiff who sought a restitutionary

[61] The rules by which compensation for torts is assessed do not invariably make such narrow assumptions about the nature and condition of someone subsequently injured by a tortious act: see, e.g., *Owens* v. *Liverpool Corporation* [1939] 1 KB 394, 400–1, per Mackinnon LJ; *Smith* v. *Leech, Brain & Co* [1962] 2 QB 405. Indeed, the law of tort would be radically restricted in its ambit were it to make such assumptions. It is clearly not necessary to make such restrictive assumptions about the victim of a wrong: so why, then, restrict the law of contract?

[62] [1974] 1 WLR 1073.

[63] [1996] AC 514, PC.

[64] See *supra* n 27 for an outline of which profits may be retained by the vendor of an asset under a contract amenable to specific performance, and which profits must pass to the purchaser of the asset.

[65] After all, the purchaser's expectations were that he would receive the asset and then exploit it in a manner decided by him; they were not that the asset would be exploited by the person from whom he acquired it.

remedy for breach of a contract amenable to specific performance are commonly such as might, very likely, have been made by the purchaser himself: they are similar to, though not constitutive of, the value of his dashed expectations.[66] In other words, a restitutionary remedy for breach of a contract amenable to a decree of specific performance will commonly resemble the compensation which could be awarded in vindication of the dashed contractual expectations; such a remedy therefore seems less at variance with the general aim of the law of contract, the vindication of expectations. However, if a restitutionary remedy is justifiable at all, there seems little reason to keep it from becoming too disproportionate to an alternative compensatory remedy, so this reason to insist on the need for a proprietary nexus to limit the extent of a restitutionary remedy for breach of contract does not have much force.

Nevertheless, there may be other, good reasons to be uneasy about the extent of a restitutionary remedy for a wrong. Such unease is, at root, about a problem of causation. Without a "proprietary nexus" between breach of contract by a defendant, and the gain in his hands which the plaintiff can capture by means of a restitutionary remedy for the breach, what is to ascertain the profit which is made by a contract-breaker "at the expense of" the other party to the contract, other than "but for", factual causation, a test which does not recognise that a profit can be the result of other, perhaps more important and more relevant, matters than the breach of contract, for example of the profit-maker's own effort and skill. When the profit in issue was generated by natural use of an asset, as is so often true of profits generated by a vendor in breach of a contract amenable to specific performance, it is simple to treat the wrongful use of the asset as the principal, relevant cause of the profit, so that it easily makes sense to award the profit to the person with an exclusive right to that asset.[67] By contrast, where the profit in question was generated in consequence of a breach of contract, but also in consequence of many other factors such as the defendant's skill and ingenuity, it is more difficult to say that the wrong is the principal, relevant cause of the profit in the defendant's hands. In short, appropriate "rules of legal causation" (i.e. rules attributing responsibility) ensure that the extent of a remedy does not become disproportionate to the cause of action upon which the remedy is based. When there is breach of a contract amenable to a decree of specific performance, use of a particular asset to delimit the extent of a restitutionary remedy for the breach of the contract ensures proportionality between the breach and a restitutionary remedy for it, though perhaps in a somewhat

[66] It is nevertheless possible to imagine circumstances where a restitutionary remedy for breach of a contract amenable to a decree of specific performance would bring benefits to the purchaser dissimilar from those he could have expected to make himself: for example, if a vendor had displayed particular care and skill in making a profit with the asset subject to the contract.

[67] Where the profit in question was generated by "unnatural" use of an asset, then it is natural to treat the cause of the profit as a combination of asset and activity, so that exclusive entitlement to the asset alone is a weaker, though not insubstantial, reason to award the entire profit to the person with an exclusive right to the asset.

rough and ready fashion; when there is breach of some other type of contract, there are no rules, even rough an ready ones, to perform that task.

The current law therefore evinces a good reason why restitution for breach of contract should only be available to remedy breach of a contract amenable to specific performance. Obviously, however, the law could change. It could make restitutionary remedies for breach of contract generally available, though, as has been noted, that would entail a significant review of the law of contract; or it could contemplate less radical change. Even if it is accepted that the grant of a restitutionary remedy for breach of contract is appropriate only where the person seeking the remedy has an exclusive claim to performance of the contract, the law could always develop "rules of causation", or attribution, to delimit the scope of a restitutionary remedy for breach of some contract which confers such an exclusive right, albeit that the right is not vindicated by specific performance *stricto sensu*.

A particular way of dealing with the problem of proportionality between a breach of contract and a restitutionary remedy for it is to measure the restitutionary award not by the profits a contract-breaker makes through breaching his contract, but by the expense he saved in doing so.[68] This was a position once advocated by Burrows,[69] but has since been rejected by him.[70] The position has been criticised on the grounds that it is difficult to distinguish between "expense saved" and "profit made".[71] Yet there is a more basic criticism of this position.

First, one may ask what is the "expense saved" by a contract-breaker who makes a profit through his breach of contract: it is the amount the contract-breaker would have to pay to obtain release from the contract in question. This might be what the plaintiff has lost by the breach of contract, what the defendant has gained through the breach of contract, or something in between. Now, to say that the "expense saved" by the contract-breaker is either what the plaintiff has lost or what the defendant has gained is to beg the question of whether or not there should be restitutionary remedies for breach of contract.[72] To say that the "expense saved" by the contract-breaker is somewhere between these two limits is to commit oneself to one of two possibilities. The first is to say that the law should follow economics, giving a remedy set at the figure the parties would have reached by negotiation. This can be criticised as involving too difficult an exercise in hypothetical bargaining, which is Burrows' objection; but furthermore, if it is to be a real, and not a fictional exercise, any mirroring of negotiations by the court would also have to take into account factors, such as the relative strength of the parties' bargaining power, which have no obvious place in any recognisably just law

[68] Smith, "Disgorgement of the Profits of Breach of Contract" (1994) 24 *Can Bus LJ* 121, 138.

[69] Burrows, *Remedies for Torts and Breach of Contract*, 1st edn (1987), 273.

[70] Burrows, *The Law of Restitution* (1993), 403; *Remedies for Torts and Breach of Contract*, 2nd edn (1994), 310.

[71] *Ibid.*

[72] This point has been seen before: see *supra* n 4.

of remedies. However, if the law is not to follow economics and grant a remedy based on a model of the parties' hypothetical negotiation, then all it is doing is plucking a figure from the air, as a "just and equitable" award, and clothing the figure in the fiction of bargaining. That is hardly satisfactory. Whichever way one looks at it, "expense saved" does not have much to comment it as a measure of recovery in this context.

Another, more plausible possible rule of causation would be to attribute profits in the hands of a defendant to a breach of contract by him only where those profits would not, as a matter of the particular facts of the case in question, have been earned by the defendant "but for" his breach, *and* those profits could not have been earned by him had he in fact adhered to his contract. This is the sort of "legal causal link" (rule attributing responsibility) employed by the House of Lords in *Target Holdings Ltd* v. *Redferns (a firm)*,[73] even though their Lordships insisted that they were simply talking about factual, "but for" causation.

**A suitable guide?**

So much for criticism of cases where specific performance was not available as a remedy for a breach of contract, but which are nevertheless alleged to be cases where a restitutionary remedy was granted, or should have been granted, for the breach. What positive reasons can be given for treating the availability of specific performance as a necessary condition for making available a restitutionary remedy for breach of contract?

The reasons have in fact already been stated, though not quite as a direct answer to this question. Given our law of contract as it now stands, remedies for breach of contract should aim principally to make good expectations. Remedies for breach of contract which look to the plaintiff's loss are generally more suited to this role than remedies which look to the defendant's gain. So, generally, remedies for breach of contract should be loss-based, unless our law of contract is modified significantly. A restitutionary remedy for breach of contract should only be allowed when such a remedy vindicates the plaintiff's rights. Restitutionary remedies for a breach of contract which could have been remedied by a decree of specific performance should generally do this, because they give full monetary effect to the plaintiff's rights, giving him the money product of the very thing to which he had an exclusive entitlement.

This is not quite to say that the restitutionary remedies arising out of the availability of specific performance are inevitably going to be what they should be, namely a monetised form of specific performance.[74] "Monetised specific performance" must mean the equivalent of performance so far as

[73] [1996] AC 421 noted [1996] L.M.C.L.Q. 161. That such a rule was used in the *Target* case was accepted by Chadwick J. in *Bristol & West B.S.* v. *May, May & Merrimans* (a firm) [1996] 2 All E.R. 801, noted [1997] C.L.J. 39.

[74] Beatson, *The Use and Abuse of Unjust Enrichment* (1991), 15–17; Law Commission Consultation Paper "Aggravated, Exemplary and Restitutionary Damages" (LCCP No 132), para. 7.21.

money can be an equivalent for performance: obviously money is but rarely an exact equivalent of performance. The most exact equivalent of performance in a case where specific performance is available to enforce a contract will be the money that is most properly and exactly equivalent to the property that should have been transferred pursuant to the contract. Equitable doctrine, developed in relation to the law of express trusts, can be used appropriately to identify the monetary equivalent of the contractual performance in issue by identifying the capital or income product of property which should have been transferred pursuant to the contract which has been breached. However, such doctrine could also be used inappropriately: if the duties of an express trustee are imposed on a contracting party, then breach of those duties could have the effect of stripping profits from the contract-breaker which bear no relation to the expected contractual performance, namely delivery of property, but which have relation to the duties of an express trustee, obligations which the contract-breaker did not assume. There is no reason why trust doctrine has to be applied so insensitively,[75] and it to be hoped that it will not be so applied. Proportionality of remedy to the cause of action is essential: this view is of fundamental importance to the arguments expressed in this chapter.

Acceptance that the availability of specific performance is a necessary pre-condition to the availability of restitutionary remedies for breach of contract would also eliminate another possible problem, namely that restitutionary remedies for breach of contract could undermine the principle of mitigation of loss. The relevance of this objection has been challenged.[76] However, even if the objection is admitted, it is immaterial whenever specific performance is available to enforce a contract. In such a case, the party injured by a breach of contract need not mitigate, but may insist on performance; questions of mitigation, and objections based on mitigation to a restitutionary remedy for the breach, are therefore irrelevant.

## 3. CONCLUSIONS

The debate about restitutionary remedies for breach of contract is not a minor, relatively unimportant discussion of marginal cases; it raises fundamental questions about the nature of contract law: what it is to make a contract, and what it is to commit the "wrong" of breaching a contract.[77] Restitution for breach of contract is, in general, incompatible with our present understanding of what it is to make and break a contract. In cases where

[75] See, for example, the case law discussed by Oakley in *Constructive Trusts*, 2nd edn (1987), 156, 163–4. Note also *Kelly* v. *Cooper* [1993] AC 205, PC.

[76] Smith, "Disgorgement of the Profits of Breach of Contract" (1994) 24 *Can Bus LJ* 121, 137.

[77] Sir William Goodhart QC, "Restitutionary Damages for Breach of Contract" [1995] *RLR* 3, 10.

a plaintiff expected a defendant to perform in some fashion, but the defendant failed to deliver such performance, the law might react in one of three ways: first, it might compensate the plaintiff if the non-performance has caused him loss, some diminution in the wealth he previously had aside from the expectation itself; secondly, the law might compensate him for the loss of his valuable expectation; and thirdly, it might take away any benefit received by the defendant in consequence of his non-performance. In the familiar terminology of the law, these responses are respectively reliance damages, expectation damages and restitution for breach of contract. Each of these responses is indicative of a different notion of contractual rights: in the first case, a contract ensures that the pre-contract estate of the innocent contracting party will not be diminished by reason of a breach of contract by the counterparty to the contract; in the second, a contract ensures that the estate of the innocent contracting party will be increased by the counterparty to the extent expected by reason of the contract; and in the third, a contract tries to ensure that there is no economic incentive for one party to breach the contract.

Such notions of contract are not mutually incompatible: English law currently accepts both the first and second of the notions listed, and it could also accept the third without rejecting the other two. What it cannot do, however, is to accept all three possible remedial responses to the defeat of expectations as remedies for breach of contract and yet still cling to an idea of the substantive law of contract which is consistent only with the first and second notions of what is entailed by making a contract. To make such an attempt would be logically incoherent: it would be an attempt to adopt a position when it is described in one way, by reference to remedies, but to reject it when described in another, by reference to rights. A point made before bears repetition: restitution for breach of contract is generally incompatible with our present understanding of contractual rights.

However, restitution for breach of contract is currently available where the contract breached was amenable to a decree of specific performance. This somewhat isolated example of restitution for breach of contract can be accommodated within the current framework of contractual doctrine. In such a case, one party to the contract, the purchaser, has an exclusive right to performance by the other, the vendor, such that a restitutionary remedy for breach of the contract is appropriate and coherent with the rights of the parties under the contract. Furthermore, the extent of the restitutionary remedy is limited in such a case by reference to the utilisation of the subject matter of the contract; this limitation ensures both that there is a causal link, as a matter of fact, between breach of contract and the profit to be captured by a restitutionary remedy for the breach, and also that the wrong is the principal, relevant cause of the profit in the defendant's hands. In other words, this limitation on the extent of the remedy ensures that it does not become unacceptably wide in scope.

Whilst the remedy of restitution for breach of contract is not coherent with current contractual doctrine, and is therefore not a development of current contractual doctrine which can be justified by reference to existing views of the law of contract, it does not follow that there should be no change to the law of contract. First, the cases reviewed in this chapter make it clear that all is not well with our law of damages: the ability of the law to monetise and assess non-pecuniary loss, to award damages where there is no market value of what the plaintiff has lost through the defendant's breach of contract or where the plaintiff has a non-pecuniary interest in performance of his contract with the defendant, is limited, to put the point mildly. However, to award restitution for breach of contract just because it is difficult to quantify loss is inappropriate: "difficulty of proof does not justify picking what on this reasoning would be an arbitrary measure".[78] Nevertheless, in order to aid a plaintiff in monetising and quantifying his loss, which can sometimes be a very difficult procedure,[79] there might be a rebuttable presumption that the loss to the plaintiff in a particular case was equivalent to the gain to the defendant, unless the defendant can show otherwise.[80]

Secondly, it might be appropriate to widen the circumstances in which specific performance of a contract will be decreed. Indeed, there are signs that the courts are more willing to grant specific remedies for breach of contract than once was the case.[81] Any such widening of the availability of specific performance would consequently increase the number of situations in which a restitutionary remedy for breach of contract will be available according to current contractual doctrine.

Indeed, it might be that more radical steps should be taken to modify the law of contract. It has been seen that a restitutionary remedy for breach of contract is consistent with contractual rights that involve one party to a contract having the exclusive right to a particular performance by the counterparty to that contract. It is possible to argue, therefore, that a restitutionary remedy for breach of contract should be available wherever a specific remedy for a breach of contract is available. This suggestion would leave the availability of a decree of specific performance as a sufficient reason to grant a restitutionary remedy for breach of contract, but would entail abandonment of the position that the availability of a decree of specific performance was also a necessary condition for the availability of such a remedy. The most important consequence of this fact would be the necessity of developing

[78] The quotation is from Burrows, *Remedies for Torts and Breach of Contract*, 2nd edn (1994), 18–19; the point was made there in criticism of the argument made by Fuller and Perdue in "The Reliance Interest in Contract Damages" (1936–37) 46 *Yale LJ* 52 and 373 that it is appropriate to award expectation damages because it may be difficult to establish reliance losses; but the point is equally valid in the present context.

[79] Witness, most recently, *Ruxley Electronic & Constructions Ltd* v. *Forsyth* [1996] 1 AC 344.

[80] Note, for example, *Jaggard* v. *Sawyer* [1995] 1 WLR 269, 291D, per Millett LJ; *Lamine* v. *Dorrell* (1705) 2 Ld Ray 1216, and *Biggerstaff* v. *Rowatt's Wharf Ltd* [1896] 2 Ch 93, 103. I am grateful to Professor Peter Watts for drawing my attention to the last two cases.

[81] See, e.g., *Cooperative Insurance Society Ltd* v. *Argyle Stores (Holdings) Ltd* [1996] Ch 286.

appropriate rules of "legal causation",[82] over and above the link of factual, "but for" causation, to limit the extent of any restitutionary remedy for breach of contract: there is no inherent, albeit slightly rough and ready, limitation to the scope of a restitutionary remedy for breach of a contract which, though capable of specific enforcement, is not amenable to a decree of specific performance. As has already been noted, one possible rule would be to attribute profits in the hands of a defendant to a breach of contract by him only where those profits would not, as a matter of the particular facts of the case in question, have been earned by the defendant "but for" his breach, *and* those profits could not have been earned by him had he in fact adhered to his contract. It is possible to imagine other rules which might be adopted.

Another, yet more radical, alteration to the law of contract would be to attach a greater importance to the performance of a contract. It has already been noted that an entitlement to restitution for breach of contract may rest on the view that a particular contractual right involves an exclusive entitlement to performance. Currently, an exclusive entitlement to performance of a contractual obligation only subsists where a specific remedy for breach of the obligation is available. So one way of attaching greater importance to the performance of a contract, is to widen the circumstances in which specific remedies for breach of contract are available, and thereby to render appropriate the wider availability of restitution for breach of contract. This approach would not necessitate modification of the currently accepted assumption that only an exclusive entitlement to contractual performance should only be admitted where there is no adequate substitute for the promised performance; it would just involve less willingness to see possible alternatives to the promised performance as an "adequate" substitute for it.

It would also be possible to attach a greater importance to the performance of a contract even without expanding the scope of specific remedies for breach of contract. The defence of an exclusive right, such as one enjoyed by a party to a contract who may compel performance of that contract, is not the only goal which may be furthered by restitutionary remedy for wrongdoing; such a remedy is appropriate where the law wishes to promote the performance of an obligation even though it may be unwilling or unable to compel such performance. So the law might choose to attach a greater importance to the performance of a contract by granting a restitutionary remedy for breach of some, or all, contracts, irrespective of whether it will specifically enforce such a contract. This is tantamount to a requirement that some, or all, contracts be performed in good faith;[83] and it would certainly entail rejection of the cur-

[82] i.e. rules by which profit in the defendant's hands is characterised as sufficiently attributable to the breach of contract, as opposed to other causes, that the plaintiff should be able to capture it by means of a restitutionary remedy.

[83] The acceptance by Israeli contract law of a principle of good faith may go a long way to explaining the result of the Israeli case *Adras Building Material Ltd* v. *Harlow & Jones GmbH* (1988), reported in English, [1995] *RLR* 235.

rent view that the function of the law of contract is simply to vindicate the expectations expressly or impliedly embodied in a contract.[84]

However, though such a change in the law would seem to involve the very widespread availability of a restitutionary remedy for breach of contract, that may not in fact be the case: it rather depends on what approach is taken to "legal causation", that is, to the process of deciding whether a defendant's wrongdoing is a sufficiently important cause of his profits to justify granting the plaintiff wronged by him a remedy extending to the amount of those profits. If a remedy were granted in respect of all profits made by the defendant which would not have been made "but for" the breach, then restitutionary remedies for breach of contract will be frequent; yet such an extensive remedy may well be thought to be incompatible with the current commercial purpose of contracts, that is to say, arm's length bargaining and exchange.[85] However, if a stricter approach were taken to questions of causation (attribution of responsibility), so that, for example, the law attributed profits in the hands of a defendant to a breach of contract by him only where those profits would not, in fact, have been earned by the defendant "but for" his breach, and the profits could not have been earned by him had he in fact adhered to his contract, then a restitutionary remedy for breach of contract would be available much less frequently.

The arguments developed so far in this chapter do not preclude these possible changes in the law. They do, however, ensure that the questions inherent in any wider acceptance are posed clearly and faced squarely. Accurate legal analysis can raise the questions which must be faced when considering any change in the law, but legal analysis cannot answer the question of whether change is desirable. In fact, the wider availability of restitutionary remedies for breach of contract would entail changes of great magnitude to the substantive law of contract which should only be adopted, if at all, after serious and direct consideration. They should not come about as the indirect consequence of changes to remedies for breach of contract which were introduced in response to perceived "hard cases", especially as any injustice inherent in such cases might be resolved within the current framework of contract law.

[84] Such a suggestion could be criticised on pragmatic, commercial grounds—that it would be very difficult in many circumstances to tell what constituted "breaching a contract in bad faith" (cf. Burrows, *The Law of Restitution* (1993), 402).

[85] Perhaps, therefore, a distinction should be made between commercial contracts, where such availability of a restitutionary remedy seems inappropriate, and other contracts, where it does not. However, the creation of any such new distinction in the law of contract would not be without a price in uncertainty and consequent litigation. Another suggestion is that restitutionary remedies for breach of contract should be available if and only if the parties would have provided for it in their contract, had they turned their minds to the issue (O'Dair, "Damages for Breach of Contract" (1993) 46(2) *CLP* 113). This approach has been criticised by Smith, "Disgorgement of the Profits of Breach of Contract" (1994) 24 *Can Bus LJ* 121 at n 77: either there would have to be outward manifestation of the parties' intention, albeit implicit rather than explicit, or the theory relies on a fiction of imputed intention. Further, agreement by the parties to a contract that a restitutionary remedy should be available for breach might well fall foul of the rules against pe- 'ty clauses (see Treitel, *The Law of Contract*, 9th edn (1995), 903–5).

# 4

# *Remedies for Breach of Contract: Specific Enforcement and Restitution—A Comment*

PETER WATTS

Mr Nolan's chapter is a careful and refined argument which warrants reflection. The chapter's central thesis seems to be that the only place for disgorgement of profits, or restitution for wrongs, in the law of contract is where disgorgement would be a near replacement for the plaintiff's lost expectations. A key passage is this[1]:

> "A restitutionary remedy for breach of contract should only be allowed when such a remedy gives effect to the plaintiff's expectations more effectively than a loss-based remedy. Restitutionary remedies for a breach of contract which could have been remedied by a decree of specific performance should do this, because they give full monetary effect to the plaintiff's expectations."

Nolan proceeds then to confirm that it is *solely* specifically enforceable contracts which are suitable for disgorgement and perhaps, even then the contract must be one for the disposition of property. Profits made from other breaches, including those that would have been subject to specific remedies such as the injunction, cannot be adequately identified, he argues, as the product of the plaintiff's defeated expectations.

It is to be inferred that Nolan sees the correlation between disgorgement and lost expectations in the assumption that the plaintiff, P, who will be the purchaser, will usually have lost the sale which the defendant, D, has made by not performing the contract, or that otherwise P would have made the profit D has made by being in occupation of the land.

The practical function of disgorgement on Nolan's thesis is very limited. Where the facts of a case match the above assumption—namely that P would, on the balance of probabilities, have made the sale D made had P been the owner of the subject property—then disgorgement would not usually be needed because it is established that expectation damages can be measured at the date of trial.[2] Where, on the other hand, the facts of a case do not match

[1] Original paper. See now *supra*, p 54.

[2] *Wroth* v. *Tyler* [1974] Ch 30; *Johnson* v. *Agnew* [1980] AC 367.

the assumption, then the correlation Nolan sees between disgorgement and lost expectations breaks down. There might be a number of reasons why profits D has made were ones that P could not have made, including those derived through D's superior marketing skills and by adventitious meetings D may have had.

There is, however, one useful role which disgorgement might perform which is consistent with Nolan's thesis. This is in establishing the measure of a *presumption* of loss. Profit-stripping performs a parallel function within the old action of money had and received in relation to the conversion of property; the converter is accountable for the actual proceeds of property converted whatever the market value of the property (reference is usually made to *Lamine* v. *Dorrell*).[3] D's wrongdoing justifies P's being freed of the burden of proving value. The resulting presumption is probably a conclusive one, since D's wrongdoing also justifies the court in not hearing any evidence D might herself wish to adduce as to value. Where title has passed to P in a contract for the sale of goods, P may be able to resort to *Lamine* v. *Dorrell* without concerning himself with the scope of disgorgement in contract law.[4]

I am not yet convinced as a result of Nolan's argument that there is not room in the law of contract for the other principal function of profit-stripping, deterrence. While contract law is unlikely to put up the candidates for deterrent remedies that the law of tort can—strong remedies may be needed against trespass to property if the peace is to be preserved (a point, I think, alluded to by Nolan)—it seems to me that there is a role for deterrent remedies in the law of contract. Although not punitive, the account will in many cases remove the incentive to break the law. Exemplary damages would be an alternative remedy; such damages have the advantage of not needing precise calculation, and by being punitive can be of greater deterrent effect. Where profiting has obviously occurred, some estimation of gain is likely nonetheless to be needed if deterrence is to result.

Before turning to what might be appropriate candidates for disgorgement, it is necessary to address a practical objection which Nolan raises to profit-stripping remedies. He argues that, outside his permitted category of specifically enforceable contracts, it is too difficult to establish causation between breach and profit. However, once one accepts that there is a role for deterrence in the civil law, it ought not to be necessary for P to show that D's gain was one P might have made.[5] It ought, prima facie at least, to be sufficient for P to prove that the profits could not have been made but for the wrong (though for a case where there was insufficient connection between wrong and gain, see *Halifax Building Society* v. *Thomas*).[6] The resulting task for the

[3] (1705) 2 Ld Ray 1216.

[4] See *Biggerstaff* v. *Rowatt's Wharf Ltd* [1896] 2 Ch 93, 103.

[5] Cf. *Reading* v. *Att-Gen* [1951] AC 507.

[6] [1996] Ch 217, as noted Watts (1996) 112 *LQR* 219. Cf. Jaffey [1996] *RLR* 92; and Birks (1996) 10 *TLI* 2.

court should be no more difficult than that already performed in cases involving infringement of intellectual property rights and cases of trespass to land.[7] What appears to be required is for the court to assess, in the light of the profits that D could not have made but for the breach, the figure at which D would have found it uneconomic to proceed to breach the contract. It is only where, in making this assessment, allowance is made to D for her skill in engineering the profit[8] that the resulting figure will tend as low as the purchase-of-rights damages awarded in cases such as *Wrotham Park Estate Co Ltd* v. *Parkside Homes Ltd*.[9]

As to the role of deterrence in contract law, I think it is bound to be small, and nowhere near as great as some have argued for. One simple reason for this is that in many cases P will indeed not be able to prove that D's profits could not have been made but for the breach. Where substitute performance was available to P, then what in most cases would there have been to prevent D fulfilling her contract with P as well as making the gain that P is alleging belongs to him? At the same time, of course, in those instances damages can adequately cover both the price of substitute performance and also the extra transaction costs incurred in obtaining it.

The account, therefore, as with the other equitable ancillary remedies, the injunction and specific performance, is likely to be warranted only where substitute performance is not available to P. Prime candidates will be negative promises. P cannot purchase elsewhere what D promised not to do. Such cases, it seems to me, involve the same exclusive entitlement to performance which Nolan sees as a feature of the specific performance paradigm. The account might, therefore, have been used in the restrictive covenant cases, such as *Wrotham Park*. The remedy might also have been available in *Surrey County Council* v. *Bredero Homes Ltd*,[10] being not dependent on the application of Lord Cairns' Act. In that case there was not present in the plaintiff the sentiment one would normally expect in the beneficiary of a restrictive covenant, but that does not seem crucial. The purpose of the relevant restriction in that case, presumably to the defendant's knowledge, was to preserve to the plaintiff access to a portion of the gain the defendant might make from further development of the affected land. Since waiver was ruled out, even expectation damages, one might have thought, could have reached to part of the defendant's profit.

It is not apparent that the account should be confined to negative promises relating to the use of property. Cases such as *Lumley* v. *Wagner*[11] would provide other examples. Indeed, the remedy of account is less invasive of liberty than the injunction in such cases. It aims to deter but does not outrightly prohibit.

[7] See, for instance, *My Kinda Town Ltd* v. *Soll* (1982) 8 FSR 147.
[8] As in *O'Sullivan* v. *Management Agency & Music Ltd* [1985] QB 428.
[9] [1974] 1 WLR 798.
[10] [1993] 1 WLR 1361.
[11] (1852) 1 De GM & G 604.

Where I am in company with Nolan is that cases such as *Tito* v. *Wadell (No 2)*[12] are not appropriate candidates for profit-stripping for wrongs, though my objections may go beyond his. In most such cases substitute performance is possible, if only the courts were prepared to take expectation damages to that length (the most recent judicial compromise is, of course, *Ruxley Electronics & Constructions Ltd* v. *Forsyth*).[13] Further, even if for some reason it is not possible by the date of trial for P to obtain substitute performance, it is most doubtful that the use of the account as a deterrent remedy could be made to turn on that fact. That being so, there is not, for the above reasons, any place for profit-stripping remedies in such cases.

In any event, an important fallacy, in my view, underlies the reasoning of those who have seen these cases as candidates for profit-stripping. No promisor makes a profit merely by not performing or by underperforming, save through keeping that which she may have been paid for performing the promise. To the extent that the promisor *has* been paid, then all that is required is true restitution to enable P to recover that payment from D. It is, of course, the case that in instances of underperformance historic bars exist to true restitution; first, in the total failure rule and, secondly, in the apparent inability of the common law in circumstances where P's consideration has not been money, as with *Tito* v. *Waddell* itself, to adjust the initial consideration agreed between the parties to take account of the underperformance (hence the law of restitution has not as yet, to my knowledge, attempted to answer the question raised by *Tito* v. *Waddell*, how much extra would the Banabans have charged the British Phosphate Commission for a lease without the repair covenant?). These problems with true restitution would not, I consider, justify the courts now resorting to restitution for wrongs.[14] But even if the courts were to do so, the maximum that could be awarded would be the consideration provided by P for the broken promise.

The crucial point is that the actual costs avoided through underperformance, which may or may not bear a close relationship to that which D has been, or was to be, paid, are not an enrichment. Put bluntly, D can be enriched only if her overall asset position, her "wealth", is increased or otherwise she receives something she wants without paying for it. D's wealth can be increased through the receipt of a saleable item or by being released from expenditure she would otherwise have been obliged by law to incur. Of these forms of enrichment, it is only the last which seems relevant in the underperformance cases. Yet it too is inapplicable. If the law did require D to incur the expenditure saved, then D would not be enriched because her liability in contract damages would not have been discharged. If, for whatever reason, the law does not require D fully to perform or to pay money that would enable that to be procured by P, then D cannot be enriched by not paying that

12 [1977] Ch 106.

13 [1996] 1 AC 344.

14 Cf. *White Arrow Express Ltd* v. *Lamey's Distribution Ltd* [1995] CLC 1251, CA.

which she was not obliged to pay. Any other conclusion would be to do by way of the account of profits that which the courts have refused to do by way of damages.

What is required, therefore, before restitution for wrongs becomes relevant in the contract context is both non-performance by D and some positive gain derived by D from X which could not have been obtained without breach of the contract with P. Such circumstances do exist in the specific performance and injunction cases discussed above.

# 5

# *The Proprietary Consequences of Contract Failure*

SARAH WORTHINGTON

## 1. INTRODUCTION

In the aftermath of *Westdeutsche Landesbank Girozentrale* v. *Islington London Borough Council*,[1] it might be thought that any paper on the proprietary consequences of contract failure should be very short. However, many would concede that the case raises almost as many questions as it answers. Moreover, in its reformulation of the law, it introduces some troubling inconsistencies. In short, it demands that more attention be given to the issue of proprietary interests, not less. In the light of the opinions expressed in that case, this chapter attempts to reconstruct an internally and theoretically consistent framework describing the proprietary consequences of contract failure.

Any discussion of the proprietary consequences of contract failure is clearly a discussion focused on interests arising by operation of law, not interests arising by agreement between the parties. The contract itself may have provided for the transfer of property interests, and when the contract fails those interests may have been successfully transferred or not. This is readily illustrated by that most familiar of contracts, the contract of sale. By the time the parties realise that the contract has failed, legal title to the sale property may—or may not—have passed from the vendor to the purchaser. The real issue is whether, by operation of law, the parties can be considered to have property interests different from those defined by the straightforward operation of the agreement itself. The contract failures which need to be considered in this context can be defined very broadly: the contract may have failed, in practical terms, because of one party's inability or refusal to perform; it may have failed in a legal and practical sense because one party elects to avoid a voidable contract; finally, it may have failed in a legal sense because the law regards the contract as void. It should not be assumed that the proprietary consequences, if any, of these three types of failure are identical.

As a starting point, it might be asked why there should be any need at all for proprietary interests arising by operation of law in a contractual context. Contract is about obligation, not property. Certainly this is, by and large, the

[1] [1996] AC 669.

view of the common law. But it is not the view of equity. We are very familiar with instances where equity regards the parties as compelled to perform a contract, and the associated, but not inevitable, proprietary interests which arise as a consequence of this.[2] It is feasible that there might also be proprietary consequences when the parties are seen, in equity, as obliged to *undo* their dealings, rather than obliged to *perform* their obligations.

This is the thesis of this chapter. The obligation to perform, or the obligation to undo, is postulated as the prime requirement for delivering proprietary consequences. The suggestion is that contract failure is visited by proprietary consequences *only* when equity sees the parties as obliged to perform their unperformed contract or as obliged to undo their performed contract. The former describes specifically enforceable contracts; the latter describes void and voidable contracts (once the election to avoid has been made). Of course, even with such equitable obligations, there can be no proprietary incidents unless there is identifiable property. This is the second and corollary requirement.[3] Only the first requirement is examined in this chapter. Moreover, the principal focus here is on the more controversial aspects of the proposition: post-*Westdeutsche*, this means that most attention must be given to void contracts.

The arguments most often advanced against the recognition of equitable proprietary interests in commercial contexts rest on both policy and principle. If the proposition advanced here is to be accepted, it must meet both these arguments.

## 2. POLICY CONSIDERATIONS

### *The Common Law Proprietary Response to Failed Contracts*

The focus of this chapter is on equitable interests. Nevertheless, it is worth revisiting the common law proprietary response to contract failure. This can be set out briefly.[4]

The common law does not anticipate contractual performance: it does not assume or deem a legal transfer of title which the parties themselves have not effected. In fact, it cannot compel the performance of an unperformed contract, much less ensure this by proprietary interests arising by operation of law. With breached and frustrated contracts, then, the common law propri-

[2] See *infra*. Similar consequences also arise outside the contractual arena, in equity's jurisdiction: see, e.g. *Attorney-General for Hong Kong* v. *Reid* [1994] AC 324.

[3] This is not to deny its practical importance: identification of the relevant property is often impossible, either because the contract itself failed to specify it, or because, over time, it has become untraceable. This acts as a significant bar to the recognition of equitable proprietary interests.

[4] For more detail, see, e.g. G.H. Treitel, *The Law of Contract*, 9th edn (1995), 262–87; Lord Goff of Chieveley and G.H. Jones, *The Law of Restitution*, 4th edn by G.H. Jones (1993), 183–97.

etary position is that effected by the parties themselves before their contract fails; no legal interests arise by operation of law.

With void contracts, the position is almost the same. Very rarely will the common law deny that legal title has been transferred in the face of a purported transfer by the parties themselves.[5] The effectiveness of the legal transfer may depend upon physical delivery or formal conveyance, rather than on the contract itself. Nevertheless, it is usually the case that the common law does nothing—statute aside—to undo the transfer even though it was motivated by a void contract.[6]

All of this perhaps makes the common law response to voidable contracts somewhat surprising.[7] It is suggested that if a contract is voidable at law and if it is effectively avoided—and this is only possible if strict *restitutio in integrum* is possible[8]—then legal title will revest in the original owner, unless the property is of the type requiring formal conveyance.[9] The practical effect of this final limitation is that the revesting rule is largely restricted to contracts for the sale of goods.

All of this is by the way. It serves only to illustrate that the common law rarely, if ever, visits contract failure with proprietary consequences. Instead, it relies upon personal remedies, whether contractual or restitutionary. There are said to be persuasive policy reasons why equity's response should be the same. This is doubted.

### *Policy Reasons Militating against the Recognition of Equitable Proprietary Interests in Failed Contracts*

Without doubt, the undesirable commercial consequences seen as associated with the imposition of equitable proprietary interests provided the primary motivation behind the reasoning of the House of Lords in the *Westdeutsche* case.[10] As Lord Browne-Wilkinson put it, "[i]f the due application of equitable principles forced a conclusion leading to these results [i.e. the imposition of a resulting trust], your Lordships would be presented with a formidable task in reconciling legal principle with commercial common sense".[11]

This articulated hostility towards the recognition of proprietary interests has a number of bases. Commercial contracts are see as founded on certainty,

[5] Although there are exceptions. See, e.g., *Cundy* v. *Lindsay* (1878) 3 App Cas 459.

[6] e.g. *Stocks* v. *Wilson* [1913] 2 KB 235.

[7] See the references cited at *supra* n 4; also see R.P. Meagher, W.M.C. Gummow and J.R.F. Lehane, *Equity Doctrines and Remedies*, 3rd edn (1992), Ch 24.

[8] This might be seen as the common law's strict enforcement of the requirement that the property be identifiable.

[9] *O'Sullivan* v. *Management Agency and Music Ltd* [1985] QB 428, 457; *Alati* v. *Kruger* (1955) 94 CLR 216, 223–4; R.M. Goode, *Commercial Law*, 2nd edn (1995), 42, 113. Although, notably, such revesting does not carry with it the *right* to demand recovery of the property *in specie*: Torts (Interference with Goods) Act 1977, s 3.

[10] See especially [1996] AC 669, 690, per Lord Goff, 703–5, per Lord Browne-Wilkinson.

[11] *Ibid*, 705.

transparency and fairness. Equitable proprietary interests, it is said, operate to deny each of these features.

**Certainty and transparency**

Certainty is frequently claimed to be essential to commercial contracts. In fact, the essence of commerce is risk-taking: there is very little certainty. What is usually meant is transparency, so that at least the commercial risks can be more readily assessed.

This alleged need for transparency reflects the popular view that commercial parties should not be faced with off balance sheet risks:[12] the ownership of assets should be clear to all. Of course, the only way to achieve this is by statutory means, with a comprehensive registration system, perhaps along the lines of the American Uniform Commercial Code. England does not yet have this. Instead it has adopted a more piecemeal approach, one which over the years has attracted considerable criticism. The end result of this is that certain proprietary interests negotiated by the commercial parties themselves can be hidden from third parties: retention of title agreements and *Quistclose*[13] trusts are obvious examples. Given this, it cannot be said that commercial transactions are transparent.

Moreover, even the introduction of a comprehensive registration system would not touch proprietary interests (whether legal or equitable) which arise by operation of law. These interests arise, despite any agreement between the parties, because justice demands them. They may put into effect the parties' intentions (although in advance of the actions of the parties themselves) or they may deny those intentions. Clearly such interests cannot possibly be registered; nor can they be known by third parties in advance of the circumstances which give rise to them.

It might be thought that such interests should not exist. English law adopts a course midway between civilian jurisdictions (where remedies are almost exclusively personal) and American and Canadian law (where remedial constructive trusts are routinely adopted). English law recognises both personal rights and proprietary interests, but the latter only as "institutions", based on rigorous and often technical legal reasoning. Before denying this heritage, and moving towards one or other alternative, as Lord Browne-Wilkinson seems to suggest we should, the consequences need very careful examination.

**Unfairness**

The House of Lords in *Westdeutsche* was clearly of the view that equitable ownership interests—however infrequently they might arise—produce commercially unacceptable side-effects. This assertion deserves closer scrutiny. Assume that A transfers money and shares to B pursuant to a void contract,

[12] See especially [1996] AC 669, 705, per Lord Browne-Wilkinson; and, less stridently, 689–90, per Lord Goff.

[13] See *Quistclose Investments Ltd* v. *Rolls Razor Ltd* [1970] AC 567.

and that the money is paid into a mixed account. Assume, further, that B then transfers funds from this account to C and, in addition, grants to D a charge over the shares to secure a loan.[14] Any of the four parties may subsequently become insolvent, bringing their unsecured creditors into the picture. The spectre of insolvency highlights the impact of proprietary interests: one party is clearly advantaged; the others (the unsecured creditors) are often assumed to be correspondingly disadvantaged. This is debatable.

*(i) Should A, the original owner, have the benefit of a trust?* This is the obvious first question, identified as such by Lord Goff:[15] why *should* A be better off simply because the contract is void?[16] Both parties believed the contract to be valid; A embarked on the commercial venture accepting the risk of B's insolvency. To say that the foundation assumptions have been removed—because A's transfer does not attract the anticipated contractual obligations due from B—does not immediately explain why the consequences should be proprietary rather than personal.

The answer really depends upon a detailed analysis of legal principles, as outlined in the second part of this chapter. For current purposes, however, the answer can be taken in two steps. First, it is generally accepted that the circumstances described are sufficient to impose on B a *personal* obligation to effect restitution, to repay the funds advanced. This is an obligation recognised both at law and in equity.[17] Moreover, the obligation does not arise simply because the consideration has failed: if B merely failed to perform, A's remedy would rest in contract.[18] A's remedy arises because there is *no* contract; it follows that, without a restitutionary remedy, B would be unjustly enriched.[19]

The second step is to explain why this personal obligation should produce proprietary consequences. The simplest answer is that this is how equity

[14] This example combines the examples considered by Lord Browne-Wilkinson, [1996] AC 669, 703–5.

[15] *Ibid*, 683–4.

[16] This statement selectively focuses on the scenario where B is insolvent. It ignores the position where both parties are solvent (as they were in the *Westdeutsche* case): then it must be said that, if A cannot have the commercial advantages of the transaction (because the contract is void), it seems patently unfair to insist that A still carries the commercial risks.

[17] Earlier cases invariably assumed this: *Moses* v. *Macferlan* (1760) 2 Burr 1005; 97 ER 676. Similarly, see Lord Goff in *Westdeutsche*, [1996] AC 669, 697. Although contrast Lord Browne-Wilkinson, *ibid*, 714–15.

[18] Unless B's failure constituted a repudiation of the contract, allowing A to terminate for breach. Then (and only then: *Lipkin Gorman (a firm)* v. *Karpnale Ltd* [1991] 2 AC 548, 579, per Lord Goff) A would have an alternative remedy in restitution; but only, it seems, if there was a total failure of consideration (*Fibrosa Spolka Akcyjna* v. *Fairbairn Lawson Combe Barbour Ltd* [1943] AC 32). This last limitation does not apply to void and voidable contracts: see below. Also see S. Worthington, *Proprietary Interests in Commercial Transactions*, (OUP 1996), Ch 7.

[19] The same argument also applies with *voidable* contracts: once an effective election to avoid is made, the contract is treated as never having existed and restitution is demanded of both parties.

invariably operates, so consistency demands precisely the same response here. There are no examples of situations where equity imposes an obligation to account or an obligation to transfer or restore property, and the asset in question is identifiable, and yet the holder of the asset is not considered to hold it on trust. This *is* how equity enforces this type of obligation. This is so whether the obligation recognised by equity is one expressly or impliedly agreed to by the parties[20] or one imposed by operation of law.[21] In addition, the cases also make it clear that, if the relevant property is identifiable, it is not to the point to try to distinguish between an obligation to account and an obligation to restore property.[22] Consistency demands the same treatment of void contracts—or a good explanation for the difference. These ideas are developed further in the second part of the chapter.

*(ii) The consequences for B, the recipient of the property, if there is a trust.* If there is a trust, the proprietary consequences for B are clear. The unfairness in this is seen as principally affecting B's general creditors. This is considered later. It is the associated personal liability of B which is more troublesome and which is seen as contributing in part to the sentiment that proprietary remedies are productive of undesirable commercial consequences. What is at stake is B's personal liability, as a "trustee", to effect compensation, to account for profits, and to be subjected to detrimental evidential assumptions in tracing exercises.

Despite the contrary views expressed by the House of Lords, it is certainly arguable that B's personal liability is purely fault-based.[23] The obligation to effect compensation is the most difficult issue. The House of Lords assumed that, with a trust, B would be *personally* liable, regardless of fault, for any subsequent payment away of the monies to third parties, even though, at the date of the payment, the "trustee" was still ignorant of the existence of any trust.[24] This must be doubted.[25] An obligation to effect compensation is imposed—in this context—in order to remedy a breach of the duty to preserve the trust fund. Such a duty is only warranted with trustees of express

[20] Consider, e.g., *Quistclose* trusts, specifically enforceable contracts and contracts dealing with future property.

[21] Consider the constructive trusts associated with tracing exercises, claims to family homes, and obligations imposed on defaulting fiduciaries to disgorge profits; also consider the resulting trusts associated with voluntary transfers, purchases in another's name, and rescission of voidable contracts.

[22] See *Attorney-General for Hong Kong* v. *Reid* [1994] AC 324.

[23] In support, see R.P. Meagher and W.M.C. Gummow, *Jacobs' Law of Trusts in Australia*, 5th edn (1986), 413–16, suggesting that, except in very special circumstances, there is *no* personal right to recovery (but also see pp. 651–2, apparently to the contrary). To the contrary, however, see A.J. Oakley, *Parker and Mellows: The Modern Law of Trusts*, 6th edn (1994), 213–17; *Re Diplock's Estate* [1948] Ch 465.

[24] [1996] AC 669, 690 per Lord Goff, 703 per Lord Browne-Wilkinson, agreeing with A. Burrows, "Swaps and the Friction between Common Law and Equity" [1995] *RLR* 15.

[25] See the discussion *infra*. The common law moderates its position using the defence of change of position.

trusts[26] and perhaps with trustees whose unconscionable behaviour has attracted the imposition of a trust by operation of law.[27]

The liability of a resulting trustee to account for profits is less problematic. Just as the issue of compensation depends upon the duty to preserve the trust fund, this liability depends upon the duty not to profit. This is not a duty imposed on resulting and constructive trustees who are unaware of the existence of the trust.[28] This limitation conceivably denies the possibility of tracing the initial asset into direct substitutions, and thereby recovering the associated capital or income gains from the trustee;[29] outside direct substitutions, it would certainly not be possible to recover the profits acquired from mere use of the asset, unless the trustee is accountable for those profits.[30]

Finally, the easiest issue. Lord Browne-Wilkinson advanced the view (*obiter*) that, since B is a trustee, if funds are traced through B's account, B will be treated as having drawn on "his own" monies first, thereby benefiting A at the expense of the unsecured creditors of B.[31] But this need not necessarily follow. There is no *presumption* (rebuttable or otherwise) that B has used his own funds first, even though this is how the position is commonly expressed. Rather, when the trust facts are known *and* when recipient is a trustee owing duties to A to preserve the trust fund, *then*—and only then—the trustee is estopped from denying that his own funds were used first;[32] but he is also estopped from denying that A's funds were used first, if that is the assumption which, in practical terms, proves more beneficial to A.[33] This estoppel rule is designed to afford the beneficiary the best protection of the trust fund when it is the trustee's duty to preserve that fund. On the facts mooted, however, B is not an active fiduciary: B does not owe fiduciary duties

[26] See I.E. Davidson "The Equitable Remedy of Compensation" (1982) 13 *MULR* 349; W.M.C. Gummow "Compensation for Breach of Fiduciary Duty", in T.G. Youdan (ed), *Equity, Fiduciaries and Trusts* (1989).

[27] This is more difficult. Consider, e.g., trusts arising with contracts which are voidable for undue influence: see *Mahoney* v. *Purnell* [1996] 3 All ER 61. On this basis, *Re Diplock's Estate* [1948] Ch 465 and other cases concerning overpaid legatees must be considered anomalous.

[28] Consider, e.g., the position of a vendor who is a constructive trustee under a specifically enforceable contract of sale: the vendor is not liable to the purchaser for profits made from the property, even while the trust operates. The same is true of parties who are made constructive trustees of the family home.

[29] A lien on the substituted asset, on the other hand, would limit proprietary recovery to the original asset's equivalent, rather than permitting recovery of the asset's equivalent *and* any profit derived from its use or replacement. In the treatment of profits, it seems that innocent volunteers should, e.g., be distinguished from fiduciaries (with equitable duties) and thieves (where the initial property acquisition was by fraud). This reflects Lord Browne-Wilkinson's view that the rule operates according to the state of the conscience of the recipient: *Westdeutsche* [1996] AC 669, 705–6. Arguably legal ownership, if it persists in substitutions, must carry with it any profits associated with the substituted asset; there is no legal equivalent of an equitable lien: see *Trustee of the Property of FC Jones and Sons (a firm)* v. *Jones* [1996] 3 WLR 703.

[30] But see P. Watts, "The Limits of Profit-Stripping for Wrongs" (1996) 112 *LQR* 219, and the cases cited.

[31] *Westdeutsche* [1996] AC 669, 704.

[32] *Re Hallett's Estate* (1879) 13 Ch D 696.

[33] *Re Oatway* [1903] 2 Ch 356.

to A to preserve the trust fund, to refrain from making a profit, to avoid conflicts of interest, and so on. The trust is "not an active one".[34] The tracing exercise discussed in *Re Diplock's Estate*[35] confirms this: the charities held the funds mistakenly paid to them on resulting trust; there was, however, no suggestion that, as volunteers, they would be penalised in any tracing exercise.

*(iii) The consequences for B's general creditors if there is a trust.* The imposition of a trust would enable A to achieve priority over B's general creditors on B's insolvency, a result seen by the House of Lords as unjust.[36] However, this perceived injustice must be doubted. In practical terms, it is hard to see the result as other than economically neutral. This is perhaps difficult to appreciate with transactions in the nature of swaps. It is more readily apparent with contracts which do not involve both parties paying sums of money.

As an illustration, consider the alternative case of the sale by A to B of shares in a private company for a price of £1 million. Assume, further, that the contract of sale is void. Also assume that B is now insolvent. Pre-*Westdeutsche*, it might have been supposed that the shares were held by B on resulting trust for A. A could therefore recover them: they could not be sold to fund B's liabilities to any general creditors. But this result is not at the expense of B's general creditors. The sale contract is void; but before equity will permit A to take advantage of any resulting trust, A will have to return the £1 million purchase price. This, rather than the shares, will then be available to B's general creditors. In this example, it is commonly assumed that B's creditors have not suffered. In financial terms, however, this is not automatically the case: the shares may in fact be worth very much more than £1 million—then, it seems the general creditors will have lost out; on the other hand, they may be worth very much less than £1 million, in which case the general creditors will have been substantially advantaged. These details of valuation are the lifeblood of commercial activity. Viewed this way, there is nothing unjust in the imposition of a resulting trust: it is simply the mechanism which ensures that the parties are restored to their pre-contractual positions. This is necessary only because the contract is void. With valid contracts, the general creditors take the benefits (or losses) delivered by the contract; with void contracts they take the benefits (or losses) afforded by restitutionary claims. The resulting trust is simply equity's means of ensuring that the contract is undone so that this can take place.[37]

[34] *Sinclair* v. *Brougham* [1914] AC 398, 421, per Viscount Haldane, with whom Lord Atkinson agreed.

[35] [1948] Ch 465.

[36] *Westdeutsche* [1996] AC 669, 689–90, per Lord Goff, 703–5, per Lord Browne-Wilkinson.

[37] The analogy with specific performance—and the proprietary interests associated with that remedy if the property to be transferred is identifiable—are apparent.

*(iv) The proprietary effects on C, a transferee from B.* If B holds an asset on trust for A, but then transfers this asset to C, A's proprietary interest will be defeated if C is a *bona fide* purchaser for value. C, and C's general creditors, will not need to concern themselves with A. On the other hand, if C receives the asset otherwise than as a *bona fide* purchaser for value, A's equitable interest will persist and A will be able to recover the asset in priority to C's general creditors. Lord Browne-Wilkinson says there is no moral or legal justification for this, since the creditors "have themselves not been enriched, in any real sense, at [A]'s expense and indeed have had no dealings with [A]".[38]

If A has no property interest in the asset in C's hands, then it is perhaps true that C and C's creditors, however much they have been enriched as volunteers, have not been enriched at A's expense. Even here, however, there is some debate. Outside the context of commercial dealings, there is some dispute about how the common law should treat C if the gift from B was motivated by B's unjust enrichment from A.[39] Even in a commercial context, the insolvency legislation, in making wide-ranging provisions for claw-back, must sometimes see C as enriched at A's (and, more particularly, at A's creditors') expense.

If A does have an equitable proprietary interest in the assets received by B and given to C, then the position must be clearer. No-one would dispute that assets *legally* owned by A, which somehow fall into C's hands as a volunteer, would enrich C and that the windfall should in no circumstances benefit C's creditors. Should the position be any different in equity? In both cases C, C's creditors and perhaps even B may all be ignorant and innocent. Consider the charities in *Re Diplock's Estate*:[40] clearly they were enriched at the residuary beneficiaries' expense; no matter what the *bona fides* of the ignorant charities and their creditors, and no matter how much the gift had been relied upon, if the property is still identifiable in the charities' hands, there seems to be no justification for dividing it between the legatees and the general creditors. It should be no different if the primary transaction is not mis-direction of trust funds in the administration of a will, but the transfer of funds subject to a void contract. The real difficulty is a moral one; it arises because both A and C are usually innocent and equally deserving: to favour one over the other can never seem "fair".[41] The same is true of the next scenario.

[38] *Westdeutsche* [1996] AC 669, 704, 716. Accordingly, he does not think that restitution should be effected by proprietary means (unless by means of a remedial constructive trust, where there is room for manoeuvre to take into account the interests of third parties).

[39] D. Hayton, "Equity's Identification Rules", in P. Birks (ed), *Laundering and Tracing* (1995), Ch 1.

[40] [1948] Ch 465.

[41] Moreover, the possibility of importing the common law change of position defence does not seem to help matters. Suppose C acquires the legal title to property which belongs in equity to A. Furthermore, suppose that C keeps this property but disposes of other property which belongs absolutely to C. To allow C the benefit of a change of position defence to A's proprietary claim suggests that A's equitable title can be retained or lost depending upon C's motivation in dealing

*(v) Consequences for D, a chargee from B.* A superficial view of orthodox equitable principles suggests that if A retains equitable ownership of the shares transferred to B, even though B has legal title, and B charges those shares to D, then D's security will *pro tanto* be defeated by A's interest. A's interest is not registrable, so the competition between A's and D's equitable interests will be judged on equitable principles. The rule is that, where the equities are equal, the first in time prevails. If the equities are equal, therefore, A's interest will prevail and, unintentionally, D will have advanced an unsecured loan to B. This does not appear fair to D. However, it must be remembered that A, too, is innocent. This is a priorities competition between two innocent parties. Inevitably if one is to win and one is to lose, the outcome cannot be based on "fairness". What equity does in these circumstances is to choose between two evils, plumbing at least for consistency if not for absolute justice. Moreover, since the first in time rule is premised on the equities being equal, there is some room for adjustment should exceptional circumstances demand it.[42]

**Summary**

In short, the commercial consequences of these equitable ownership interests—for all parties—is simply to effect a timing difference in the commercial risk. The contract is either regarded as completed when in fact it is not, or is regarded as unperformed when in fact it has been performed. This reallocation of risk does not occur in every instance of contract failure. In fact, it occurs in very few instances: only those where the interests of justice demand, from the contract's inception, that it be performed or, again from its inception, that it be undone. The effect of this on the contracting parties cannot be seen as commercially unacceptable. On policy grounds, therefore, this type of proprietary intervention need not necessarily be denied.

The next issue is whether equitable principle supports this particular type of proprietary intervention.

## 3. THE PRINCIPLES GOVERNING EQUITABLE OWNERSHIP

Even if the interests of justice demand intervention in contractual performance, why should the intervention be proprietary rather than personal? As noted earlier, the trite answer is that this is how such equitable intervention always works: if equity imposes a mandatory obligation to deal with identified property in a particular way, then, because equity regards as done whatever ought to be done, the net effect is proprietary.

not with A's property, but with C's property. This is not orthodox English property law, no matter how appropriate motivation may be as a factor determining C's *personal* liability to A.

[42] This should not entail the review of every priority dispute. But see A.J. Oakley, "Judicial Discretion in Priorities of Equitable Interests" (1996) 112 *LQR* 215.

Consider equity's exclusive jurisdiction. This is where the obligations imposed on the parties are recognised only in equity. There we are familiar with—and ready to accept—that equity's intervention is proprietary. There are many familiar examples: legal owners of property can be seen, in equity, as obligated to hold property for the benefit of others, with proprietary consequences, in express trusts, purchase money resulting trusts, voluntary transfer presumed resulting trusts, constructive trusts of family homes, and constructive trusts of the profits derived from breaches of fiduciary obligations. The reason for the proprietary response is that equity regards as already done that which ought to be done. If identified property ought to be transferred, then equity regards that as already done, and equitable ownership is the result.

In the auxiliary and concurrent jurisdiction, the same themes are evident: if the legal owner of property is obliged, in equity, to deal with that property in a particular way, then equity regards as already done that which ought to be done. The result is often equitable ownership, whether via a resulting or a constructive trust. The real question, then, is when can one party be obliged to deal with identified property in a particular way.

The matter is best examined by considering separately the different forms of contract failure. Equity's response, and the commercial consequences, are most clearly seen by considering particular examples. Take three simple contracts: a sale of goods; a sale of shares; and a loan contract. To add a note of commercial realism, assume that the nominated sale price or loan amount is £1 million. A contract which requires A, the purchaser or lender, to pay £1 million to B, the vendor or borrower, may fail for any number of reasons. The proprietary consequences, if any, depend upon the form of failure.

### *Contracts which Fail because of Breach or Frustration*

The most common form of contract failure is breach of contract: one of the contracting parties simply refuses, or is unable, to perform. In a few instances this inability to perform arises because the contract is frustrated. Outside the cases of frustration, the common law response is to allow the injured party to claim damages for breach of contract. This remedy is personal, and seeks to provide the injured party with the monetary equivalent of contract performance. Sometimes the breach is considered so serious that the injured party is justified in terminating the contract. This puts to an end the prospective contractual obligations for both parties.[43] The injured party can then elect to sue for restitution rather than for contractual damages. Restitutionary remedies are only available when the contract has been terminated.[44] In addition,

[43] But not their prior obligations. This makes a terminated contract something quite different from void and voidable contracts.

[44] *Lipkin Gorman (a firm)* v. *Karpnale Ltd* [1991] 2 AC 548, 579, per Lord Goff.

such remedies have traditionally been regarded as only available when there is a total failure of consideration.[45]

In *none* of these circumstances (unless the contract is specifically enforceable[46]) will equity intervene to reallocate property ownership; this is because equity does not require that contractual performance be either completed or undone.[47]

### *Failure to Perform a Specifically Enforceable Contract*

It is widely accepted that, if a contract to transfer property is specifically enforceable and if the property to be transferred is sufficiently well identified, then the intended recipient is the owner in equity of the property.[48] The trust is a constructive trust.[49] This form of equitable intervention is possible with both real and personal property.[50] It is the result of a decision in equity that the contract *must* be performed. Equity then regards as done that which ought to be done. Because this response is widely accepted, the coverage here can be restricted to a few important points.

Given the accepted general rule, the critical factor regulating equitable ownership is clear: it is whether the contract is specifically enforceable. Equity's decision on this is discretionary, although it is grounded in well-accepted principles. It follows that it is often relatively easy to predict whether a contract

[45] *Fibrosa Spolka Akcyjna* v. *Fairbairn Lawson Combe Barbour Ltd* [1943] AC 32. This requirement has been eliminated by statute if contract performance is frustrated: Law Reform (Frustrated Contracts) Act 1943. The position is not the same with void and voidable contracts. Also see P. Birks, "Inconsistency between Compensation and Restitution" (1996) 112 *LQR* 375.

[46] See the next section *infra*.

[47] This says nothing of the incidence of equitable liens rather than equitable ownership interests. See S. Worthington, *Proprietary Interests in Commercial Transactions* (OUP, 1996), Ch 9.

[48] See, e.g., J.E. Martin, *Hanbury and Martin's Modern Equity*, 14th edn (1993), 28; J.D. Heydon, W.M.C. Gummow and R.P. Austin, *Cases and Materials on Equity and Trusts*, 3rd edn (1989), para 629; I.C.F. Spry, *The Principles of Equitable Remedies*, 4th edn (1990), 648. For further details, see S. Worthington, "Proprietary Remedies: The Nexus between Specific Performance and Constructive Trusts" (1996–7) 11 *JCL* 1. Note that not all specifically enforceable contracts generate proprietary interests; if the property is not sufficiently well-identified, there can be no ownership interest in it, even if the contract is specifically enforceable: e.g. *Mac-Jordan Constructive Ltd* v. *Brookmount Erostin Ltd (in rec)* [1992] BCLC 350; *Re London Wine Co (Shippers) Ltd* [1986] PCC 121.

[49] This area of the law is beset by problems of semantics. The trust here is regarded as a constructive trust because the vendor who, before the contract, was the full legal owner of the property, is now, after the contract, regarded as bound in conscience to hold that property for the benefit of the purchaser. In contrast, as will be seen later, it is suggested that the trust which arises with void and voidable contracts is a resulting trust: this is because the property results back, in equity, to its original owner. With void contracts this happens *eo instanti*. With voidable contracts it happens after a period where the purchaser is full legal owner of the property. With voidable contracts, it is perhaps a moot point whether the contract is called a resulting trust or a constructive one: it is resulting in the sense that the property "results back" to the vendor; it is constructive in the sense that the purchaser is seen as unable, in conscience, to retain full legal title to property previously owned absolutely. The practical consequences, whatever the nomenclature adopted, are the same. This is amplified in the discussion which follows.

[50] e.g. *Lysaght* v. *Edwards* (1876) 2 Ch D 499, 507; *Falcke* v. *Gray* (1859) 4 Drew 651, 62 ER 250.

will be specifically enforced or not. To return to the examples cited earlier, a contract for the sale of goods will not be specifically enforced unless the goods have particular qualities (rarity, beauty, etc) which would render damages inadequate.[51] A contract for the sale of shares will usually be specifically enforceable if the shares are private company shares, but not if they are public company shares freely available in the market.[52] Finally, contracts of loan are rarely, if ever, specifically enforced.[53]

This general rule suggests that specific enforceability depends largely upon the nature of the property to be transferred. However, it must not be forgotten that the remedy is discretionary and so particular circumstances sometimes suggest that it is not warranted. Contracts for the sale of land, for example, are traditionally regarded as specifically enforceable. However, this is not invariably the case and then the purchaser will not become the owner in equity of the sale property.[54] This reinforces the idea that equitable proprietary interests depend upon the existence of a mandatory obligation to transfer identifiable property and upon equity then regarding as done that which ought to be done. It also reinforces the idea that, although equity's principles give rise to general rules, these rules are subject to exceptions when the particular facts demand a different equitable response.

This idea that proprietary interests depend upon equity regarding as done only what the vendor is obliged to do is reinforced by equity's response to conditional sale contracts. If a vendor is not required to transfer the sale property until certain conditions are met, then no equitable proprietary interest will arise until that time.[55] This lends further support to the general rule advanced here.

In short, if equity considers that a contract *must* be performed (and if the relevant property is identifiable), then equity regards the contract as already performed, in advance of legal performance. The rule is important, although its practical impact must not be exaggerated: few contracts for the sale of personalty will specifically identify the property in advance of the transfer of legal ownership; fewer still are specifically enforceable.

### *Contracts which Fail Because of One Party's Election to Avoid a Voidable Contract*

Contracts may be voidable either at law or in equity. As might be expected, many more contracts fall into the latter category than into the former. This

[51] e.g. *Falcke* v. *Gray* (1859) 4 Drew 651, 62 ER 250. Furthermore, it should be noted that with such contracts the *legal* title generally passes at the time of the contract; equitable intervention is then unnecessary. Moreover, equitable intervention is severely circumscribed by the restrictive analysis of the Sale of Goods Act 1979 derived from *Re Wait* [1927] 1 Ch. 606.

[52] *Duncuft* v. *Albrecht* (1841) 12 Sim 189, 59 ER 1104.

[53] *Loan Investment Corp of Australasia* v. *Bonner* [1970] NZLR 724.

[54] e.g. *Wroth* v. *Tyler* [1974] 1 Ch 30.

[55] *Brown* v. *Heffer* (1967) 116 CLR 344. The position is not vastly different if the purchaser can waive the condition: *Wood Preservation Ltd* v. *Prior* [1969] 1 WLR 1077.

is because equity takes a more expansive view of the factors which will permit an injured party to elect to undo a contract; equity also takes a more lenient view of whether the parties are still in a position where they can be compelled to undo their agreement (i.e. whether *restitutio in integrum* is possible).

If a contract is voidable in equity and if the entitled party effectively elects to avoid the contract, then the contract is avoided *ab initio*. Both parties are seen as never having been obliged to perform, and there is an obligation in equity to undo the contract.[56] If the sale property remains identifiable despite its transfer—and the contract will not be voidable unless it is[57]—then the vendor will be regarded as its owner in equity; the purchaser will hold the property on resulting trust.[58] Again, this approach is widely accepted, so it merits only brief attention here.[59]

The trust which arises in these circumstances is regarded as a traditional resulting trust, since the property "results back" to its original owner.[60] In truth, as noted earlier,[61] the issue is one of semantics. What is important is *why* the trust is imposed by operation of law. The argument here is that it is imposed because equity sees the parties as obliged to act to undo their contract. Equity enforces this obligation by regarding as done that which ought to be done.

This equitable response should not be seen as surprising, given the parallel response at law.[62] However, once again the practical impact of the rule is severely constrained, not just because few contracts are voidable, but because, once this possibility is discovered, the sale property is often no longer identifiable.

[56] This is subject to the statutory discretion granted to the court by the Misrepresentation Act 1967, s 2(2): in cases where a contract can be rescinded for innocent or negligent misrepresentation, the court can declare that the contract subsists and award damages instead. See, e.g., *William Sindall Plc* v. *Cambridgeshire CC* [1994] 1 WLR 1016. This will exclude the operation of any proprietary remedies.

[57] This is certainly the orthodox position, but see *Mahoney* v. *Purnell* [1996] 3 All ER 61.

[58] *O'Sullivan* v. *Management Agency and Music Ltd* [1985] QB 428, 458–9 per Dunn LJ, 464–9 per Fox LJ, 471–3 per Waller LJ; *Alati* v. *Kruger* (1955) 94 CLR 216, 223–4 per Dixon CJ; *El Ajou* v. *Dollar Land Holdings Plc* [1993] 3 All ER 717, 734 per Millett J. Also see R.P. Meagher, W.M.C. Gummow and J.R.F. Lehane, *Equity Doctrines and Remedies*, 3rd edn (1992), 655–7 and th cases cited there.

[59] Although there are some recent and surprising unsupported *dicta* to the contrary, suggesting that equitable title does not revest: see *Re Goldcorp Exchange Ltd (in rec)* [1995] 1 AC 74, 102–3, suggesting that, even if the bullion investors had rescinded their contracts with Goldcorp (which they had not), their rights would have been personal; rescission would not, by operation of law, have carried with it any proprietary interest. Although this was no doubt true on the facts (the purchase money being unidentifiable), it must be wrong in theory: it ignores equitable doctrine. See the criticisms in D. Hayton, "Ascertainability in Transfer and Tracing of Title" [1994] *LMCLQ* 449, 452; P. Birks, "Establishing a Proprietary Base (*Re Goldcorp*)" [1995] *RLR* 83, 88. However, the same conclusions were also suggested in *Eldan Services Ltd* v. *Chandag Motors Ltd* [1990] 3 All ER 459, 462 per Millett J (*dicta*).

[60] It is also true that, in the circumstances, it can be seen as unconscionable for the purchaser to retain the property. Equity's recognised response to this is a constructive trust.

[61] See *supra* n 49.

[62] See the earlier discussion of common law remedies.

In the few cases where an equitable proprietary interest can be asserted, its effect on the parties, should insolvency intervene, cannot be seen as commercially unacceptable. If a contract is voidable, then the initial transfer of property is effective both at law and in equity. Returning to the earlier examples, if shares are transferred to A under the terms of a voidable contract, then A becomes their legal and beneficial owner. Before the contract is avoided, B, the vendor, has no equitable interest in them. B has, at most, a mere equity. This means that, before avoidance, A has an absolute right to deal with the shares and, should A become insolvent, A's general creditors will benefit from the acquisition. Once the contract is avoided, however, the shares will belong in equity to B. An effective election to avoid the contract occurs by the act of the injured party, and the contract is avoided from the time this election is made. It follows that B will be the owner in equity of the shares from this moment. However, it is also true that B cannot effectively elect to avoid the contract unless both parties are in a position to effect *restitutio in integrum*, at least according to equity's more lenient standards. This means that B must return the £1 million purchase price to A. It follows that A, and—on insolvency—A's general creditors, will not benefit from the shares, but they will instead benefit from the returned purchased price. This cannot be regarded as working an unfairness on A or A's general creditors, even though it does put the parties in their pre-contractual positions and thus denies to A the potential advantages (or disadvantages) associated with the contract.

Once again, the rationale behind equity's response is the obligation to deal with identifiable property in a particular way. Here, the obligation is to undo a sale contract which has, at law, been performed. Equity sees such obligations as arising whenever a transfer has been induced by fraud, undue influence, misrepresentation and so forth: the contract is then voidable in equity.

### *Contracts which Fail because they are Void*

With void contracts the parties do not have the luxury, or the ability, to elect whether to confirm the contract or not. The contract is in law regarded as void *ab initio*. If the parties perform, they do so gratuitously; the contractual obligations of both are, from the start, a nullity. The effect—if equity regards as done that which ought to be done—is that equity from the start would see the contract as not performed, or, if performed, as needing to be undone immediately. The reasons for this are amplified below.

If the consequences of this type of equitable obligation is proprietary in other circumstances, then consistency would seem to demand that it be proprietary here too. Of course, such an assertion runs directly counter to the opinions advanced by the House of Lords in the *Westdeutsche* case. On that basis, the proposition advanced here may be seen as doomed. However, the bounds within which *Westdeutsche* can and should be confined have not yet been settled. Moreover, the decision itself suffers from the serious criticism that the House of Lords was unable to hear full argument on these important doctrinal issues. Given this, it seems necessary to expound the theoretical arguments fully before any further steps are taken.

In this chapter there is obviously not the space to rehearse in detail the reasons for disagreement with the conclusions of the House of Lords. These reasons can, however, be summarised. The clear sense from Lord Browne-Wilkinson's opinion—and it was he who provided the most comprehensive analysis—was that both policy and principle mandated against a resulting trust being the appropriate response to a void contract. The policy issues have already been dealt with. The arguments based on principle had three quite distinct roots. Each merits some attention.

**"Retention" of an equitable interest is technically impossible**

This assertion is derived from the well-known starting point that a person solely entitled to the full beneficial ownership of property, both at law and in equity, does not enjoy an equitable interest in that property: the legal title carries with it *all* the rights.[63] There is ample authority for this view.[64] From this it follows that, unless and until there is a separation of the legal and equitable estates, there is no separate equitable title. On this basis it is meaningless to talk about the bank "retaining" its equitable interest in the funds: it had no separate equitable interest before the funds were transferred. But this argument is really one of semantics, and can easily be taken too far. Moreover, there is something wrong with an argument which supposes it to be impossible to *retain* an equitable interest which has no prior existence, but which regards it as unexceptional to *transfer* such an interest.[65]

In truth, all that is meant by the assertion that the equitable title is "retained" is that, for some reason recognised by equity, "the property comes back to [the beneficiary] after it has been given away, *although in truth the beneficial interest may never have left [the beneficiary]*".[66] What is critical is

[63] *Westdeutsche* [1996] AC 669, 706.

[64] See, e.g., *Commissioner of Stamp Duties (Queensland)* v. *Livingston* [1965] AC 694, 712, per Viscount Radcliffe; *Vandervell* v. *IRC* [1967] 2 AC 291, 311, per Lord Upjohn, 317 per Lord Donovan; *Re Cook* [1948] Ch 212; *Underhill and Hayton, Law of Trusts and Trustees*, 15th edn (1995), 866.

[65] As frequently happens: e.g. declarations of trust by a settlor, purchase-money resulting trusts, constructive trusts of bribes or unauthorised profits. See, too, Lord Browne-Wilkinson's analysis of *Chase Manhattan Bank NA* v. *Israel-British Bank (London) Ltd* [1981] Ch 105 in *Westdeutsche* at [1996] AC 669, 714–15. He regarded it as impossible for the paying bank to *retain* (by operation of law) an equitable interest in the funds transferred when, prior to payment, there was no existing separate equitable interest. However, at a later date it was regarded as perfectly possible for the recipient bank to *transfer* (by operation of law) an equitable interest in those same funds, notwithstanding that prior to this transfer there was, again, no existing separate equitable interest. (Lord Browne-Wilkinson also had other reasons for disagreeing with the reasoning—but not the conclusions—in this case: see especially the later discussion on the role of knowledge.)

[66] R.P. Meagher and W.M.C. Gummow, *Jacobs' Law of Trusts in Australia*, 5th edn (1986), 263 (emphasis added). When a resulting trust arises because of an election to avoid a voidable contract, the beneficial interest returns after it has been given away; when a resulting trust arises because of a voluntary transfer, the beneficial interest never leaves the donor.

not the matter of semantics: whether the equitable title was "retained" or whether it passed with the legal title and then, immediately, resulted back to the transferor. What *is* critical is the *reason* why equity sees this as an appropriate response. It is also critical that the transferor is seen as being *immediately* entitled to this equitable interest. On both counts, void contracts clearly differ from voidable contracts.[67]

**The traditional principles which underpin presumed resulting trusts deny their existence in the context of void contracts**

The starting point for this view is the assertion that, under existing law, a presumed resulting trust can only arise where A makes a voluntary payment to B[68] and the circumstances are such that there is a *presumption* that A did not intend to make a gift to B. In this context, "voluntary" is used in the sense of "gratuitous". The money or property is then held on resulting trust for A. However, the presumption is easily rebutted either by the counter-presumption of advancement or—more importantly in this context—by direct evidence of A's intention to make an outright transfer.[69] According to Lord Browne-Wilkinson, the legal effect of A's intention to transfer is not altered merely because both A and B are acting under a misapprehension that the transfer was being made pursuant to a valid contract.

With respect, this misconceives the traditional operation of resulting trusts. The law, as stated above, is clear. The suggestion that evidence of an intention to make an outright transfer will suffice to rebut the presumption of a resulting trust must be treated with some caution. It is correct, but not comprehensive; it assumes an underlying voluntary (i.e. gratuitous) transfer and, moreover, a transfer intended as such. In these circumstances a resulting trust will certainly be rebutted by evidence of an intention to make an outright transfer. Nevertheless, what the evidence in rebuttal must really show is *an intention to make an absolute and voluntary (i.e. gratuitous) transfer*. Only this is sufficient, in the eyes of equity, to allow the recipient volunteer to assert legal and beneficial ownership of the property transferred.[70]

None of this is directly at odds with the arguments advanced by Mr William Swadling[71] and accepted by the House of Lords. The cases examined by Mr Swadling clearly demonstrate that *any* evidence of an intention to make an absolute and voluntary transfer will oust the presumption of a resulting

[67] And very different from contracts which a party simply refuses, in breach of contract, to perform.

[68] Or pays (wholly or in part) for the purchase of property which is vested either in B alone or in the joint names of A and B.

[69] *Westdeutsche* [1996] AC 669, 708 per Lord Browne-Wilkinson, citing *Underhill and Hayton*, 317 *et seq*; *Vandervell* v. *IRC* [1967] 2 AC 291, 312 *et seq*; *Re Vandervell (No. 2)* [1974] Ch 269, 288 *et seq*.

[70] Moreover, it would be very strange if equity paid regard to the quality of the bank's intention to transfer in cases where a contract might be *voidable*, but chose to ignore the more acute demand for equitable intervention when the contract was *void*.

[71] W.J. Swadling, "A New Role for Resulting Trusts?" (1996) 16 *Legal Studies* 110.

trust. This is so even if the transfer was motivated by an incorrect view of the facts. Thus, a gift from A to B, intended as such but mistakenly motivated by the view that B was not already provided for,[72] or that A's wife should be denied any interest,[73] are examples where there *is* evidence of a positive donative intent (albeit a mistaken one) and so there is no resulting trust.[74]

This is effective to deal with transfers which are intended to be absolute and voluntary, whether based on mistaken motive or not. But it says nothing of transfers intended to be absolute but *not* intended to be voluntary.[75] The latter problem is of much greater concern in a commercial context. Mistaken liability payments are the classic example, but so too are payments made pursuant to a void contract. Lord Browne-Wilkinson dealt with this separate issue with the simple assertion that, here too, an intention to effect an absolute transfer was simply and clearly inconsistent with the presumption of a resulting trust. Equity could not *presume* that the bank did not intend to part with beneficial ownership in the face of clear evidence that it did.

All of this sounds eminently reasonable, but only so long as the underlying contract is valid. Then the bank clearly does intend to transfer absolutely (although not voluntarily), and it matters not that the contract turns out to be less commercially advantageous than expected, or that, had this been known, the bank would not have proceeded with the deal. In other words, if the contract is effective, then it matters not that the intention to transfer absolutely was mistakenly motivated: the transfer will stand, both at law and in equity.[76]

But to say that it matters not that the underlying contract is *void* misconceives the situation. Because the contract is void—and was from the start, even though this was not known to either of the contracting parties—this means that the bank in fact paid the funds to the local authority without being contractually obliged to do so; moreover, it did this in circumstances which rendered the local authority not liable to satisfy any of the agreed counter-obligations. Given this, if we say that the bank intended the local authority to have the funds absolutely, and cannot invoke a resulting trust, we are effectively saying that the bank must be seen as intending a voluntary and absolute

[72] Also, in this context, see *Lady Hood of Avalon* v. *Mackinnon* [1909] 1 Ch 476, where Eve J rescinded a second, forgotten, deed of appointment. This is not inconsistent with the proposition advanced here. However, such rescission is not the same as imposing a resulting trust on property mistakenly transferred. It is more akin to allowing a plaintiff to renege on a promise to make a gift, something which is unexceptional with promises not embodied in a deed. Even with a deed, promises to make a gift are not specifically enforceable in equity; nor could the donee obtain damages for breach of contract, since no loss could be proved. But contrast Lord Goff of Chieveley and G.H. Jones, *The Law of Restitution*, 4th edn by G.H. Jones (1993), 121–2.

[73] *Fairhurst* v. *Griffiths* (H Ct of the Isle of Man, His Honour the Deemster Corrin, 4 May 1989).

[74] Equity distinguishes between an *intention to give* and the *motive for giving*.

[75] And, in this context, a transfer is only voluntary if it is made for "no consideration", not if it is made for a consideration which simply fails.

[76] Unless, for other reasons, the contract is voidable.

transfer to the local authority. We cannot solve this by saying that the bank was mistakenly motivated by the thought that the contract was valid. This mistake in itself denies the suggestion that the transfer was intended to be voluntary. This, in turn, means that the presumption of a resulting trust is not rebutted. As both Lord Goff and Lord Browne-Wilkinson assert, the traditional view is that a presumed resulting trust arises whenever "A makes a *voluntary* payment to B . . . and there is [an unrebutted] presumption that A *did not intend to make a gift to B*".[77] On the assumed facts, the presumption is not rebutted; on the contrary, it is proved to accord with the true facts.

Furthermore, it must be remembered that what is at issue here is a resulting trust, a trust arising by operation of law, not by agreement or expressed intention. It is important not to conflate the requirements of each type of trust. A resulting trust is not premised on the transferor's intention to create a trust.[78] Lack of intention to create a trust would negate the creation of an *express* trust; it says nothing of a resulting trust. What is important is that the transferor does not intend an absolute and voluntary transfer; the further logical step, that therefore the transferor must intend a trust, will not have been consciously taken by the transferor:[79] this is the role of the law; it creates the necessary trust.

In the same vein, a resulting trust is not premised on a proven intention that the trust fund should be kept separate and identifiable. This is not even an essential feature of express trusts,[80] and is quite irrelevant to resulting and constructive trusts.[81]

#### There cannot be a trust (including a resulting trust) unless the trustee is aware of the factors alleged to affect conscience

According to Lord Browne-Wilkinson,[82] there cannot be a trust unless the potential trustee is "aware that he is intended to hold the property for the benefit of others in the case of an express or implied trust, or, in the case of

[77] *Westdeutsche* [1996] AC 669, 708, per Lord Browne-Wilkinson (emphasis added), and, in similar terms, at 689, per Lord Goff.

[78] See W.J. Swadling, (1996) 16 *Legal Studies* 110, *supra* n 71. And still less on the *transferee's* intention, despite the comments of Lord Browne-Wilkinson that resulting trusts are considered to give effect to "the common intention of the parties. A resulting trust is not imposed by law against the intentions of the trustee (as is constructive trust) but gives effect to *his* presumed intention": [1996] AC 669, 708 (emphasis added). With respect, this is not true. Such trusts are considered to operate according to the *presumed* intentions of the *transferor*, not the trustee. Moreover, if the transferor actually intended to create a trust, the trust would be express, not resulting.

[79] If it has, the trust will be express, or will be the type of resulting trust which arises because the intended express trust fails.

[80] See, e.g. *Stephens Travel Service International Pty Ltd (Rec & Man apptd)* v. *Qantas Airways Ltd* (1988) 13 NSWLR 331, 341–2, 349.

[81] But, to the contrary, see *Westdeutsche* [1996] AC 669, 712, per Lord Browne-Wilkinson. Of course, there cannot be a resulting or constructive trust unless the trust property can be identified with certainty; however, the parties need not *intend* the property to remain separate and identifiable.

[82] *Ibid*, 705–6.

a constructive trust, of the factors which are alleged to affect his conscience".[83] If this is true, then it follows that there could be no trust of the funds advanced by the bank: at the time when the potential trust property was identifiable,[84] the local authority was unaware that the contract was void, hence its conscience could not be affected. For this reason Lord Browne-Wilkinson is also critical of the reasoning adopted in *Chase Manhattan Bank NA* v. *Israel-British Bank (London) Ltd*.[85] To his mind, the conscience of the recipient bank could not be affected before it was aware of any mistake, although he accepted that, two days later, when the mistake was discovered, retention of the monies with knowledge of the mistake might be sufficient to give rise to a constructive trust.[86]

With respect, this is not orthodox equity. Here again we encounter problems of semantics.[87] The *existence* of a trust has never depended upon the state of knowledge of the trustee. This is true of both express trusts and trusts arising by operation of law. The fallacy in the reasoning arises because of the tendency to equate the *existence* of a trust with the *imposition* of the full gamut of fiduciary obligations traditionally imposed on trustees of express trusts.[88] A trust is traditionally seen as existing whenever there is a separation of legal and equitable ownership.[89] However, as Lord Browne-Wilkinson himself recognised, this separation of titles does not automatically attract the

[83] *Ibid*, 705.

[84] It seems to have been assumed that the funds were no longer traceable, having been paid into an account which was subsequently overdrawn. The possibility of tracing withdrawals from this account into assets purchased using those funds was, it seems, not pursued.

[85] [1981] Ch 105. See *Westdeutsche* [1996] AC 669, 714–15.

[86] It follows that he accepts the result in the case as probably correct and well-founded, but on alternative reasoning: *ibid*.

[87] This time it is over the meaning of the terms "trust", "constructive/resulting trustee" and "fiduciary" and whether there is any necessary degree of overlap in the different ideas behind these words. Here, "trust" is used to indicate a division of legal and equitable ownership; this says nothing of the "fiduciary" duties of the "trustee". The view subscribed to here is that the particular fiduciary duties (if any) imposed on resulting and constructive trustees depend upon the circumstances. There is no necessary congruence with the duties imposed on trustees of express trusts (and even those are subject to wide variation depending upon the circumstances). The precise content of fiduciary duties cannot be known in advance of the scenarios giving rise to them: see P.D. Finn, *Fiduciary Obligations* (1977), 1–2. Lord Browne-Wilkinson, on the other hand, would wish to use the word "trust" only when the "trustee" is subject to the full gamut of fiduciary obligations: see *Westdeutsche* [1996] AC 669, 707. On this basis, in what seems to be a reversal of conventional reasoning, his view is that, if the trustee is not accountable for profits from the use of the funds (because of lack of knowledge sufficient to affect conscience), then those funds cannot be held on trust.

[88] A matter which was particularly important in the *Westdeutsche* context, because it was seen to relate to the local authority's potential liability to compound interest.

[89] Whether that separation arises by agreement (an express trust) or by operation of law (a resulting or constructive trust). Furthermore, the separation must be of *ownership* interests if there is to be a trust. Other less potent equitable rights which are enforceable against the legal owner (e.g. lien, equity of redemption, right to rectification or subrogation) are not sufficient to constitute a trust. But see *Westdeutsche* [1996] AC 669, 707 per Lord Browne-Wilkinson: perhaps this traditional formulation will not survive, given the semantic difficulties described above.

onerous duties of trusteeship.[90] This disjunction is not a problem: it is possible for third parties to have the benefits of equitable ownership without all the additional protections potentially afforded by fiduciary obligations;[91] the reverse is also possible.

To repeat, equity does not regard a recipient's conscience as affected only when there is some appropriate degree of knowledge: equity is not examining the *bona fides* of the recipient in obtaining or dealing with the property, but simply determining whether the recipient is entitled to retain what has been received. Were it otherwise, priority problems would be resolved on the basis of the time at which the potential trustee acquired the necessary knowledge rather than the time at which the property was received.[92] This has plainly never been the case. Nor will it do, in this context, to distinguish between resulting and constructive trusts and to assert that with the former there needs to be knowledge of the trust obligation, whereas with the latter there needs to be knowledge only of the circumstances which affect the recipient's conscience. Both forms of trust are imposed to ensure that a recipient cannot unconscionably retain property.

With volunteers this objective is easily achieved, and the recipient's state of knowledge has never been an issue. The justice and morality of this is self-evident, even to the common law, which demands personal restitution (it not having at its disposal any proprietary remedies). Where property is put into the name of X without X's knowledge but in circumstances where no gift to X was intended, it is orthodox equity that X holds the property on resulting trust for the transferor, and does so from the time of receipt.[93] To see these cases as explicable on the ground that X's conscience was affected only from the time X became aware of the true facts and only *thereafter* did X hold the property on resulting trust[94] is to re-interpret these cases and impose upon them an analysis and justification which is not evident in the primary decisions. X is seen as holding the property on resulting trust from the moment of receipt. There is no presumed re-transfer of the beneficial interest from X to the original owner at the time that X is made aware of the true facts.

[90] *Ibid*, noting in particular that a constructive trustee without some necessary degree of knowledge is not personally liable to account as trustee: See *Re Diplock's Estate* [1948] Ch 465, 478; *Re Montagu's Settlement* [1987] Ch 264; *Underhill and Hayton*, 369–70. The position is perhaps more uncertain than this comment suggests.

[91] See the earlier discussion of policy issues. The contrary view (*Westdeutsche* [1996] AC 669, 689, per Lord Goff and 707, per Lord Browne-Wilkinson) seems to be derived from an unsubsantiated comment in A. Burrows, "Swaps and the Friction between Common Law and Equity" [1995] RLR 15, 27.

[92] Or, with constructive trusts arising as the result of voidable contracts, at the time at which an election to avoid was properly made.

[93] The tracing process applied with this type of case reinforces this assertion: property can be traced from its receipt, not from some later date when the appropriate degree of knowledge can be established.

[94] Which is Lord Browne-Wilkinson's approach: *Westdeutsche* [1996] AC 669, 705, citing *Birch* v. *Blagrave* (1755) Amb. 264; *Childers* v. *Childers* (1875) 1 De G & J 482; *Re Vinogradoff* [1935] WN 68; *Re Muller* [1953] NZLR 879.

Where knowledge *is* critical is in assessing the *duties* owed by the trustee to the beneficiaries. This is amply illustrated by the different approaches to constructive trustees: if the defendant is a trustee under an express trust[95] or a "knowing recipient" of trust property, then the full force of fiduciary obligations to act in the beneficiary's interests and to abstain from making a profit or misusing position ensure that any evidential difficulties are resolved to the beneficiary's advantage, that any profits generated are held for the beneficiary, and that orders for compensation recognise the beneficiary's assumed loss of profits. Where the constructive trustee is an innocent volunteer unaware that a trust exists, however, the rigours of this approach are substantially modified: evidential difficulties are resolved by balancing the parties' respective interests, arguably the profits need not be accounted for, and compensation orders are not grounded in an obligation to maximise the beneficiary's interests. Lord Browne-Wilkinson expressly recognises this in his discussion of innocent third-party recipients of trust property: they are regarded as constructive trustees (because there is a severance of legal and equitable titles), but they are under no personal liability to account.[96]

This is all in accordance with the general principle, recognised by Lord Browne-Wilkinson, that "equity operates on the conscience of the owner of the legal interest . . . [and] requires him to carry out the purposes for which the property was vested in him (express or implied trust) or which the law imposes on him by reason of his unconscionable conduct (constructive trust)".[97] The error is to see all these purposes as identical. The true position is that there can be a trust (a separation of legal and equitable title) in many circumstances; however, the particular equitable duties imposed on the trustee (the legal owner) as a result of this separation vary according to the circumstances giving rise to the trust.

It follows that, even if traditional resulting trust principles suggest that the local authority does hold the transferred funds on trust for the bank, this says nothing of the obligations imposed on the local authority in dealing with those funds. The resulting trust defines the bank's *proprietary* rights to the funds; it says nothing of the *personal* remedies available to the bank. In particular, it says nothing of the local authority's obligation to pay compound interest.

To reiterate, what is postulated here is that, if a contract is void, then equity will regard the contract as not performed; if the parties do perform their con-

[95] Or a person in a fiduciary relationship, not necessarily holding trust property.

[96] *Westdeutsche* [1996] AC 669, 707. Moreover, as Lord Browne-Wilkinson recognised, there is no authority for the proposition that the trustee of a trust arising by operation of law—he confined his comments to a constructive trust—is (inevitably) accountable for his or her deeds from the date of receipt of the property: *ibid*, 705–6. This is true; the obligation to account—to remedy breaches of duty—only arises when the trustee has such duties. Moreover, there is no reason in principle or practice why resulting trusts should not be analysed on precisely the same lines: where there is a disposition for no consideration in circumstances where a gift was not intended (to use Lord Browne-Wilkinson's words), the resulting trust should be seen as imposing no positive duties on the recipient until he is aware of the existence of the trust.

[97] *Ibid*, 705.

tract, then equity can oblige them to undo their transaction. This mandatory obligation gives rise to proprietary interests rather than personal rights, by analogy with the reasoning applied to voluntary transfers.

## 4. CONCLUSION

In summary, the proposition advanced here is that contract failure is visited with proprietary consequences only when one party is obliged to act—whether to *perform* or to *undo* the contract—and the property which must thereby be dealt with is identifiable. This simple rule accords with the principles underpinning all of equity's proprietary intervention: equity regards as done that which ought to be done. Such proprietary interests do not deliver undesirable and unacceptable commercial consequences: they merely ensure that an interrupted contract is either performed or reversed; they put the parties, and their general creditors, in either the pre-contractual or post-contractual position. They only do this with those contracts which equity sees the parties as compelled to perform or compelled to undo. In the scheme of things, this limitation means that very few contracts are affected: most contracts are not specifically enforceable or void or voidable. The commercial impact of this when insolvency intervenes is not to deliver a windfall to either party, or to the general creditors. It is simply to shift the risk time-frame to pre- or post-contractual performance.

# 6

# *The Proprietary Consequences of Contract Failure—A Comment*

JANET ULPH

## Policy issues

In any discussion of equitable proprietary rights in insolvency, it is easy to become absorbed with the issue of *identification* of property. The value of the paper written by Sarah Worthington is that, whilst it explicitly recognises the importance of this issue, it removes this layer of law (and, where this is relevant, the further layer concerning whether the parties *intended* in their contract to create proprietary rights[1]) to consider what is the quintessential issue: when will contract failure give rise to equitable proprietary rights and, more specifically, to a resulting trust?

### Identification

In *Westdeutsche Landesbank Girozentrale* v. *Islington London Borough Council*,[2] which involved an interest rate swap which was outside the powers of a local authority, the House of Lords held that the bank, as the other party to the transaction, merely had a personal restitutionary claim at common law. It therefore appears that equitable proprietary rights are not an automatic consequence of the termination of a contract in these circumstances. But a distracting element in *Westdeutsche* was the fact that the money had been spent shortly after it had been received. In this respect, *Westdeutsche* appeared to be reminiscent of *Re Goldcorp Exchange Ltd*,[3] decided some time previously by the Privy Council. The facts of *Goldcorp* were far removed from those of *Westdeutsche*; in *Goldcorp*, the plaintiffs were ordinary people who had been misled into investing in non-existent gold bullion. There was, however, this similarity: in both cases, the transferees had enjoyed complete freedom to

[1] See, for example, the *Quistclose* line of cases based upon *Barclays Bank* v. *Quistclose Investments Ltd* [1970] AC 567.

[2] [1996] AC 669.

[3] *Re Goldcorp Exchange (In Receivership); sub nom. Kensington* v. *Unrepresented Non-Allocated Claiments* [1995] 1 AC 74.

spend the money received and there was no property which the plaintiffs could point to and claim as their own. In *Goldcorp*, the plaintiffs put forward a variety of arguments to suggest that they had an equitable interest in any bullion matching the contract description or in the purchase money. The Privy Council rejected all of these arguments, returning time and time again to the point that the contracts were for "unallocated" bullion and that there was no property which could be described as impressed with a trust. The impossibility of *identifying* the plaintiffs' property became the driving force behind this judgment.

If one turns to consider *Westdeutsche*, one can see that, if the facts had been different and the money received from the bank had been put into an account where it remained until after it was discovered that the transaction was *ultra vires*, there should have been no difficulties in establishing some form of trust, be it resulting or constructive. However, given that the bank's money was spent so promptly after its receipt, one suspects that there was almost a spontaneous reaction to deny a trust in these circumstances. Superficially, it might even appear that, once the money had been spent by the local authority, the plaintiff bank in *Westdeutsche* was thrown onto the same arid wasteland as the unsuccessful litigants in *Bishopsgate Investment Management Ltd* v. *Homan*;[4] in that case, unable to point to a specific asset as their own, those litigants attempted in vain to argue that there was a trust embracing the defendants' general assets. But this is to confuse the matter. The bank in *Westdeutsche* was not attempting to make a proprietary claim. As Sarah Worthington points out,[5] it is vital to appreciate that, in maintaining that money received is held upon resulting trust, it is not essential to prove that it was *intended* that the money would be placed in a separate account as a trust fund. Fundamentally, the parties are obliged to return the property which they have received under a contract which is *ultra vires* and void and the only issue is whether this is correctly analysed in terms of a resulting trust. The issue of whether the property exchanged under the contract still exists when the parties discover that the contract is void should only be relevant at a second stage, in determining what a particular plaintiff can recover if he wishes to assert proprietary rights.

An excessive preoccupation with identification can lead to a blinkered vision, where one fails even to raise other questions. A reference to a related area—specific performance—will suffice by way of illustration. According to the Sale of Goods Act 1979, and its predecessor, specific performance is only available in relation to contracts for the sale of goods where the goods are "specific or ascertainable".[6] As the Act is viewed as a codification, it has been suggested that this provision has had a broader influence and has led the

[4] [1995] 1 Ch 211. See Further, L. D. Smith, "Tracing, Swollen Assets and the Lowest Intermediate Balance" (1994) 8 *TLI* 102.

[5] See Worthington, *supra* text to n. 81.

[6] Sale of Goods Act 1979, s 52(1).

courts, in cases such as *Re* Wait,[7] forcefully to reject arguments attempting to claim equitable proprietary rights in sale transactions.[8] Looking at the matter afresh from the standpoint of the parties' obligations and, in particular, the seller's obligations, may lead one to alternative conclusions.[9] If not, there will still have been a benefit obtained in testing a proposition in an invigorating way. This is what Sarah Worthington's chapter sets out to do: its mission is to establish a framework in which the proprietary consequences of contract failure are defined. Its focus is upon equity, which provides for proprietary consequences where the parties are obliged to perform their contract (by awarding specific performance) or obliged to undo their contract (because the contract is either void or has been rescinded).

**Size of the Threat**

It is difficult to avoid the conclusion that decisions relating to equitable proprietary rights are policy driven. A limited role for trusts is acceptable where they can be viewed as merely short-term expediencies which will inject some much needed capital to prop up a moribund company, as in the case of *Quistclose*[10] trusts. Arguments that an express trust exists, involving relatively small sums of money, may also be sympathetically received.[11] However, where there may be a multiplicity of claims, as in the case of retention of title clauses, the courts adopt a cautious approach. The claim in *Westdeutsche* would therefore have given cause for concern. Over a million pounds remained outstanding and there were other local authorities facing similar claims. Assuming, as the House of Lords did, that any recognition of a resulting trust would *necessarily* have the consequence of giving plaintiffs access to the more draconian tracing rules and other advantages[12] enjoyed by beneficiaries under a conventional trust, this could be seen as posing a severe threat to the insolvency regime.

**Consequences of a Resulting Trust Analysis**

Some of the consequences of a resulting trust analysis remain largely unexplored. Sarah Worthington's discussion is particularly valuable in this regard.

[7] [1927] 1 Ch 606.

[8] M. G. Bridge, *The Sale of Goods* (Oxford, 1997), 532; W. Goodhart and G. Jones, *Specific Performance*, 2nd edn (Butterworths, 1996) (hereafter "*Goodhart and Jones*"), 147, 150.

[9] See, e.g., Law Reform Commission of Western Australia, Discussion Paper on "Equitable Rules in Contracts for the Sale of Goods" (Project No. 89, 1995), para. 5.6. The question is raised in the Discussion Paper as to whether, if the contract provides for the appropriation of goods by the seller from an identified bulk, a decree of specific performance could be awarded to enforce this contractual obligation. This possibility was not directly raised by the English and Scottish Law Commissions when they were considering reform of this area of law: "Right to Goods in Bulk" (W.P. No. 112, 1989), "Sale of Goods Forming Part of a Bulk" (Law Com. No. 215, 1993).

[10] See *supra* n 1.

[11] A classic example is *Re Chelsea Cloisters Ltd* (1981) 41 P & CR 98, involving tenants' deposits.

[12] See Worthington, *supra* text to nn 23–35.

Taking a slightly different approach from her chapter, I would argue that a determination of these consequences depends upon whether one sees the recipient transferee as a *wrongdoer*. If one does not (and this is my view of the matter) then her chapter's arguments appear eminently persuasive.[13] Why should the more draconian tracing presumptions be available to the plaintiff transferor in these circumstances? Furthermore, why should the recipient be obliged to account for any profits which he may have made with the property transferred (such as speculation in shares)?[14] On the same lines, I have great sympathy for the argument that Lord Browne-Wilkinson erred in assuming that if there was a resulting trust, a recipient would automatically be personally liable if he paid the money or property away before becoming aware of such trust's existence. Fault is surely relevant. Where I part company with Sarah Worthington is in relation to the question of where the issue of fault should be located. I would suggest that a recipient of property could be made personally liable if he pays property away which is subject to a resulting trust. However, it should be open to such a recipient to rely upon the defence of change of position;[15] any question of fault should be deliberated over at this point. It had been mooted that such a defence was not available because the recipient was a wrongdoer: Lord Browne-Wilkinson was content to accept this.[16] The matter surely needs to be explored further: arguably, this defence should be available in these circumstances.

**Unfairness and the Need for Coherence**

From a policy viewpoint, favourable treatment to any class of claimant has to be objectively justifiable to avoid the erosion of the statutory insolvency regime which provides for *pari passu* distribution amongst unsecured creditors. A claimant who possesses equitable proprietary rights has priority over such creditors where the property remains identifiable. At the same time, it has to be accepted that there inevitably will be injustices. As in any major disaster, a claimant may end up being in the wrong place at the wrong time.[17] One has to reconcile oneself to this and seek consistency so that the law relating to equitable proprietary rights does not become fragmented and disconnected as a whole.

[13] See Worthington, *supra* text to nn 23–35.

[14] Resulting trustees do not owe fiduciary obligations: see L. D. Smith, "Constructive Fiduciaries?" in P. Birks (ed), *Extending Obligations* (OUP, 1997).

[15] *Lipkin Gorman* v. *Karpnale Ltd* [1991] 2 AC 548; *Goss* v. *Chilcott* [1996] AC 788. See further, P. Birks, "The English Recognition of Unjust Enrichment" [1991] LMCLQ 473; E. McKendrick, "Restitution, Misdirected Funds and Change of Position" (1992) 55 MLR 377.

[16] *Westdeutsche* [1996] AC 669, 703. Lord Browne-Wilkinson relied upon an article by A. Burrows, "Swaps and the Friction between Common Law" [1994] *RLR* 15, 27. The possibility that the recipient could rely on the defence of change of position until he is aware that the contract is void was raised, *ibid*, at 28.

[17] See, e.g., *Re Lewis's of Leicester Ltd* [1995] BCC 514, 517, where the ability to claim equitable proprietary rights upon a company's insolvency depended upon the type of agreement made and whether the company had paid the money received (gross takings from the sale of goods) into separate accounts.

## Resulting Trusts and *Westdeutsche*

As Sarah Worthington's chapter sets out, Lord Browne-Wilkinson's judgment is based upon the following principles:[18]

### Retention of equitable interest is technically impossible

This principle is rightly questioned in her chapter. In considering whether there is an invariable rule to this effect, it is easy to be diverted. It has to be accepted that one cannot be a trustee of one's own property. If the entire legal and equitable estate are vested in one person, the legal and beneficial interest are combined.[19] This situation must be distinguished from one where an owner purports to transfer the bare legal estate in property. In these circumstances, when does separation of legal and equitable title take place? In Lord Browne-Wilkinson's view *in Westdeutsche,* it takes place at the point of receipt and not at the point of transfer.[20] First instance cases in the field of retention of title bolster this analysis.[21] No doubt the general rule should be that, when property is transferred the equitable interest will be transferred with the legal interest: the House of Lords recognised as much in *Vandervell* v. *IRC*.[22] This is because it is what the parties usually intend.[23] But it can be argued that it is excessive to state that it is never possible to retain the equitable interest whatever the parties may intend. The matter requires further exploration, not least because it has caused controversy in other jurisdictions.[24] It raises fundamental issues relating to the flexibility of the operation of equity.[25]

It is submitted that the speeches in *Westdeutsche* were dominated by policy concerns. In particular, Lord Browne-Wilkinson frequently expressed fear lest equity be permitted to inject uncertainty into commercial law.[26] Yet the

[18] The three principles, as minor headings, are taken *verbatim* from her chapter for ease of cross-referencing; see Worthington, *supra* text to fn 63 *et seq.*

[19] See *Re Cook* [1948] 1 Ch 212, 215; *Commissioner of Stamp Duties (Queensland)* v. *Livingstone* [1965] AC 694, 712.

[20] [1996] AC 669, 706, 714. Lord Browne-Wilkinson relied on the above cases and *Vandervell* v. *IRC* [1967] 2 AC 291, as authority for this proposition.

[21] *Re Bond Worth Ltd* [1980] Ch 228; *Stroud Architectural Services Ltd* v. *John Laing Construction Ltd* (1993) [1994] BCC 18. See further G. McCormack, "Proprietary Claims and Insolvency in the Wake of *Westdeutsche* " [1997] J.B.L. 48, 63–64.

[22] *Vandervell* v. *IRC* [1967] 2 AC 291.

[23] *Vandervell* v. *IRC* [1967] 2 AC 291, 311, per Lord Upjohn; 317, per Lord Donovan.

[24] See J.D. Heydon, W.M.C. Gummow and R.P. Austin, *Cases and Materials on Equity and Trusts* (Butterworths, 1993), para. 718. In *DKLR Holding Co. (No 2) Pty Ltd* v. *Commissioner of Stamp Duties* (1982) 149 CLR 431, although the High Court of Australia was unanimously of the opinion that the equitable interest had been transferred with the legal interest and had then been granted back, Mason J (with whom Stephen J concurred) considered that, having examined the particular instrument, this was what had been intended: *ibid* at 449–50. The majority view was that the equitable interest could not be retained: *ibid.*, 442–3, per Gibbs CJ; 464, per Aickin J; 473–4, per Brennan J.

[25] See Heydon, Gummow and Austin, *supra* n 24, who criticise the majority view in *DKLR Holding Co*, *supra* n 24 as "inconsistent with the flexible nature of equitable interests".

[26] [1996] AC 669, 704–5, 709, 712.

emphasis appeared to be not upon how equity would affect the life-blood of commercial law but upon how it would affect its death throes. But if insolvency was the true focus, then it is unfortunate that the law relating to preferences was not considered in conjunction with the issue of whether a transferor can retain an equitable title. If the recipient is a company and it purports to transfer the equitable interest in property back to the original transferor then this transaction may be struck down either as a charge[27] or as a preference.[28] It will be as a preference where it can be shown that the insolvent company had been influenced in fact by a desire to put the plaintiff in a better position than other creditors.[29] Lord Browne-Wilkinson's analysis in *Westdeutsche* casts a shadow over a number of decided cases. *Quistclose* loan trusts are less vulnerable to a successful attack because they are trust arrangements to which an impecunious company submits in desperation rather than with any subjective intention to prefer; it is trusts such as in *Re Kayford*,[30] involving consumer prepayments for goods, which are less secure. In *Re Kayford*, Megarry J asserted that either the transferors (the prepaying customers) or the transferee (the recipient company) could impress the money transferred with a trust. *Re Kayford* has been followed in a number of decisions since then.[31] What is to become of these types of trust? Surely an absolute rule that equitable title cannot be retained by the transferor under any circumstances is a dangerous and inflexible one, which risks distorting the law in other ways.[32] Arguably Lord Goff's approach, in which he accepted Lord Browne-Wilkinson's analysis as a *general* rule, is the better one.[33]

**The traditional principles which underpin presumed resulting trusts deny their existence in the context of void contracts**

The crux of the argument in Sarah Worthington's chapter is that Lord Browne-Wilkinson assumed that a transfer of property under a void contract should be seen as an absolute voluntary transfer which would be effective to vest the property in the transferee both at law and in equity. This is questioned and, in effect, it is suggested that the transfer can hardly be described as *voluntary* where both parties assume that there is a valid enforceable contract in existence when in fact the contract is invalid and unenforceable.

[27] See M.G. Bridge, "The *Quistclose* Trust in a World of Secured Transactions" (1992) 12 OJLS 333, 346–7.

[28] Insolvency Act 1986, s 239.

[29] See *Re M C Bacon Ltd* [1991] Ch 127. See further *Re Lewis's of Leicester Ltd* [1995] BCC 514, 522–3, where an express trust was not viewed as a preference where the company made this agreement in a last ditch effort to keep itself afloat.

[30] [1975] 1 WLR 279.

[31] See *Re Lewis's of Leicester Ltd* [1995] BCC 514; *Re English & American Insurance Co Ltd* [1994] 1 BCLC 649; *Re Eastern Capital Futures Ltd* [1989] BCLC 371.

[32] One obvious risk is that, in attempting to uphold *Kayford* trusts, the courts may weaken the test for preferences set out by Millett J in *Re M C Bacon Ltd* [1991] Ch 127.

[33] *Westdeutsche* [1996] AC 669, 689–90.

It is unfortunate that, for various reasons, this matter did not receive a full airing before their Lordships in *Westdeutsche*. The arguments in the chapter are persuasive and are reinforced by the fact that, where a valid contract is avoided, then equitable proprietary rights are revested in the transferor at that stage. Logically then, if a contract is void *ab initio*, it should follow that the transferor has equitable proprietary rights in the property transferred. If this argument had been accepted by their Lordships, an analysis in terms of a resulting trust could then have been embraced. The fact that the case was not dealt with in this way is explicable, in this writer's view, on the grounds of policy. This is discussed further below.[34]

**There cannot be a trust (including a resulting trust) unless the trustee is aware of the factors alleged to affect conscience**

The effect of this principle can be exposed in an example on similar lines to *Chase Manhattan Bank NA* v. *Israel-British Bank (London) Ltd)*.[35] What if the transferee, X Co Ltd receives £1 million pounds one day and then, due to an administrative error, receives the same amount the next day? According to Lord Browne-Wilkinson, there is merely a personal restitutionary obligation to repay in these circumstances. The plaintiff transferor can only make a proprietary claim (by way of a constructive rather than resulting trust) when the transferee's conscience is affected. If this is the correct interpretation of his Lordship's speech it would mean that, if X Co becomes insolvent a week after receipt of the overpayment, the plaintiff's hopes of recovering the payment will depend upon what X Co knew or did not know.

At first glance, this principle may not necessarily appear unsatisfactory. After all, whether one can recover one's property can turn upon fine timing.[36] Looking at the position from a trusts angle it may even have a superficial attraction. The requirement of knowledge is currently still the test for imposition of liability under a constructive trust: these are the so-called "knowing receipt" cases.[37] However, knowledge is used there to decide whether personal liability should be imposed. The *proprietary* remedy available to beneficiaries to allow them to recover the property itself or its value in a substitute product (using the process of tracing) has always been one of strict liability, not dependent upon knowledge.[38] This requirement of knowledge to ground a proprietary restitutionary remedy appears odd and could lead to a disjointed

[34] See Part C: Survey.

[35] [1981] Ch 105; discussed by Lord Browne-Wilkinson in *Westdeutsche* at [1996] AC 669, 714–15.

[36] e.g. *Neste Oy* v. *Lloyds Bank Plc* [1983] 2 Lloyds Rep 658. In the retention of title context, whether goods can be reclaimed will depend upon whether they have been resold or entered the manufacturing process: see, e.g., *Re Peachdart* [1984] Ch 131.

[37] See e.g. *Carl-Zeiss Stiftung* v. *Herbert Smith and Co (No 2)* [1969] 2 Ch 176; *Re Montagu's S.T.* [1987] Ch 264.

[38] But subject to the defences of *bona fide* purchase and change of position.

picture of the law.[39] If one could simply accept that loose terminology was in play in Lord Browne-Wilkinson's speech and that his Lordship was really preoccupied with the issue of personal liability, such difficulties would disappear.[40] Further elucidation is needed.

## Survey

Sarah Worthington's chapter admirably surveys the response of the common law and equity to contract failure. Proprietary consequences can hardly be described as the norm. Specific performance of a contract (or specific restoration of the property where there is conversion of the goods) is rarely available.[41] Although proprietary restitutionary consequences follow where the contract is rescinded,[42] the right to rescind is hedged around with restrictions.[43] The common law right to rescind depends upon strict *restitutio in integrum* being possible. Although equity is more flexible and there is scope for partial rescission, the courts have a discretion,[44] in relation to innocent or negligent misrepresentation, to award damages instead.[45] The right to rescind can be lost by lapse of time, affirmation with knowledge, or where the property is acquired by a third party.[46] If the other party becomes insolvent before the contract is rescinded then it will be too late to rescind and thereby obtain priority over any secured creditor.[47] Rescission is therefore limited in its impact upon the insolvency regime.

The House of Lords' speeches in *Westdeutsche* have limited the scope of equitable proprietary rights where there are void *ultra vires* contracts. Where

[39] In the area of resulting trusts, the courts have concentrated on the conduct and supposed intentions of the *transferor* (and not on the recipient's state of mind): see P. Birks, "Trusts Raised to Reverse Unjust Enrichment" [1996] *RLR* 3, 20. It is not anticipated that the effect of *Westdeutsche* will be that the courts will decide that a resulting trust exists in situations outside the traditional fact situations: *ibid.*, 22.

[40] This argument is advanced by L.D. Smith, *supra* n 14, who suggests that, when Lord Browne-Wilkinson referred to a "trust", he was considering the issue of personal liability rather than the question of whether equitable proprietary rights existed. Arguably, indirect support for this interpretation can be found in Millett L.J.'s judgment in *Bristol & West B.S.* v. *Mothew* [1997] 2 WLR 436, 454. Loose terminology has bedevilled trusts and fiduciary obligations: P. D. Finn, *Fiduciary Obligations* (Sydney, 1977), 1.

[41] See *Goodhart and Jones*, *supra* n 8, 31 *et seq.*

[42] On the grounds for avoiding a contract at common law and in equity: see S. Worthington, "Proprietary Restitution—Void, Voidable and Uncompleted Contracts" (1995) 9 *TLI* 113. See further, D. Friedmann, "Valid, Voidable, Qualified, and Non-existing Obligations: An Alternative Perspective on the Law of Restitution": Ch 10 of A. Burrows (ed), *Essays on the Law of Restitution* (Oxford, 1991) 247, 266 (hereafter "Friedmann").

[43] *Goodhart and Jones*, *supra* n 8, 198 *et seq.*

[44] See J. W. Carter and G. Tolhurst, "Rescission, Equitable Adjustment and Restitution" (1996) 10 *JCL* 167, discussing *Vadasz* v. *Pioneer Concrete (SA) Pty Ltd* (1995) 184 *CLR* 102.

[45] Misrepresentation Act 1967, s 2(2).

[46] See Friedmann, *supra* n 42, 268, who argues persuasively that a plaintiff should be able to trace his property into the purchase money where his goods are sold to a *bona fide* purchaser.

[47] *Re Goldcorp Exchange Ltd* [1995] 1 AC 74.

a contract is voidable, there are no proprietary consequences until the contract is avoided. After *Westdeutsche*, it would appear that, in relation to void contracts, there are no proprietary consequences until the recipient has the requisite degree of knowledge. Thus proprietary rights are conveniently contained.

What wider ramifications can be anticipated? From a contract perspective, although equity has intervened where there is a mistake of fact to mitigate the inflexibility of the common law,[48] equity has no role where frustration is argued.[49] Indeed, it may be that the fact that contracts which are frustrated attract only a personal and not a proprietary response influenced the House of Lords in their decision in *Westdeutsche*. This would be reinforced by the consideration that generally contract termination only leads to a personal remedy.[50] If, as Sarah Worthington emphasises, equity acts to impose obligations upon the parties to either do or undo a contract, this may mean that equity's role becomes more restricted in the contract sphere. Could *Westdeutsche* encourage judges to exercise their discretion to award damages rather than rescission? Could *Westdeutsche* suggest a more limited role for equity in the future where there is a mistake of fact?

In relation to trusts, it had been hoped that *Westdeutsche* would do away with the necessity of finding a fiduciary relationship before tracing in equity was permissible.[51] Disappointingly, their Lordships drew back from scrapping this requirement. As a result, the concept of a fiduciary relationship will continue for the moment to be under strain, used for different purposes which may pull in different directions. Furthermore, the thrust of the judgment can be as an attempt to restrict the scope of trusts in the commercial sphere. Thus, despite the emphasis placed by Lord Browne-Wilkinson upon a constructive trust being imposed where a recipient's conscience is affected, it is clear that there is no intention to give plaintiffs wider proprietary rights under a substantive constructive trust.[52] Whether this may lead their Lordships to look

[48] A contract will generally be void at common law where the mistake of fact is so fundamental that it operates to prevent any genuine agreement between the parties. The court has wider discretion in equity. See Friedmann, *supra* n 42, 251 *et seq*. See further *Solle* v. *Butcher* [1950] 1 KB 671.

[49] E. McKendrick, *Contract Law*, 2nd edn (1994), 244–5.

[50] *Westdeutsche* [1996] AC 669, 704–5, per Browne-Wilkinson LJ. Usually a plaintiff will seek to recover damages, which are designed to protect his expectation interest. Interestingly, where goods are rejected, property in these goods revests in the seller: *Kwei Tek Chao* v. *British Traders and Shippers Ltd* [1954] 2 QB 459; yet the buyer's remedy is a personal one in these circumstances. If the price has been paid, it can be recovered as a personal restitutionary claim for money had and received if there has been a total failure of consideration. As to the extent to which the failure must be total in order to ground a restitutionary claim, see Lord Goff of Chieveley and G. Jones, *The Law of Restitution*, 4th edn by G. Jones (1993) 417 *et seq*.; P. Birks, "Failure of Consideration": Ch 9 of F. D. Rose (ed) *Consensus Ad Idem (Essays on the Law of Contract in Honour of Guenter Treitel)* (1996).

[51] See W.J. Swadling, "Forsaking the Fiduciary Requirement" (1995) 9 *TLI* 101.

[52] See Birks [1996] *RLR* 3, 21–3.

afresh at situations where proprietary rights have been granted despite the insolvency implications, most notably in the context of bribes[53] and proprietary subrogation,[54] is a moot point.

Can one perceive, in Lord Browne-Wilkinson's suggestion that remedial constructive trusts might be a more satisfactory way for the law to develop,[55] the beginnings of a new trend in the law, where a different line is taken when a plaintiff claims proprietary rights according to whether the possessor of the property is insolvent or not? As the constructive trust has always been a substantive institution in this country, the development of a doctrine of remedial constructive trusts will mean that judges will be turning their backs on history. It will also require a degree of judicial activism with which as yet English judges are not familiar[56] (and which would be far more radical than if their Lordships had permitted the equitable jurisdiction to award compound interest to be bolted on to the personal common law restitutionary claim in *Westdeutsche*). It may be simpler to find an alternative way of watering down proprietary rights in insolvency, if this is seen by the judiciary as a desirable goal. This could be done by recognising that the process of tracing through substitutions involves an exercise of a power *in rem* and that property rights do not crystallise until the power is exercised and proprietary rights in relation to particular assets are asserted.[57] This would have the effect, where a defendant is insolvent, of deferring a plaintiff's rights to those whose property rights have already crystallised (such as a bank, which will usually be a secured creditor with a floating charge).[58]

As Sarah Worthington's chapter points out in its opening paragraph: *Westdeutsche* raises as many questions as it answers.

[53] *Attorney-General for Hong Kong* v. *Reid* [1994] 1 AC 324. See further, e.g., P. Birks, "Obligations and Property in Equity: *Lister* v. *Stubbs* in the Lime Light" [1993] LMCLQ 30; P. Millett, "Bribes and Secret Commissions" [1993] *RLR* 7; D. Crilley, "A Case of Proprietary Overkill" [1994] *RLR* 57.

[54] *Lord Napier and Ettrick* v. *Hunter* [1993] AC 713, criticised by C. Mitchell, *The Law of Subrogation* (Oxford, 1994), 82 *et seq*. See further, *Boscawen* v. *Bajwa, Abbey National Plc* v. *Boscawen* [1996] 1 WLR 328. *Lord Napier and Ettrick* v. *Hunter* was acknowledged by Lord Brown-Wilkinson in *Westdeutsche* without demur: [1996] AC 669, 707.

[55] *Ibid*., 716.

[56] See, e.g., *Lac Minerals Ltd* v. *International Corona Resources Ltd* (1989) 61 D.L.R. (4th) 14, discussed by W.M.C. Gummow, "Unjust Enrichment, Restitution and Proprietary Remedies": Ch 3 of P. D. Finn (ed) *Essays on Restitution* (1990) 47, 74; D.W.M. Waters, "The Nature of the Remedial Constructive Trust": Ch 13 of P. Birks (ed), *The Frontiers of Liability* Vol. 2 (Oxford, 1994) 165; S. Gardner, "The Element of Discretion": Ch 14, *ibid*., 186.

[57] P. Birks [1996] *RLR* 3, 24; P. Birks, "Mixing and Tracing" (1992) 45 *CLP* 89–96. For a different view, see L.D. Smith, *The Law of Tracing* (OUP, 1997).

[58] This would be similar to the difficulty faced by the plaintiffs in *Re Goldcorp* [1995] 1 AC 74: claims to equitable proprietary rights based on misrepresentation, mistake and total failure of consideration failed because the contracts were still on foot when the company went into receivership: the claimants wished to avoid their contracts but by that stage it was too late to obtain rights in priority to the bank: see P. Birks, "Establishing a Proprietary Base" [1995] *RLR* 83, 87.

# 7

# *Restitution Under Article 85(2) of the EC Treaty: Can it be Done?*

FELICITY TOUBE*

## 1. INTRODUCTION

Article 85 of the EC Treaty reads as follows:

> "(1) The following shall be prohibited as incompatible with the common market: all agreements between undertakings, decisions by associations of undertakings and concerted practices which may affect trade between Member States and which have as their object or effect the prevention, restriction or distortion of competition within the common market, and in particular those which:
> (a) directly or indirectly fix purchase or selling prices or any other trading conditions;
> (b) limit or control production, markets, technical development, or investment;
> (c) share markets or sources of supply;
> (d) apply dissimilar conditions to equivalent transactions with other trading parties, thereby placing them at a competitive disadvantage;
> (e) make the conclusion of contracts subject to the acceptance by other parties of supplementary obligations which, by their nature or according to commercial usage, have no connection with the subject of such contracts.
> *(2) Any agreements or decisions prohibited pursuant to this Article shall be automatically void.*[1]
> (3) The provisions of paragraph 1 may, however, be declared inapplicable in the case of:
> — any agreement or category of agreements between undertakings;
> — any decision or category of decisions by associations of undertakings;
> — any concerted practice or category of concerted parties;
>
> which contributes to improving the production or distribution of goods or to promoting technical or economic progress while allowing consumers a fair share of the resulting benefit, and which does not:
> (a) impose on the undertakings concerned restrictions which are not indispensable to the attainment of those objectives;

* Barrister, 3–4 South Square, London. The author wishes to thank those who attended the SPTL Conference, in particular Alison Jones, for their useful suggestions and comments on an earlier draft of this chapter.

[1] Emphasis added.

(b) afford such undertakings the possibility of eliminating competition in respect of a substantial part of the products in question."

An agreement which offends against Article 85(1) and which is not granted a block exemption or an individual exemption under Article 85(3) is therefore void. This nullity is retroactive in effect.[2] As a result, parties who have treated themselves as acting pursuant to and governed by a binding agreement, in many cases for a significant number of years, may find that they are, and have been, in fact parties only to a void agreement. In such a case, one party or the other may consider it beneficial to claim the return of monies or the value of goods passed or services rendered under that contract. Alternatively such a party may wish to claim restitutionary damages for the breach of Article 85. This chapter is concerned both with whether that restitution of benefits is permitted and whether recovery of restitutionary damages is available to a litigant.

This chapter can be little more than an introduction to this highly complex area. As rights of action based upon restitutionary concepts are analytically still in the process of development, it becomes necessary to consider the interaction between such causes of action and other complex areas of the law. As a result there is often a build-up of problems waiting to be recognised and solved. This chapter cannot offer solutions to the large number of such problems, but it attempts to raise the questions which need to be answered.[3] There are a number of imponderables which complicate an already difficult question. In attempting to suggest the manner in which answers may be found, this chapter concentrates upon the effect of Article 85(2), a directly effective provision of the EC Treaty,[4] but also refers to the possible different effect of contracts rendered void by the operation of Article 86.

This chapter does not attempt to tackle: (a) domestic competition law legislation; or (b) which agreements and concerted practices are contrary to Article 85(1), and which agreements may be exempted under Article 85(3).

The following matters are considered in this chapter:

(a) Is a cause of action in autonomous unjust enrichment available as a result of the effect of Article 85(2)?
(b) What is the effect of voidness under Article 85(2)? Is the whole contract void if a provision offends against Article 85(1)?
(c) What is the effect of the decision in *Westdeutsche Landesbank*

[2] *Brasserie de Haecht* v. *Wilkin-Janssen* [1973] CMLR 287.

[3] The answers to these questions are not provided by EC law, where the questions of restitution in this area have not been considered. Indeed, as the question of the proper remedy for breach of the competition rules is a matter for national law, this chapter does not consider the growing body of EC jurisprudence in respect of restitution which arises principally in the area of state aids. It may be that some guidance may be drawn, in time, from those areas.

[4] *Brasserie de Haecht* v. *Wilkin-Janssen* [1973[ CMLR 287; *Delimitis* v. *Henninger Brau* [1995] 5 CMLR 210.

*Girozentrale* v. *Islington London Borough Council*[5] upon the law of restitution? Does it introduce a new "unjust factor" under which recovery can be made, namely "absence of consideration" or "no consideration"? Would the introduction of such a new "unjust factor" be beneficial to the development of the law of restitution?

(d) How does any restitutionary cause of action which is available interact with the potential illegality of an agreement which breaches Article 85?

(e) Are restitutionary damages available in respect of the wrong of a deliberate breach of Article 85?[6] What exactly is the wrong? Are restitutionary damages available in respect of all wrongs? How should the possibility of such recovery of restitutionary damages interact with the availability of punitive damages?

(f) What are the practical difficulties of bringing a claim in restitution or for restitutionary damages under Article 85(2)? How should such a case be pleaded? What problems may be faced with respect to burden of proof? What are the problems relating to discovery?

## 2. IS A CAUSE OF ACTION IN AUTONOMOUS UNJUST ENRICHMENT AVAILABLE AS A RESULT OF THE EFFECT OF ARTICLE 85(2)?

In considering this question, it must be borne in mind that not all provisions which offend against Article 85(1) are void. Some are exempted by way of block exemptions. Others are exempted by way of individual exemptions. Still others are dealt with as special cases.[7]

In addition there is the added complication that an agreement can be notified to the Commission under Regulation 17/62. If the agreement is not

[5] [1994] 4 All ER 890 (hereafter "*Westdeutsche*"), at first instance and in the Court of Appeal; [1996] AC 669, in the House of Lords, where the question of the ground upon which restitution could be awarded was not before their Lordships, though comments were made *obiter* in respect of the appropriate unjust factor.

[6] I distinguish between a cause of action in autonomous unjust enrichment and recovery for restitution for wrongs, in which restitutionary damages are available for the deliberate breach of an obligation in contract or tort or for an equitable wrong. For expansion of this distinction see Goff and Jones, *The Law of Restitution*, 4th edn (1993); P. Birks, *An Introduction to the Law of Restitution* (rev. edn, 1989); and A. Burrows, *The Law of Restitution* (1993).

[7] An important special case in practice, for example, is that of transactions in securities entered into by parties to a merger after the Commission has suspended the merger for being anti-competitive. The relevant regulation is Regulation 4064/89. Securities are defined, by Article 7(5), in the second paragraph of the Regulation, as being "securities including those convertible into other securities admitted to trading on a market which is regulated and supervised by authorities recognized by public bodies, which are operated regularly and is accessible directly or indirectly to the public". Where a merger has been suspended by the Commission such transactions are not invalid unless the buyer and the seller knew or ought to have known that the transaction was carried out in contravention of a suspension. This rule is clearly intended to overcome the difficulties of voidness under Article 85(2). Property in the securities is intended to pass even if the full rights deriving from ownership cannot be exercised.

notified, it is open to the court to find that it is clearly not caught by Article 85(1), or that it clearly is caught by Article 85(1), or that it falls within a block exemption. If the agreement does not fall within a block exemption, or the court is unsure whether it does so, the court can refer the case to the European Court of Justice.

If the agreement is notified and either clearly would or clearly would not offend against Article 85, the court can proceed. If it is possible that the case might fall within an exemption, the national court may choose to stay the proceedings or take interim measures to deal with the matter. Therefore until an exemption is given, the agreement will be void. On exemption, the agreement will be retrospectively exempted and the voidness will be overcome.[8]

Therefore when a contract is notified, it will be very difficult for a party to claim restitution based upon its voidness. At present there is a considerable backlog of notifications which will take a number of years to process. Until exemption is given, the parties may carry out their obligations under a contract in the belief that it will be exempted, only to discover after the Commission has considered the matter that it was in fact void. It is at this stage that a claim in autonomous unjust enrichment may be considered.

### *Effect of Voidness under Article 85(2)*

If the agreement as a whole contravenes Article 85, the contract will be void.[9] However, if only certain provisions of the contract are void, and if the provisions which offend against Article 85(2) are capable of being severed from the rest of the agreement, the agreement is not void as a whole.[10] The law of severance which is to be applied is that of the national courts.[11]

In the UK, the question of severance is governed by the principles expressed in *Chemidus Wavin Ltd* v. *Société pour la Transformation et l'Exploitation des Resines Industrielles S.A.*,[12] where Buckley LJ stated:

> "where in a contract there are certain clauses which are annulled by reason of their being in contravention of Article 85, paragraph (1), of the Treaty, one must look at the contract with those clauses struck out and see what the effect of that is in the light of the domestic law which governs the particular contract. In the present case, we have to consider what effect the invalidity, if any, of the clauses in the licence agreement by reason of Article 85 would have upon the contract as a whole . . . It seems to me that, in applying Article 85 to an English contract, one may well have to consider whether, after the excisions required by the Article of the Treaty have

[8] Old agreements—those which were entered into before Regulation 17/62 came into force—have a provision validity until a decision has been taken not to exempt them. Therefore, the problem with regard to them is not so acute.

[9] *Windsurfing International Inc* v. *EC Commission* (Case 193/83).

[10] *La Technique Minière* v. *Maschinenbau Ulm GmbH* (Case 56/65) [1996] CMLR 357.

[11] *Société de Vente de Ciments et Betons de l'Est* v. *Kerpen & Kerpen GmbH & Co KG* [1985] 1 CMLR 511. See also *VAG France SA* v. *Establissements Magne SA* (Case 10/86) [1988] 4 CMLR 98.

[12] [1978] 3 CMLR 514, 519–20.

been made from the contract, the contract could be said to fail for lack of consideration or on any other ground, or whether the contract would be so changed in its character as not to be the sort of contract that the parties intended to enter into at all."

Goff LJ came to the same conclusion, relying upon the decision of Salter J in *Putsman* v. *Taylor*, where the judge had stated that:[13]

> "If a promisee claims the enforcement of a promise, and the promise is a valid promise and supported by consideration, the court will enforce the promise, notwithstanding the fact that the promisor has made other promises, supported by the same consideration, which are void, and has included the valid and invalid promises in one document."

Therefore, in considering whether the whole agreement fails, it is necessary first to look at the contract and consider whether there is any consideration left to support it at all, and secondly to consider whether the excision of the invalid parts is such that the scope and intention of the contract are completely changed from that for which the parties had bargained.[14]

### *What is the Effect of the Decision in* Westdeutsche?[15]

Assuming that the offending clauses cannot be severed without doing damage to the fundamental nature of the contract, the agreement will be void. The question then becomes whether there can be restitution of any benefits conferred under the contract before it was found to be void. It is first necessary to identify the ground upon which a cause of action in restitution can be based, the "unjust factor".

One potential unjust factor was raised in *Westdeutsche*. At first instance Hobhouse J relied upon a number of the old annuity cases in holding that there was a right to restitution in respect of payments made under void contracts triggered by an unjust factor which was distinct from the unjust factors of total failure of consideration and mistake of fact. The judge used the phrase "absence of consideration" to identify this new unjust factor which is applicable where there had never been a contract. Despite the fact that Hobhouse J recognised that "the phrase 'failure of consideration' has very frequently been used in connection with void contract",[16] he was not prepared to hold that the applicable unjust factor was failure of consideration.

[13] [1927] 1 KB 639.

[14] See *Atwood* v. *Lamont* [1920] 3 KB 571, 580, per Lord Sterndale MR.

[15] *Westdeutsche Landesbank Girozentrale* v. *Islington LBC* [1996] Ac 669. The facts of *Westdeutsche*, a case also considered elsewhere in this book, are well known and need not be rehearsed here. In dealing with this case, I confine myself to the question of the effect of the new unjust factor, that of "absence of consideration" or "no consideration", which was introduced by Hobhouse J at first instance, and do not consider the other matters raised in the case.

[16] [1994] 4 All ER 890, 924h. The judge mentioned, in particular the argument in *Fibrosa Spolka Akcyjna* v. *Fairburn Lawson Combe Barbour Ltd* [1943] AC 32, 36.

In the Court of Appeal Dillon LJ upheld the application of the "no consideration" unjust factor rather than rely upon partial or total failure of consideration:[17]

> "[T]o hold that as the interest swap transaction and contract were ultra vires and void there was no consideration for the payment by Westdeutsche of the £2.5 million and therefore the balance which has not so far been repaid by Islington can be recovered by Westdeutsche in quasi contract as money had and received or on the grounds of unjust enrichment is warranted by early cases decided under the Grants of Life Annuities Act 1777."

This conclusion was reached despite the fact that the phraseology used by Dillon LJ elsewhere in his judgment was, with respect, equally consistent with a finding that there had been a total failure of consideration.[18] In the House of Lords, although the question of the unjust factor was not before the House,[19] views were expressed by their Lordships that the correct unjust factor was failure of consideration and not "no consideration". Lord Goff[20] stated:

> "I think it right to record that there appears to me to be considerable force in the criticisms which have been expressed[21]; and I shall, when considering the issues in this appeal, bear in mind the possibility that it may be right to regard the ground of recovery as failure of consideration."

In addition, Lord Goff noted, correctly, that in the annuity cases the courts regarded the ground of recovery as total failure of consideration. Lord Goff stated that the concept of total failure of consideration does not require that there should be a failure of consideration subsequent to the making of the

[17] [1994] 4 All ER, 961e. The formulation of Legatt LJ was more forthright: "There can have been no consideration under a contract void ab initio. So it is fallacious to speak of the failure of consideration having been partial" (*ibid*., 969b–d).

[18] See in particular the consideration of *Fibrosa* v. *Fairburn* at 959d–e, where Dillon LJ noted that total failure of consideration "is a well-known category for cases in which the full amount of contract or intended contract can be recovered. It applies . . . where the supposed contract has for some reason been void or was voidable and has been rescinded". See also at 962g–h, where Dillon LJ stated that "the purpose for which the £2.5 million was paid by Westdeutsche to Islington has wholly failed".

[19] A matter which Lord Goff referred to as "an extraordinary feature" of the appeal, particularly in the light of the "important questions in the law of restitution, which are of great interest to lawyers specializing in this field": [1996] AC 669, 681. His Lordship also noted, "If restitution lawyers are hoping to find in your Lordships' speeches broad statements of principle which may definitively establish the future shape of this part of the law, I fear that they may be disappointed": *Ibid*., 686.

[20] *Ibid*., 683. Although dissenting on the question of simple or compound interest, together with Lord Woolf, all their Lordships were *ad idem* on the question of the unjust factor. It was, perhaps unsurprisingly, Lord Goff who made the most comprehensive survey of the potential bases for allowing a personal claim in restitution.

[21] Here his Lordship referred in particular to the following articles: Birks, "No Consideration: Restitution after Void Contracts" (1993) 23 *UWALR* 195; Swadling, "Restitution for No Consideration" [1994] *RLR* 73; Burrows, "Swaps and the Friction between Common Law and Equity" [1995] *RLR* 15.

contract. His Lordship indicated that there could also be a total failure of consideration where a contract was not initially binding. This view is clearly correct.

Lord Browne-Wilkinson stated that the Court of Appeal were correct to hold "that the swap moneys were paid on a consideration that wholly failed".[22] In fact with respect to his Lordship, it appears that the Court of Appeal actually held, as has been set out above, that the moneys were treated as having been paid for no consideration. The restatement by Lord Browne-Wilkinson is more accurate.

However, as the views expressed by the House of Lords were, strictly speaking *obiter*, it cannot be said with certainty that the newly created unjust factor can be dismissed out of hand.[23] It may be necessary to deal with the *Westdeutsche* decision as a matter of principle rather than strict precedent. This new unjust factor is of application to all contracts which are void *ab initio*. It is therefore potentially capable of overrunning any attempt to confine the unjust factors within distinct boundaries in order to provide some certainty of application for potential litigants. Is such a replacement necessary or to be desired?

Contrary to the suggestion made by Hobhouse J at first instance in *Westdeutsche*, there is no lacuna in the law which requires filling with a separate cause of action grounded on "no consideration". The fact that a contract is void *ab initio* does not mean that there cannot be recovery on the basis of the existing unjust factor of total failure of consideration.[24] In *Rover International Ltd* v. *Cannons Film Sales Ltd*,[25] for example, the Court of Appeal held that, where a contract was void *ab initio* as a result of the non-incorporation of a company, there had been a total failure of consideration and could be restitution upon that ground. There was no suggestion that the true ground was in fact no consideration. There is therefore precedent, of equal authority to Court of Appeal decision in *Westdeutsche*, for the common sense argument that there need not be a valid contract for there to be consideration which has failed. Support for this conclusion can also be found in *Chillingworth* v. *Esche*,[26] where the court permitted the recovery of sums paid as a deposit under a transaction expressed to be subject to contract where the

[22] [1996] AC 669, 710H. This point was repeated at 714B.

[23] Although it might be possible to persuade a court that the comments of their Lordships were persuasive authority.

[24] The requirement that there should be a total failure of consideration does not sit easily with the more developed law on restitution which provides for the possibility of counter-restitution of the value of benefits received by both parties, so that the loss should not fall upon one party rather than the other, where the failure is partial. There is not space in this chapter to deal with this question more fully, and I have therefore treated the total failure requirement as representing the present state of the law. But see Birks, "Failure of Consideration", Ch 9 of F.D. Rose (ed.), *Consensus Ad Idem (Essays on the Law of Contract in Honour of Guenter Treitel)*; *Goss* v. *Chilcott* [1996] AC 788.

[25] [1989] 1 WLR 912, a case which Hobhouse J considered in *Westdeutsche* [1994] 4 All ER 890, 928 to 929, and yet surprisingly still went on to develop a new unjust factor.

[26] [1924] 1 Ch 97.

contract was not concluded through the actions of the payer. The ground for recovery was total failure of consideration even though there was no contract. If further precedent is required, it can be found in *Martin* v. *Andrews*,[27] where conduct money had been paid to a subpoenaed witness. When the action was settled before the trial, Lord Campbell CJ permitted an action for money had and received. He stated:[28]

> "We have therefore to consider the general question whether money so paid to a party on a subpoena is, or is not, recoverable as money had and received. I think it is. *The consideration has failed.* The money was paid for the purposes of defraying the expense of the witness's journey. If there was no journey there was no expence, and *the consideration fails*; and then an action lies for money had and received."

There was no suggestion in any of these cases that there was required to be a contract in order for there to have been a total failure of consideration. This point appears to have been recognised by the House of Lords in *Westdeutsche*, and has also been noted by textbook writers.[29]

There may also be a potential ground for recovery based upon the unjust factor of mistake. In many cases, the mistake which has been made is one of law, or at least is not one as to the existence of some fact, and therefore as the law stands at present there can be no recovery.[30] This unjust factor was not available for recovery in *Westdeutsche* because of the problem of the mistake of law bar. There is a need for the law to be reformed along the lines which were suggested by the Law Commission,[31] namely removing the mistake of law bar, which is already undermined by the large number of exceptions to it.

The reason why the unjust factor of failure of consideration was not properly analysed in *Westdeutsche* was that the swaps were regarded as one complete transaction[32]. As a result there was no proper consideration of the individual transactions and there was no consideration of whether the consideration failed in respect of each individual swap. In the case of an anti-competitive contract in which the parties have received and conferred the benefits for which they bargained, there is, of course, no total failure of consideration. The same is true of a fully performed contract where the mistake as to validity has not caused any loss or gain.

[27] (1856) 7 E & B 1; 199 ER 1148.

[28] (1856) 7 E & B 1, 4 (emphasis added).

[29] See, e.g., *Chitty on Contracts*, 27th edn (1994), para 29-034, where Professor Beatson states: "Although the principle is not confined to contracts, most of the cases are concerned with ineffective contracts". See also Burrows, *The Law of Restitution*.

[30] The situation is different under Scottish law, where in *Morgan Guaranty Trust of New York* v. *Lothian Regional Council* [1995] SLT 299, the court held that in a swaps case the relevant mistake was one of law, and that recovery could be made in respect of it.

[31] See the Law Commission, "Restitution: Mistakes of Law and Ultra Vires Public Authority Receipts and Payments" (Law Com No 227, 1994).

[32] Much as was the case in *Lipkin Gorman* v. *Karpnale* [1991] 2 AC 548.

In *Westdeutsche*, Hobhouse J held that in considering the application of this new unjust factor of no consideration, it was irrelevant whether the swap had been completely performed.[33] The failure to make such a distinction is incorrect. There should not be any recovery in the case of an anti-competitive contract which has been carried through in such a way that each party received exactly what he bargained for.[34] One measure of the enrichment which has been received by a party is that the party has shown that he valued the benefit which he received by reason of the price which he was prepared to put upon it when bargaining. If that party then receives that for which he bargained, he should not be permitted subjectively to devalue the benefits which he has received simply because the transaction into which he has entered turns out to have been void.

Therefore, if the parties took a risk that the contract would be anti-competitive and both received benefits under it, there should be no restitutionary remedy permitted. The fact that the contract is anti-competitive means that it should not continue to be enforced, and may also give rise to recovery by third parties, but it should not unwind the contract as between the two parties to the contract.

In any event, the availability of a restitutionary cause of action does not depend upon the voidness of the contract per se, but rather upon the reason why that contract became void. There is no room for a "no consideration" unjust factor which may have the effect of confusing and eliding the categories upon which a restitutionary claim can at present be based. There is a potential for such a new unjust factor to consume the existing categories into one ill-defined and underdeveloped whole.[35]

### *Interaction with Illegality*

Even if restitution on the ground of failure of consideration, mistake or, potentially, no consideration is *prima facie* available, the general policy of the law in this area is that a cause of action in restitution should not proceed if it would require the court to lend its aid to a person who founds his cause of action upon an illegal or immoral act.[36] An anti-competitive agreement is illegal, and can be visited with fines because of its illegality.[37]

[33] [1994] 4 All ER 890, 937b–c.

[34] As was the case with respect to the majority of the swap transactions in *Westdeutsche*.

[35] It is interesting to note that views have been expressed by practitioners in the USA that, where there is a contract which is void by reason of the *ultra vires* act of a municipal body, the law of municipal finance suggests that there will probably be no recovery. See "Legal Uncertainty May Allow Issuers to Ignore Contracts", *The Bond Buyer*, 9 December 1995. Thanks to Homer D Schaaf of Brown & Wood, New York, for having identified and provided this article to me.

[36] This principle is often referred to by its Latin tag: *ex turpi causa non oritur actio*.

[37] There is, however, an interesting question whether they are sufficiently illegal to warrant the operation of the general common law rule. There are also, of course, many types of anti-competitive agreement, some of which are clearly regarded as more obviously illegal than others. There is therefore an interesting problem as to whether the anti-competitive agreement is sufficiently illegal to affect recovery, or whether all cases should be regarded as equally illegal.

Considerations of illegality did not feature in *Westdeutsche*, as the court found as a fact that no illegality was involved. The swaps contracts were not illegal and Hobhouse J held that there was no overriding principle of illegality or public policy which could prevent the recognition of the rights and remedies which the court found were available to the local authority.[38]

This approach may mean that one party to an illegal contract is permitted to benefit from that contract at the expense of the other party. However, benefiting one of the parties to the illegality is not the primary aim of this principle; it is merely a side effect. As Lord Mansfield put it in *Holman* v. *Johnson*:[39]

> "The objection, that the contract is immoral or illegal as between plaintiff and defendant sounds at all times very ill in the mouth of the defendant. It is not for his sake, however, that the objection is ever allowed; but it is founded in general principles of policy, which the defendant has the advantage of, contrary to the real justice, as between him and the plaintiff, by accident, if I may say so. The principle of public policy is this: *ex dolo malo non oritur actio*. No court will lend its aid to a man who founds his cause of action upon an immoral or an illegal act. If from the plaintiff's own stating or otherwise, the cause of action appears to arise *ex turpi causa*, or the transgression of the law of this country, there the court says he has no right to be assisted. It is upon that ground that the court goes; not for the sake of the defendant, but because they will not lend their aid to such a plaintiff."

Therefore, if the plaintiff in an action must rely upon his own illegality to establish his claim, he will fail.[40] Considerations such as concern for outraging the public conscience do not come into the equation.[41]

The effect of the illegality of the anti-competitive agreement may be different in some Article 85 cases, and all Article 86 cases brought by the non-monopolistic party. Where the parties are *non in pari delicto*, the party which is more "innocent" may be permitted to recover from the other party. That is in particular the case where there is an offence against Article 86:

> "In the case of an abuse of a dominant position, it would be unthinkable that Article 86 should be held indiscriminately to avoid contracts in a manner detrimental to the victims of the abuse or to third parties."[42]

The principle in *Kiriri Cotton Co Ltd* v. *Sewani*[43] should be applied, as "the duty of observing the law is placed on the shoulders of the one rather than the other".[44] In order to make out the *non in pari delicto* exception to the ille-

[38] In particular, the court found that the swaps contracts were not illegal gaming contracts. See [1994] 4 All ER 915c–e. This difference may provide a ground for distinguishing *Westdeutsche* so that the new unjust factor does not apply in this area.

[39] (1775) 1 Cowp 341, 343; 98 ER 1120.

[40] See also *Berg* v. *Sadler and Moore* [1937] 2 KB 158; *Bowmakers Ltd* v. *Barnet Instruments Ltd* [1945] KB 65.

[41] *Tinsley* v. *Milligan* [1994] 1 AC 340.

[42] *Greenwich Film Production* v. *SACEM* [1980] 1 CMLR 629, 640, per Warner AG.

[43] [1960] AC 192.

[44] *Ibid.*, 204, per Lord Denning, delivering the opinion of the Privy Council.

gality bar, it will therefore be necessary for a litigant to show that the burden of avoiding an illegal contract was more upon one party than upon the other.

### *Summary*

Recovery by way of a restitutionary cause of action as a result of the effect of Article 85(2) is not a special result of the voidness of the contract, but is a question to be answered by reference to normal restitutionary principles. In the case of a contract which has not been completed and which is found to be anti-competitive, there may be grounds for recovery for failure of consideration or mistake and, in Article 86 cases, duress.

There may be many cases in which restitution is not available at all because of the interplay with illegality, unless the parties are *non in pari delicto*. In addition, where contracts have been completed and both sides have received that for which they bargained, neither party should be viewed as having been enriched, and restitution should not be available.

There is no room in this area for the use of an unjust factor of no consideration which is potentially far-reaching in nature. Such a widely drawn unjust factor could take over from all other unjust factors which are at present available where there is a void contract, thereby removing much of the benefit of the clear analysis of restitution which has begun to be adopted in this country. In addition such a widening of the categories of restitution could fuel claims that lawyers are over-ambitious in their attempts to have restitution recognised as a discrete and disciplined subject which is fundamental to our national legal system.

## 3. RESTITUTION FOR WRONGS

An alternative method for recovering the value of benefits conferred under an anti-competitive agreement is to bring an action for restitutionary damages. This is not necessarily a means of escaping the problems which have been raised in the consideration of an action for autonomous unjust enrichment, but it may be an alternative manner of pleading a claim. In considering an alternative possible remedy for breach of Articles 85 and 86, the first problem is to identify the nature of the wrong in respect of which restitutionary damages can be sought.

### *What is the Wrong?*

It is for the national courts to apply Articles 85 and 86 to relations between individual companies. By the making of an express provision for the civil sanction of voidness, the Treaty postulates that national law gives the courts power to preserve the rights of enterprises which are victims of anti-competitive practices.[45] In principle, the concept that there should be reparation for breach of Articles 85 and 86 is a reasonable one. As Van Gerven AG stated in *Banks* v. *BCC*[46]:

> [Competition law] prohibitions are aimed at safeguarding undistorted competition and freedom of competition for undertakings operating in the common market, with the result that breach of that system must be made good in full.

In addition, the Commission has stated, in response to a question in the European Parliament, that claims for damages could prove useful support for enforcement actions taken by the Commission.[47] The Commission does not have any power to award damages by itself,[48] and therefore it is clearly intended that the remedies should be complementary.

There are several potential wrongs for which there could be an action under Articles 85 and 86. It is clear that Articles 85 and 86 have direct effect in UK law, and therefore they give rise to direct rights under UK law,[49] but otherwise the state of the law is by no means certain.

**Breach of statutory duty**

The leading case is *Garden Cottage Foods* v. *Milk Marketing Board*,[50] in which the House of Lords expressed a view, *obiter*, that there could be recovery for damages for breach of statutory duty where there had been a breach of Article 86. As Lord Diplock put it:[51]

> "A breach of the duty imposed by Article 86 . . . can thus be categorised in English law as a breach of statutory duty that is imposed not only for the purpose of promoting the general economic prosperity of the common market but also for the benefit of private individuals to whom loss or damage is caused by breach of that duty . . . I can see [no other cause of action] that would be capable of giving rise to a civil cause of action in English private law on the part of a private individual who sustains loss or damage by reason of a breach of a directly applicable provision of the Treaty of Rome . . . I, for my own part, find it difficult to see how it can ultimately be successfully argued . . . that a contravention of Article 86 which causes damage to an individual does not give rise to a cause of action in English law of the nature of a cause of action for breach of statutory duty."

45 *Automec* v. *Commission* [1992] 5 CMLR 431.

46 [1994] 1 ECR 1209, 1260. The case was brought under a similar provision in the ECSC. However, unlike Articles 85 and 86, the provision of the ECSC did not have direct effect, and therefore there were no direct rights available in national law at all, so that the Court eventually determined that damages should not be available.

47 Question Number 519/72; 1973 OJ C67/54.

48 And indeed, although it has the power to adopt interim measures (see *Camera Care* v. *Commission* [1980] 1 CMLR 334) it has rarely done so. The Commission does, of course, have the power to fine under Regulation 17/62.

49 *BRT* v. *SABAM* [1974] ECR 51.

50 [1984] AC 130.

51 *Ibid.*, 141D–E, 151E–F, 144B–C. Lord Wilberforce declined to express an opinion upon the question of damages, believing it inappropriate to consider the question at an interlocutory hearing.

The *Garden Foods* decision has since been followed in Scotland in *Argyll* v. *Distillers Co*,[52] and in England in *An Bord Bainne Co-operative* v. *Milk Marketing Board*,[53] *Barretts & Baird* v. *IPCS*,[54] *Bourgoin SA* v. *Ministry of Agriculture Fisheries and Food*[55] and *Plessey Co Plc* v. *General Electric Co Plc and Siemens*.[56]

In order to make out the tort of breach of statutory duty, there is a four-stage test. First, that the loss suffered is within the scope of the statute; second, that the statute gives rise to a civil cause of action; third, that there has been a breach of statutory duty; and, fourth, that the breach has caused the loss of which it is complained.[57]

The provision of a remedy in damages for breach of statutory duty is generally justified by the claim that it complies with the rules of the EEC which demand that there should not be discrimination between UK and non-UK parties in granting a remedy. Under the Restrictive Trade Practices Act 1976, there are two breaches of statutory duty which are capable of giving rise to void agreements and thereby to damages for breach of statutory duty.[58] In addition, there are also some cases in which an action lies for infringements of the provisions of the Resale Prices Act 1976 in respect of collective and individual resale price maintenance. However, there are equally a number of cases in respect of which no remedy is available.[59]

Damages are clearly a better deterrent to those indulging in anti-competitive behaviour than an injunction. However, there are seen to be two disadvantages in the provision of a remedy in damages for breach of the Treaty. Of these two disadvantages the former is more persuasive. First, there is a possibility that a potential litigant would be tempted to forum shop in an attempt to find those jurisdictions which provide a claim in damages for breach of the Treaty. Second, it is unclear whether the national courts are experienced

52 [1986] 1 CMLR 764.

53 [1984] 1 CMLR 519, *affirmed* [1984] 2 CMLR 584.

54 [1987] IRLR 3, where Henry J noted: "There is clearly an arguable case for a similar cause of action here for a breach of statutory duty based on what might be called a Eurotort".

55 [1985] 1 CMLR 528; *rvrsd* [1986] 1 CMLR 267. This case was concerned with damages where a member state acted in breach of the EEC Treaty, Act 30, but the judgments in the Court of Appeal also dealt with the competition law rules. The case was settled before it went to the House of Lords.

56 [1990] ECC 384. See also in *Cutsworth* v. *Mansfield Inns* [1986] 1 WLR 558, 563G per Sir Neil Lawson: "It is clear on the relevant authorities that breaches of the relevant provisions of the EEC Treaty give rise to a cause of action in the domestic courts by a plaintiff who contends that he is the victim of such breached".

57 Causation is tested on the "but for" basis.

58 Under ss 2(1) and 35(1), which provide that contractual provisions which are prohibited are void. The sections apply where particular have not been furnished in due time to the Director General of Fair Trading, and to agreements which are found by the Restrictive Practices Court to be contrary to the public interest.

59 The non-discrimination argument is more apt in respect of Article 85 than it is in respect of Article 86. There are rights to remedies in damages under the Restrictive Trade Practices Act 1976 referred to above, but there is no right under the Competition Act 1980 or any other equivalent of Article 86 in domestic law.

enough in dealing with the quantity of detailed economic information which would be required to be considered in determining whether there should be restitution.[60] It may furthermore be the case that, where two parties are equally in breach of a statute, an action for breach of statutory duty is not open to them in respect of one another's wrong. In this way the effect of the illegality bar may be imported into the question of restitutionary damages for the tort, and the question of the level of illegality which can be countenanced without preventing recovery will again have to be considered.

**Economic torts**

Another possible wrong which is committed by a party who is in breach of Articles 85 or 86 is one of the economic torts.

*(i) Unlawful interference with trade or business.* In order to prove this tort it is necessary to show that there has been an unlawful act which foreseeably caused injury to the interest of another or which was done with the intention of harming another. The advantage of this tort is that liability is not strict.[61] The need to show that the unlawful act was directed towards the other person or that it was intended to harm him allows the tort to be more flexible. However, as the primary justification for the provision of a remedy is that it is to be non-discriminatory, it should be borne in mind that a cause of action based upon an economic tort is not provided by domestic law.

In addition there are three further problems. First, it is difficult to see what is the "unlawful act" for the purpose of the tort. In general, breach of a domestic statutory obligation will not suffice for this requirement to be satisfied,[62] although it may suffice where one person intends to harm another.[63] Secondly, if Articles 85 and 86 are in fact intended to be strict duties so that they act as a deterrent, this tort is clearly not a suitable "wrong". Thirdly, where both parties are equally to blame, it may be that there can be no cause of action based upon this economic tort at all.

*(ii) Conspiracy.* A third possible wrong is that of conspiracy. Liability for civil conspiracy[64] has two potential forms:[65] first, where two or more parties

[60] The mere fact that courts are not yet experienced in dealing with such matters should not, it is suggested, cause such a claim to be abandoned.

[61] Since directly effective provisions of Community law impose clear and unconditional duties, liability for breach of statutory duty based upon the breach of those provisions is likely to be strict.

[62] *Lonrho* v. *Shell Petroleum Company (No. 2)* [1982] AC 173, although see *contra Barretts & Baird (Wholesale)* v. *IPCS* [1987] IRLR 3, where Henry J considered that breach of a statutory duty was in itself unlawful.

[63] This is suggested by some remarks of Stuart-Smith LJ in *Associated British Ports* v. *TGWU* [1989] 1 WLR 939, 970.

[64] Breach of the rules of competition cannot amount to a criminal conspiracy: Criminal Law Act 1977, s 5.

[65] The best analysis is that provided in *Lonrho Plc* v. *Fayed* [1992] 1 AC 448.

combine, with the predominant intention of causing injury to another, where the means used are lawful; and, second, where two or more parties intentionally injure another by use of unlawful means even where the primary purpose is to further their own ends. The act of combination by itself is not enough to constitute an actionable economic tort where there is no unlawful act.[66] Again, it is unclear whether where there has been a breach of Articles 85 and 86 there are unlawful means such that there could be said to have been the commission of an economic tort. For example, in *Mogul Steamship Co Ltd* v. *McGregor Gow & Co*,[67] the court held that it was not an unlawful act to act in restraint of trade per se. There is also clearly a problem where the action is brought by one of the parties to the conspiracy—in which case there may not be an action available in respect of the tort at all.

### (c) Innominate tort

A fourth potential cause of action was that suggested by Lord Denning MR in *Application des Gaz SA* v. *Falks Veritas*,[68] namely that there could be a cause of action in innominate tort created by the Treaty, with each Treaty provision creating a new tort. This approach was doubted in *Valor International* v. *Application des Gaz*,[69] and in the *Garden Cottage Foods* case.[70]

### (d) No wrong

It may be that there should be no wrong at all. As Jacob J held in *Newport AFC Ltd* v. *Football Association of Wales Ltd*[71]:

> "It is well settled that a contract or other arrangement in unreasonable restraint of trade is merely void and unenforceable. As such it creates no wrong, either to the parties to the arrangement or to third parties."

This view is to be doubted in relation to third parties in the light of the *Garden Cottage Foods* case but, as adverted to above, may be relevant where the parties are equally to blame.

## *Restitutionary Damages*

Whatever the wrong which is most appropriate in this area, it next falls to be considered whether restitutionary damages are available in respect of it. It is relatively clear that restitutionary damages are available in respect of at least

[66] *Crofter Hand Woven Tweed* v. *Veitch* [1942] AC 435.
[67] [1892] AC 25.
[68] [1974] Ch 381.
[69] [1978] 3 CMLR 87.
[70] *Supra* n 50.
[71] [1995] 2 All ER 87.

some torts,[72] equitable wrongs,[73] and possibly in respect of breach of contract.[74]

It has been suggested that the remedy should be confined to protecting facilitative institutions[75] but the better view is that it should be available wherever there is a deliberate exploitation of wrongdoing.[76] Generally there is a sound policy in favour of deterring a party from deliberately committing a wrong. A remedy which has no penal element, but which merely requires a party to disgorge his gain is a useful measure to remove the temptation to cause a wrong, without serving to suffocate normal commercial activities. A party may enter into a contract willing to take the risk that he is entering into an anti-competitive agreement. In that case, he will pay for that risk by disgorging his gain. The law would therefore neither encourage risk-taking nor prevent it.

There is no good policy reason why there should be any deliberately committed wrongs which are insulated from the possibility of an award of restitutionary damages. In the case of anti-competitive agreements, therefore, where there has been a deliberate breach of Articles 85 or 86, recovery of restitutionary damages should be available, measured not by way of loss to one party but by reference to the gain of the party which deliberately breaches the Treaty provisions.[77]

### *Punitive and Exemplary Damages*

There may therefore be compensatory damages, restitutionary damages, or recovery under a restitutionary cause of action available to the potential litigant. Whether there should be a greater disincentive to those entering into an anti-competitive agreement is a complex question which the writer merely raises. Exemplary damages are available in England law where a party involved in wrongdoing has cynically breached an obligation upon the

[72] *Lamine* v. *Dorrell* (1701) 2 Ld Raym 1216; *Chesworth* v. *Farrar* [1967] 1 QB 407 (conversion); *Oughton* v. *Seppings* (1830) 1 B & Ad 241; *Strand Electric and Engineering Co Ltd* v. *Brisford Entertainments Ltd* [1952] 2 QB 246 (trespass to goods); *Whitwham* v. *Westminster Brymbo Coal and Coke Co* [1896] 2 Ch 538; *Penarth Dock Engineering Co* v. *Pounds* [1963] 1 Ll Rep 358; *Bracewell* v. *Appleby* [1975] Ch 408 (trespass to land); *Colbeam Palmer Ltd* v. *Stock Affiliates Property Ltd* (1968) 122 CLR 25; *My Kinda Town Ltd* v. *Soll and Grunts Investments* [1982] FSR 147 (breach of copyright and infringement of trademark).

[73] *Regal* v. *Gulliver* [1967] 2 AC 134n; *Boardman* v. *Phipps* [1967] 2 AC 46 (secret profits); *Attorney-General for Hong Kong* v. *Reid* [1994] AC 324 (bribes); *AG* v. *Guardian Newspapers (No 2)* [1990] 1 AC 109; *LAC Minerals* v. *International Corona Resources Ltd* (1989) 61 DLR 4th) 14 (breach of confidence).

[74] *Wrotham Park Estate Co* v. *Parkside Homes Ltd* [1974] 1 WLR 798. But see *contra Surrey CC* v. *Bredero Homes Ltd* [1993] 1 WLR 1361.

[75] See Jackman, "Restitution for Wrongs" [1989] *CLJ* 302; Burrows, *The Law of Restitution*, 000.

[76] See Birks, *An Introduction to the Law of Restitution.*

[77] Again, in many Article 85 cases it is likely to be difficult to show that one party is more to blame for a deliberate breach than the other.

assumption that to breach it will be more profitable than to abide by it.[78] Of course such damages are only available for torts which were in existence prior to 1964. At that time there were no Community law rights available in this country. There is certainly a respectable argument that there should be exemplary damages available for the deliberate breach of Community rights, remedies for which existed in Community jurisprudence in 1964. If this were the case, then there would be a remedy available which was similar to the American remedy of treble damages.[79] Whether it should be available is clearly a matter of policy and is best left to statute to deal with. If restitutionary damages are available,[80] it would not, however, seem strictly to be necessary that there should be exemplary damages.

## 4. PRACTICAL PROBLEMS

The first problem which is likely to be met by the practitioner is in framing a claim in restitution or for restitutionary damages. It is difficult to identify how a claim should be formulated. It is clear from the analysis in the foregoing sections that there are several potential unjust factors, although in my opinion the unjust factor of "absence of consideration" should not be adopted.[81] In addition, if a claim is sought to be made for restitutionary damages, such a claim can be made either in respect of the cynical commission of the tort of breach of statutory duty, or an economic tort, or an innominate tort. At present the best solution is to plead all the options in the alternative.

Once a choice has been made as to how to plead the claim, there comes the question of discovery. As there is always a potential action by the Commission in Article 85 cases for the collusive action which may give rise to a penalty, the question of self-incrimination is bound to be a matter of considerable importance when giving discovery. In *Rio Tinto Zinc Corp* v. *Westinghouse Electric Corp*,[82] the House of Lords held that the privilege was available in Article 85 cases, as the production of documents would expose the parties to fines.

78 *Rookes* v. *Barnard* [1964] AC 1129. To that extent it is therefore similar to the situation where restitutionary damages are available.

79 This remedy is available under the Sherman Act, s 7, which states: "Any person who shall be injured in his business or his property by any other person or corporation by reason of anything forbidden or declared to be unlawful by this Act may sue therefor and shall recover threefold the damages by him sustained and the cost of suit, including a reasonable attorney's fee". The Clayton Act, s 4 is in a similar form. It appears that in American law, the fact that the parties are in *pari delicto* will not prevent a party from recovering treble damages. This remedy is not restitutionary in character as it requires not only disgorgement but also has a punitive element. In the USA the fear of treble damages actions is recognised as being one of the most effective means of persuading an individual to refrain from entering into an anti-competitive contract. See Neale and Goyder, *The Antitrust Laws of the United States of America*.

80 As, it is suggested by the writer, should be the case.

81 If it has not already been eliminated by the *dicta* of the House of Lords in *Westdeutsche*.

82 [1978] AC 547.

Where there has already been an investigation by the Commission, there may also be a number of documents which are in the possession, custody or control of the Commission, and therefore would be discoverable if the Commission were a party to the action in which restitution or restitutionary damages are sought. Although the matter is unclear, it may be possible to get discovery from the Commission where it is a third party. If that is the case, the Commission has an obligation to make all documents available which were obtained during the course of any investigation, except internal documents of the Commission, those concerning business secrets, and any other confidential information.[83]

At trial, it is clear that the burden of proof lies upon the person who is asserting that there has been a breach of Articles 85 or 86. What standard of proof is required is unclear. In *Shearson Lehman* v. *Watson*,[84] Webster J held that, as an infringement of Article 85 carries with it a liability to penalties, a higher degree of proof was required than that upon the ordinary balance of probabilities, although such standard was still lower than the criminal burden of proof. However, the Irish High Court held in *Masterfoods* v. *HB Ice Cream*,[85] that the appropriate standard of proof should be the ordinary civil standard. In principle, this approach appears to be the better one.

Finally, it is also necessary to consider how to frame a contract when drafting it so that one's client does not have to address this problem in litigation at all. When drafting a contract, it is vital to consider whether the client intends to enforce it, in which case it should be drafted so that it does not offend against Articles 85 and 86, or alternatively it should be notified to the Commission for an exemption if it is felt that it does not comply with the treaty provisions and is unlikely to fall within an exemption. Of course, if the other party is the one who is to front-load all the costs, it may tactically e useful to include a potentially anti-competitive clause, as it is the other party who will take the monetary risk that the contract is void. A void provision may prove at a later stage to be a useful tool for renegotiation of the contract.

## 5. CONCLUSIONS

The UK courts have not yet had to face the question of whether restitution or restitutionary damages can be granted for contravention of Articles 85 and 86. Whatever approach is taken by the courts, they should not seek to avoid the complexities of the question.[86] As Megarry V-C noted in *ICI* v. *Berk*,[87] the courts

[83] *Re the Polypropylene Cartel: S.A. Hercules Chemicals NV* v. *EC Commission (Case T-7/89)* [1992] 4 CMLR 84.

[84] [1989] 3 CMLR 429.

[85] [1992] 3 CMLR 830, 873.

[86] The courts must consider the jurisprudence of the Commission and economic considerations: *Delimitis* v. *Henninger Brau* [1992] 5 CMLR 210.

[87] [1981] 2 CMLR 91; [1981] FSR 1.

should not adopt the attitude that, where there is a Euro-defence argued, it should necessarily survive an application under RSC Order 14 simply because of its complexity.[88] Such careful consideration was undertaken by the High Court in *Merson* v. *Rover Group*[89] in refusing to order summary judgment under RSC Order 14A with damages to be assessed, where the plaintiff claimed that it was the victim of unlawful abuse under Article 86.[90] The same level of consideration is necessary in applications to strike out a plaintiff's statement of claim which is based upon breaches of Articles 85 and 86.

The House of Lords Select Committee suggested in 1993[91] that in due course harmonising measures may be required, probably by way of Directive, to provide a systematic approach to enforcement at national level throughout the European Union. An attempt to move towards such co-operation was made by the Commission in the same year, by the issuing of a Notice of Co-operation[92] by which national courts were provided with a procedure whereby they could obtain assistance from the Commission, including a right to consult the Commission on points of law.[93]

However, as the question whether restitution is available is a matter for national law, even if further harmonisation does take place it is unlikely that there will be any detailed consideration of the possibility of restitution, nor should there be. It is a matter for national law. It is to be hoped that there will be no suggestion by the UK courts that restitution for "no consideration" should have any place in this area. The courts must face up to the potential danger of such an unjust factor. Before developing the law in such a direction the courts need to consider the potentially far-reaching effects which such a development could have.

The best solution would be to allow restitution based upon the unjust factors of failure of consideration and mistake of fact or law, if there is no question of illegality blocking recovery, where contracts have not provided that for which the parties bargained. No restitutionary cause of action should be available where the parties have received that for which they bargained,

[88] Despite this dicta, the Court of Appeal in *Lansing Bagnall* v. *Buccaneer* [1984] FSR 241 stated that, until the European Court of Justice had given guidance on Article 86, it would be necessary for Euro defences to be allowed provided that they were properly pleaded and properly particularised. With respect, more analysis is required than is suggested by that judgment.

[89] Unreported, 22 May 1992.

[90] The abuse in question had been condemned by the Commission and the Commission's decision had been upheld in *British Leyland* v. *Commission* [1987] 1 CMLR 185; [1993] 2 CMLR 66; [1992] IRLR 84. The fact of the previous decision distinguishes the case from so many of these competition cases where courts often proceed upon the assumption that Articles 85 and 86 are applicable. However, like many other competition cases, the case was settled before it was heard by the Court of Appeal.

[91] HL Select Committee, "Report on Enforcement of Community Competition Rules" (HL Paper 7, 7 December 1993), paras 138 and 164.

[92] Notice on co-operation between national courts and the Commission in applying Articles 85 and 86 of the EEC Treaty [1993] OJ C39/6.

[93] Para 38.

because there is no enrichment which falls to be returned. In addition the courts should be prepared to countenance recovery of restitutionary damages based upon the wrong of the deliberate breach of statutory duty of such other deliberately committed wrong as may be deemed appropriate by national law.

What national courts must not do is to treat the question whether there can be restitution where Article 85(2) has been breached as a question which must be answered in a vacuum. The growing case law and jurisprudential analysis on the law of restitution should be fully considered. Unless such careful consideration is given to the question, the courts may be tempted to invent another unsuitable unjust factor. Such invention would be neither necessary nor desirable.

# 8

# *Restitution Under Article 85(2) of the EC Treaty: Can it be Done?—A Comment*

ALISON JONES*

This note is not so much a comment on Felicity Toube's chapter as a complement to it. Her paper establishes that the position of a plaintiff who has paid money to another under a contract, or contractual provision, that is subsequently found to be void for infringing Article 85 (or 86) is unclear.

Her chapter identifies two important potential problems for those seeking to recover at common law. The first, in relation to money claims, is that no action for money had and received lies where there has only been a partial failure of consideration for the payment made. A plaintiff seeking to recover monetary payments made under such a contract will, therefore, have to establish that a personal action for money had and received is available either on the ground that consideration for his payments had "totally failed" or, possibly, on the ground that he received "no consideration" for the payments made. In the light of *dicta* in the recent case of *Westdeutsche Landesbank Girozentrale* v. *Islington LBC*,[1] however, it is now doubtful that an action for money had and received will lie on the grounds of no (or an absence of) consideration. The question of recovery may depend, therefore, on the extent to which the concept of failure of consideration can be stretched. A plaintiff seeking restitution for goods provided or services rendered under the contract should, however, be able to bring an action for either a *quantum valebat* or a *quantum meruit*, the defendant having freely accepted the goods or services.[2]

Secondly, a very serious problem is that any restitutionary claim whether for money, goods or services, may well be barred by the operation of the principle *in pari delicto*. Both Articles 85 and 86 of the EC Treaty clearly prohibit contracts concluded in contravention of their rules. Their intention is to deter and prevent conduct which distorts competition within the common market

* With thanks to Jack Alexander Keen, who was kind enough to be born on Monday, 23 September 1996.

[1] [1996] 2 WLR 802.

[2] For a more detailed discussion, see Jones "Recovery of Benefits Conferred under contractual obligations prohibited under Article 85 or 86 of the Treaty of Rome" (1996) 112 *LQR* 607, at 609–12.

and/or interferes with other important Community objectives (such as the goal of integrating the single market). Although a contravention of the competition rules does not attract criminal sanctions, it may well be that a prohibited contract would be considered to be "illegal" for the purposes of the *in pari delicto* rule. The principle has developed broadly and has been applied to a variety of situations where the courts have deemed it correct to deny rights to persons for reasons of public policy. Indeed, in *Inntrepreneur Estates (CPV) Plc* v. *Milne*,[3] Mitchell J considered that on the basis that contractual terms infringing Article 85(1) were "void, they must also be illegal. I was reminded yesterday that the Commission has jurisdiction to fine in the event of a breach. The illegality of the 'tie' provision is, as I understand it common ground".

If the principle of *in pari delicto* applies, recovery will be barred unless the plaintiff can establish that the parties were not *in pari delicto*.[4] It will, therefore, have to be established that the purpose of the EC Treaty provisions was to protect a particular class of persons which includes the plaintiff (the *Kiriri* principle).[5] A strong argument could be constructed that this is the case in certain instances (for example, where the plaintiff was a "smaller" entity and in a weaker bargaining position[6]). However, such reasoning may be defeated by the counter-argument that the purpose of the provisions is not primarily the protection of any class of plaintiff but the protection of a wider economic interest, for example, the public economic policy in seeing that markets remain competitive and the protection of the competitive structure of the market. An English court would have to interpret the *Kiriri* principle more liberally than has previously been the case if it is to be dissuaded from concluding, as Mitchell J did in *Inntrepreneur Estates Ltd* v. *Milne*, that Article 85 does not identify, even in general terms, any parties to prohibited agreements as constituting a class of persons designed to be protected.

From this brief introduction,[7] it can be seen that (a) it may be the position that no action for the recovery of monetary payments will be available where it cannot be established that consideration for the payments has totally failed[8]; and (b) a restitutionary action, whether in relation to money, goods or services, may be barred by the operation of the principle of *in pari delicto*. This will be the position even though, for example: (i) the plaintiff was ignorant that he had contravened the community competition rules; (ii) a rule of no

[3] Unreported, July 1990. The defendant publican was not, however, represented.

[4] It will not be possible to avoid pleading the illegality by relying on a legal or equitable property interest in the money or goods transferred under the void contract, see Jones, "Recovery of Benefits Conferred under contractual obligations prohibited under Article 85 or 86 of the Treaty of Rome" (1996) 112 *LQR* 607, 614–17.

[5] See *Kiriri Cotton Co* v. *Dewani* [1960] AC 192.

[6] See Jones, "Recovery of Benefits Conferred under contractual obligations prohibited under Article 85 or 86 of the Treaty of Rome" (1996) 112 *LQR* 607, 618–22.

[7] For a more in-depth discussion, see Jones, "Recovery of Benefits Conferred under contractual obligations prohibited under Article 85 or 86 of the Treaty of Rome" (1996) 112 *LQR* 607.

[8] An exception to the general rule barring recovery for mistake of law may, however, exist where the payor can establish that he is not *in pari delicto* with the payee.

recovery may allow one guilty party to benefit at the expense of another; (iii) the plaintiff was a smaller entity compelled to conclude the bargain, some of the terms of which he considered to be unacceptable, by a larger and more powerful counterpart; (iv) the parties to the contract may be fined and, consequently, punished by the European Commission for participating in an offending contract *and* pursued in civil proceedings by third parties that have been injured by their conduct; (v) permitting recovery may in some circumstances actually encourage the enforcement of the competition rules (a party may be more inclined to withdraw from the contract if it can recover any benefits it has conferred on the other); and (vi) in many cases, given the wide policy objectives pursued by the Commission in enforcing the competition rules, it is extremely hard to characterise an entity that has contravened the rules either as a wrongdoer or as being guilty of morally reprehensible behaviour.

Although the fate of a plaintiff seeking a restitutionary claim in English law is not at all certain, it must not be forgotten that the dispute arises from the contravention of the EC Treaty competition rules. The impact of Community law must therefore be considered.

In the first place, it is Community law which establishes that the Treaty competition rules are directly effective. Consequently, individuals are both entitled to rely on rights derived from the provisions before national courts and are bound to respect obligations laid down in them.[9] In *Belgische Radio en Televisie* v. *SABAM*, the Court of Justice ruled that "[a]s the prohibitions of Article 85(1) and 86 tend by their nature to produce direct effects in relations between individuals, these Articles create direct rights in respect of individuals concerned which the national courts must safeguard".[10]

Further, it is Community law that determines the circumstances in which a contract infringes Article 85(1) or Article 86. National courts are, therefore, obliged to look to the jurisprudence of the European courts and the practice of the Commission to determine whether or not the particular contract before it does indeed contravene the Treaty provisions.[11]

Community law also spells out at least some of the consequences arising from an infringement of either Article 85 or 86. For example, Council Regulation 17/62 authorises the Commission to fine undertakings it finds to be acting in contravention of the competition rules. Article 85(2), as interpreted by the Court of Justice,[12] establishes that the agreement as a whole, or the contractual provisions contravening the rules where those provisions can successfully be severed from the remainder of the agreement, are void.

In addition, given the limited resources of the Commission and its consequent inability to enforce the competition rules adequately throughout the

[9] The EC Treaty Articles are capable of horizontal direct effect.

[10] (Case 127/73) [1974] ECR 51, 62.

[11] If the national court is uncertain on whether or not this is the case, it may make a reference to the European Court of Justice seeking clarification of this point (see Article 177 of the Treaty).

[12] See *Societe Technique Miniere* v. *Maschinenbau Ulm GmbH* (Case 56/65) [1966] ECR 235, 250.

entire Community, the Community authorities have actively been encouraging the enforcement of the competition rules at the national level (see, for example, "Notice on Co-operation between National Courts and the Commission in Applying Articles 85 and 86 of the EEC Treaty"[13], *Stergios Delimitis* v. *Henninger Brau AG*[14]). Strangely, however, the Court of Justice has not, so far, been prepared to give the national courts much guidance on what remedies should be available where individuals seek to enforce the competition rules before them. In *Société de Vente de Ciments et Betons de l'Est SA* v. *Kerpen & Kerpen GmbH & Co KG*[15] the Court of Justice held that the consequence of nullity under Article 85(2) on any orders and deliveries made and the resulting financial obligations was not a matter for Community law. The consequences were to be determined by the national court according to its own law.

This appears at first sight to leave the answer to the question of whether benefits conferred under a contract should be recoverable entirely up to the laws of the individual national court in which the dispute arises. Were national courts to apply their own national rules the availability of a remedy may, therefore, vary radically from member state to member state. A plaintiff in member state A may be able to recover any benefits conferred together with interest (where appropriate); a plaintiff in member state B may, *prima facie*, be entitled to recover but may find his claim barred by the operation of an extremely strict limitation period; and a plaintiff in member state C may not be able to recover at all, either perhaps because there is no ground for recovery or because recovery is barred by a principle such as that of *in pari delicto*. This would appear to be the case even though Community law has made the scope and effect of the Treaty provisions clear and, consequently, the cause of the action is identical in each member state.

The approach of the Court in the *Ciments et Betons* case is not, however, unusual. Although forthright about the existence, scope and effect of Community rights and their impact on national courts, Community law is not particularly developed in the field of remedies. In the absence of harmonising Community rules, the Court of Justice has largely been forced to rely on national courts to protect Community law and rights. The principle of national procedural autonomy has dictated that national rules determine the forum, procedural conditions, scope and nature of any relief available to a plaintiff whose Community rights have been infringed. The Court of Justice has itself, however, on occasions, talked about this regrettable absence of Community harmonisation rules. It has expressed dissatisfaction that such a vital matter as the availability of remedies should be left for resolution at a national level.[16] Consequently, it has not been prepared to embrace or to

[13] [1993] OJ C 39/6.

[14] (Case C-234/89) [1991] ECR I-935.

[15] (Case 319/82) [1980] ECR 4173.

[16] See *Express Dairy Foods Ltd* v. *Intervention Board for Agricultural Produce* (Case 130/79) [1980] ECR 1887.

accept the principle of national procedural autonomy wholeheartedly. By relying on the duty of cooperation set out in Article 5 of the EC Treaty, it has managed to achieve at least a partial harmonisation of the rules. It has stressed the obligation of the national courts to ensure the protection of the directly effective Community rights of the individual and directly effective Community law. Thus it has insisted, in order to limit national discrepancies and to ensure the effectiveness of Community law, that national procedures (a) must not be less favourable than those relating to similar claims of a domestic nature (the principle of non-discrimination) and (b) must not make it impossible or impossible in practice to exercise the rights that the national courts are obliged to protect (the principle of effectiveness).

If an English court were to deny a right to restitution to a plaintiff seeking to recover a benefit conferred under a contract which infringed the Treaty competition provisions either on the ground that no restitutionary action lies or on the ground that an action was barred by the principle of *in pari delicto*, it would not be applying national rules which were less favourable than those relating to similar domestic claims. The denial of a restitutionary remedy may, however, make it impossible for the plaintiff to exercise Community rights which those courts are obliged to protect. In spite of the Court's ruling in the *Ciments et Betons* case (which in fact appeared to enable the plaintiff to pursue his restitutionary action under German law[17]) it may be that, for two different but inter-connected reasons, Community law demands that a plaintiff should, *prima facie*, have a right to restitution.

First, a plaintiff could rely on series of cases in which the Court of Justice has demanded that a right to restitution should exist. For example, the jurisprudence of the Court establishes that where a plaintiff has made a payment to a national authority under rules which infringe Community law:

> "entitlement to the repayment of charges levied by a Member State contrary to the rules of Community law is a consequence of, and an adjunct to the rights conferred on individuals by the Community provisions prohibiting charges . . .".
>
> "[W]hilst it is true that repayment may be sought only within the framework of the conditions as to both substance and form, laid down by the various national laws applicable thereto, the fact nevertheless remains, as the Court has consistently held, that those conditions may not be less favourable than those relating to similar claims regarding national charges and they might be so framed as to render virtually impossible the exercise of rights conferred by Community law".[18]

[17] The German court sought to discover from the Court of Justice whether or not the sanction of nullity laid down in Article 85(2) of the EC Treaty precluded a supplier from recovering in respect of assets delivered under the void contract on the basis of the German rules of unjust enrichment.

[18] *Amministrazione delle Finanze dello Stato* v. *San Giorgio* (Case 199/82) [1983] ECR 3595, 3612. See also *Barra* v. *Belgium* (Case 309/85) [1988] ECR 355 and *Pigs & Bacon Commission* v. *McCarren & Co. Ltd* (Case 177/78) [1979] ECR 2161.

Similarly, a line of cases establishes that where a member state has paid out money in breach of the Community state aid rules, that member state may be obliged to seek restitution of the monies so paid. The power of the Commission to require recovery is necessary to achieve the practical elimination, past and future, of Treaty infringements.[19]

By analogy to these cases the plaintiff may be entitled to recover any benefits conferred either as a consequence of, and an adjunct to, the rights conferred on him prohibiting the conclusion of contracts in breach of Community rules, or on the ground that the objectives of the Treaty would be thwarted if he could not recover benefits conferred under a contract concluded in breach of the rules. Non-recovery would enable a wrongdoer to retain a benefit that should never have been conferred of it. Further, it has already been pointed out that the right of recovery might actually encourage the private enforcement of the rules and the abandonment of contracts concluded in contravention.

Secondly, a strong argument could be presented establishing that the principle of unjust enrichment is a general principle of Community law and that national courts, when acting in a field touched by Community law, are bound to respect those principles.[20]

If either of these arguments were accepted, then a plaintiff's fate would not be left entirely to the law of an individual member state. Rather a national court would be obliged to set aside national rules which inhibit the recovery of benefits conferred contrary to Community law. Although in *Rewe-Handelsgesellschaft Nord GmbH* v. *Hauptzollamt Kiel*[21] the Court of Justice held that national courts only had to make national remedies available in aid of Community law and that they were not obliged to create new remedies, in view of the many developments that have since occurred this can no longer be said to be an adequate statement of the law. If no restitutionary action were available, for example a money claim failed because there was no total failure of consideration, this would render the exercise of a Community right impossible. Thus, a national remedy may have to be adapted, extended or even created to ensure the "effectiveness" of Community law. It would seem unlikely in these circumstances that an English court would fail to permit a restitutionary claim enabling a plaintiff to recover benefits conferred under a contract or contractual provision found to be void for infringing the Community competition rules.[22]

[19] See, for example, *Commission* v. *Germany (Kohlgesetz)* (Case 70/72) [1973] ECR 813. For a more detailed discussion of all of these relevant cases, see Jones, "Regional Digest: European Union" [1996] *RLR* 190–213.

[20] See Jones, *ibid.*, sections V and VI.

[21] (Case 158/80) [1981] ECR 1805.

[22] See especially, the approach of the House of Lords in both *R* v. *Secretary of State for Transport, ex parte Factortame Ltd (No. 2)* [1991] 1 AC 60 and *Woolwich Equitable Building Society* v. *Inland Revenue Commissioners* [1993] AC 70 (particularly Lord Goff).

Assuming that an action were potentially available, we have seen that such action may nonetheless be barred by the *in pari delicto* principle. The Court of Justice has ruled that reasonable national rules limiting or barring the right of recovery are acceptable. National courts may apply reasonable limitation periods,[23] deny recovery where the plaintiff has "passed on" its loss[24] and apply rules designed to protect a recipient's legitimate expectations.[25] A national court must, however, set aside rules which impair the effectiveness of Community law such as evidential rules which make it impossible in practice for a plaintiff to exercise his right[26] or a statutory provision denying recovery.[27] In this case it would be for the Court of Justice, not a national court, to determine whether the principle of *in pari delicto*, as applied by the English courts in the Article 85 or 86 context, was an acceptable limitation on the right of recovery or an impediment to the effective exercise of a Community right.

[23] For example, *Rewe Zentralfinanz eG and Rewe Zentral AG* v. *Landwirtschaftskammer fur das Saarland* (Case 33/76) [1976] ECR 1989.

[24] For example, *Hans Just I/S* v. *Danish Ministry for Fiscal Affairs* (Case 68/79) [1980] ECR 501.

[25] For example, *Deutsche Milchkontor GmbH* v. *Federal Republic of Germany* (Case 205, 215/82) [1983] ECR 2633.

[26] For example, *Amministrazione delle Finanze dello Stato* v. *SpA San Giorgio* (Case 199/82) [1983] ECR 3595.

[27] For example, *Amministrazione della Finanze delo Stato* v. *Simmenthal SpA* (Case 106/77) [1978] ECR 629.

# 9

# *Restitution for Termination of Contract in German Law*

GERHARD DANNEMANN*

## 1. INTRODUCTION[1]

Termination (*Rücktritt*) is normally a remedy for breach of a hitherto valid contract. Termination (or, sometimes used synonymously in English language, avoidance or rescission) must be distinguished from two other situations. The first concerns contracts which are void *ab initio* (or *nichtig* in German), e.g. because one of the parties lacks capacity, because the contract violates a statutory prohibition, or because a form requirement has not been observed. The second relates to situations where a contract is voidable (*anfechtbar*) by the aggrieved party in cases of mistake, fraudulent misrepresentation and duress. Such *Anfechtung* will render a contract void *ab initio*. In both of these situations, if parties perform under what turns out to be a void contract, this is a straightforward case for the law of restitution (*ungerechtfertigte Bereicherung* or unjustified enrichment). On the other hand, termination of a valid contract is subject to more specific contractual rules, in particular §§ 327, 346–361 of the *Bürgerliches Gesetzbuch* ("BGB": German Civil Code). A translation of the most important provisions is at the end of this chapter.

* I am grateful to Professor Peter Birks, All Souls College, Oxford, for his detailed comments, and to Dr Simon Whittaker, St John's College, Oxford, for his advice.

[1] See further the following selected reading list on German law.

*A.* General textbooks and commentaries: Esser/Schmidt, *Schuldrecht Bd. 1, Allgemeiner Teil*, 7th edn (1992); Jauernig/Sclechtriem/Stürner/Teichmann/Vollkommer, *Bürgerliches Gesetzbuch*, 7th edn (1994); Medicus, *Schuldrecht I Allgemeiner Teil*, 8th edn (1995); Palandt, *Bürgerliches Gesetzbuch*, 55th edn (1996); Schlechtriem, *Schuldrecht Allgemeiner Teil*, 2nd edn (1994), Kap, 9; Staudinger, *Kommentar zum Bürgerlichen Gesetzbuch mit Einführungsgesetz und Nebengesetzen*, 13th edn, §§ 328–61 (1995); Markesinis, Lorenz and Dannemann, *The German Law of Contract and Restitution* (OUP, 1997).

*B.* Monographs and essays on termination of contract: von Caemmerer, "Mortuus redhibetur". Bemerkungen zu den Urteilen BGHZ 53, 144 und 57, 135, Festschrift Larenz I (1973), 621–42; Glaß, "Gefahrtragung und Haftung beim gesetzlichem Rücktritt" (1959); Leser, "Der Rücktritt vom Vergrag" (1975).

In this chapter, the following abbreviations have been used in particular: BGH = Bundesgerichtshof (Federal Court of Justice); BGHZ = Entscheidungen des Bundesgerichtshofs in Zivilsachen, Amtliche Sammlung; JZ = Juristenzeitung (periodical); MDR = Monatsschrift für deutsches Recht (periodical); NJW = Neue Juristische Wochenschrift (periodical); OLG = Oberlandesgericht (regional court of appeal); RG = Reichsgericht (the former Imperial Court); RGZ = Entscheidungen des Reichsgerichts in Zivilsachen, Amtliche Sammlung.

As the present chapter deals with restitution for termination of contract, little will be said about those situations which can give rise to a right to terminate a contract.[2] Suffice it to say that such a right will normally arise from the other party's serious breach of contract, or else because such a right has been stipulated. The former is called a statutory right to termination (*gesetzliches Rücktrittsrecht*) and the latter a contractual right to termination (*vertragliches Rücktrittsrecht*).[3]

Termination occurs when the aggrieved party makes a declaration to this effect (BGB §349). It should be pointed out that a slightly different remedy exists in German law for termination of sales or works contracts on the ground of defects of the goods, or of the work. This is called *Wandelung*, and effectuated when both parties agree on termination of the contract (BGB §§465, 634(4)), or else when a court finds that the aggrieved party has a right to terminate the contract because of the defects.[4] *Wandelung* will be considered in this present chapter, as its effects are the same as those of *Rücktritt*.[5]

The provisions which govern consequences of termination of contract (BGB §§ 346–361) occupy a central position within the German law of contract and are thus, at least in space, far removed from the law of unjustified enrichment (BGB §§ 812–822). According to the modern German view, termination does not render a contract void.[6] Rather, the contract turns into a different set of obligations whereby parties are essentially required to return what they have received from each other. Some elements of the contract do indeed survive in German law. For example, according to BGB §346 the contract will continue to define the value which is to be attached to benefits exchanged. This marks an important difference to English law, about which more will be said below. Also, liability under BGB §§ 346 *et seq* is generally stricter than liability for unjustified enrichment. In particular, while change of position is not a defence under BGB §§ 346 *et seq*, it is recognised under BGB §818(3); again a point which will be taken up below. Suffice it to say at this stage that there is this

[2] See e.g. Dannemann, *An Introduction to German Civil and Commercial Law* (1993), 27–31, 44 (where, however, *Rücktritt* has been translated with "rescission" rather than with "termination"). A much more detailed account will be given in Markesinis, Lorenz and Dannemann, *The German Law of Contract and Restitution* (OUP, 1997). I am indebted to Professor Lorenz for the benefit of having read in draft his Ch 8 on "Remedies for Breach of Contract".

[3] A cross-bred is contained in BGB §455. According to this provision, if the seller retains title in the goods sold until full payment of the purchase price, it is presumed that the seller is entitled to terminate the contract once the buyer defaults with payments. This presumption makes it a contractual, rather than statutory, right to terminate the contract.

[4] In practice, the difference between unilateral (*Rücktritt*) and consensual termination (*Wandelung*) is not overwhelming. In both situations, if the party in breach does not give up voluntarily what it has received under the (terminated) contract, the innocent party will have to go to court.

[5] For the effects of *Wandelung*, BGB §§ 467 and 634(4) refer to the provisions on *Rücktritt* in BGB §§ 346 *et seq*.

[6] While termination was considered to render a contract void in 19th century Germany, the now prevailing view that (part of) the contract survives gained ground after Heinrich Stoll wrote *Die Wirkungen des vertragsmäßigen Rücktritts* (1921); see e.g. Jauernig-Volkommer, § 346 1c, who quote BGB 8.12.1989, NJW 1990, 2068, at 2069, in support.

conceptual difference between German and English law. How much of a difference this means in practice will be evaluated at the end of this chapter.

On the other hand, this dichotomy between consequences of termination of a valid contract (contractual rules) and consequences of performance under a void contract (unjustified enrichment rules) is no longer as clear as it originally was intended. It was precisely the stricter liability under the contractual rules which, in the view of the courts, caused problems when applied to the innocent party.

The solution which courts have found to this problem builds on the somewhat curious fact that BGB §§ 346–361 have been drafted for the much rarer case of a contractually stipulated right to terminate the contract. It is only by reference in BGB §327 that the same provisions also apply to statutory rights to terminate the contract for breach. However, this same BGB §327 contains a rather oblique sentence 2. According to this sentence, if termination of the contract has been declared against a party which is not to blame, this party is liable under the more lenient provisions on unjustified enrichment rather than under the contractual rules. However, there is practically no case where a statutory right to terminate the contract does arise against a party which is without fault. In nearly all cases, such a right arises as a remedy for a serious breach of contract by the other party, for which this party is indeed to blame.[7] What the courts have done for the last 65 years, though, is to apply this provision by analogy to innocent parties who terminate a contract for the other party's breach.[8] This leads to the unusual situation where a provision, which by many is considered to be a drafting error, survives by its application by analogy. Be that as it may, the case law has it that different models of liability apply to the innocent party and to the party in breach in cases of termination for breach of contract. It is therefore only to the exercise of a contractual right to terminate a contract that BGB §§ 346 *et seq* apply without reservation.

In a nutshell, German law has three different models for what English law would classify as restitution for failure of consideration. If the contract is void, the restitutionary consequences are conceived to arise solely in the law of unjustified enrichment. If the contract has been terminated in exercise of a right stipulated in the contract, restitution occurs under what—at least in the structure of the BGB—is entirely within the law of contract. If the contract has been terminated for breach of contract (i.e., in exercise of a statutory right), a mixed contractual/unjustified enrichment model applies. It is the latter situation that this chapter will be concerned with most, as breach of contract is much more common than a stipulated right to termination.

[7] The only agreed exception is BGB §636. Under this provision, the client may have the right to terminate a contract for works if the work is not completed within the envisaged time, even if the contractor is not responsible for the delay.

[8] Since RG 24.10.1930, RGZ 130, 119, at 123. This practice is very controversial amongst scholars. See e.g. Medicus, 250 *et seq* (in support); against: Schlechtriem no. 443; Emmerich, *Münchener Kommentar zum Bürgerlichen Gesetzbuch*, Bd. 2, 3rd edn 1994, § 327 no. 13.

For this purpose, and even more in order to facilitate the comparison with English law, a first distinction will be made between the innocent party (i.e. the party who is entitled to, and does, terminate the contract) on the one hand, and the party in breach on the other (i.e. the party against whom the contract is terminated).

The second distinction is between restitution of money paid, and restitution for benefits in kind. This is, in principle, a preoccupation of English law, whereas German law allows or disallows restitutionary claims regardless of whether or not they concern money. Nevertheless, there are some problems which cannot arise for money claims, in particular destruction, deterioration, and, normally, valuation. Also, the comparison between English and German law becomes easier if one follows this distinction.

Taken together, this leads to four different situations, which will be considered in turn. The first concern the innocent party, and the second the party in breach seeking restitution of money paid. The third situation relates to the innocent party, and the fourth to the party in breach seeking restitution for benefits in kind.[9]

## 2. INNOCENT PARTY SEEKING RESTITUTION OF MONEY PAID

The general rule in BGB §346 is that parties have to return to each other what they have received in performance of the contract which now has been terminated. For money paid, this rule is very straightforward: the party in breach has to return all payments made by the innocent party under the contract.[10]

### *Total Failure of Consideration?*

It may come as a surprise to English lawyers that there is no requirement of total failure of consideration in German law, or indeed of any failure of consideration. If the innocent party does have the right to terminate the contract, it can, in principle, require restitution of all payments made under the contract, regardless of whether the other party has not performed at all, has performed badly, partially, or completely. Nor is there any equivalent in German law to the rule in *Thomas* v. *Brown*,[11] according to which no restitution is allowed against a party which has always been willing to give full perfor-

[9] Note that both Goff and Jones, *The Law of Restitution*, 4th edn by Gareth Jones (1993) (hereafter "Goff and Jones") 417 *et seq*, and Burrows, *The Law of Restitution* (1993) (hereafter "Burrows"), 262–81, employ the same four categories for their descriptions of failure of consideration in contracts discharged for breach.

[10] This is also the position of English law: see Goff and Jones, *supra* n 9, 417 *et seq*.

[11] (1876) 1 QBD 714. In this case, no recovery was allowed of a deposit made under an unenforceable contract for the sale of a shop, because the vendor had always been willing to perform the contract. See Burrows, supra n 9, 257. The case did therefore not concern termination of contract, but the rule has been thought to be general. But see the criticism of the total failure of consideration requirement in, e.g.Goff and Jones, *supra* n 9, 413.

mance. The only bar in German law is that no statutory right to terminate the contract will arise in the first place if the other party has done everything as it should have done under the contract. At least to that extent there does have to be a failure of consideration (in the sense in which that word was used in *Fibrosa Spolka Akcyjna* v. *Fairbairn Lawson Combe Barbour Ltd*)[12] even in German law.

It should be mentioned that this difference between German and English law has become less marked. The requirement that failure of consideration must be total has come under attack, and, while lip service was paid to it in *Rover International Ltd* v. *Cannon Film Sales Ltd (No 3)*, the rule was nevertheless somewhat eroded in substance,[13] and more generally excluded from cases where apportionment can be carried out in the recent case of *Goss* v. *Chilcott*.[14]

### *Escape from a Bad Bargain*

When a contract is terminated, a party who initially made a bad bargain may see some hope of doing better than it could ever have done had the contract been fully performed. For such a person, getting back to square one is obviously advantageous. Can therefore an innocent party use termination as an escape from a bad bargain? It seems that the answer is yes in English law.[15] BGB §346 itself provides the authority for German law: performances made under the contract are to be returned, and no exception is provided for bargains which are unfavourable to either party.[16] But see below, Part 5, for the other party's counterclaim for benefits in kind.

### *Interest*

The party in breach must pay interest on all payments received under the contract, whereby interest starts to run from the time when the payment was received: BGB §347. This marks a difference from English law, in particular if the innocent party's claim is based on failure of consideration. Such an action does not accrue until consideration has indeed failed, so that under the Supreme Court Act 1981, s 35A, interest cannot be awarded for a time between receipt of the money and the subsequent failure of consideration.[17]

[12] *Fibrosa Spolka Akcyjna* v. *Fairbairn Lawson Combe Barbour Ltd* [1943] AC 32, HL.

[13] *Rover International Ltd* v. *Cannon Film Sales Ltd (No 3)* [1989] 1 WLR 912; in particular because both parties had performed part of what they owed under the contract. However, *Rover* did not concern termination, but a contract which, unbeknown to both parties, was void *ab initio*.

[14] *Goss* v. *Chilcott* [1996] 3 WLR 180, PC, 187–8; see also McKendrick, "Total Failure of Consideration and Counter-Restitution: Two Issues or One?", in Birks (ed), *Laundering and Tracing* (1995), 217–42; Birks, "Failure of Consideration", Ch 9 of F.D. Rose (ed), *Consensus Ad Idem (Essays on the Law of Contract in Honour of Guenter Treitel)* (1996).

[15] Goff and Jones, *supra* n 9, 412 *et seq*; Burrows *supra* n 9, 265.

[16] See, however, *infra* Part 4 for benefits which cannot be returned in kind.

[17] See also Burrows, *supra* n 9, 258 *et seq*, 30.

On the other hand, the statutory interest rate is fixed at a low 4 per cent per annum in general (BGB §246) and 5 per cent in commercial contracts (*Handelsgesetzbuch* (HGB, Commercial Code), §352) in German law; if a different rate has been stipulated in the contract, this takes precedence. If the innocent party can prove that the other party has reaped more than the statutory rate of interest, the entire gain must be given up under BGB §§347 sent. 2, 987.[18]

### *Impossibility of Counter-Restitution*

BGB §§ 350–353 contain regulations which are somewhat equivalent to the English rule that impossibility of counter-restitution is a defence to a restitutionary claim. However, this rule has to be taken with several pinches of salt.

Neither English nor German law require a party to return objects in the very condition in which they were received in order to claim back the contractual price.[19] In *Erlanger* v. *New Sombrero Phosphate Co*,[20] an account of profits was sufficient compensation for the fact that the object of the contract, a phosphate mine, had been worked before it was returned. BGB §§ 346, 347 would have led to the same solution. Most benefits which are not capable of being returned in kind (such as the mere use of an object) are replaced by their financial value (BGB §§ 346, 347: see below) rather than amounting to a bar to recovering the contractual price.

However, the picture changes once the object which was transferred to the plaintiff under the contract can no longer be returned at all. Technically speaking, this is not a defence to a restitutionary claim in German law, but rather to the preceding termination of contract—although the practical implication of this difference is very limited.[21] Under §§ 351–353, a party cannot terminate a contract if it is responsible for the fact that the very object which it has received under the contract has been destroyed, seriously damaged, or for other reasons cannot be returned. BGB §352 specifies that further processing of this object by the recipient will also exclude this party's right to terminate the contract. To this effect, impossibility of counter-restitution amounts to a bar to recovery for the contractual price.

On the other hand, BGB §350 provides that a party may terminate a contract and claim restitution even if an object which this party has already received under the contract has been fortuitously lost or destroyed. This provision is in clear contrast with the English position on impossibility of counter-restitution. German scholars have criticised BGB §350 for a number

[18] BGH 27.10.1982, NJW 1983, 929 (in this case: 8% interest p.a.).

[19] This, however, was the position of the Prussian ALR (General Law of the Land) as concerned remedies for defective goods: see von Caemmerer, *supra* n 1, 621.

[20] *Erlanger* v. *New Sombrero Phosphate Co* (1878) 3 App Cas 1218, 1278, per Lord Blackburn, but *dub.* Lord Cairns, LC at 1241.

[21] It is for this reason that this question is considered in the present chapter, although it does not, strictly speaking, concern a consequence of termination of contract.

of reasons. Most seriously perhaps, in sales contracts, it provides an astonishing exception to the rule that the risk passes to the buyer on the transfer of possession (BGB §446).

Some have tried to justify the rule on the ground that it is typically inherent defects of the goods which cause their subsequent destruction or damage,[22] and there are indeed some cases where this was the reason. In one such case, the plaintiff was a farmer who had bought a used combine harvester from the defendant.[23] The machine was defective to the point that it rapidly deteriorated during its use. The Bundesgerichtshof used this opportunity to affirm that under BGB §350 a buyer is always entitled to recover for the full purchase price if the destruction or deterioration of the goods has been caused by a defect for which the seller would be liable under a valid contract.

However, BGB §350 would also have applied in this case if the machine had instead been destroyed by lightning or flash flood, for these are both circumstances for which the buyer would not have been responsible. In these situations as well, the buyer would have been allowed to recover the full purchase price in exchange for scrap. This is questionable as a result, but difficult to avoid as long as BGB §350 remains in force.

In consequence, there has been some pressure to use a rather wide concept of "fault" or "responsibility" in order to bring cases under BGB §351 rather than §350. In particular, some scholars have argued that any conduct by the recipient which increases the danger of the object's being lost or damaged should qualify as fault under BGB §351.[24] However, a line is normally drawn where some deterioration has occurred due to the normal use of goods sold, such as by driving a car. A case decided by the Reichsgericht concerned a car which was sold as brand new (which it was); what the buyer had not been told, however, is that the car had suffered an accident during transport.[25] The Reichsgericht held that the buyer was not at fault for having used the car until he discovered the defect. In consequence, the fact that he could only return a used car was no bar to his claim for recovery for the purchase price.[26]

There are both English and German cases which concern stolen cars. In on case before the Bundesgerichtshof, the plaintiff buyer returned the car to its true owner and terminated his contract with the defendant seller. The defendant argued that the plaintiff should have returned the car to him instead, and was therefore to blame for his impossibility to do so now.[27] The Bundesgerichtshof held that the owner's proprietary claim was stronger than the defendant's restitutionary counterclaim in the car, so that the plaintiff was not to blame for his impossibility of returning the car to the defendant. This

[22] See Jauernig-Vollkommer, *supra* n 1, §350(2)(b).
[23] BGH 9.10.1980, BGHZ 78, 216.
[24] von Caemmerer, *supra* n 1, 627 *et seq*; see Medicus, *supra* n 1, 252.
[25] RG 3.7.1934, RGZ 145, 79.
[26] In these cases, the buyer will nevertheless have to pay for the use of the car; see below Part 5
[27] BGH 28.3.1952, BGHZ 5, 337.

can be compared to *Rowland* v. *Divall*,[28] where, however, the buyer had resold the car to a third party, where it was seized by the police. After the buyer had refunded the purchase price to the third party, he was allowed to recover the price he had paid, even though he could no longer return the car. However, the English case succeeded on the ground that failure of consideration had been total, rather than on the fact that the plaintiff was not to blame for the impossibility of counter-restitution.

It should be emphasised that the rules in BGB §§ 350–353 on impossibility of counter-restitution apply only if the impossibility occurred before the contract was terminated. If restitution in kind becomes impossible after the contract has been terminated, BGB §347 applies with its reference to BGB §989. According to these provisions, parties are liable for any negligent deterioration or destruction of objects which they have received under the terminated contract. Impossibility of counter-restitution which occurs after the termination will, therefore, not operate as a bar to recovery, but will rather replace the claim for return of the object by a claim for damages for their destruction or deterioration. It should be mentioned, though, that a party who terminates e.g. a sales contract and then goes on to use the goods may, depending on the circumstances of the individual case, be estopped from claiming back the purchase price.[29] At this point, German rules on good faith (BGB §242) converge with English rules on total failure of consideration.

### *Change of Position*

In the German law of unjustified enrichment, change of position is generally available as a defence to the innocent party. Under BGB §818(3), claims are limited to the enrichment which has survived in the hands of the defendant. However, and perhaps not surprisingly, change of position is not available as a defence against the innocent party's claim for return of money paid under a terminated contract. This follows from BGB §347 and its reference to BGB §§ 987, 989, the proprietary provisions on the unauthorised possessor's liability towards the owner, where, unlike in BGB §818(3), change of position is not generally allowed as a defence.

Therefore, if the defendant has managed to sell a 14-year-old Volkswagen Golf as a vintage car, and if the buyer terminates the contract when it turns out that the vintage aspect consists in the car being a safety hazard (BGB §§ 467, 346), the defendant cannot raise in defence that the purchase price has been spent on a holiday trip to the Fiji islands, even if the defendant was entirely unaware that the car was unsafe.

[28] *Rowland* v. *Divall* [1923] 2 KB 500; see also Birks, *supra* n 14, 247.
[29] BGH 8.2.1984, NJW 1984, 1525.

## 3. PARTY IN BREACH SEEKING RESTITUTION OF MONEY PAID

Once a contract has been terminated by the innocent party, the party in breach can recover all payments made under the contract: BGB §346. Typically, this concerns situations where the party in breach has paid part, but not all of the contract price, for a party which has paid all which was due will not normally be in breach of contract.

The English position is less clear. A party in breach was allowed to recover for money paid under a terminated contract in *Dies* v. *British and International Mining and Finance Co*;[30] interestingly enough, the basis of this claim was held to be contractual rather than restitutionary. However, a similar claim was disallowed in *Hyundai Heavy Industries Co Ltd* v. *Papadopoulos*.[31] *Dies* was distinguished in the latter case on the ground that it concerned a contract of sale rather than shipbuilding, as in *Hyundai*; the fact that the shipbuilders had already started with their work made the difference.

### *Total Failure of Consideration?*

Again, under German law there is no need for failure of consideration to be total, or for any failure of consideration at all. At the end of the day, however, the party in breach will not keep any benefit, for it must also make restitution under BGB §§ 346 *et seq*.

### *Escape from a Bad Bargain*

The bad bargain issue can arise if, for instance, a tenant has rented accommodation from the innocent party, paid the deposit, but defaults with the first monthly rent payment. This can give the landlord as the innocent party the right to terminate the contract, and thus escape what might have been a bad bargain by paying back the deposit under BGB §346.

### *Interest*

In principle, as the innocent party should be liable under the more lenient unjustified enrichment rules according to BGB §§ 327 sent. 2, 818, interest should be considered as another form of "use of an enrichment", and the innocent party should only be liable to the extent that it actually gained bene-

[30] *Dies* v. *British and International Mining and Finance Co* [1939] 1 KB 724. See Birks, *supra* n 14, 236 *et seq*; Goff and Jones, *supra* n 9, 429–31.

[31] *Hyundai Heavy Industries Co Ltd* v. *Papadoupoulos* [1980] 1 WLR 1129; see Burrows *supra* n 9, 275. Had *Hyundai* been governed by German law, the action would have failed, for one can no longer sue for the contractual price after having terminated the contract in German law. Rather than terminating the contract, the plaintiffs would have sued for damages under BGB §326.

fit from using this money. However, lower courts have occasionally awarded statutory interest from the time when the money was received without proof of any specific gain, in particular where the innocent party was a businessperson.[32]

### *Change of Position*

Under BGB §§ 327 sent. 2, 818(3), the innocent party can rely on a change of position which occurred before it was aware of the other party's breach of contract. This implies that the innocent party need not return payments made under the contract to the extent that it can establish that (a) it has spent the money, (b) it would not have spent this money had it not been for the payment by the party in breach, and (c) there is no substitution or other increase in the innocent party's assets which is connected with the spending of this money. Blowing the enrichment on a luxury cruise or by gambling are textbook examples.[33] It is particularly point (b) which makes change of position a difficult defence in termination of contract cases, for it will not operate if the innocent party (e.g., a building contractor) would have entered into a similar contract with another party (a different client) had it not chosen to contract with the party in breach. It is maybe for these reasons that there are hardly any cases where the innocent party was indeed allowed to rely on change of position against the other party's claim for recovery of money.

There is one case in which a contract for the construction of a ship was terminated by the defendant contractor during the times of hyperinflation in the 1920s, when the plaintiff buyer refused to pay more than the agreed price. The plaintiff sued for return of payments made (1.7 million Mark), converted into some (meanwhile stabilised) RM 300,000. Of this sum, RM 10,000 were disallowed for what appears to be change of position, but it remained entirely obscure what this sum represented.[34]

[32] OLG Hamburg 24.9.1973, MDR 1974, 42. The court argued that a commercial business will normally put money to economical use, and the defendants had not pleaded that they had either kept the amount in cash or left it in a no interest current account. This amounts to a reversal of the burden of pleading and proof. See also Jauernig-Vollkommer *supra* n 1, §347(3)(c); Palandt-Heinrichs, *supra* n 1, § 347(3)(c).

[33] However, in a recent case the Oberlandesgericht Hamm disallowed the gambling defence on what essentially are causation arguments: OLG Hamm 6.11.1989, NJW-RR 1991, 155. The defendant had tried to defeat an argument that he was *mala fide* by claiming that he had been expecting an outstanding payment from a third party, which he actually received a few weeks after allegedly having lost the plaintiff's money by gambling. The court held that, by disallowing change of position, the defendant was merely put in the position which would have existed had he not mistaken the source of the payment, in which case he would have wasted his own money by gambling. For a critical view, see Schlechtriem, *JZ* 193, 185, at 189. Again, this is not a termination of contract case.

[34] RG 24.10.1930, RGZ 130, 119. It appears that the plaintiff had made the mistake of pleading that the sum claimed would be RM 10,000 less if awarded under unjustified enrichment.

### *Knowledge Causes "Loss of Innocence"*

If the innocent party does indeed deserve leniency, it is because it could reasonably rely on the contract being fulfilled to its full satisfaction. The picture changes, however, once the innocent party becomes aware of the other party's breach. For from this moment, the innocent party is aware that the benefits which it has received under the contract will have to be given back to the party in breach, at least if it terminates the contract. Therefore, from this moment the innocent party loses the protection afforded by BGB §818.[35] BGB §819 applies, which invokes BGB § 987, 989 and thereby the very same provisions which are invoked by BGB §347 for the liability of the party in breach. In other words: once the innocent party has knowledge of the breach of contract, for which the contract is eventually terminated, both parties become equally liable, and what has been said above about the liability of the party in breach applies *mutatis mutandis* to the liability of the innocent party. In particular, the innocent party cannot rely on any change of position which occurs after it has gained knowledge of the breach of contract. On the other hand, it can continue to rely on any previous change of position.

## 4. INNOCENT PARTY SEEKING RESTITUTION FOR BENEFITS IN KIND

BGB §§ 346, 347 govern the liability of the party in breach for benefits in kind which it has received under the contract. Again, there is no need to show for the innocent party that failure of consideration was total; but then, this does not seem to be a requirement in English law when an innocent party seeks restitution for benefits in kind rather than for money paid.[36]

### *Restitution in Kind*

The party in breach must return to the innocent party all benefits in kind to the extent that this is possible: BGB §346. If, for instance, the seller terminates the contract because the buyer has defaulted on payments, the buyer must return any goods or real property to the seller. If the benefit consists in an object which has been damaged, destroyed, or for another reason cannot be returned to the innocent party, the party in breach is liable in damages under BGB §§ 347, 989.

However, BGB §989 requires that the damage, destruction or loss has been caused negligently. This seems to leave the innocent party without protection whenever this negligence on the side of the party in breach is lacking. On the other hand, the innocent party need not choose termination of contract as a remedy in these situations, but will instead go for damages for breach of

[35] Jauernig-Vollkommer, *supra* n 1, §347 3c.

[36] Goff and Jones, *supra* n 1, 413; but see Birks, *supra* n 14, 226 *et seq*.

contract, or sue for the purchase price. Therefore, if the buyer defaults with payment and the goods have been destroyed without the buyer's fault, a seller will not terminate the contract, but instead sue the buyer for the purchase price and recover in addition damages for delay (BGB §286).

On the other hand, if the very loss of the benefit has caused another gain to the party in breach, this party must give up that gain to the innocent party under BGB §281. In one case, a buyer of land had sold the land to a third party and thus violated a clause in the contract according to which the land was not to be sold to third parties until buildings had been erected on the property. The seller terminated the contract for this breach, and was allowed to claim from the buyer the purchase price which the third party had paid.[37]

### *Nature of Benefit Prevents Restitution in Kind*

If the benefits which the innocent party has conferred on the party in breach cannot, by their nature, be returned in kind, these benefits are replaced by their value in money. This is explicitly stated in BGB §346 for cases where the benefit consists in the use of an object, or in services, but the provision is also applied to e.g. building contracts. So far, this corresponds with English law. For example, in *Chandler Bros Ltd* v. *Boswell*,[38] plaintiffs were allowed to claim a *quantum meruit* for work on the excavation of a tunnel. However, an important difference to English law is that any contractual price which has been stipulated for the benefit in question will continue to determine its value under BGB §346. German law does therefore not only have a contractual ceiling. Rather, the contractual price remains in force for the better or for the worse (but see also *infra*, 'Escape from Bad Bargain').

The party in breach is also liable for other benefits which it has gained from using the object of the contract. Such benefits are called *Nutzungen* and defined in BGB §100. They include the mere advantage of using the property, e.g. by living in a house. This rule would cover e.g. the hire-charge which defendants were made to pay in *Strand Electric and Engineering Co Ltd* v. *Brisford Entertainments Ltd*.[39] As the German case law seems too centre around vehicles, one might mention that the use of a new car tends to be taxed at 0.67 per cent of its worth per 1,000km driven (assuming a car-life of 150,000km), and quite regardless of whether this is the "stricter" liability of

[37] BGH 27.10.1982, NJW 1983, 929. This case concerned the exercise of a contractual right to terminate the contract.

[38] *Chandler Bros Ltd* v. *Boswell* [1936] 3 All ER 179; see Burrows *supra* n 9, 267 *et seq*.

[39] [1952] 2 QB 246; see Birks, *supra* n 14, 330. In this case, the defendants continued to use the plaintiff's theatre lighting equipment for their theatre after a deal with a prospective buyer of the theatre, who had initially rented the theatre and obtained the equipment, had fallen through. This is, therefore, not a case of termination of contract. It is nevertheless interesting that the hire-charge was awarded as damages, not as restitution.

the party in breach under §§ 347, 987, or the "more lenient" liability of the innocent party under §818(2).[40]

If the terminated contract was for the sale of a business, the party in breach is also liable for an account of profits. In one case, the plaintiff had sold a petrol station to the defendant company. Shortly afterwards, the defendant became insolvent, with most of the purchase price being unpaid. The seller terminated the contract, reclaimed the petrol station, and was also awarded a full account of profits. However, the Bundesgerichtshof affirmed that this would exclude any profits which were due to the particular personal skills of the new owner—which, however, were obviously lacking in this case.[41]

The party in breach must also compensate for any use which it has negligently failed to make: BGB §§ 347, 987(2). This concerns in particular contracts for the sale of real property which the buyer, without reason, fails to rent out or use in another way; it could, in principle, also concern badly-run businesses. However, the case law is far from abundant.[42]

In situations which do not concern an account of profit, the party in breach will find it difficult to deduct its expenditure on the object from the value of the use which it must give up to the innocent party. BGB §347 sent. 2 refers to proprietary remedies in BGB §§ 994, 995, which in turn invoke *negotiorum gestio* liability under BGB §§ 667 *et seq*. This implies that the party in breach can recover for necessary expenditure in full only if this corresponded to the actual or the implied will of the innocent party. Otherwise, the innocent party is liable only under the unjustified enrichment model and can therefore rely on change of position (BGB §818(3)). If the expenditure was not necessary to start with, then the party in breach cannot recovery at all, unless the innocent party consented to the expenditure (BGB §§ 996, 1001). Nevertheless, the Bundesgerichtshof allowed one party who had bought a snack bar business with its business name, stock, and inventory, to claim back not only its part payments of the purchase price, but also the rent which it had to pay to a third party for the business premises. The court argued that there was no other way in which the business could have been kept alive except by continuing to pay this rent.[43]

[40] See e.g. OLG Hamm 29.6.1993, MDR 1994, 138; Jauernig-Vollkommer, *supra* n 1, §347 2b (for liability under BGB §987); Palandt-Heinrichs, *supra* n 1, §347 3b (for liability under BGB §818(2)).

[41] BGH 12.5.1978, NJW 1978, 1578.

[42] Staudinger-Kaiser, *supra* n 1, §347 no. 77 quotes some cases, which, however, are not accessible to me.

[43] BGH 11.1.1978, NJW 1978, 1256. The contract was actually terminated by the buyer on the ground that the snack bar did not conform with statutory requirements. Nevertheless, the stricter liability under §§ 346, 987 applied because the rent had been paid after the buyer had knowledge of the other party's breach, see *infra* Pt 5. We must presume that no profit was made from the operation of the snack bar. See also Staudinger-Kaiser, *supra* n 1, §347 no. 84.

### *Escape from Bad Bargain*

It is in particular the above-mentioned rule in BGB §346 which keeps the contractual price agreement alive which contrasts with the common law position on the restitutionary liability of the party in breach for benefits in kind. This is illustrated by the well-known American case of *Boomer* v. *Muir*,[44] where the plaintiffs were allowed to claim another (nearly) $258,000 for work in building a dam, even on the assumption that they had already been paid all but $20,000 of what they were owed under the contract. While this decision remains controversial in England, it has nevertheless often been said that English law would decide just the same.[45] German law takes the opposite view. This may seem inconsistent with the situation where the innocent party seeks repayment of money: it has been stated above that German law does allow the innocent party to escape a bad bargain in these cases. More will be said about this *infra*, Part 6.

### *Change of Position*

The party in breach is not allowed to rely on change of position as regards benefits in kind. There is one exception, though. As has been mentioned above, fortuitous loss, destruction or damage of an object exonerates also the party in breach from providing restitution. However, as has also been said above, this is more of a seeming exception, as the innocent party will find little point in terminating the contract in the first place and instead go for damages, or claim the contract price.

## 5. PARTY IN BREACH SEEKING RESTITUTION FOR BENEFITS IN KIND

If the innocent party seeks restitution of money paid (or terminates a contract before having paid the agreed contract price), the (counter-)claim of the party in breach will normally be for restitution for benefits in kind, provided that the party in breach has made some performance. If, on the other hand, this performance has been full and without deficiencies, there is no breach of contract and hence no statutory right to termination.[46] Therefore, in this category we are most likely to be looking for restitution for the benefits in kind conferred by some incomplete or deficient performance.

[44] 24 P2d 570 (1933). However, the court held that the contractual price would apply if provided specifically for portions of the work, which have been fully performed and fully paid.

[45] Burrows, *supra* n 9, 268–70; Goff and Jones, *supra* n 9, 425–8 (who take a critical view).

[46] Of course, there is always the possibility that the "innocent" party had a contractual right to terminate the contract without any breach on the other side. This does not happen often in practice. In this case, §346 applies without restrictions, and the party against whom the contract is rescinded has therefore the same rights as an innocent party seeking restitution for benefits in kind (see at Pt 4).

### *Restitution in Kind*

If the benefits which have been provided are capable of being returned in kind, this is what the party in breach can require under BGB §346. If a buyer terminates the contract because the goods are defective, the seller must return the purchase price, but can require the buyer to give back the deficient goods. English law arrives at a similar conclusion via the total failure of consideration doctrine: if the buyer does not reject (and presumably: return) the goods, failure of consideration is not total.

We have already looked at the situation above where the benefits, while capable of being returned in kind, have been destroyed or substantially damaged. If the "innocent" party is to blame, it loses the right to terminate the contract (BGB §§ 351–353). However, if the loss if fortuitous, the innocent party can require return of its payment (§350) and at the same time is not liable for this loss or damage. On the other hand, if the very loss of the benefit has caused another gain to the innocent party, this party must give up that gain to the party in breach under BGB §818(1). If we take again the case of the defective combine harvester[47] and assume that this machine was insured against, and destroyed by, an accidental fire, the seller of the harvester can require the farmer to give up the claim against the insurance company in exchange for return of the contract price.

### *Nature of Benefit Prevents Restitution in Kind*

The difference between English and German law becomes more obvious when we look at benefits which, by their nature, cannot be returned in kind. Under BGB §346, these benefits are generally replaced by their value in money. This is explicitly stated in BGB §346 for cases where the benefit consists in the use of an object, or in services. It has been mentioned above that the use of a new car tends to be taxed at 0.67 per cent of its worth per 1,000km driven (assuming a car-life of 150,000km), and quite regardless of whether this is the "stricter" liability under §§ 347, 987, or the "more lenient" liability under §818(2).[48]

This indicates a general trend: the value of the use will often be calculated to represent that fraction of the expected normal life of the object which the innocent party has used up. In a recent case, the innocent party (a hotel business) terminated a contract under which it had bought 163 beds, on finding out that they were deficient. As the seller refused to take back the beds, they were used in the hotel for a total of eight months before they were finally returned. The innocent party was allowed to claim back the purchase price of

[47] BGH 9.10.1980, BGHZ 78, 216.

[48] See e.g. OLG Hamm 29.6.1993, MDR 1994, 138; Jauernig-Vollkommer, *supra* n 1, §347(2b) (for the stricter liability); Palandt-Heinrichs, *supra* n 1, §347(3b) (for liability under BGB §818(2)).

DM 47,116.15 plus interest, but the seller was allowed to set-off with a counterclaim for use which amounted to DM 32,303.34, i.e. more than two-thirds of the purchase price.[49]

The last case also illustrates that even the innocent party must pay the value of the use from the time when it received the object, rather than from the time when the contract is terminated. This is only fair, because the innocent party can likewise claim interest from the time when it paid the contract price to the party in breach.[50] The case also shows that the seller of defective goods can sometimes improve his or her position by an initial refusal of the termination of contract: the longer the buyer keeps the goods, the more this party will have to pay for their use.[51]

However, the innocent party is only liable for any use which it has actually made. If, for instance, the innocent party has obtained possession of real property under the contract which it subsequently terminated, it will have to give up any rent it may have collected from letting the property to a third party (after deducting reasonable expenses) BGB §§ 327 sent.2, 818(1). But if the innocent party has made no use of the real property, it will not be charged for having failed to use this opportunity before the contract was terminated.

In a recent case, the buyer had terminated a contract for the combined sale of a motor yacht, a trailer and a Range Rover on the ground of (alleged) serious defects of the yacht. The buyer had used the car and the trailer to take the yacht to what was then Yugoslavia on 11 May 1989 for a holiday. The yacht allegedly suffered engine failure on 13 May, and on 18 May the buyer declared termination of the entire contract.[52] The Bundesgerichtshof affirmed that any benefit of use gained before knowledge of the right to terminate the contract was subject to unjustified enrichment principles, and approved of the Appeal Court's finding that this aborted trip to Yugoslavia did not amount to an enrichment. Considering that all three objects sold had undeniably been used, this looks puzzling at first sight. However, the underlying reason why the claim was denied is in all likelihood linked to the intended purpose of use: a holiday which is aborted on its second or third day gives everything but the leisure, pleasure and relaxation which the buyer had sought when buying the yacht. This illustrates that the purpose of the failed contract may have a bearing on what is considered benefit of use and what is not.

The most obvious difference to English law, however, is the fact that the party in breach is allowed to recover at all for such benefits in kind.[53] Similar claims were rejected in both *Sumpter* v. *Hedges*[54] and in *Bolton* v.

[49] BGH 26.6.1991, BGHZ 115, 47.

[50] RG 3.7.1934, RGZ 145, 79, at 82.

[51] This problem was discussed in OLG Köln 22.6.1979, OLGZ 1980, 210. Nevertheless, the court held explicitly that the seller's refusal to take back the car, which led to longer use by the plaintiff, did not prevent the seller from counter-claiming the value of use under BGB §§ 347, 987.

[52] BGH 1.4.1992, NJW 1992, 1965.

[53] Goff and Jones, *supra* n 9, 438 *et seq.*

[54] [1898] 1 QB 673.

*Mahadeva*.[55] Both cases concerned construction contracts which were either only partially completed (*Sumpter*) or where the work was deficient (*Bolton*). The defendants terminated the contracts, and the plaintiffs were denied any claim for *quantum meruit*. Under German law, the defendants would have been liable in both cases to the extent that there was a surviving benefit (BGB §818(2), (3) ) at the time when the contract was terminated.[56] This also shows that the rule in BGB §346, replacing value for benefit, is not limited to use of an object and services, but is applied to all situations where benefits cannot be returned due to their very nature.[57]

However, the benefit must be of a kind that was bargained for. In one leading case,[58] the plaintiff leased the defendant's agricultural property and erected a massive building without permission by the defendant, who then terminated the lease. The plaintiff claimed from the defendant the value of this building. This building had been erected not in performance, but in violation of the lease contract, and did therefore not fall under BGB §346. In addition, the Bundesgerichtshof disallowed the claim under unjustified enrichment rules, arguing that the building was imposed on the defendant against his will, and that the building could only be put to commercial use by incurring considerable additional expenses. Rather than paying for the value of the enrichment, the defendant was entitled to remove the building or, if this was unreasonable because of the costs involved, to require the plaintiff to remove the building. The case also illustrates that subjective devaluation can be used as a defence in termination of contract cases only if it concerns a benefit which the recipient had not bargained for.

### *Escape from Bad Bargain*

It has been mentioned that, under BGB §346, where parties have fixed a contractual price for benefits which cannot be returned in kind, this price agreement remains in force in spite of the contract being terminated. This provision is undoubtedly applied in favour of the innocent party (i.e., where the contract price to be paid by the innocent party is lower than market value). There is some uncertainty as to whether it is also applied against the innocent party (i.e. where the innocent party should have paid more than the market value). It would be consistent with the idea of analogous application of BGB §327 sent. 2 (i.e., by applying general unjustified enrichment principles under BGB §818) not to use this provision against the innocent party, which would then be allowed to escape a bad bargain on this account as well, but there seems to be no clear judgment on this question.

[55] [1972] 1 WLR 1009.

[56] This is in fact a solution which is favoured by Burrows, *supra* n 9, 277–9.

[57] Jauernig-Vollkommer, *supra* n 1, §346(4b), Palandt-Heinrichs, *supra* n 1, §346(2cc).

[58] BGH 21.12.1956, BGHZ 23, 61, at 64–5.

### *Change of Position*

The main difference between the liability of a party in breach under BGB §§ 346 *et seq* on the one hand, and of the innocent party under BGB §§ 327 sent. 2, 818 on the other, is that only the latter is allowed to rely on change of position: BGB §818(3).

On second look, however, change of position comes less to the aid of the innocent party which has received benefits in kind than one would think at first sight. As has been mentioned above, BGB §§ 351–353 are nevertheless applied to this party, so that an innocent party which is responsible for the destruction or serious damage to an object which it has received under the contract will not be able to rely on change of position. It has also ben said that there is little difference between BGB §§ 346, 347 on the one hand, and BGB §§ 327 818(1) on the other, when it comes to placing a value on the use which the innocent party has made of an object in its possession. Furthermore, situations will be rare where the innocent party can defeat an action for the value of this use by relying on change of position, and that is mainly for reasons of causation. It will often be assumed that the innocent party would have entered into a contract similar to the one which it terminated, had it not been for the breach of the other party. Therefore, if the innocent party had not bought, e.g., a defective car from the party in breach, it would probably have bought a different car and have suffered depreciation of this car's value by its use. The fact that the innocent party did not suffer such depreciation because it terminated the contract will be considered a saving, so that the use of the car figures as a surviving benefit. For the same causative reasons, the innocent party may not be allowed to deduct those expenses for the upkeeping etc of the enrichment object under change of position which it cannot deduct at any rate from any profit which it has made by the use of the object.[59] However, if the very defects which give rise to the innocent party's right to terminate the contract necessitate additional expenses for upkeep or repair, these could be deducted either directly from what is due for use of the object, or else under change of position.

### *Knowledge Causes "Loss of Innocence"*

It has been mentioned above that, from the time when the innocent party learns of the breach of contract, it will lose the protection afforded by the more lenient unjustified enrichment liability under BGB §§327 sent.2, 818, and fall under the stricter liability according to BGB §§ 346 *et seq*, which has been detailed above at D. It has also been said that the more lenient liability remains in place for any liability which accrued before the innocent party

[59] If it were not for lack of causation, such expenses could be deducted under change of position, see BGH 11.1.1980, NJW 1980, 1790 (concerning construction on real property). See also Schlechtriem, *Schuldrecht Besonderer Teil*, 4th edn (1995) no. 703.

gained knowledge of the breach of contract. However, this rule is not always observed in practice. There are decisions where the innocent party was held liable under BGB §§ 346, 347, 987 for the entire use it had made of goods which it had received under a sales contract, i.e., including use made before knowledge of the defects. One such example is the case which involved the sale of 163 beds to a hotel, which has been discussed above.[60] On the other hand, since there is not much difference between calculating the benefit of use under BGB §818(1) and under §§ 347, 987 respectively, the consequences of this deficiency are often more of an aesthetic than of an economic nature.

## 6. CONCLUSIONS

### *Total Failure of Consideration*

From the perspective of English law, it seems surprising that there is no requirement of total failure of consideration in German law, or indeed of any failure of consideration. As has been shown above, however, this difference can be explained by the following reasons.

(a) With very limited exceptions, a statutory right to terminate a contract arises both in German and English law only for serious breaches of contract. This implies that the innocent party which seeks recovery of money paid will, in one way or another, not have obtained what it should have under the contract.

(b) At any event, the party which seeks recovery of money paid under the contract must in turn give up everything which it has received itself under the contract, be it in kind, or be it in value. Therefore, under both English and German law, one cannot recover the money and keep the benefit at the same time.

(c) A party who nevertheless attempts to do this—i.e. who terminates a contract but continues to use goods or other benefits obtained—may be estopped from claiming back the purchase price under German law.[61]

It is argued that these three rules serve the very same purpose which is behind the English total failure of consideration requirement. However, some differences remain in the practical application. Most obviously, *Hunt* v. *Silk*[62] would have been decided differently by German courts. The tenant would have been allowed to claim back the £10 he had paid for the lease, and be liable for a counterclaim for these of the house under BGB §§ 327 sent. 2, 818(1) for the first 10 days, and under §§ 347, 987 for the few more days he stayed on after it was clear that the landlord would not effectuate the

[60] BGH 26.6.1991, BGHZ 115, 47.

[61] BGH 8.2.1984, NJW 1984, 1525.

[62] (1804) 5 East 449, 102 ER 1142.

promised repairs. On the other hand, an English court in 1997 would not necessarily reach the same decision that was made 1804, i.e. to refuse the tenant's claim in its entirety on the ground that failure of consideration was not total. A point of convergence between German and English law is feasible: the (serious) breach of contract which German law requires in order for the innocent party to terminate the contract could at the same time indicate failure of consideration under English law.

### *Escape from Bad Bargain*

German law allows a party to escape from a bad bargain by terminating the contract if (a) no more has been performed than the payment of money, or (b) if benefits transferred in kind can be returned in kind. However, the picture changes as soon as the nature of the benefit conferred under a contract prevents its restitution in kind, e.g. in construction contracts. Any contractual price on which parties have agreed for this benefit remains in force: BGB §346. This is the only substantial difference to English law on this point.

It can be argued that the rule in BGB §346 creates inconsistency. Why should this be the only situation where a party is not allowed to escape from a bad bargain by terminating the contract? The justification may lie precisely in the different situation. If all benefits conferred under the contract can be returned, the same situation exists as would have without the contract; this is the very purpose of termination of contract. However, if benefits cannot be returned due to their nature, the contract, although terminated, has irreversibly changed the parties' positions. If the contract therefore has this irreversible effect, it might as well serve to determine all the reversal that can be made, i.e. in money. The fact that, e.g., the defendant failed to pay in time for works provided by the plaintiff does not alter the act that the parties have agreed on what the works are worth. The price agreement is not normally affected by the deficiency which leads to the termination of contract. Relying on the price agreement can also avoid lengthy arguments about the value of services provided, or of other benefits.

### *Fortuitous Destruction*

It has been shown *supra*, Parts 2 and 4, that the fortuitous destruction of an object received under the contract does not prevent restitution of the price for this object. Termination of the contract can therefore lead to the situation where one party can claim back its money, while the other gets nothing at all. In case of fortuitous damage to the object, at least the damaged object must be returned, but no compensation is paid for the damage. This operates both ways, i.e. regardless of whether it is the innocent party, or the party in breach, who claims back the object. While the innocent party can avoid this consequence by not terminating the contract, no such choice is given to the party in breach. It does not always seem fair that the risk of fortuitous destruction of goods rests with the seller after these goods have been handed over to the buyer, even if the seller is often to blame for some breach of contract.

### *Survival of the Contract?*

It has been mentioned above that, according to the modern German view, the contract survives in spite of its termination. Rather than making the contract disappear, BGB §§ 346 *et seq* are considered to turn this agreement into a framework for returning the benefits which have been conferred.

This view is not purely terminological. It has been pointed out that the price agreement between the parties continues to determine the value of benefits which, due to their nature, cannot be returned in kind. While English law differs on the last point, it probably agrees on a related issue: the fact that one party has agreed to pay for a certain benefit in the (now terminated) contract prevents this party from raising subjective devaluation as a defence.[63]

It has also been shown in the case of the defective yacht[64] that even a terminated contract will have a bearing on what is and what is not considered a benefit. Furthermore, under both German and English law, parties are free to negotiate consequences of termination in the very contract which subsequently is terminated (subject to general policing, e.g. as regards forfeiture clauses),[65] provisions which therefore survive the termination of contract. Consequently, it is also the intentions of the parties in the (terminated) contracts which decide whether securities provided for the performance of the contract can instead be used to secure the restitutionary claims under BGB §§ 346 *et seq*.[66] Similarly, the contract may have a bearing on the place of performance of restitution, e.g. whether goods need to be brought back to the seller's place, or whether the seller must collect them from the buyer.[67]

Whatever the conceptual approach, it seems fair to say that under both English and German law, the question is not whether some parts of the contract survive, but rather, which parts.

What is striking for English lawyers, though, is that termination of contract excludes all claims for damages for expectation loss in German law.[68] The

[63] See Burrows, *supra* n 9, 269.

[64] BGH 1.4.1992, NJW 1992, 1965.

[65] See e.g. Medicus, *supra* n 1, p. 247, §10 No. 7 AGBG (Standard Contract Terms Act); §§ 13, 18 VerbrKrG (Consumer Credit Act) prevent contract terms which are less favourable to the consumer than §§ 346 *et seq* BGB for hire purchase agreements. For English law, see *Mayson* v. *Clouet* [1924] AC 980; Burrows, *supra* n 9, 272.

[66] BGH 18.11.1968, BGHZ 51, 69, at 73; BGH 26.3.1976, BGHZ 66, 171; see also Jauernig-Vollkommer, *supra* n 1, §346(4a).

[67] According to OLG Hamm 14.9.1981, MDR 1982, 141, the contractual place of performance determines the place of performance of restitution under §346; *contra*: OLG Nürnberg 25.6.1974, NJW 1974, 2237. As regards termination for defective goods (*Wandelung*), however, it is generally agreed that the place where the goods are to be according to the contract is the place of performance for restitution.

[68] BGH 8.12.1989, NJW 1990, 2068. See Schlechtriem, *supra* n 59, no. 428 with further references, and Leser, *supra* n 1, 138 *et seq*.

argument is that since both parties no longer own fulfilment of the main obligations under the contract, they can no longer be liable for failing to perform these obligations. But this is a very conceptual argument, and fails to produce convincing results.[69] At least, the consequences of this doctrine are somewhat mitigated.

First, by terminating a contract, a party does not lose the right to claim damage caused by delay up to the time of termination.[70] Secondly, damage which e.g. defective goods have caused to the buyer's other property must also be compensated.[71] Thirdly, and perhaps most important, in many situations a party will be allowed to reject the other party's performance and claim damages without terminating the contract. This is in particular true for breach of warranty in the sale of goods.[72] Likewise, when a buyer defaults with payment, a seller who has retained title in the goods may claim both damages and return of the goods (the latter under property law).[73] Nevertheless, there remains a residue of cases where a party must face the choice of either claiming back its performance, or damages. But the same can also be true for English law.[74]

It may be worth mentioning that the UN Convention on Contracts for the International Sale of Goods provides restitutionary relief in cases of termination under Arts 81–84. The solutions which this Convention offers do somewhat resemble the position of German law, in particular as regards the survival of some of the contract[75] and the ability of the buyer to terminate the contract even if return of the goods is impossible, as long as the buyer is in no way to blame for this impossibility.[76] On the other hand, the CISG does allow the innocent party to claim damages, and thus avoids this questionable aspect of German law.

### *Preferential Treatment of Innocent Party*

In principle, it is a feature common to English and German law that the innocent party will be treated better than the party in breach when a contract is terminated for breach. It has been said that German courts have achieved this by applying the more lenient model of unjustified enrichment liability to the innocent party from the time when it receives performance or part performance until it gains knowledge of the other party's breach.

[69] It is interesting that the same conceptual approach can be found in *Boomer* v. *Muir* 24 P2d 570 (1933), 577: "But, if the contract is rescinded, the prices fixed by the contract are also rescinded". This fails to explain why the innocent party can nevertheless claim damages, while the German viewpoint fails to explain why BGB §346 provides that the contractual price remains in force.

[70] BGH 24.6.1983, BGHZ 88, 46.

[71] Jauernig-Vollkommer, *supra* n 1, §346(4a), so-called *Mangelfolgeschaden*.

[72] BGB §463, so-called *großer Schadensersatz*; see Jauernig-Vollkommer, *supra* n 1, §463 4c bb.

[73] Jauernig-Vollkommer, *supra* n 1, §326 3b aa.

[74] Burrows, *supra* n 9, 265–6.

[75] CISG, art 81(1).

[76] CISG, art 82(1)(a).

However, if one looks through the case law, one will need a magnifying glass to find any case where this preferential treatment did indeed make any difference.

The fact that only the innocent party is allowed to rely on change of position has the largest potential for preferential treatment. It does indeed account for the most obvious difference when it comes to restitution of money paid under a contract. However, as has been stated above, there are hardly any cases where an innocent party could actually defeat a claim for repayment of money by relying on change of position. And change of position as a defence against restitution for benefits in kind it limited in its practical application. First, BGB §§ 351–353 take precedence so that an innocent party cannot rely on its own negligent damaging or destruction of an object it has received. Secondly, there is very little, if any, difference between calculating benefits of use under BGB § 818(1) on the one hand, and BGB § 987 on the other. It is true that the innocent party cannot be made liable for having failed to make good use of objects in its possession, but then, there is an apparent lack of cases where a party in breach has been held liable on this ground.

All in all, while it is true that the liability imposed on the innocent party is less taxing, it is equally true that this seems rarely to have made any difference in practice.[77] One wonders, therefore, whether it was worth spilling all that ink, and leading such heated discussions, on whether or not BGB § 327 sent. 2 should be applied by analogy in order to protect the innocent party.

Moreover, courts seem occasionally forgetful of the distinction they have created. In all cases where the innocent party continued to use the object for some time after gaining knowledge of the other party's breach, courts should, in principle, calculate the value of the use under BGB §§ 327 sent. 2, 818(1) for the time from the receipt until knowledge of the breach, and under BGB §§ 347, 987 from that time until the time of the return of the object. However, one can find many judgments where courts have simply not made this distinction, including the hotel bed case decided by the Bundesgerichtshof.[78]

If, on the other hand, this analysis is wrong, and the different model of liability really does make difference, it becomes difficult to justify this difference in treatment when compared with the exercise of a contractually stipulated right to terminate the contract. As BGB §§ 346 *et seq* are directly applicable, no exception can be made for the innocent party. This may be justified on the ground that a party which has stipulated a termination clause in a contract is always aware that it may eventually have to return benefits. On the other hand, in practice, contractual rights to terminate a contract are usually stipulated as a remedy for breach of contract, and in particular for delay. This means that a party who was prudent enough to stipulate a right to terminate

[77] Similarly Staudinger-Kaiser, *supra* n 1, §347 no 59.

[78] BGH 26.6.1991, BGHZ 115, 47. Staudinger-Kaiser, *supra* n 1, §347 no 59 quotes seven OLG judgments where no such distinction was made; unfortunately, these judgments are not accessible to me at the moment.

a contract as soon as the other party delays performance will be held more strictly liable than a party which has not stipulated such a right and instead goes through BGB §326 in order to terminate the contract on the ground of delay. Thus, the prudent, but not terribly clever party might be punished—a result which German law would normally be keen to avoid.

*BGB (German Civil Code)*[79] *§§ 327, 346–353*

**§ 327 [Regulation of the statutory right to terminate a contract]**
The rules on a contractually stipulated right to terminate a contract under §§ 346–356 apply accordingly to the right to terminate a contract under §§ 325, 326. If termination occurs due to a circumstance for which the other party is not responsible, that party is only liable under the rules which govern the return of an unjustified enrichment.

**§ 346 [Effects of termination]**
If in a contract one party has reserved his right to terminate, and if termination occurs, the parties are obliged to return to each other the performances which they have received. For services rendered, or for permitting the use of a corporeal object, the value must be paid; if the contract specifies a counter-performance in money, this must be paid.

**§ 347 [Liability in case of return]**
In case of termination, claims for damages for deterioration, perishing, or impossibility of return for any other reason, are determined, from the time of receipt of the performance, by those provisions which apply to the relationship between the owner of a corporeal object and the possessor from the time when an action for return of the object becomes pending. The same applies to claims for the surrender, or for the value of any benefits, and to claims for reimbursement of expenditure. A sum of money carries interest from the time when it was received.

**§ 348 [Performance upon tender of counter-performance]**
Obligations between parties which arise from the termination are to be performed upon tender of counter-performance. The provisions of §§ 320, 322 apply accordingly.

**§ 349 [Declaration of termination]**
Termination occurs by declaration towards the other party.

[79] Headings in square brackets are not part of the Code, and are modelled on those chosen for the C.H. Beck edition of the German original. Translation by G. Dannemann.

**§ 350 [Accidental perishing]**
Termination is not excluded by the fact that an object, which the party entitled to termination has received, has accidentally perished.

**§ 351 [Culpable perishing]**
Termination is excluded if the party entitled to termination is to blame for the fact that the object received has materially deteriorated or perished, or that its return has become impossible in another way. Perishing of a considerable part of the object is equal to material deterioration, and culpability of another party for which the entitled party is responsible under §278 is equal to the entitled party's own culpability.

**§ 352 [Processing or transformation]**
Termination is excluded if the party entitled to termination has changed the object received into another object by way of processing or transformation.

**§ 353 [Passing on or encumbrance]**
(1) If the party entitled to termination passes on, or charges with third party rights, the object received, or a considerable part thereof, termination is excluded if the requirements set forth in §351 or in §352 have been met in the hand of the person who has received the object by such disposition.

(2) A disposition which occurs by enforcement of a judgment or attachment order, or by an administrator in bankruptcy, is treated the same as a disposition by the party entitled to terminate the contract.

# 10

# *Failure of Long-Term Contracts and the Duty to Re-negotiate*

ERICH SCHANZE

## 1. INTRODUCTION

One scarcely expects to find in the standard textbook treatment of contract remedies a chapter on a remedy providing a duty to re-negotiate a contract. This is at least true for important legal orders, such as the English and American common law, French law or German law. Even in more specialised texts on frustration and contracts, such as the recent treatise of Professor Treitel on frustration and *force majeure*, the keyword "duty to re-negotiate" does not show up, and there are only a few remarks on contract modification under the general heading of "mitigations of the principle of discharge".[1] Treitel makes specific reference to the German doctrine of the disappearance of the base of contract (*Wegfall der Geschäftsgrundlage*) and the French doctrine of *imprévision* where under very limited circumstances a contract may be modified by court intervention only.[2] Although there are slight differences from a comparative law perspective, the legal principle remains the discharge of obligations under specified extremely narrow defined circumstances.

As a matter of commercial practice, however, contracts which become impracticable, are frequently re-negotiated by the parties, even under factual pressures or circumstances which would not amount to the classical legal standard for discharge. Moreover, in the drafting process, parties stipulate "soft" excuse clauses in advance, particularly on specific "hardships" relating to the contract. There is a rich literature in the international contract setting on the various types of clauses basically informing the draftspersons of complex contracts for contract planning.[3] In a comparative report[4] Professor Horn lists—in addition to those instances where *force majeure*, impossibility or

[1] G.H. Treitel, *Frustration and Force Majeure* (London, 1994), 530–5.

[2] *Ibid.*, 530.

[3] Excellent concise treatment in M. Bartels, *Contractual Adaptation and Conflict Resolution* (Frankfurt, Deventer, 1985). Cf. also W. Peter, *Arbitration and Renegotiation of International Investment Agreements* (Dordrecht et al., 1986); H. Merkt, *Investitionsschutz durch Stabilisierungsklauseln* (Heidelberg, 1990) and N. Nassar, *Sanctity of Contract Revisited* (Dordrecht et al., 1995).

[4] N. Horn, "Die Anpassung langfristiger Verträge im internationalen Wirtschaftsverkehr", in H. Kötz et al. (eds), *Die Anpassung langfristiger Verträge* (Frankfurt, 1984), 9–71.

special risks are defined in a contract as reasons for excuse—a set of clauses which are geared toward adaption of the "internal" balance of contracts including:

(a) clauses in which one party may implement and change the contract in view of new information on changed circumstances;
(b) escalation clauses concerning prices, qualities and other items; clauses against currency risks;
(c) most favoured clauses;
(d) stabilisation clauses concerning the change of local laws;
(e) tax adjustment clauses; and
(f) general revision clauses of the contract.

All these clauses may eventually lead to re-negotiation of the contract if they do not change the contract automatically.

## 2. TOWARD A NEW GENERAL DUTY TO RE-NEGOTIATE CONTRACTS IN CASES OF CONTRACT FAILURE?

### *Two Schools of Thought*

There are two fundamental doctrinal reactions to the visible divergence between a relatively stiff "legal" treatment of discharge by court intervention and the relatively liberal treatment of re-negotiation in contracting practice.

One school of thought, including contract lawyers, such as Professors Fontaine[5] in Belgium, Horn[6] in Germany and Schmitthoff[7] in England, have inferred from contractual practice that there is an implicit change of general contract rules. Put simply: courts should observe contract practice and align their rules to this "softer" practice. Hence, scholars such as Horn argue that there is a general principle of a duty to re-negotiate contracts which are impracticable. In a similar direction Schmitthoff has advanced the view that standardised hardship clauses including re-negotiation clauses should be used in a commercial context.[8]

The other school of thought points out that courts ought to maintain their rigid position precisely in view of the factual drafting options. Again put simply: the more courts emphasize the strict principle of enforcement of the original contract, the more parties are forced to stipulate in detail the risk distribution in clauses for specific contractual contingencies.

[5] M. Fontaine, "Les clauses de hardship" (1976) 2 *DPCI* 51 *et seq.*
[6] N. Horn, *supra* n 4.
[7] C. Schmitthoff, "Hardship and Intervener Clauses" [1980] *JBL* 82 *et seq.*
[8] *Supra* n 7.

### *The New Lando Proposal*

The first school of thought who would invite courts to take a more interventionist stance has recently received support from a group of distinguished comparative lawyers from a number of major European jurisdictions who have formed a working group for formulating "Principles of European Contract Law" headed by the senior Danish contract lawyer Professor Ole Lando.[9] For the problem of contract failure the Lando group has formulated "a general principle" of a "duty to re-negotiate". This duty is not only proposed for specific classes of contracts, such as long-term contracts, but for all situations in which, during the time between the conclusion of the agreement and its execution, there are "changes of circumstances" that may make "the performance of the contract excessively onerous".

Article 2.117 of the Principles of European Contract Law reads:

> " (1) A party is bound to fulfil his obligations even if performance has become more onerous, whether because the cost of performance has increased or because the value of the performance he receives has diminished.
>
> (2) If, however, performance of the contract becomes excessively onerous because of a change of circumstances, the parties are bound to enter into negotiations with a view to adapting the contract or terminating it, provided that:
>
> (a) the change of circumstances occurred after the time of conclusion of the contract, or had already occurred at that time but was not and could not reasonably have been known to the parties; and
>
> (b) the possibility of a change of circumstances was not one which could reasonably have been taken into account at the time of conclusion of the contract; and
>
> (c) the risk of the change of circumstances is not one which, according to the contract, the party affected should be required to bear.
>
> (3) If the parties fail to reach agreement within a reasonable period, the court may:
>
> (a) terminate the contract at a date and on terms to be determined by the court; or
>
> (b) adapt the contract in order to distribute between the parties in a just and equitable manner the losses and gains resulting from the change of circumstances; and
>
> (c) in either case, award damages for the loss suffered through the other party refusing to negotiate or breaking off negotiations in bad faith."

In explaining the principle of "excessive onerosity" the Lando group also envisages increased cost[10]:

> "The 'excessive onerosity' may be the direct result of increased cost in performance—for example, the increased cost of transport if the Suez Canal is closed and

[9] O. Lando and H. Beale (eds), *Principles of European Contract Law* (Dordrecht et al., 1995); reprinted in F.D. Rose, *Blackstone's Statutes on Contract, Tort and Restitution*, 7th edn (London, 1996) 374.

[10] Beale and Lando, *supra* n 9, at p. 115.

ships have to be sent round the Cape of Good Hope. Or, as the paragraph states, it may be the result of the expected counter-performance becoming valueless; for example if the cost of building work which has already been executed is to be determined by reference to some index of a price which collapses in a quite unforeseeable way. In neither situation is it possible to give precise rules to cover the diversity of situations which may arise.

*Illustration* 1: A canning business buys the whole of a producer's future crop of tomatoes at 10 pence per kilo. It cannot demand renegotiation when by harvest time the market price has fallen to 5 pence per kilo because of an unexpected flood of imported tomatoes.

*Illustration* 2: A contract is made to supply for irrigation for 50 years at a fixed price but the price becomes derisory through inflation. The supplier may be able to demand renegotiation."

If the required renegotiation is not conducted in good faith, there may be damages for the harm caused by the refusal to renegotiate and so on. If the negotiation fails, the court may intervene.

The Lando group seems to be aware that the proposed "principle" deviates substantially from the conventional principles of national European contract laws. Thus they state that "the mechanism reflects the modern trend towards giving the court some power to moderate the rigours of freedom and the sanctity of contract". Moreover, the group points to the non-mandatory nature of the "principles".[11]

### *Criticism of the Lando Proposal and a General Hardship Clause*

Is it really correct that the tendency reflects a *new trend* towards giving the court more power to moderate the "sanctity" of contract? It is true that—for a period of 20 years between 1965 and 1985—courts seemed to assume a more interventionist position in contract law.[12] In the areas of labour law and consumer law these trends persisted and were strengthened by EC directives. But this practice never reached commercial transactions.

It was especially the law and economics movement starting in the middle of the 1970s which pointed to the excessive cost of paternalism.[13] The more recent contract literature, by applying the insights of the modern economics of information and risk-bearing, has isolated specific instances where paternalism is warranted or where it leads to mere redistribution. The argument of the Lando group that the rule of a duty to re-negotiate is non-mandatory helps very little. It would require extreme sophistication of the parties to pick and choose among the single rules of the "principles" of European contract law for an individual contract. Either the rule makes sense as an appropriate system of risk distribution for all contracts, or it should be abandoned.

[11] Beale and Lando, *supra* n 9, at 113.

[12] cf. E. Schanze, "New Directions in Contract Research", in B. Dahl and R. Nielsen (eds), *New Directions in Business Law Research* (Copenhagen, 1996), 61–72.

[13] Summary: M.I. Trebilcock, *The Limits of Freedom of Contract* (Cambridge Mass., 1993), 147–63.

This situation is similar to that of recommending general hardship clauses with a duty to renegotiate as in the earlier proposals by Professor Schmithoff. To be very brief on this point, which has been discussed in more detail in the international contract literature[14]: from an empirical viewpoint general hardship clauses of this kind are much rarer than one would assume from the theoretical literature in contract practice. In the 1980s we have studied 200 major mining contracts, and we did not find a single *general* hardship clause. Most well-advised parties try to spell out the contractual risks and, if needed, look for automatic adjustment clauses. The reasons are fourfold:

(a) There are no proper criteria for the seriousness of "re-negotiations" e.g., what degree of compromise is sufficient? The determination of a violation of a duty to renegotiate in good faith is largely discretionary.
(b) The bargaining process refers to the classical situation of the bilateral monopoly where results are unpredictable.
(c) The necessity of renegotiation may be used as a stratagem for impeding final decisions of the parties.
(d) Discharge or suspension poses the correct incentive for effective re-negotiation.

### *Re-negotiation and Pre-existing Duties*

A duty—or its possible corollary, a right—to re-negotiate, implies a sufficient *reason* for change. The law and economics literature has pointed out that opportunism of the party benefitting from change would be invited if "easy" re-negotiation options would be granted.

Indeed, policing this issue seems to be a fundamental concern of contract law. According to the Lando proposal those situations should eventually give rise to a re-negotiation where there is a risk which was unforeseen by either party. Nevertheless, even in this case one might leave the new risk where it lies for encouraging the parties to make a reasonable risk analysis *ex ante*.

It is frequently sound to devise overshooting sanctions for enhancing a specific value maximising behaviour. Thus, for example, a sensible rule for allowing "efficient" breach would probably add a lump sum damage item to the expectation damages for policing opportunistic behaviour of the breaching party in view of the procedural risks of enforcing the damage claim. Such a proposal would add some realism to the model theory of efficient breach.

If one looks at the civil law literature on re-negotiation and adaptation this point is frequently overlooked. At least on first inspection, German law, for example, would enforce a re-negotiated contract simply if it is "voluntary". The defendant party who has signed the new contract would have to show that the factual pressure of the other side was *contra bonos mores*.[15] As far as

[14] Cf. references *supra* n 3.
[15] BGB §138.

I can see, there is no systematic relation between the requirements for contract termination (in long-term contracts: "serious reason": "wichtiger Grund") and the validity of the new contract.

Despite some criticism voiced by my distinguished colleague Professor Hein Kötz,[16] I support the common law doctrine of pre-existing duty as a part of the doctrine of consideration in its recent modification in the case of *Williams* v. *Roffey Bros and Nicholls (Contractors) Ltd.*[17]

Even if one does not subscribe to all arabesques of the doctrine of consideration, the modern variant of the pre-existing duty rule shows concern for policing unreasonable re-negotiation by technically shifting the burden of proof. In essence *Williams* v. *Roffey* leaves it to the party striking the advantageous new deal to show that it was beyond the pre-existing contractual duty. The court speaks of "commercial advantage to both sides".[18]

The economist Professor Dnes has pointed to the important fact that the miscalculation was completely on the subcontractor's side, hence it was his risk.[19] However, under the circumstances which involved no duress, the contractor himself had made the commercially sound proposal to go ahead under the new agreement.

Unlike the well-known authorities on the pre-existing duty doctrine, this re-negotiation literally did not happen on the high seas. Glidewell LJ correctly points to a necessary compliance between the pre-existing duty doctrine and the doctrine of economic duress as an excuse for breach, and hence a reason for "termination" of the old agreement.[20] This does not mean that the pre-existing duty rule is part of a more general doctrine of economic duress.[21]

If one takes the lesson from this related problem and applies it to the problem of re-negotiation, re-negotiation only makes doctrinal sense if the party aggrieved by the breach either freely offers a new contract, or both parties are entitled to terminate the agreement anyway. This is at least all that the *law* can say in regulating the problem. If the parties realise in this situation that there are mutual gains from the new agreement, as in the situation of *Williams* v. *Roffey*, they will conclude that agreement. To argue, however, that the parties in this instance have a *duty* to re-negotiate is overshooting paternalism; they have a mere *option* to re-negotiate. Again, if we find empirically a high frequency of re-negotiation we cannot infer that this practice is based on an implicit legal rule. The standard reason is mutual benefit, or in the terms of *Williams* v. *Roffey*, "commercial advantage to both sides".[22]

[16] H. Kötz, *Europäisches Vertragsrecht* (Tübingen, 1996), 106–7.

[17] [1991] 1 QB 1, CA.

[18] *Ibid.*, 22, per Purchas LJ.

[19] A.W. Dnes, "The Law and Economics of Contract Modifications: The Case of *Williams* v. *Roffey*" (1996) 16 *International Review of Law and Economics*.

[20] [1991] 1 QB 1, at 13 seq.

[21] But see Kötz, *supra* n 16.

[22] *Supra* n 18.

Thus, the general rule of requiring—as a matter of law—renegotiation in cases of change of circumstances as proposed in Article 2.117 of the Principles of European Contract Law, or to invite parties to use general hardship clauses with the same effect, is much too broad.

## 3. DELIMITING THE SCOPE OF A DUTY TO RE-NEGOTIATE TO APPROPRIATE CASES—AND ALTERNATIVES

### *Duration*

Adaptation of contracts will be a necessary item on the agenda of drafting if the contract runs over an extended time period. Mention was made of the practice of using automatic adjustment clauses, for example escalation clauses or currency clauses. Another option is to ask an expert, e.g. an engineer, to make discretionary adjustment in accordance with standard engineering and business practice. In their cases and materials, Beale, Bishop and Furmston refer correctly to the ICE conditions.[23] Similar approaches are found in the FIDIC conditions. These schemes underline the argument against general re-negotiation clauses. The expert party is empowered with discretion precisely because it is assumed that the parties will not reach an agreement by re-negotiation. And if they want to re-negotiate they will reach an agreement before the expert steps in.

The mere duration of a contract does not warrant a different treatment of contracts. The character of performances and risks may be asserted for the future. Indeed, contracts are, as Lon Fuller has correctly argued in his famous article on the reliance interest,[24] instruments which make future values into present values respecting the fact that in view of the protection of the expectation interest other opportunities are foregone. In this sense all legally relevant contracts are always "long-term", because they relate to future events.

Even if future acts are planned through present consensus it is instructive that contract doctrine has largely neglected the aspect of the difference of contracts of long duration and the example of the sales transaction. The writing of Ian Macneil[25] has drawn special attention to long-term relations although—as I have detailed elsewhere—it was largely a misunderstanding of economists such as Goldberg and Williamson that ultimately lead to a new theory of long-term contracting. Macneil has a different contract theory in mind, which was never conceived as a theory of long-term contracts.[26]

[23] H.G. Beale, W.D. Bishop and M.P. Furmston, *Contract—Cases and Materials*, 3rd edn (London, 1995), Ch 28.

[24] L.L. Fuller and W.R. Perdue Jr., "The Reliance Interest in Contract Damages (1936) 46 *Yale L.J.* 52, 59–63.

[25] I. Macneil, *The New Social Contract* (New Haven, 1980).

[26] I have explained that in detail: E. Schanze, "Symbiotic Contracts: Exploring Long-Term Agency Structures Between Contract and Corporation", in Ch. Joerges (ed), *Franchising and the Law: Theoretical and Comparative Approaches in Europe and the United States* (Baden-Baden, 1991) 67, 87–8.

### *Treatment of Some Long-Term Contracts in the German Civil Code*

In the civil law literature long-term contracts have been an old topic. In Germany, for example, some types and problems of long-term contracting were treated explicitly in the Civil Code. There, for example, the simple society is treated in the law of obligations[27]—a matter which would never have been treated in an English text on contract. Likewise, labour law[28] and landlord and tenant law[29] are covered, in more or less detail, in the Code. Here, issues of adaptation and modifications are standard.

Neither the German law of societies, nor of services nor of leases, contain duties to re-negotiate in a simple form. Specific systems of adaptation were either in the Code or evolved over time. In the area of landlord and tenant adaptation was originally treated by concluding sequential contracts of a specific time. Since the problem of hold-up is evident, we nowadays face a complicated adjustment scheme regulated in a specific statute on adaptation of leases which contains a limited duty of re-negotiation within a certain price range.[30]

For labour contracts the adjustment took an even more elaborate structure through the German system of collective bargaining, which has a much stronger normative component than the British or American counterpart. In case of successful collective bargaining it is standard that the result is declared universal (*Allgemeinverbindlichkeitserklärung*).[31]

The most sophisticated system of "re-negotiation" takes place in the system of the law of societies which is the basis of company law. Here, the fundamental structure of the relation is formulated in the contract. The contract itself is a scheme of adaptation through voting, including the important idea of majority vote.

It is clear that the practice of international drafting has tried to introduce all these mechanisms derived from qualified long-term relations into international long-term business relations which require adaptation.

[27] German Civil Code (BGB), §§ 705 *et seq.*

[28] *Ibid.*, §§ 611 *et seq.*

[29] *Ibid.*, §§ 535 *et seq.*

[30] Statute Concerning the Regulation of the Amount of Rent of December 1974, BGBL I, pp. 3603, 3604.

[31] cf. Statute on Collective Bargaining (*Tarifvertragsgesetz*).

### *Hostages and Sunk Investment as Characteristics of Long-Term Contracts*

Returning to contract theory, a preliminary theoretical synthesis was reached when Goldberg[32], Klein,[33] Williamson[34] and others analysed long-term relations from an incentive perspective and stressed that not only duration and intensity of the relation matter but that "hostages" and "sunk investment" may be characteristic of these relations.

Combining these insights with the Coasean paradigm of markets and hierarchies,[35] it was Williamson in particular who pointed out that a discrete structure of "hybrids" was discernible—located between market (= contract) and hierarchy (= firm, corporate organisation).[36]

The economic literature is difficult for lawyers to understand, because it uses contract in two meanings. Contract in Williamson's terms is basically the market contract, e.g. the sales transaction. Contract, in terms of Alchian and Demsetz,[37] is also a general mode of bilateral and multilateral transacting embracing the corporation as a "nexus of contracts" between the corporate actors, and "hybrids" as special forms of complex "contract".

### *Symbiotic Arrangements*

By introducing the term of "symbiotic arrangements"[38] I have tried to isolate phenomena between classic contract (covered by contract law) and

[32] V.P. Goldberg, "Toward an Expanded Economic Theory of Contract" (1976) 10 *Journal of Economic Issues*; "Regulation and administered contracts (1976) 7 *Bell Journal of Economics*, 426; "Relational Exchange-Economics and Complex Contracts", (1988) 23 *American Behavioral Scientist* 337; (ed), *Readings in the economics of contract law* (Cambridge-New York et al., 1989).

[33] B. Klein, R.G. Crawford and A.A. Alchian, "Vertical Integration, Appropriable Rents, and the Competitive Contracting Process" (1978) 27 *Journal of Law and Economics* 297.

[34] O.E. Williamson, "The economics of defense contracting: incentives and performance", in National Bureau of Economic Research (ed), *Issues in Defense Economics* (New York, 1967) 218; "Franchise bidding for natural monopolies—in general and with respect to CATV" (1976) 7 *Bell Journal of Economics* 73.

[35] R.H. Coase, "The Nature of the Firm" (1937) 4 *Economica* 386, reprinted with comments in R.H. Coase, *The Firm, the Market and the Law* (Chicago and London, 1988) 33; cf. also R.H. Coase, "Lectures: The Nature of the Firm: Origin, Meaning, Influence" (1988) 4 *Journal of Law and Economics* 3 and the related papers by Rosen, Williamson, Joskow, Hart, Demsetz, Winter, Masten and Klein, *ibid.*, 49–213. Cf. also the earlier collection of views and comments on the nature of the firm, with contributions by Bösmann, Williamson, Brinkmann and Kübler, Manne, Schanze, Furubotn, Bonus, Albach, Baetge and Fischer (1981) 137 *Journal of Institutional and Theoretical Economics* 665–732.

[36] For detail cf. E. Schanze, *supra* n 26, and "Symbiotic Arrangements" (1993) 149 *Journal of Institutional and Theoretical Economics* 691–7.

[37] The classic is: A.A. Alchian and H. Demsetz, "Production, Information Costs and Economic Organization" (1972) 62 *American Economic Review* 775–95. For a recent review of the literature cf. O. Hart and B. Holmström, "The Theory of Contracts", in T.F. Bewley (ed), *Advances in Economic Theory* (Cambridge et al., 1987) 71–153. Cf. also the collection by G. Bamberg and K. Spremann (ed), *Agency Theory, Information and Incentives* rev. ed. (Heidelberg, 1989).

[38] See *supra* n 36.

corporation (covered by company law) which share some characteristics of either but are, indeed, "hybrids" in the sense that they employ both features of contract law as well as features of company law. Six properties of these arrangements, which include *inter alia* complex forms of franchising, of subcontracting and of joint venturing, may be specified[39]:

(1) a voluntary, tendentially Pareto superior long-term engagement of discrete firms;
(2) that is typically spelled out, and ratified in a contractual document;
(3) a strong conceptual link between the partners that is typically expressed in a branded product, a design, or a specific common task; hence: "cooperation by concept";
(4) the dedication of sizeable non-recoverable assets in view of the engagement;
(5) an implicit or overt asymmetry between the partners (substantial parity is a special case);
(6) the stipulation of various rights to determine, to monitor, and to sanction "contractual" behaviour and performance of the other party—the introduction of partially crossing principal-agent relations on various transactional levels of the general relation based on a contractual interface.

Professor Collins, in his textbook,[40] and in a couple of articles,[41] has clarified the meaning of crossed principal-agent relations. In standard contracting, either the character of performance or at least the result is specified. In symbiotic contracting the parties are tied in a working relationship which is constantly adapted by both parties to the requirements of the outside market. The franchisor revises constantly the franchise scheme, and he polices the performance of the adapted scheme among his franchisees. The franchisees, on the other hand, are required to produce constant feedback on the practical implementation. In a sense, there is an ongoing re-negotiation, and explicit duties to re-negotiate in pursuance of the goal of optimising the overall economic scheme.

Interestingly enough, some franchise systems have introduced "councils" which may vote on specific issues.[42] Moreover—especially in the area of automobile franchises—we find forms of "collective bargaining". Dealers create

[39] E. Schanze, "Symbiotic Arrangements", *supra* n 36, at 691–7.

[40] H. Collins, *The Law of Contract*, 2nd edn (London et al., 1993), especially 9–10 and 280–2; "Independent Contractors and the Challenge of Vertical Disintegration to Employment Protection Laws" (1990) 14 *OJLS* 353.

[41] H. Collins, "Why are There Contracts of Employment?" (1993) 149 *Journal of Institutional and Theoretical Economics* 762; "Legal Regulation of Dependent Entrepreneurs—Comment" (1996) 152 *Journal of Institutional and Theoretical Economics* 263.

[42] E. Schanze, *supra* n 26, at p. 96.

coalitions for interest representation, including pressure groups which have, for example in the USA, successfully influenced the franchise legislation.[43]

Further research on these alternatives to "duties to re-negotiate" in long-term relations is critically needed. I have noted with pleasure that there is an increasing interest in Great Britain to investigate these issues, which go beyond classical contract law and remedies.

[43] St. Macaulay, "Long-Term Continuing Relations: The American Experience Regulating Dealerships and Franchises", in Ch. Joerges (ed), *Franchising and the Law* (Baden-Baden, 1991) 179.

# 11

# *Failure of Long-Term Contracts and the Duty to Re-negotiate—A Comment*

GEOFFREY SAMUEL

Professor Schanze's chapter on the duty to re-negotiate in long-term contracts is of interest to comparative lawyers on two levels. The first level is the immediate topic itself. Here Professor Schanze raises a number of legitimate concerns with respect to the Lando Commission's provision in the Principles of European Contract Law that EU contract law ought to recognise a duty to re-negotiate in situations where "performance of the contract becomes excessively onerous because of a change of circumstances".[1] Professor Schanze is concerned that this duty is far too widely stated and he questions the Lando view that the provision reflects "the modern trend towards giving the court some power to moderate the rigours of freedom and the sanctity of contract". He refers to the English decision of *Williams* v. *Roffey & Nicholls (Contractors) Ltd*[2] to make the point that these factual situations which involve an apparent re-negotiation do not, and should not, be used as the basis for the induction of a general duty. *Roffey* is a situation best explained by its own particular facts and it gives rise, not to a *duty* to re-negotiate, but merely to an *option*. Whatever the other civil lawyers might make of this view, there are probably few common lawyers who would dissent from this opinion of Professor Schanze. Leaving aside the general reluctance of the English judiciary ever to extend a precedent beyond its own facts, *Roffey*, although probably rightly decided, is a case confined to its own rather special circumstances, involving, not the question of any "duty" to negotiate, but the descriptive existence or non-existence of consideration and duress. A small change of fact might well have led to a very different outcome. Common lawyers are, of course, more than prepared to think in terms of duties, but only in a particular way. They are on the whole reluctant to consider duties outside of either the remedy (damages, rescission, injunction) or any sets of facts through, or within, which the duty finds expression. For example, in the

1 Art 2.117(2).
2 1991] 1 QB 1.

law of tort, the attempt in *Anns* v. *Merton LBC*[3] to locate duty in an abstract normative proposition has been abandoned; the approach to reasoning is now one that functions only at the level of the facts themselves which, in effect, means that the "complex syllogism"[4] has been replaced by reasoning by analogy and policy.[5] In contract the House of Lords has shown a similar distaste for the broad normative principles such as good faith in its judgment in *Walford* v. *Miles*.[6] Outside of statute, good faith is something that finds expression in the common law only indirectly through particular remedies or specific rules dealing with specific kinds of circumstances.[7]

The second level at which Professor Schanze's chapter engages the comparative jurist is the more abstract one of ideas. Professor Schanze's analysis alludes to a number of rather interesting themes and notions, of which several are deserving of comment. However, for reasons of space, this commentary will restrict itself to the most powerful theme underpinning his chapter. This theme is the notion of time as it relates to the law of obligations.

The theme of a duty to re-negotiate in long-term contracts raises the whole question of time in relation to law and to legal reasoning. This theme has directly emerged in one or two recent tort cases—for example in the "historic pollution" problem of *Cambridge Water Co* v. *Eastern Counties Leather Plc*[8]—and it is fundamental to the remoteness cases in contract. A contractor is liable, according to the Code Civil, only for the damages that could have been contemplated (*ont été prévus*) at the time of the contract.[9] Going back in time in order to contemplate, or foresee, a future which has in fact matured in a particular way illustrates the paradoxes that face any "scientific" (*scientia iuris*) model that tries to rationalise what is essentially a huge and complex empirical object more than prone to the uncertainties generated by chaos. It is the existence of chaos which acts as the *raison d'être* of the scientific model; yet the problem facing the contract model is that there is an inherent tension, not just between the time factors surrounding the litigation facts and the formation of the contract, but also between certainty and reasoning. A long-term contract is an attempt to control the uncertainties of the long-term future and it might seem obvious that the starting point of those who have to interpret and apply the contract is the highly developed normative proposition that contracts have the binding force of legislation.[10] Time and circumstance are not factors to be taken into consideration when it comes to enforcing what the parties have clearly agreed between themselves.[11] However the reasoner,

[3] [1978] AC 728.
[4] *FA & AB Ltd* v. *Lupton* [1972] AC 634, 658–9.
[5] See e.g. *Goodwill* v. *Pregnancy Advisory Service* [1996] 1 WLR 1397, 1399.
[6] [1992] 2 AC 128, 138.
[7] *Interfoto* v. *Stiletto Visual Programmes Ltd* [1989] QB 433, 435, 439, 445.
[8] [1994] 2 AC 264.
[9] Code Civil, art 1150; *Hadley* v. *Baxendale* (1854) 9 Exch 341; 156 ER 145.
[10] Code civil, art 1134.
[11] See, e.g., Cass. civ. 6.mars 1876, D.1876.I.193.

when faced with specific factual litigation problems, not only cannot in truth ever infer a result from a normative proposition however clear the text—for there is always an *entre deux* between proposition and solution.[12] The reasoner may in addition be faced with counterbalancing concepts such as *l'intérêt général*, whose normativity, or quasi-normativity, can be equally powerful in suggesting a solution.[13] Reasoning in law is not a matter of inference, but a question of argumentation; and, once this point is properly appreciated—as indeed it is even in civil law[14]—the easier it becomes to see that time can exert its influence in ways that cannot always be captured by the symbolic representations of knowledge functioning in terms of an algorithm. In other words, there is more to legal knowledge than the propositional rule.

Take for example *Staffordshire Area Health Authority* v. *South Staffs Waterworks*.[15] In this case a Health Authority sought a declaration as to whether a contract under seal made in 1929 between it and a water company could be determined by the water company on reasonable notice and without the consent of the Health Authority. Lord Denning MR explained the background to the case:[16]

> "The water company feel that the time has come when the hospital authorities should pay a more reasonable rate. In order to accomplish this, they assert that the 1929 agreement is determinable by six months' notice. Accordingly, on 30th September 1975 they gave notice to the hospital authorities to terminate the agreement as from 30th April 1976. They said that they were quite prepared to supply 5,000 gallons a day free of charge, but they would have to charge for the excess at their normal rate. The area health authority refused to accept this notice as valid. So an originating summons was taken out to determine the matter. Foster J held that the agreement of 1929 was to last forever: and that the hospital authorities could take all the water they desired from the mains at the rate of seven old pence (that is 2.9p) per 1,000 gallons in perpetuity. The water company appeal to this court"

The problem of course was the inflation that had occurred since 1929. Now, for Lord Denning MR, this inflation over time was something of which the court should directly take account when interpreting the written contract of 1929. However, rather than focusing upon the words themselves, Lord Denning in effect created a hypothetical factual situation:[17]

> "As I understand this modern rule, we are no longer to go by the strict construction of the words as judges did in the 19th century. We are to put ourselves in the same situation as the parties were in at the time they drew up the instrument, to sit

[12] Ost and Van de Kerchove, *Le droit ou les paradoxes du jeu* (Paris, PUF, 1992), 50–70.

[13] See, e.g., CE 30 mars 1916; D.1916.3.25, *Gaz de Bordeaux*.

[14] Bergel, *Théorie générale du droit*, 2nd edn (Paris, Dalloz, 1989) 267–81; Stamatis, *Argumenter en droit: Une théorie critique de l'argumentation juridique* (Paris, Publisud, 1995).

[15] [1979] 1 WLR 1387; noted Rose (1980) 96 *LQR* 177.

[16] [1979] 1 WLR 1387, 1393–4.

[17] *Ibid.*, 1395.

> in their chairs with our minds endowed with the same facts as theirs were, and envisage the future with the same degree of foresight as they did. So placed we have to ask ourselves: what were the circumstances in which the contract was made? Does it apply in the least to the new situation which has developed? If events occur for which they have made no provision, and which were outside the realm of their speculations altogether, or of any reasonable persons sitting in their chairs, then the court itself must take a hand and hold that the contract ceases to bind"

The image created by the judge was one of two humans incapable of speculating so far into the future and from this image he went on to induce a proposition:[18]

> "I do not think that the water company could have determined the agreement immediately after it was made. That cannot have been intended by the parties. No rule of construction could sensibly permit such a result. But, in the past 50 years, the whole situation has changed so radically that one can say with confidence: 'The parties never intended that the supply should be continued in these days at that price'. Rather than force such unequal terms on the parties, the court should hold that the agreement could be and was properly determined in 1975 by the reasonable notice of six months. This does not mean, of course, that on the expiry of the notice the water company can cut off the supply to the hospital. It will be bound to continue it. All that will happen is that *the parties will have to negotiate fresh terms of payment*"

Lord Denning was indeed suggesting, within this particular factual situation, a principle of re-negotiation; and, had he been supported by the other two judges in this approach, the *Staffordshire* case might well have stood as something of an authority in support of the Lando principle. In fact the other two judges, although they supported the determination of the contract, arrived at their conclusions on the basis of an interpretation of the written agreement itself. Yet even if they had taken a similar approach to the Master of the Rolls, the way in which the time and inflation factor operated was not actually through the development of an abstract principle to re-negotiate as such. The approach was to create an image of two particular human contractors negotiating this particular agreement; it was, in other words, a matter of arriving at a principle of re-negotiation (symbolic knowledge) from a pictorial image which attempted to capture the full dimension of time, place and circumstance (non-symbolic knowledge). It was a question of arriving at symbolic knowledge (the principle of re-negotiation) from non-symbolic imagery.[19] Time, of course, cannot be reduced to symbolic propositions and so, while Cumming-Bruce LJ preferred to base his decision on the construction of the agreement, he, like Lord Denning, was unable to found his reasoning upon any actual proposition. "The words of the agreement are, of course, a factor to take into account, and a factor of great importance", said

[18] [1979] 1 WLR 1387, 1393–4, 1398 (emphasis added).
[19] Delacour, *Le cerveau et l'esprit* (Paris, PUF, 1995), 121.

Cumming-Bruce LJ.[20] But they were not "sufficient to displace the inferences to be drawn from the other circumstances attending the formation of the agreement".

The effect of the Lando proposal on change of circumstances is that it will fundamentally alter the role played by time in that it will effect a shift from the descriptive and quasi-descriptive to the purely normative. Time will be reduced to a duty. Now there may be compelling arguments in favour of this—although Professor Schanze is sceptical on economic grounds—but the comparative lawyer ought immediately to be aware that, the moment it is reduced to a proposition in the form proposed by Lando, the method of reasoning becomes one of dialectical contradiction, since the principle of re-negotiation is immediately severely limited by a counter-proposition. A long-term contract will not be subject to the principle of re-negotiation when the change of circumstances is one that could reasonably have been taken into account at the time of the conclusion of the contract and the risk is one that one party affected should be required to bear.[21] This limitation is a counter-proposition in as much as it seeks to impose on the contractors a notion of time and events which is by definition different from the one facing the contractors at the time they made the contract; the dissymmetry is analogous to imposing on the certain memory of an event the uncertain expectation of some future event.[22] This is not to suggest that the metaphysics of time should exclude legal intervention. What needs to be stressed is that to subject contractors to post-contractual duties, perhaps leading to a damages claim,[23] is create a contradiction at the level of the contractual *vinculum iuris* itself; for contract is about creating stability of interest and risk in a present-future factual world where change of circumstance is one of the compelling factors behind a law of contract.

This dialectical contradiction is not of course untypical of abstract legal propositions—one thinks of the famous absolute right to enjoy and to dispose of property in article 544 of the Code Civil. Not only did the proposition contradict the actual thinking of the time,[24] but the second limb (restricting the "absolute" right where statute or regulations prohibit a usage) of the article completely undermines the first limb. In a sense these kinds of propositions are themselves creating an image: in the case of article 544 the first limb creates the idea of an absolute and single *vinculum iuris* between person and thing which was needed to counteract the old feudal images of property. The second limb reflects the image of the Napoleonic State. However, the comparative lawyer interested in epistemological questions might well conclude that, despite the bi-polar nature of law and legal argumentation (a party either

[20] *Ibid.*, 1406.
[21] Art 2.117(2)(b)–(c).
[22] Barreau, *Le Temps* (Paris, PUF, 1996) 4–5.
[23] Art 2.117(3).
[24] Halpérin, *Histoire du droit privé français depuis 1804* (Paris, PUF, 1996), 37.

wins or loses), time and social fact are simply not reducible to two-dimensional oppositions.[25] Law involves the interpretation of fact as much as text.[26] Knowledge of the common law has never been a matter of rules applied via an *ars hermeneutica*; it is a work of construction and reconstruction of factual situations around institutional representations of "persons" and "things", often in relation to "actions", and it is the image created by these constructions that produces the basis for solutions.[27] This view of legal knowledge may not be as user-friendly as a code of normative propositions. But its great strength is that it can model complexity. In the *Staffordshire* case this constructed image was complex enough to encompass not just the world of contract, with its emphasis on benefit and detriment (important in the judgments of Goff and Cumming-Bruce LJJ), but equally the public law element. It did this in the reference to the principles of statutory interpretation to be applied in this case to the contract (Lord Denning MR), in the relation of negotiation to the various statutory provisions which have governed the supply of water, and in the oblique mentioning of public health problems which forced the hospital to abandon its own well. Within the symmetry of the image of the general interest, which of course had played such a vital role in the French *imprévision* case of 1916, *Gaz de Bordeaux*, was secreted the institution of the public. As Legrand has recently implied, the Lando type approach—that is to say the reduction of images to norms—is likely to be epistemologically meaningless since "the sources of credibility . . . differ in the two legal traditions".[28] Therefore, as regards the mentality of common law, Lando is not just imposing, historically speaking, one scientific stage (axiomatic) upon another (inductive), but is doing it at a time when there is an increasing scepticism, even in parts of the civil law world, about legal knowledge itself.[29] The provision will simply impose, at the two-dimensional level of the conceptual norm, the meaningless contradiction that long-term contracts will be both binding and non-binding.

A better approach, as far as legal knowledge is concerned, would be to model these contradictions thrown up by the time element in long-term contracts in terms of the law of actions. This, indeed, is the traditional approach of both the common law and Roman classical law. The equitable remedy of rescission would have the twin advantages of introducing the principle of unjust enrichment into the area of long-term contracts and allowing the court to attach terms upon which it is granted.[30] Furthermore, it would permit the construction of more complex symmetries when it comes to constructing reasoning patterns. A good analogous example of this approach is to be found

[25] cf. Berthelot, *L'intelligence du social* (PUFJ 1990), 82.
[26] Ivainer, *L'interprétation des faits en droit* (Paris, LGDJ, 1988).
[27] See generally Samuel, *Foundations of Legal Reasoning* (Antwerp, Maklu, 1994).
[28] Legrand, "European Legal Systems are not converging" (1996) 45 *ICLQ* 52, 69.
[29] See e.g. Atias, *Épistémologie du droit* (Paris, PUF, 1994).
[30] See *Solle* v. *Butcher* [1950] 1 KB 671.

in the tort case of *Miller* v. *Jackson*,[31] where the time element assumed importance in regard to the playing of cricket. The plaintiffs in this case were seeking the equitable remedy of an injunction to stop the playing of cricket in a field situated next to the plaintiffs' house; cricket balls were quite regularly hit into the plaintiffs' garden and they were understandably concerned about personal injury should they be sitting in their garden on a weekend when cricket was being played. A majority of the Court of Appeal refused the injunction. Lord Denning MR, although he actually thought that the playing of cricket did not amount to a nuisance (a view not shared by the other two judges), abandoned the law of obligations as such and constructed a reasoning model around the remedy of the injunction itself:[32]

> "This case is new. It should be approached on principles applicable to modern conditions. There is a contest here between the interest of the public at large and the interest of a private individual. The *public* interest lies in protecting the environment by preserving our playing fields in the face of mounting development . . . The *private* interest lies in securing the privacy of his home and garden without intrusion by anyone. In deciding between these two conflicting interests, it must be remembered that it is not a question of damages . . . No, it is a question of an injunction . . . As between their conflicting interests, I am of opinion that the public interest should prevail over the private interest . . . In my opinion the right exercise of discretion is to refuse an injunction"

Now it may well be that Lord Denning's solution was both wrong, in terms of precedent, and unfortunate in terms of result. Certainly *Miller* v. *Jackson* is a questionable case and the analysis of the factual situation by both Lord Denning MR and Cummings-Bruce LJ is, at best, controversial and at worst distasteful. But the strength of the case is to be found in its approach to problem-solving: the common law was able to construct a very sophisticated reasoning model around the notion of an interest which in turn was generated by the remedy of the injunction. Of course there was a contradiction between the rights in the tort of nuisance and the interests attaching to the remedy of the injunction. Yet that contradiction was formally modelled through the differing, but interconnected, symmetries of the law of obligations and the law of actions, a point that becomes very evident when Lord Denning MR's analysis is compared with that of the dissenting judge, Geoffrey Lane LJ. This makes the case very open in respect of external examination in that the institutional image constructed by each judge is not hidden behind some two-dimensional linguistic proposition which tends to exclude the way that legal facts themselves are constructed. Transferred to the area of long-term contracts, the tension between the law of obligations (contract as binding private legislation) and the law of actions (rescission based on unjust enrichment and change of circumstances) can be resolved through the use both of institutions

[31] [1977] QB 966.
[32] *Ibid.*, 981–2.

(persons, things and actions) and of quasi-normative notions such as interest, damage and fault. And the advantage of such a complex reasoning model is that it operates at, and within, the facts, which, of course, is exactly what the Lando normative proposition is attempting to achieve in its world of symbols and algorithmic logic. The advantage of operating the contradiction in the separate dimension of the law of actions is that the binding force of justified enrichment can be upheld in one dimension, while in another dimension, the law of remedies can assert that a means of justified enrichment will not be permitted to become a vehicle of abuse, oppression and (or) unjustified enrichment. This three-dimensional symmetry worked with particular effect in the celebrated *High Trees* case.[33]

None of this is to decry the notion of codification. Codes are an excellent means of orientating legal thought; and they can act as the bridge between legal education, legal research and legal practice. In addition they can inject form and symmetry into legal analysis in a way that is sometimes more efficient than by means of analogy or metaphor.[34] Nevertheless, they are fundamentally two-dimensional in the way that they seemingly rely upon symbolic knowledge; their very abstraction means that they are incapable of managing complexity and thus, even if they are easily assimilated by the mind, they suffer from a major loss of information.[35] The problem with long-term contracts is that the time and circumstances are highly complex factors in need of fairly complex legal models if they are to be modelled with success. Professor Schanze's chapter goes far in appreciating this point.

[33] *Central London Property Trust Ltd* v. *High Trees House Ltd* [1947] 1 KB 130.

[34] Cf. *Spartan Steel & Alloys* v. *Martin & Co* [1973] 1 QB 27, 35.

[35] Delacour, *supra* n 19, 34–5.

# 12

# *Le Mythe de la Responsabilité Contractuelle en Droit Français*

CHRISTIAN LAPOYADE DESCHAMPS

"Responsabilité contractuelle"? L'expression, largement consacrée, devrait pourtant surprendre puisqu'elle résulte de l'assemblage des deux mots-clef du droit des obligations et de ses deux sources principales mais fort différentes: le contrat et la responsabilité civile.

Or, les deux mots ne jurent-ils pas d'être accouplés? Monstre sacré, la "responsabilité contractuelle" fait-elle partie de ces institutions qui exposent au crime de lèse-majesté tous ceux qui oseraient la désacraliser?

Pour impertinente qu'elle puisse paraître, la question mérite d'être posée: "la responsabilité contractuelle existe-t-elle?"[1]

A première vue, l'interrogation semble triplement saugrenue, puisque l'institution figure tant dans les textes[2] que dans la jurisprudence (comme rubrique à part entière de la plupart des revues) et dans les ouvrages (où elle occupe une place de plus en plus considérable).

Il nous semble néanmoins qu'insensiblement, ce que l'on appelle la responsabilité contractuelle est devenue un véritable mythe, à bien des égards:

(i) d'un point de vue sémantique, l'expression n'a guère de sens: entendue comme l'obligation de réparer un dommage, la "responsabilité" ne peut naître d'un contrat (à moins de lui donner une signification beaucoup plus large).[3] Le contrat n'engendre pas une obligation de réparer,mais des obligations spécifiques à chaque convention; certes, l'inexécution de ces obligations peut entraîner un dommage réparable, mais la responsabilité n'est alors qu'un effet du contrat et non une source d'obligations. A moins d'admettre, à l'instar de certains auteurs[4] que s'opère une métamorphose de l'obligation contractuelle, au cas d'inexécution, en une obligation de réparer. L'explication est ingénieuse mais ne saurait trouver aucun appui législatif.

[1] Elle vient d'ailleurs d'être formulée en ces termes par P. Jourdain, *Les principes de la responsabilité civile* (Dalloz 1996), 31.

[2] l'art. 1147 du code civil essentiellement—v. aussi l'art. L. 133-3 du code de la consommation.

[3] cf. Mourlon, juriste du XIX° siècle: "un contrat, c'est une responsabilité convenue d'avance".

[4] cf. récemment Le Tourneau et Cadiet, *Droit de la responsabilité* (Dalloz, 1996), no. 222.

(ii) Textuellement, en effet, le code civil n'use jamais du terme "responsabilité" en matière contractuelle, mais donne à la matière un intitulé très différent: "des dommages et intérêts résultant de l'inexécution de l'obligation". Et ce n'est pas une périphrase, puisque le texte essentiel -l'art. 1147- détaille le formule dans les termes suivants: "le débiteur est condamné, s'il y a lieu, au payement de dommages et intérêts, soit à raison de l'inexécution de l'obligation, soit à raison du retard dans l'exécution, toutes les fois qu'il ne justifie pas que l'inexécution provient d'une cause étrangère qui ne peut lui être imputée, encore qu'il n'y ait aucune mauvaise foi de sa part". Peut-on sérieusement classer cet article parmi les textes relatifs à la responabilité alors que n'y figure aucun des termes habituels du droit de la responsabilité civile? Ni le mot "dommage" (du moins isolément), ni celui de "faute", ni même le verbe "causer".

(iii) Théoriquement ce que l'on nomme (improprement, donc) la "responsabilité contractuelle" n'a pas rigoureusement pour objet une "réparation", mais plus exactement un "paiement", l'équivalent (en argent) de la prestation promise et inexécutée, lorsque précisément il n'est pas possible de sanctionner autrement la violation du contrat (c'est d'ailleurs certainement le sens du "s'il y a lieu" de l'art. 1147).

(iv) Concrètement, l'hypothèse de la "responsabilité contractuelle" suppose la réunion de plusieurs conditions, dont la dernière n'est guère "contractuelle":
   (a) l'esistence d'un contrat valablement formé;
   (b) l'inexécution ou le retard dans l'exécution d'une obligation née de ce contrat;[5]
   (c) un dommage résultant de cette inexécution, condition qui ne figure pas expressément au texte et qui, justement, est susceptible de transformer la responsabilité dite contractuelle en une responsabilité civile ordinaire. En effet, l'inexécution constitue, en ellemême, un préjudice pour le créancier. Pour le compenser, il lui suffira, non pas exactement de demander "réparation", mais plus simplement l'équivalent monétaire de la prestation inexécutée (le prix de la marchandise non livrée, par exemple). En revanche, lorsque l'inexécution cause un dommage spécifique, et donc supplémentaire, la sanction s'apparentera effectivement à une véritable responsabilité, de sorte que la responsabilité contractuelle y perdra toute son originalité. Or c'est exactement ce qui se produit lorsque la jurisprudence ne se contente pas de sanctionner l'inexécution des obligations prévues au contrat, mais indemnise aussi le créancier des dommages causés par cette inexécution (y compris l'inexécution d'obligations accessoires et générales, qui n'ont plus rien de contractuelles . . .).

[5] Remarquons que l'art. 1147 n'évoque pas la mauvaise exécution.

Malgré tout, le droit positif français demeure fermement attaché à la distinction entre la responsabilité contractuelle et . . . les autres responsabilités civiles (dites, pour cette raison, "extracontracuelles"); sans doute moins à cause de différences profondes (il s'agit chaque fois de la violation d'un devoir préexistant, tout spécialement au cas de manquement à l'obligation de sécurité) que de disparités "techniques" (telle la mise en demeure ou la prescription, restée à 30 ans en matière contractuelle . . . par paresse législative?) En réalité, la responsabilité contractuelle ne se singularise que sur deux points, qui constituent les obstacles les plus résitants à l'unification des responsabilités (car les règles de preuve se sont d'elles-mêmes harmonisées, la distinction entre les obligations de résultat et les obligations de moyens aidant . . .): la réparation des seuls dommages prévisibles et la faculté d'insérer des clauses élusives ou limitatives de responsabilité.

Quoiqu'il en soit, le maintien de la distinction entraîne cette conséquence déplorable (et inconnue de la plupart des systèmes juridiques, notamment en droit anglais) que l'on connait en France sous l'horrible appellation de la règle du "non-cumul": la Cour de cassation rappelle obstinément que "le créancier d'une obligation contractuelle ne peut se prévaloir, quand bien même il y aurait intérêt, des règles de la responabilité délictuelle."[6] Ce motif, où perce expressément une pointe de regret, résume à lui seul le degré d'incohérence auquel conduit le cloisonnement entre les deux responsabilités: la première Chambre civile défend contre vents et marées une responsabilité qui, le plus souvent, n'a plus rien de contractuel!

Une récente décision de la même Chambre[7] témoigne à merveille des contorsions juridiques auxquelles le juge français doit se livrer pour "sauver" la responsabilité contractuelle: les parents d'une fillette de 4 ans, blessée par la rupture d'un cerceau dans la cour d'une école privée, ont pu mettre en jeu, d'une part la responsabilité délictuelle du distributeur en tant que vendeur professionnel pour le défaut de sécurité de ses produits, avec cette précision capitale qu'"il en est responsable tant à l'égard des tiers que de son acquéreur", d'autre part la responsabilité de l'établissement d'enseignement "contractuellement tenu d'assurer la sécurité de ses élèves", pour les "dommages qui leur sont causés non seulement par sa faute, mais encore par le fait des choses qu'il met en oeuvre pour l'exécution de son obligation contractuelle": d'un côté l'arrêt aménage une responsabilité délictuelle sur le modèle contractuel, de l'autre il forge une responsabilité contractuelle sur le modèle délictuel!

Ce chassé-croisé est révélateur de l'indécision du juge français: soucieux à juste titre d'indemniser les victimes d'un dommage subi dans un cadre contractuel, il s'épuise à sauvegarder la responsabilité contractuelle, tout en lui administrant des doses massives de règles empruntées à la responsabilité délictuelle.

[6] 1° Ch.Civ. 11 janvier 1989, JCP 1989.II.21326, note C. Larroumet.
[7] 1° Ch.Civ. 17 janvier 1995, D. 1995.350, note P. Jourdain.

La coexistence artificielle de *deux* responsabilités civiles ne nous parait donc plus tolérable car, dans la réalité, elles ne sont mêmes plus distinctes! L'observateur du droit positif français constate en effet:

(i) d'une part que la responsabilité délictuelle réinvestit progressivement le territoire de la responsabilité contractuelle (*1ère partie: La reconquête*);
(ii) d'autre part, que là où la responsabilité contractuelle "résiste", elle emprunte largement les règles de la responsabilité délictuelle (*2ème partie: La colonisation*).

## 1. LA RECONQUETE

Dans le conflit territorial qui oppose les deux ordres de responsabilité, de nombreux signes montrent que le domaine de la responsabilité contractuelle est à nouveau occupé par celui de la responsabilité délictuelle.

Il faut reconnaître que la responsabilité contractuelle avait été exagérément dilatée (et l'est encore dans les situations quelle continue de régir) sous l'effet de plusieurs phénomènes conjugués (et développés infra):

(a) principalement, la découverte d'obligations accessoires—l'obligation de sécurité en particulier—qui engagent le débiteur sans que ce dernier ne l'ait expressément voulu;
(b) également dans les hypothèses où le débiteur est déclaré responsable à l'égard d'une victime qui n'est pas son cocontractant;
(c) plus généralement, chaque fois que le juge distend le lien de causalité entre le dommage et le contrat.

Pour des motifs rationnels ou de circonstance, la jurisprudence et le législateur se sont alors efforcés de replacer la responsabilitié contractuelle dans son orbite naturelle, du moins lorsque l'application d'une responsabilité extra-contractuelle ne nuisait pas à l'intérêt des victimes.

Un double repli de la responsabilité contractuelle a été ainsi opéré, dans le temps et dans l'espace.

### *La Reconquête du Temps Contractuel*

Autant il est logique que la responsabilité délictuelle ait vocation à s'appliquer dans les phases précontractuelle et postcontractuelle, autant cette incursion peut sembler plus étonnante lorsque le dommage survient pendant le contrat, mais en dehors de son exécution.

Avant la formation du contrat, il ne saurait y avoir place, faute d'accord, pour le moindre lien de droit.

Mais d'une part, le principe de libre rupture cède devant une possible responsabilité lorsque les pourparlers sont rompus abusivement ou de mauvaise foi: cette responsabilité ne peut alors être que délictuelle ou, si l'on préfère, précontractuelle.[8]

D'autre part, l'absence d'obligation durant cette période n'a pas empêché la jurisprudence d'y imposer un devoir de renseignement, dont la transgression est, là encore, sanctionnée par une responsabilité délictuelle (malgré une doctrine dissidente qui considère que les fautes précontractuelles doivent être rattachées au contrat dès lors qu'elles ont une incidence sur l'exécution de celui-ci: J. Huet, thèse n⁰ 292—M. Fabre-Magnan, thèse n° 281).

Aprés l'extinction du contrat se développent, symétriquement mais plus timidement, des obligations qui semblent prolonger la convention expirée: obligation de non-concurrence ou de confidentialité, notamment.

Par principe, la responsabilité encourue entre les anciens contractants est naturellement de nature délictuelle, puisqu'ils ne sont plus liés par la convention: ce sera, par exemple, le cas pour des actes de concurrence déloyale commis par l'ex-salarié.

Par exception, la responsabilité sera contractuelle parce que l'obligation inexécutée n'est pas un devoir général mais résulte bien d'une clause du contrat (cf. le débat classique sur la validité des clauses de non-concurrence).

Entre les parties contractantes, mais hors de l'exécution du contrat, la jurisprudence a longtemps considéré que la responsabilité ne pouvait être que contractuelle.

L'illustration la plus significative concerne le contrat de transport de personnes, lorsqu'un accident survient à un moment où le voyageur, muni d'un billet, subit un dommage avant ou après la période du transport proprement dit (accident de quai).

Dans les années 1970, la jurisprudence opérait un savant découpage de l'obligation contractuelle de sécurité du transporteur, tenu d'une obligation de résultat pendant le trajet, mais d'une simple obligation de moyens dans les phases antérieure ou postérieure, la responsabilité contractuelle étant, en tout état de cause, appliquée de bout en bout.

Un revirement a été opéré par le lère Chambre civile le 7 mars 1989.[9] Désormais, la responsabilité du transporteur, en dehors de la phase d'exécution du contrat, "est soumise aux règles de la responsabilité délictuelle".

Cette solution a connu un certain retentissement,[10] mais n'a pas connu le succès qu'elle méritait (elle n'a pas été étendue au contrat de remonte-pente, par exemple), probablement parce qu'elle s'est contentée de corriger ponctuellement les inconvénients de la solution ancienne (qui faisait

[8] Avec un possible recours à la théorie de l'apparence, cf. Riom 10 juin 1992, Revue trimestrielle de droit civil 1993.343 observations. J. Mestre—et avec, pour sanction, l'octroi de dommages et intérêts et non la conclusion forcée du contrat.

[9] Arrêt Valverde, Dalloz 1991.1 note P. Malaurie.

[10] Elle a été appliquée notamment à un incident survenu dans un grand magasin: 2° Civile 5 juin 1991, Dalloz 1992.409 note C. Lapoyade Deschamps—de même, il a été récemment jugé que le commerçant n'est pas tenu d'une obligation contractuelle de sécurité à l'égard des personnes se trouvant dans son magasin: 1° Chambre civil 29 mai 1996, JCP 1996.IV.1638)

injustement un sort différent au voyageur et à l'accompagnateur accidentés dans les mêmes conditions). Au surplus, le nouveau découpage (entre les responsabilités et non plus entre les obligations) n'est pas à l'abri de critiques: outre l'idée, certainement excessive, qu'avec cette jurisprudence, le contrat ne serait conclu que par son exécution,[11] l'on peut soutenir que le transporteur, comme tout autre contractant, doit veiller à la sécurité de son partenaire, en dehors même de la phase d'exécution; sinon tout se passe comme si le dommage était survenu lors de la période précontractuelle.[12] Il n'en reste pas moins que cette décision a l'immense mérite de dissocier la formation du contrat de ses effets et de rattacher la responsabilité contractuelle au seul critère suggéré par l'article 1147 du code civil: l'exécution du contrat.

## *La Reconquête de l'Espace Contractuel*

Elle se produit non seulement dans la "périphérie" du contrat, en réduisant ainsi la sphère d'application de la responsabilité contractuelle, mais affecte aussi les personnes concernées, en limitant en principe le jeu de la responsabilité contractuelle au seul cercle des parties.

### 1. La sphère contractuelle

Pour définir le domaine d'application de la responsabilité contractuelle, se posent tout à la fois un problème de territoire et un problème de frontières.

Quant au territoire régi par la responsabilité contractuelle, des restrictions de plus en plus nombreuses ont été opérées par la jurisprudence:

(i) tout d'abord, parce que la responsabilité contractuelle suppose l'existence d'un contrat valable, au cas d'annulation de celui-ci, le dommage subi par le créancier ne peut être réparé qu'au titre de la responsabilité délictuelle, sauf si ce dommage est la conséquence de la nullité. La jurisprudence la plus récente consacre ainsi la pleine autonomie de l'action en responsabilité, déclarée recevable même si la victime se désiste de son action en nullité;[13]

(ii) ensuite, la responsabilité délictuelle l'emporte lorsqu'il n'y a qu'une "apparence" de contrat, ce qui est le cas du passager clandestin ou en situation irréguliere, ou encore pour celui qui poursuit le voyage au-delà de sa destination (le "trespasser", en droit anglais). Sur ce point, la jurisprudence est constante, même si une justification plausible fait défaut car, dans le fond, la solution est la même que celle qui est adoptée pour la responsabilité post-contractuelle, alors que les situations sont bien différentes;

[11] Cf. Malaurie note précitée.

[12] cf. également la critique de R. Nérac, Dalloz 1995 chronique 35, qui propose de maintenir la responsabilité contractuelle hors du trajet mais de ne charger le transporteur que d'une obligation de résultat . . . atténuée.

[13] En l'occurrence pour dol: 1° Chambre civile 18 octobre 1994, Dalloz 1995.180, note C. Atias.

(iii) la responsabilité contractuelle est encore exclue lorsque le lien entre auteur et victime ne peut être considéré comme un rapport contractuel. La principale difficulté concerne l'hypothèse des actes de dévouement ou d'assistance pour lesquels la jurisprudence française est passablement incertaine. La comparaison entre deux arrêts rendus dans des espèces similaires est, à cet égard, édifiante: l'un voit une véritable convention d'assistance dans le service rendu entre deux frères,[14] l'autre estime au contraire qu'il n'y a qu'un pur acte de courtoisie dans l'aide bénévole fournie par un employé municipal à un particulier.[15]

(iv) enfin, c'est le législateur lui-même qui décide parfois d'écarter, dans certaines situations, les règles de la responsabilité contractuelle. L'illustration la plus importante de cette tendance[16] concerne le régime des accidents de la circulation, régi par la loi du 5 juillet 1985, texte qui déroge nettement aux règles habituelles de la responsabilité civile, dans le souci d'une meilleure indemnisation. L'article 1er dispose en effet que la loi s'applique aux victimes d'un accident de la circulation "mêmes lorsqu'elles sont transportées en vertu d'un contrat" (à l'exception des accidents de chemin de fer, selon l'idée—assez peu convaincante—que les trains ne sont pas mêlés à la circulation . . .)

Quant aux frontières de la responsabilité contractuelle, deux limites doivent être tracées:

(a) une première restriction, bien connue, est celle qui est apportée par l'art. 1150 du code civil, texte qui, en matière contractuelle, limite la réparation au dommage prévisible,[17] sauf dol ou faute intentionnelle du débiteur. La justification habituelle de cette limitation—l'engagement est circonscrit par la volonté des parties—est probablement insuffisante car, au cas de dommage imprévisible, c'est plutôt l'équivalent contractuel qui fait défaut, et l'on retrouve donc cette idée que la pseudo responsabilité contractuelle n'a pas exactement pour fonction la réparation des dommages mais plutôt le paiement, sous forme d'équivalent, de la prestation inexécutée;

(b) la seconde restriction éventuelle est à la fois plus importante et plus incertaine: pour que puisse être mise en jeu une responsabilité contractuelle, il faut qu'il y ait une relation suffisante entre le dommage et le contrat et, plus précisément, entre le dommage et l'inexécution. C'est le problème du critère de la faute contractuelle: certes d'un côté, c'est une faute spécifique, directement en rapport avec les stipulations du contrat, stipulations qui ne traduisent aucune exigence morale ou

[14] 1° Chambre civile 27 janvier 1993, Bulletin I. n° 42.

[15] 2° Chambre civile 26 janvier 1994, Revue Responsabilité civile et assurance 1994, n° 114.

[16] En attendant que le parlement français se décide à transposer la directive du 25 juillet 1985 sur les produits défectueux, où il n'est fait aucune distinction entre les responsabilités.

[17] Solution analogue en droit anglais, depuis l'affaire Hadley en 1854.

normative;[18] mais d'un autre côté, faute contractuelle et faute délictuelle tendent à se rapprocher, d'une part parce que des règles générales de conduite ont été intégrées dans le contrat (obligation de loyauté et surtout de sécurité), d'autre part parce que le comportement de l'auteur du dommage est apprécié de la même manière dans les deux types de responsabilité, du moins chaque fois qu'il s'agit d'une obligation de moyens (appréciation in abstracto, par référence au critère du bon père de famille).

Ce rapprochement rend particulièrement difficile la recherche d'un critère distinctif et, à cet égard, l'incertitude jurisprudentielle contraste avec la perspicacité de la doctrine: malgré la tentative d'une décision pour exiger un "lien nécessaire" avec le contrat,[19] la jurisprudence actuelle est assez anarchique et a tendance, lorsqu'elle l'estime opportun, à rattacher de manière artificielle le dommage à l'inexécution contractuelle.[20]

Les auteurs se sont pourtant efforcés de dégager des critères rigoureux de délimitation entre les deux responsabilités. A partir du fil conducteur que constitue l'exécution du contrat,[21] trois critères ont été principalement suggérés: l'un tiré de la situation des parties, la responsabilité étant de nature délictuelle lorsque le créancier subit un préjudice "dans des conditions de fait où pourrait se trouver identiquement un tiers",[22] l'autre tiré de l'objet du contrat, selon lequel la responsabilité sera contractuelle lorsque le dommage est causé par un bien objet du contrat ou à un bien sur lequel porte l'exécution du contrat,[23] un troisième critère s'attachant plutôt à "l'intérêt lésé par l'inexécution".[24]

## 2. Le cercle des contractants

Normalement, la responsabilité contractuelle n'a lieu "qu'entre les parties contractantes" en vertu du principe fondamental de l'effet relatif des contrats, proclamé par l'art. 1165 du code civil (comparable au principe de "privity of contract", en droit anglais).

Mais cette conception individualiste du contrat, qui en fait une sorte de "club privé", est de plus en plus difficile à concilier avec le phénomène de socialisation du contrat et surtout avec les impératifs économiques, qui ren-

[18] cf. G. Viney, Introduction à la responsabilité, LGDJ n° 168.

[19] A propos de la glissade d'un malade, 1° Chambre civile 28 avril 1981, Bulletin I n° 137, Revue trimestrielle de droit civil 1982 p. 144, observations G. Durry.

[20] Voir notamment 2° Chambre civile 26 mai 1992, Revue responsabilité civile et assurance 1992. n° 33, chronique C. Lapoyade Deschamps, qui, à propos de l'incendie d'une voiture survenu lors de la réparation d'un chaudière, estime, de manière extrêment vague, qu'il "ne saurait être fait abstraction de la convention pour apprécier la responsabilité engagée".

[21] cf. l'arrêt Valverde, précité.

[22] J. Huet, thèse précitée n° 363.

[23] G. Durry, observations Revue trimestrielle de droit civil 1979.610.

[24] N. Dejean de la Batie, Responsabilité délictuelle, édition Librairies techniques 1989 n° 94 p. 218.

dent nécessaire de relier entre elles des opérations juridiques au sein d'une même activité.

Cette absence d'étanchéité entre le contrat et les tiers conduit à examiner deux situations d'inégale importance, selon que le tiers est responsable ou victime.

*(a) La responsabilité des tiers envers un contractant.* C'est une hypothèse relativement exceptionnelle, quis suppose l'incursion d'une personne étrangère au contrat et dont l'intervention explique l'inexécution ou la mauvaise exécution de celui-ci: le tiers, en quelque sorte complice de l'inexécution, pourra être déclaré responsable, si du moins il est démontré qu'il a eu connaissance du contrat ("Inducement of breach of contract" ou "Interference with contractual relation", en droit anglais). L'hypothèse classique est celle du débauchage d'un salarié ou, inversement, du réembauchage d'un salarié tenu par une clause de non-concurrence. Malgré le lien indiscutable avec le contrat, la jurisprudence[25] a toujours fondé l'action en responsabilité sur l'art. 1382 du code civil.[26]

La solution est analogue lorsqu'un tiers se rend complice de l'inexécution d'une promesse unilatérale ou d'un pacte de préférence: si le tiers connaissait l'existence de la promesse, il pourra être rendu délictuellement responsable avec, comme réparation, l'annulation de la vente qui lui a été consentie.[27]

*(b) La responsabilité du contractant envers les tiers.* À l'égard d'un tiers totalement étranger au contrat, il a toujours semblé difficile (faute notamment de transposition de la directive du 25 juillet 1985, précitée) de justifier l'action du tiers, sauf à admettre l'existence d'une faute détachable du contrat. Cette analyse, qui revient à considérer la violation de l'obligation contractuelle comme une faute délictuelle à l'égard d'un tiers, a pourtant été implicitement reprise par l'importante décision de la 1ère Chambre civile rendue le 17 janvier 1995 (affaire du cerceau, précitée), ce qui montre bien que l'exigence de sécurité n'est pas spécifiquement contractuelle.

La responsabilité d'un contractant au sein d'un groupe de contrats a récemment donné lieu en France à un débat acharné—et à un véritable "feuilleton" jurisprudentiel: à la question de savoir quelle est la nature de la responsabilité encourue entre deux participants d'un ensemble ou d'une chaîne contractuelle, la 1ère Chambre civile de la Cour de cassation répondait que la responsabilité était "nécessairement" de nature contractuelle, alors que la 3ème Chambre civile constatait qu'en l'absence de lien contractuel direct entre auteur et victime, la responsabilité éventuelle ne pouvait être que délictuelle. Contre toute attente, l'Assemblée plénière de la Cour de cassation a entériné

[25] A partir de la thèse de P. Hugueney, *De la responsabilité du tiers, complice de la violation d'une obligation contractuelle* (1910).

[26] Depuis, le code du travail a d'ailleurs entériné cette solution dans l'art. L 122–15.

[27] Civ. 22 mars 1968, Dalloz 1968.412, noteJ. Mazeaud.

cette dernière solution, à propos d'un contrat de sous-traitance et sous le visa de l'art. 1165 du code civil.[28] L'argument le plus solide au soutien de la solution adoptée par la 1ère Chambre civile—l'action reste contractuelle comme accessoire du bien transmis—a néanmoins permis à la jurisprudence postérieure d'admettre encore une action en responsabilité contractuelle dans les chaines homogènes[29] et ce malgré la condamnation implicite de ce raisonnement par la Cour de Justice des Communautés Européennes.[30] La 1ère Chambre civile en tire cette conséquence qu'est opposable au maître de l'ouvrage qui agit sur le terrain contractuel contre le fabricant, une clause limitative de responsabilité, alors qu'il ne s'agit pas d'une chaîne homogène où pourrait jouer la théorie de l'accessoire.[31]

Le conflit territorial entre les deux responsabilités est donc loin d'être apaisé. Et l'insécurité juridique à laquelle conduisent toutes ces tergiversations est d'autant plus regrettable que là où une responsabilité contractuelle est retenue, les règles appliquées ne diffèrent pas fondamentalement de celles qui gouvernent la responsabilité délictuelle.

## 2. LA COLONISATION

Alors qu'il est classique de remarquer que la responsabilité délictuelle a longtemps puisé dans la matière contractuelle pour parfaire son régime,[32] force est de constater, inversement, qu'en s'inspirant de plus en plus des règles de la responsabilité délictuelle, la responsabilité contractuelle tend à devenir une responsabilité civile ordinaire, ce qui lui fait perdre toute singularité et justifie donc la remise en cause de la distinction traditionnelle.

Il s'agit même d'une double infiltration, qui se réalise d'un côté par un "forçage" du contrat (l'expression est de Josserand) et de l'autre par un renforcement de la responsabilité contractuelle, sur le canevas de la responsabilité délictuelle.

### *Le "Forçage" du Contrat*

Il résulte tout à la fois d'une découverte et d'une invention.

(a) La découverte est bien connue: depuis le début du siècle, et par souci d'indemnisation des victimes, la jurisprudence française a cru bon d'ajoindre des obligations accessoires aux obligations contractuelles principales.

[28] Arrêt Besse, 12 juillet 1991, Dalloz 1991.549, note J. Ghestin, JCP 1991.II.21743, note G. Viney.

[29] En particulier lorsque cette action est intentée par un sous-acquéreur: 1° Chambre civile 27 janvier 1993, Revue Contrat, Concurrence, Consommation 1993, chronique 5 par L. Leveneur.

[30] CJCE 17 juin 1992, JCP 1992.II.21927, note C. Larroumet.

[31] 1° Chambre civile 7 juin 1995, Dalloz 1996.395, note D. Mazeaud.

[32] L'exonération par la force majeure et le dommage réparable, notamment—cf. J. Carbonnier, droit civile, 4, n° 154.

C'est principalement la découverte d'une obligation de sécurité (totalement ignorée du droit anglais) mise à la charge de certains débiteurs qui a profondément modifié la physionomie de la responsabilité contractuelle. La métamorphose résulte tant du fondement que des conséquences de ces nouvelles obligations:

(i) quant au fondement des obligations accessoires, les explications habituellement fournies par la doctrine ne sont guère convaincantes: l'une, "volontariste", justifie une telle découverte par la volonté tacite des parties avec, comme support textuel, l'article 1156 du code civil; mais il est parfaitement artificiel et illusoire de faire "parler" ainsi le contrat car cette prétendue volonté est au pire inexistante, au mieux non concordante. L'autre, qui est une justification plus "légale", s'appuie essentiellement sur l'art. 1135 du code civil, texte visé par nombre de décisions, et selon lequel "les conventions obligent non seulement à ce qui y est exprimé, mais encore à toutes les suites que l'équité, l'usage ou la loi donnent à l'obligation d'après sa nature"; mais il ne s'agit que d'un texte d'interprétation, qui n'autorise que des alluvions aux obligations figurant *déjà* au contrat.

En réalité, cette oeuvre de "remplissage" du contrat s'inscrit dans une politique jurisprudentielle d'indemnisation des dommages accidentels, qui consiste à greffer des obligations accessoires dans le seul but de rendre le débiteur responsable du préjudice subi par le créancier. Cette responsabilité de "complaisance" n'a donc plus rien de contractuel: à partir d'un dommage constaté chez le créancier, le juge crée de toutes pièces une obligation de circonstance, pour constater aussitôt (et évidemment!) que le débiteur ne l'a pas exécutée.[33]

(ii) quant à la portée de cette découverte, il est évident qu'en incluant dans le contrat des devoirs *généraux*, il est inévitable que l'on raisonne comme s'il s'agissait d'une responsabilité de droit commun. Il faut notamment remarquer que l'obligation contractuelle de sécurité est l'équivalent de l'obligation générale de prudence sous-jacente à l'article 1382 du code civil. L'on pourrait certes objecter qu'il convient de veiller davantage à la sécurité du cocontractant qu'à celle d'un tiers[34] mais chacun doit tout de même veiller à la sécurité d'autrui, notamment lorsqu'il y a un lien entre la victime et celui qui est à l'origine de "l'insécurité". Dans le fond, il s'agit peut être davantage d'un problème de causalité que de pure responsabilité.

Surtout, l'obligation de veiller à l'intégrité corporelle d'autrui ne nous semble pas de l'essence du contrat, dont l'objet est purement patrimonial,

[33] Cf. Josserand, Mélanges Gény, p. 345, qui écrivait déjà: "en réalité, les obligations que l'on insère ainsi dans certains contrats ne sont plus à base de consentement, mais à base d'autorité".

[34] En ce sens cf. J.A. Jolowicz, Droit anglais, Dalloz n° 202 p. 146: "vous devez protéger ceux qui se fient à vous".

économique: le dommage corporel n'est pas l'affaire du contrat! (ce pourquoi le préjudice corporel subi lors d'une intervention médicale ou chirurgicale ne devrait pas, selon nous, relever de la responsabilité contractuelle).

(b) L'invention est encore plus célèbre: il s'agit de la fameuse distinction, proposée en 1928 par R. Demogue, entre les obligations de résultat et les obligations de moyens. On sait que cette nouvelle classification a été concue dans un objectif probatoire et il faut bien reconnaître qu'elle a eu effectivement pour conséquence d'aboutir à un parallélisme quasi parfait des règles de preuve en matière contractuelle et délictuelle. Certes, dans la première hypothèse, le créancier, victime de l'inexécution dommageable, est théoriquement dispensé de prouver une faute du débiteur, puisque celle-ci se déduit de l'inexécution, alors qu'en matière délictuelle la victime doit prouver le comportement fautif de l'auteur du dommage, du moins selon le droit commun des articles 1382 et 1383 du code civil.

Mais cette différence s'est progressivement estompée, tout d'abord parce que, selon la jurisprudence, le débiteur contractuel n'est parfois tenu que d'une obligation de moyens, ce qui oblige le créancier à prouver une conduite fautive, ensuite, et inversement, parce que la jurisprudence fait de plus en plus souvent peser sur l'auteur du dommage, en matière délictuelle, une "présomption de responsabilité". La symétrie entre les règles de preuve se vérifie encore avec le système intermédiaire de la présomption de faute, auquel correspond la récente "obligation de résultat atténuée" (mise à la charge notamment du garagiste réparateur ou du teinturier).

### *Le Renforcement de la Responsabilité Contractuelle*

De manière générale, il faut tout d'abord remarquer que, malgré des finalités a priori distinctes (bien que toutes deux tendent à réparer un dommage, la responsabilité délictuelle est surtout préoccupée d'indemnisation, alors que la responsabilité contractuelle "n'est qu'un remède parmi d'autres à l'inexécution du contrat": P. Jourdain, les principes de la responsabilité civile, p. 33), la responsabilité contractuelle n'a pas échappé au phénomène de "socialisation", à l'instar de ce qui s'était produit, bien avant, dans le domaine de la responsabilité délictuelle: en fait, notamment lorsque le débiteur est une collectivité (comme la SNCF) ou un contractant professionnel (presque toujours obligatoirement assuré), comme en droit, avec le développement de la responsabilité contractuelle sans faute, où "le débiteur reste tenu de tout ce qui n'est pas force majeure démontrée".[35]

De manière plus précise, ce renforcement de la responsabilité contractuelle se traduit par une double évolution: d'une part elle s'étend maintenant à des hypothèses qui étaient jusqu'à présent l'apanage de la responsabilité délictuelle, d'autre part elle est dotée d'une force devenue comparable à celle de la responsabilité délictuelle.

[35] J. Carbonnier, op. cit. n° 159, p. 303, qui y voit une application de la théorie du risque.

**L'extension de la responsabilité contractuelle**
Elle a été réalisée dans deux directions et sur le modèle des régimes spéciaux de la responsabilité délictuelle.

Alors que l'article 1147 n'envisage, semble-t-il, qu'une inexécution *personnelle* du débiteur, la jurisprudence admet maintenant que celui-ci soit contractuellement responsable du fait d'autrui et du fait des choses.

*(a) La responsabilité contractuelle du fait d'autrui.* Si l'on met à part les rares hypothèses où le code civil rend responsable certains débiteurs pour le dommage causé par des tiers[36] la question s'est posée de savoir s'ils pouvaient, de manière plus générale, être responsables du fait d'un tiers volontairement introduit dans l'exécution du contrat.

Alors qu'il n'y a, en l'occurence, aucune disposition comparable à celle de l'article 1384 du code civil, la jurisprudence n'a pas hésité à retenir la responsabilité contractuelle du fait d'autrui, qu'il s'agisse de personnes substituées ou de simples auxiliaires (transporteur responsable du vol commis par son chauffeur, chirurgien responsable du dommage causé par l'anesthésiste, société de surveillance responsable des cambriolages de son préposé, etc . . .).

Il faut remarquer que l'admission d'une telle responsabilité n'a pas donné lieu aux controverses particulièrement vives qui ont agité la responsabilité délictuelle, à la suite de l'arrêt, d'ailleurs peu explicite, rendu par l'Assemblée Plénière le 29 mars 1991.[37] L'explication pourrait être recherchée dans le fondement de ces responsabilités: alors qu'il est difficile de justifier l'existence d'une responsabilité générale du fait d'autrui, sur le plan délictuel, dans la mesure où l'article 1384 établit une liste limitative, l'admission d'une responsabilité contractuelle du fait d'autrui peut s'expliquer plus aisément: le débiteur est personnellement tenu des obligations figurant au contrat, qu'il les accomplisse lui-même ou qu'il en confie l'exécution à un autre. Il ne s'agirait donc pas vraiment d'une responsabilité contractuelle du fait d'autrui . . . mais d'une responsabilité contractuelle tout court.[38] L'on pourrait d'ailleurs tout aussi bien justifier cette extension en rappelant que l'article 1147 n'institue pas une véritable responsabilité.

*(b) La responsabilité contractuelle du fait des choses.* Le débat est un peu similaire au précédent: tout d'abord, il n'y a aucune difficulté lorsque la chose, objet du contrat, ne satisfait pas le créancier puisqu'en ce cas, il n'y a pas de problème de responsabilité mais de simple inexécution. Lorsqu'en revanche le dommage est causé par une chose utilisée lors de l'exécution du contrat, la règle du non-cumul semble devoir exclure l'application d'une responsabilité

[36] Le locataire, selon l'art. 1735 du code civil—l'hôtelier, selon l'article 1953.

[37] Affaire Blieck, Dalloz 1991.324, note C. Larroumet.

[38] En ce sens C. Larroumet, note précitée—adde D. Rebut "De la responsabilité contractuelle du fait d'autrui et de son caractère autonome", Revue de la recherche juridique, droit prospectif 1996-2.

délictuelle, de sorte que se pose de nouveau le problème d'une responsabilité contractuelle du fait des choses. Certes, là aussi, l'on pourrait simplement constater que le dommage résulte d'un manquement à une obligation contractuelle et qu'il y a lieu d'appliquer directement l'article 1147, d'autant qu'il n'existe pas d'équivalent de l'art. 1384 alinéa 1er en matière contractuelle.

Reste néanmoins l'hypothèse délicate où le dommage est causé par une chose, dans un contrat où le débiteur n'est tenu que d'une obligation de moyens. Jusqu'à une époque récente, une jurisprudnce assez confuse esquivait la difficulté, soit en appliquant l'art. 1384 al.1er malgré l'existence d'un contrat (arrêt Valverde), soit en chargeant le débiteur d'une obligation de sécurité de résultat.[39]

Une étape décisive a été franchie par l'arrêt, déjà cité, rendu par la 1ère Chambre civile le 17 janvier 1995, dans un motif très "doctrinal", manifestement inspiré de la tournure de l'art. 1384 alinéa 1er: à la suite de l'accident causé par un cerceau, l'établissement d'enseignement, rappelons-le, a été déclaré "responsable des dommages . . . causés non seulement par sa faute, mais encore par le fait des choses qu'il met en oeuvre pour l'exécution de son obligation contractuelle". De cette manière, la Cour de cassation esquive le raisonnement, purement contractuel, qui aurait obligé à distinguer entre l'obligation de résultat et l'obligations de moyens (car, dans ce type de contrat, la jurisprudence avait plutôt tendance à considérer que l'obligation n'est que de moyens). La décision préfère opposer responsabilité pour faute et responsabilité sans faute, de la même manière qu'en matière délictuelle. Malgré tout, la haute juridiction n'a pas voulu aller jusqu'au bout de sa logique et a cru bon, pour rester dans le giron de la responsabilité contractuelle, d'imaginer un critère spécifique (et plus restrictif: celui des choses "mises en oeuvre . . ."), alors qu'il aurait été plus simple d'abandonner tout raisonnement fondé sur une obligation de sécurité, afin d'avoir les mains libres pour appliquer . . . l'art. 1384 alinéa 1er du code civil!

Quoi qu'il en soit, cet arrêt montre parfaitement que, bien souvent, l'affirmation d'une responsabilité contractuelle est purement formelle et que son régime s'imprègne de plus en plus des règles de la responsabilité délictuelle.

**La force de la responsabilité contractuelle**

En supposant que le principe de la responsabilité a été admis, l'intensité de la dette va pouvoir être mesurée selon deux indicateurs: la faculté d'exonération, qui va déterminer le poids exact de la responsabilité, et l'étendue de la réparation, qui va déterminer le montant définitif de la dette.

[39] Notamment 1° Chambre civile 22 janvier 1991, Bulletin civil I n° 30, Revue trimestrielle de droit civil 1991.539 observations P. Jourdain.

*(a) Le poids de la responsabilité.* L'exonération, qui consiste précisément à "enlever du poids", est sans aucun doute la meilleure mesure de la responsabilité.

Or il est remarquable de constater que les causes d'exonération ne sont envisagées par aucun texte du droit commun de la responsabilité (sauf le cas particulier de la responsabilité parentale) et que la jurisprudence applique uniformément les textes écrits pour la matière contractuelle.[40]

De même, l'intervention d'un tiers ou de la victime elle-même, non prévue par le code civil, exerce une influence similaire dans les deux types de responsabilité:

(i) dans les deux cas, le fait du tiers est traité comme un cas particulier de force majeure et, s'il en revêt les caractères, est une cause d'exonération totale; et il en va de même pour le fait de la victime, qu'il soit ou non fautif (avec cette remarque qu'une telle exonération totale n'est pas concevable si le défendeur est fautif, qu'il soit l'objet d'une action délictuelle—fondée sur l'article 1382—ou d'une action contractuelle—fondée sur une obligation de moyens);

(ii) en revanche, mais toujours dans les deux types de responsabilité, la faute de la victime, même si elle ne présente pas les caractéres de la force majeure, est une cause d'exonération partielle (son fait non fautif n'ayant aucun effet libératoire).

*(b) le poids de la réparation.* Bien que ce soit l'aspect où la responsabilité contractuelle présente le plus d'originalité, des points de convergence peuvent être relevés:

(i) tout d'abord, et dans chacune des responsabilités, l'indemnisation est de plus en plus tributaire de la gravité de la faute commise par l'auteur ou la victime, avec des modalités certes différentes, mais selon une politique commune qui, tenant probablement compte de l'"usure" de la faute ordinaire, réintroduit un facteur de culpabilité dans le droit de la responsabilité civile: ainsi, non seulement la faute intentionnelle ou dolosive entraîne, en matière contractuelle, la réparation des dommages imprévisibles, mais elle est aussi une cause légale d'exclusion de garantie en droit des assurances; en outre, la faute lourde ou inexcusable infléchit les règles d'indemnisation dans les régimes spécialement institués pour les accidents (du travail et de la circulation, de même dans le transport aérien et maritime);

(ii) ensuite, les conventions relatives à la réparation, annulables en matière délictuelle (mais la solution est critiquée et elle ne s'applique pas aux conventions conclues après la réalisation du dommage), sont certes autorisées en matière contractuelle au nom du principe de l'autonomie de la volonté; mais, en raison de abus auxquels ces clauses peuvent

[40] Essentiellement l'article 1147 et l'article 1148 du code civil relatif à la force majeure.

donner lieu (elles sont le plus souvent imposées dans des contrats d'adhésion et favorisent la négligence du débiteur), le principe de validité recoit tant d'exceptions . . . qu'il n'est pas loin d'être renversé! En effet, les conventions affectant le droit à indemnisation sont inefficaces si le dommage est causé par la faute intentionnelle ou dolosive (à laquelle est assimilée la faute grave) du débiteur, si elles concernent une obligation "essentielle" du contrat,[41] si elles visent une atteinte à l'intégrité physique ou encore si elles peuvent être considérées comme abusives, à l'égard d'un consommateur . . .

(iii) enfin, la clause pénale, qui est assurément une "exclusivité" contractuelle, connaît actuellement une telle situation de crise que son avenir est passablement compromis: d'une part quant à sa qualification, avec ce paradoxe que celui qui l'insère en conteste ensuite l'existence . . . pour en éviter la réduction, d'autre part et précisément quant à sa possible révision, la jurisprudence allant jusqu'à supprimer la pénalité en l'absence de préjudice,[42] ce qui, au moins dans ce cas, ôte à la clause pénale toute fonction d'intimidation (cf. le droit anglais, qui interdit la clause pénale . . . mais autorise les parties à s'accorder pour fixer le montant des dommages-intérêts).

Ces dernières orientations du droit positif n'effacent pas la distinction entre les règles d'indemnisation, mais amorcent certainement, dans les deux types de responsabilité, un mouvement favorable au principe de réparation intégrale.

Absorbée peu à peu par la responsabilité délictuelle ou imprégnée de son régime, la responsabilité contractuelle occupe une place inconfortable, en quelque sorte "en porte-à-faux", de sorte qu'il paraît nécessaire, en conclusion, de s'interroger sur l'avenir de l'institution.

Deux directions peuvent être imaginées:

(a) la première consisterait, de manière radicale, à supprimer la distinction entre les responsabilités: soit en s'efforçant de les uniformiser (en rapprochant leur régime), soit en cherchant à les unifier, par une application systématique du droit commun de la responsabilité délictuelle ou par l'instauration d'un régime autonome, mais forcément extracontractuel;[43]

(b) la seconde maintiendrait la dualité des responsabilités, soit en conservant le statu quo . . . avec son lot de contradictions et d'injustices, soit par une recomposition des différents régimes de responsabilité: un auteur propose ainsi de "soustraire des situations à l'alternative entre les deux régimes opposés" pour les soumettre à un régime autonome, donc débarrassé de l'interdiction du "cumul" (les troubles de voisinage, les

[41] cf. 1° Chambre Civile 23 janvier 1994, JCP 199.I.3809, observations G. Viney. Affaire Chronopost, Com. 22 Octobre 1996. Dalloz 1997. p. 121, note A. Seriaux.

[42] Com. 16 juillet 1991, Dalloz 1992.365, note critique D. Mazeaud.

[43] Sur cette option, voir P. Jourdain, note précitée au Dalloz 1995, spécialement p. 355.

responsabilités professionnelles), avec une réduction des différences entre les deux responsabilités "au minimum qu'exige le respect du contrat."[44]

Cette dernière proposition s'harmonise effectivement assez bien avec les orientations du droit positif, où la victime est traitée de la même manière, qu'elle soit contractante ou tiers: loi du 5 juillet 1985 sur les accidents de la circulation, directive du 25 juillet 1985, arrêt du 17 janvier 1995.

Nous estimons, pour notre part, qu'il convient surtout de mieux cloisonner des institutions fondamentalement différentes et, par un "pélerinage aux sources", ramener la pseudo "responsabilité contractuelle" à son étiage naturel: la sanction de l'inexécution contractuelle par l'octroi de dommages-intérêts au seul créancier, et uniquement pour le préjudice patrimonial directement causé par le manquement aux obligations figurant au contrat; tous autres dommages pourront ainsi être réparés par un mécanisme de responsabilité civile, et non par une technique contractuelle qui a amplement montré qu'elle n'était pas appropriée.

De cette manière, la dualité des sources d'obligations pourrait être finalement respectée, car il ne faut pas confondre le respect de la parole donnée—fondement du contrat, issu des volontés individuelles—et l'obligation de réparer les conséquences dommageables de ses actes—fondement de la responsabilité civile, issue de la volonté publique.[45]

## SOMMAIRE

La "responsabilité contractuelle" existe-t-elle?

Question impertinente (l'institution figure aussi bien dans les textes que dans la jurisprudence ou dans les ouvrages), mais qui mérite plus que jamais d'être posée, car la responsabilité dite contractuelle est devenue un véritable mythe: une responsabilité ne peut naître d'un contrat et l'article 1147 du code civil n'évoque que les "dommages et intérêts résultant de l'inexécution de l'obligation" (et non les dommages causés *par* l'inexécution).

La jurisprudence française maintient poourtant la distinction entre la responsabilité contractuelle et la responsabilité délictuelle avec, pour fâcheuse conséquence, la règle du "non-cumul", tout en s'efforçant de sauver la responsabilité contractuelle en lui administrant des doses massives de responsabilité délictuelle![46]

D'une part, la responsabilité délictuelle reconquiert donc le territoire de la resopnsabilité contractuelle, d'autre part, et dans le large domaine qu'occupe encore la responsabilité contractuelle, celle-ci est "colonisée" par les règles de la responsabilité délictuelle.

[44] G. Viney, opus cité, p. 426, 444 et s., 452.

[45] C'est la dissociation qu'opérait déjà Charles Sainctelette, en 1884, dans son ouvrage intitulé "de la responsabilité et de la garantie".

[46] cf. affaire du "cerceau" – 17 janvier 1995..

*1. La Reconquête*

Double repli de la responsabklité contractuelle:

**La reconquête du temps contractuel**, avec une application prépondérante de la responsabilité délictuelle, non seulement dans les périodes précontractuelle (rupture abusive des pourparler, violation du devoir de renseignement) et post-contractuelle (obligation de non-concurrence), mais aussi lorsque le contrat est formé mais que le dommage se produit hors de son exécution (revirement de jurisprudence par l'arrêt Valverde du 7 mars 1989, qui soumet les accidents de quai à la responsabilité délictuelle).

**La reconquête de l'espace contractuel**, limité d'une part à la stricte sphère contractuelle (la responsabilité délictuelle s'applique si le contrat est nul, si les relations ne sont pas vraiment contractuelles ou lorsque le législateur édicte des régimes spéciaux, tel celui des accidents de la circulation, régi par la loi du 5 juillet 1985, ou enfin à défaut de lien suffisant entre le dommage et l'inexécution), d'autre part au cercle des contractants (rejet de la théorie des groupes de contrats par l'Assemblée Plénière, dans l'arrêt Besse du 12 juillet 1991).

*2. La Colonisation*

Double imprégnation de la responsabilité contractuelle par les règles de la responsabilité délictuelle:

**Par "forçage" du contrat**, avec d'une part la découverte d'obligations accessoires, telle surtout l'obligation de sécurité, difficile à justifier sinon par une politique d'indemnisation, et de nature comparable aux devoirs généraux qui fondent la responsabilité délictuelle, d'autre part l'invention de la distinction entre les obligations de résultat et les obligations de moyens, qui aboutit à un système de preuve symétrique de celui de la responsabilité délictuelle.

**Par renforcement de la responsabilité contractuelle**, étendue tout d'abord à la responsabilité du fait d'autrui et, plus récemment, à la responsabilité du fait des choses, dotée ensuite d'une force équivalente, dans la mesure où les deux responsabilités admettent des causes d'exonération similaires et où les disparités tenant à la réparation ont tendance à s'estomper.

Dès lors, l'avenir de la responsabilité contractuelle doit être redessiné, soit en ramenant les deux responsabilités civiles à l'unité, soit en maintenant leur dualité, quitte à mieux les cloisonner.

## ENGLISH SUMMARY[47]

Contractual Liability—does it exist?

An impertinent question (the institution can be found both in the legal texts and in caselaw or doctrinal writings), which deserves, however, more now

[47] English translation of the Summary by S. Banakas, University of East Anglia.

than ever before, to be asked; because the so-called contractual liability has become a real myth: contract cannot give birth to liability, and article 1147 of the Code Civil refers only to "compensation of losses resulting from the non-performance of the obligation" (and not to losses caused by the non-performance).

Nevertheless, the courts in France have sustained the distinction between contractual and delictual liability with the rule of non-cumulation, an irritating repercussion, while, at the same time, they do their best to save contractual liability by administering to it massive doses of delictual liability![48]

Thus, on the one hand, delictual liability reconquers the territory of contractual liability while, on the other hand, and in the large domain still occupied by contractual liability, the later is "colonised" by rules of delictual liability.

### 1. *The Reconquest*

Double recoil of contractual liability:

**The reconquest of contractual time**, with a predominant application of delictual liability, not only in the pre-contractual (abusive termination of negotiations, breach of the duty of information) and post-contractual (obligation of non-competition) periods, but also when the contract has been made but the damage is caused outside its performance (change of precedent in the decision Valverde of 7 March 1989, that places the accidents of the quay under the regime of delictual liability).

**The reconquest of the contractual space**, on the one hand restricted to the strict contractual sphere (delictual liability applies if the contract is void, if relations are not truly contractual or where the legislator imposes special regimes, such as that of traffic accidents, governed by the Law of 5 July 1985, or, finally, because of lack of sufficient causal link between the damage and the non-performance), and on the other hand restricted to contractual parties only (rejection of the theory of "groups of contracts" by the Plenary Assembly of the Cour de Cassation, in the decision Besse of 12 July 1991).

### 2. *The Colonisation*

Double impregnation of contractual liability by rules of delictual liability:

**With the "stretching" of contract**, with, on the one hand, the discovery of accessory obligations, especially the obligation of security, difficult to justify except on the basis of a policy of compensation, and of a comparable nature to that of the general duties that are the foundations of delictual liability, and, on the other hand, with the invention of the distinction between obligations of result and obligations of means, that leads to a system of proof symmetrical to that of delictual liability.

[48] See the case of "cerceau"—17 January 1995).

**With the strengthening of contractual liability**, extended, first of all, to liability for another's acts or omissions and, more recently, to liability for damage caused by things, and then endowed with a force of equal value, to the extent that the two liabilities accept similar defences and also to the extent that the disparities with regard to assessment of damages tend to blur.

From this moment the future of contractual liability must be re-designed, either by bringing back together the two civil liabilities in unity, or by maintaining their duality, at least by divising them better.

# 13

# *The Myth of Contractual Liability in French Law—A Comment*

MALCOLM CLARKE

## Future Shock?

In his elegantly constructed chapter, Professor Lapoyade Deschamps has pointed up what he describes as the myth of contractual liability in French law. This comes as something of a shock to the English lawyer who expects there to be contractual liability (doesn't everyone have it?) and especially to the English lawyer with some knowledge of French law, who will surely have heard with some wonder of the separation of contractual and delictual liability under the principle of *non-cumul*.

On a closer reading of the chapter, however, it becomes apparent that the myth lies not in the existence of contractual liability in French law but in the belief that contractual liability has a distinct and significant role. In particular, Professor Lapoyade Deschamps shows how in practice the separation of contractual and delictual liability is not observed and that, once they come together, it is delict that has taken over contract.

In the course of this deconstruction, there are many points that might be raised. Here are some.

## Has English Law Become More French than French?

If a repairer who has contracted to repair pipes does not repair the pipes properly, there is liability for consequent leaks of water, oil etc in England. There is liability in France too but there, we are told,[1] the liability in contract has lost all its "originality". In England this cannot be said because, for example, the theory of compensation that can be obtained from the defaulting repairer is what Lord Diplock called one of secondary promises and implied consent[2]—unless, of course, with the departure of Lord Diplock we have ditched this part of Lord Diplock's legacy of common law theory together with others such as his common law theory of subrogation.

[1] *Supra*, p. 176.

[2] See e.g. *The Heron II* [1969] 2 QB 659, CA.

Another example concerns the liability of the carrier for goods in his charge pre- and post- the period of actual transport.[3] Instead of importing ideas from tort, although there is of course have some subjacent bailment, English law bases liability mainly on implied terms, if there are gaps in any applicable contract. English courts do not, like those in France, look for solutions in tort.

Finally, when it comes to fault and the influence of delict on contract which, we are told,[4] is marked in French law, English law is more ambivalent. On the one hand, English law retains a number of strict contractual ideas in the commercial sphere, whereby there is a notion of risk assumption by a promisor which no amount of "frustration" or difficulty will excuse.[5] On the other hand, in the non-commercial sphere, tort does sometimes influence contract.[6]

A condition in a householder's insurance policy required the insured to "take all reasonable steps to safeguard any property insured and to avoid accidents which may lead to damage or injury". One January, the insured and family set out for the Dover ferry on holiday. In a case measuring 12 inches by 6 inches in the locked glove compartment of the car was valuable jewellery. The reason, as the insured had previously told the insurer's agent, was that, having had a burglary at home, he felt the jewellery would be safer with him than back at home. Being early for the ferry, they stopped to have a quick look at Dover Castle. The car park was unattended. What were they to do about their things? Having discussed the matter, they took their money and travellers cheques but left everything else in the car. On their return 15 minutes later, they found that the car had been ransacked. The insurer argued that the insured was in breach of the condition—that the insured should either have taken the jewellery with him to the Castle or left one of the party behind in the car. In the response of the Court of Appeal we see the template of tort. The Court approached the issue of construction of the contract and its application to the case as if confronted with the issue whether a defendant had been in breach of a duty of care actionable in tort. The gravity of the risk (thieves like jewellery) and the triviality of the occasion (a casual unscheduled visit to Dover Castle) counted against the claimant. However, the small chance of theft (short absence from empty car park in January) and the difficulty of taking adequate precautions counted in his favour. On balance, held the Court, the insured might have been careless but had not been reckless; he was not in breach of the condition of care (strictly construed), and his claim against the insurer succeeded.

[3] *Supra*, p. 179.

[4] *Supra*, p. 189ff.

[5] See *Intertradex SA* v. *Lesieur Tourteaux SARL* [1978] 2 Lloyd's Rep 509, CA.

[6] See e.g. *Sofi* v. *Prudential Assurance Co Ltd* [1993] 2 Lloyd's Rep 559, CA.

**Hard Lines and Parallel Presumptions?**

If there is a greater tendency to *présomption de responsabilité* in delict in France,[7] as we are told by Professor Lapoyade Deschamps, are there not similar signs in England, signs seen, for example, in the doctrine of *res ipsa* and also in nuisance since the *Cambridge Water* case?[8] Do we now share on each side of the Channel, with or without fires in the Tunnel, a greater sense of the danger of things and less trust in technology and in those in authority who tell the man who, having left the Clapham bus to eat roast beef on a restaurant car speeding through the Channel Tunnel: "enjoy your meal! there is nothing to worry about"?

**Are the French really any less French?**

We are told that *non-cumul* is defended in form but that, in substance, it has survived only by means of *des contorsions juridiques*. The suggestion is that the substance is rather different from the form, and that the cross-breeding of ideas is such that the apartheid is now artificial. If any English lawyer, having read Lord Goff of Chieveley's speech in *Henderson* v. *Merrett*,[9] is tempted to say "we told you so", that would not be very polite: for one thing, at the end of his chapter Professor Lapoyade Deschamps expresses a personal preference for a return to the essential duality. For another thing, it would be inappropriate. The lack of any such division in the common law has not led to lack of rigidity in other respects. Whereas, for example, in France there seems to be a more developed notion of liability during pre-contractual negotiations,[10] in England this area is still something of a void between contract and tort. Why has English law taken so long to listen to Professors Jones, Birks, Burrows and Beatson?

As for the intrinsic merits on *non-cumul*, what can we say? Best nothing perhaps; but we must wonder perhaps whether *non-cumul* (or a Euro-version of it), if transplanted, would ever take in the common law climate. The past suggests that elegant academic distinctions will be overlooked by busy judges, who are bent on solving particular disputes as seems best in the circumstances—those same judges who have been told of the virtues of the incremental development of the law and who, consequently, tend to suffer judicial agoraphobia when they do not have some close analogy to hand on to.

[7] *Supra*, p. 180.
[8] *Cambridge Water Co* v. *Eastern Counties Leather plc* [1994] 2 AC 264.
[9] [1995] 2 AC 145, 193–4.
[10] See J. Schmidt, *Negotiation et Conclusions des Contrats* (Paris, 1982).

# 14

# *Contract, Unjustified Enrichment and Concurrent Liability: A Scots Perspective*

HECTOR L. MACQUEEN*

When in 1985 Peter Birks published the article which represents the beginning of the modern study of the Scots law of unjustified enrichment,[1] his first concern was to distinguish the subject from the law of contract. He was prompted to do so by the appearance of the second edition of David Walker's *Law of Contracts and Related Obligations in Scotland*, the last chapter of which dealt with unjustified enrichment.[2] Although, as Birks noted, Walker's treatment did not suggest that enrichment liabilities were contractual ones, and justified dealing with them in a contract book on grounds of practical and functional rather than analytical or conceptual overlap, nevertheless the conjunction of two analytically distinct branches of the law of obligations risked dangerous confusion. The risk was that contractual notions would enter, possibly delimit, and distort enrichment law. It was a risk which had befallen English law, but from which Scots law ought to be safe if it looked to its inheritance from the past. The institutional writer Stair had made clear in the seventeenth century the distinction between voluntary or conventional obligations such as contract, created by the will of the parties, and involuntary or "obediential" obligations imposed by law, such as arose in the law of delict and unjustified enrichment. He had rejected the potentially confusing Roman term of "quasi-contract" to denote the latter subject. This had been the analytic base for Scots law ever since and, while there was in addition a doctrine of implied contract, that had not swallowed up or restricted the independence of enrichment law.[3]

By and large, it remains true that Scots law distinguishes contract and unjustified enrichment, and modern work in the two fields continues to reflect this. Although the third edition of Professor Walker's work on *The Law of*

* I am grateful to Niall Whitty for helpful comment on an earlier draft.

[1] "Six Questions in Search of a Subject: Unjust Enrichment in a Crisis of Identity" 1985 *JR* 227.

[2] 2nd edn (1985), Ch 35. A 3rd edn was published in 1995.

[3] For the foregoing see Birks, *supra* n 1, 227–33.

*Contracts and Related Obligations in Scotland* (1995) retains its final chapter on "Obligations Arising from Unjust Enrichment", the editors of the tenth edition (also 1995) of *Gloag & Henderson's Introduction to the Law of Scotland*, the standard introductory work on Scots law, have retitled as "Unjustified Enrichment" the chapter known in previous editions as "Quasi-Contract", and it has been moved from its previous position within the treatment of the general law of contract to a much later and completely separate treatment alongside salvage. William Stewart's *Law of Restitution in Scotland* (1992), the first book-length treatment of the subject, scrupulously leaves contract law out of consideration. Volume 15 of the *Stair Memorial Encyclopedia*, which deals with the Scots law of obligations and was published in 1996, distinguishes the voluntary obligations of contract and promise from obligations imposed by force of law and obligations arising from a wrongful act, and includes unjustified enrichment and *negotiorum gestio* in the second category.

## 1. INSTRUMENTAL REASONS FOR CALLING ENRICHMENT QUESTIONS CONTRACTUAL

### *Prescription*

There are few instrumental reasons in Scots law for calling enrichment contractual. For example, the law of prescription makes explicit reference to obligations "based on redress of unjustified enrichment", those "arising from *negotiorum gestio*" and those "arising from, or by reason of any breach of, a contract or promise".[4] For all of these, and also for obligations of reparation under the law of delict, the prescriptive period of five years begins to run from the date upon which the obligation becomes enforceable. There is therefore no advantage for prescription purposes to be gained from calling an obligation delictual rather than contractual, one of the reasons which Andrew Burrows has recently given for favouring concurrent contractual and tortious liability under English law.[5] An interesting case on the interface between contract and enrichment for the purposes of prescription may suggest that there is also no particular advantage to be gained by switching from contract to enrichment. In *NV Devos Gebroeder* v. *Sunderland Sportswear Ltd*[6] a seller of goods claimed recompense in circumstances where, because a part of the goods supplied had been defective, it had been held unable to claim the

[4] Prescription and Limitation (Scotland) Act 1973, Sch 1, para 1(b), (c) and (g). For the comparative position, see I. Englard, "Restitution of Benefits conferred without Obligation", Ch 5 of P. Schlechtriem (ed), X *International Encyclopedia of Comparative Law* (1991), §§ 309–317.

[5] A. Burrows, "Solving the Problem of Concurrent Liability" (1995) 48(2) *CLP* 103, 114–24; a surprisingly pragmatic conclusion from an author who elsewhere in the same article favours "the discipline of clarity and rationality imposed by categorisation" (at 104). But Scots law reaches the same conclusion: *Robertson* v. *Bannigan* 1965 SC 20.

[6] 1990 SC 291.

contract price in respect of the goods which were not defective. The supply had taken place in or before December 1982, and the judicial decision that the price was irrecoverable occurred in 1986. It was only in 1988 that the recompense claim was mounted. It was held to be defeated by prescription. The seller had argued that it had no enforceable enrichment claim until the decision in 1986 that the contract price was not payable. The court held that the contract ceased to be a basis for the seller's claim, not on the judicial decision of 1986, but on their material breach before December 1982. The proper approach for the seller would have been to make a case on recompense from the outset as an alternative pleading to the claim based on contract, or to have introduced an amendment to the pleading before the expiry of the prescriptive period.

Another interesting aspect of the *Devos* case is its application of the rule that, if a "relevant claim" is made by the creditor under an obligation that interrupts the running of prescription, this has the effect of putting the clock back to the beginning and in effect giving the creditor a further five years' grace. In *Devos* the seller argued that the unsuccessful claim for the contract price was a relevant claim preventing prescription running against him in respect of an action of recompense based on the same facts. The court rejected this argument by a majority, holding that the contractual obligation to pay was distinct from that of recompense. Under the prescription statute a relevant claim is "a claim made by or on behalf of the creditor for implement or part-implement of the obligation". Lord President Hope commented:[7]

> "In my opinion there is no doubt that an obligation to pay the price due under a contract and an obligation to make recompense are based upon different principles of law. The obligation to pay the price is constituted by agreement, that is to say, by the agreement of the parties to the contract which they have entered into. The obligation of recompense is a remedy which is independent of contract, so much so that it is excluded if the matter in question is the subject of a contract which can still be enforced . . . [T]he legal basis for these two obligations is separate and distinct . . . [T]he quantification of the sum to be paid in order to discharge the obligation is different. On the one hand the price due is fixed by the contract, whereas the amount to be paid by way of recompense has to be assessed by reference to the extent to which the defenders have been enriched."

Lord Coulsfield dissented from this approach, concerned by the seeming oddity of the result that the buyers would not have to pay for goods which they had admittedly used and for the value of which the sellers had been suing for several years, the claim having been prescribed for lack of action. He said:[8]

> "It seems to me to be singularly artificial to say that the pursuers made no 'relevant claim' . . . prior to . . . December 1987 . . . [It] is true that the claim founded on the 1987 amendment is a claim grounded on the equitable rule of recompense,

[7] *Ibid.* at 303–4.
[8] *Ibid.* at 310.

> not a claim founded on the terms of the original contract. I do not question that these are different legal grounds of claim or that the value of the claim of recompense is different from that of the claim for the contract price. Nevertheless, in the circumstances of this case, the proper view is, in my opinion, that the pursuers' claim in the action as originally raised was a claim for what was due to them out of the transaction by which they supplied goods which the defenders used. The fact that the pursuers' claim was originally based on the terms of the contract should not, in my view, require that claim to be read so narrowly as to exclude another legal ground derived from exactly those facts and circumstances which have all along formed the subject matter of the action."

While there may be a good deal of sympathy for Lord Coulsfield's approach in the circumstances of the case, the analysis of the majority must be preferred, at least as a matter of the interpretation of the statutory language concerning relevant claims. The statute speaks of *relevant* claims made for *implement* of an obligation. To be relevant, a claim must relate to the obligation which it is now sought to enforce. None of the judges oppose the proposition that payment of a contract price and recompense are different kinds of obligation; a contractual claim cannot implement an obligation of recompense, nor *vice versa*. The real problem with the *Devos* case is that it got off on the wrong foot with a holding that the seller's material breach disabled him from recovering payment. Under the law as it stood at the time of the case, a buyer confronted with the supply of a consignment of goods part of which was faulty had to reject the whole consignment (in which case he was not liable for the price) or else accept the whole consignment, pay the price and offset it with a claim for damages.[9] So, had the case been correctly decided in the first place, there would have been no need to contemplate alternative means of reaching the just result. It is fortunate in these circumstances that the court resisted the temptation to distort the basic structure of the law and the words of the prescription statute.

The case is important, however, for its recognition that unjustified enrichment can arise in the setting of performances which were rendered under a contract. As we shall see in more detail later, this is consistent with a number of other earlier authorities and also, I shall suggest, with principle. The upshot is that a party may frame a claim in terms of contract and enrichment as alternative juridical bases for the action and, indeed, would be well advised to do so lest one fail when it is too late to turn to the other. The competency of such alternative pleading has been further recognised in *Bennett* v. *Carse*.[10] It may also be very important in cases where the facts may give rise to claims of implied contract or of enrichment, to be discussed below.

[9] *Aitken Campbell & Co Ltd* v. *Boullen & Gattenby Ltd* 1908 SC 490. See now the Sale of Goods Act 1979, s 35A, added by the Sale and Supply of Goods Act 1994, s 3.

[10] 1990 SLT 454.

## *Jurisdiction*

Another important area of Scots law where instrumentalism has been resisted is in the application of the Civil Jurisdiction and Judgments Act 1982, which implements in the United Kingdom the Brussels Convention on Jurisdiction and the Recognition of Judgments in Civil and Commercial Matters 1968. The Act confers jurisdiction upon certain courts other than those of the defender's domicile in matters "relating to" a contract, delict and quasi-delict, but makes no reference to matters relating to unjustified enrichment.[11] In *Strathaird Farms Ltd* v. *G A Chattaway & Co*[12] Chattaway, a firm domiciled in England, supplied goods and services under a contract to Strathaird, a company domiciled in Scotland. Strathaird raised an action in the Inverness sheriff court for repayment of an overpayment of £5,000. The question was whether this was a matter relating to a contract so that the courts for the place of the performance of the obligation in question had concurrent jurisdiction with those of the English defender's domicile. Scots law holds that it is a debtor's duty to pay or perform at the creditor's place of business. Sheriff Principal Ireland held that the action was a *condictio indebiti*, in which "the obligation arises not *ex contractu*, by virtue of any promise or agreement by the debtor that he will pay, but *ex lege*, because it would be unjust to allow the debtor to retain what he has received".[13] Thus the creditor was entitled to be paid in Scotland and argued that the Scottish courts therefore had jurisdiction. Following Scottish authority binding upon him if relevant,[14] Sheriff Principal Ireland took the view that "relating to a contract" meant "based on a contract", which did not include a case such as the present one where "the existence of the contract between the parties is only part of the historical background explaining why the payment was made".[15] Sheriff Principal Ireland also thought that, had the statutory expression been "*related* to a contract" rather than "relating", the outcome would have been different:[16]

> " 'A matter *related* to a contract' clearly denotes something other than a contract which nevertheless has a relationship with the contract (*Oxford English Dictionary*, s v 'related', 2a). On the other hand the phrase 'in matters *relating* to a contract' need not import a reference to something outside the contract; the words 'in matters relating' are a prepositional expression equivalent to 'with reference to' (*Oxford English Dictionary*, s v 'relate' II 7). I am conscious that in the construction of European legislation words are often found to mean something different from what

[11] For commentary on "matters relating to a contract", see P.R. Beaumont, *Anton and Beaumont's Civil Jurisdiction in Scotland*, 2nd edn (1995), paras 5.17–5.28 and 9.18.

[12] 1993 SLT (Sh Ct) 36.

[13] *Ibid.* 37I.

[14] Which was debatable, since they were cases on delict. For another recent Scottish case on "matters relating to a contract" in a delictual context, see *William Grant & Sons Ltd* v. *Marie-Brizard & Roger International SA* 1996 GWD 23–1347.

[15] 1993 SLT (Sh Ct) 36, 39L.

[16] *Ibid.* at 40B–D.

> may at first appear to be the proper construction. Nevertheless, on the assumption that the draftsman . . . was an accurate and fastidious craftsman, I see no reason why he should not be supposed to have used the word 'relating' deliberately, so that the matters referred to in the clause would be confined to contracts, to the exclusion of matters which are not contracts, even if they have some connection with them. If he had intended to include such non-contractual matters he would, on the assumption which I have just made, have used the word 'related'."

No doubt this "relatively narrow construction of matters relating to a contract"[17] will have to be reconsidered in the light of the finding by a majority of the English Court of Appeal in *Kleinwort Benson Ltd* v. *Glasgow District Council*,[18] one of the many cases arising out of the decision in 1990 that "swaps" transactions between various finance houses and local authorities were *ultra vires* the authorities and therefore void. In the *Kleinwort* case the action for restitution of payments made under the void transaction was raised in England but the Scottish defendants argued that, the matter not being one relating to a contract, the only appropriate court was the one of their domicile, presumably the Court of Session or the Glasgow sheriff court. At first instance this plea was successful;[19] on appeal the Court of Appeal first made a reference of the issue to the European Court of Justice, which declined jurisdiction to make a ruling;[20] the Court of Appeal, Leggatt LJ dissenting, then took the view that the claim was a matter relating to a contract and that, England being the place of performance of the obligation, the English courts had concurrent jurisdiction in the case.

The reasoning of the majority is interesting. Millett LJ expressly rejects the view that "relating to a contract" means "based on a contract'. The word "contract" includes "a void contract"; there is a real difference between the case where negotiations had not led to a concluded contract, where there was no contract at all, and the case where they had led to a contract, so that there was a contract in fact, but one of the parties lacked contractual capacity, so that there was no contract in law. In the proceedings before the European Court of Justice three member States and the European Commission had submitted that the claim was one relating to a contract, while only one (Germany) had taken the opposite stance.[21] It would be strange if the court deciding the issue of validity could not also decide the consequences of the invalidity. The wording of the legislation was deliberately vague to deal with the notorious difficulty of distinguishing contractual from restitutionary claims, and the fact that different States dealt with the overlap in different

[17] Beaumont, *supra* n 11, 227.

[18] [1996] QB 678.

[19] [1993] QB 429.

[20] (Case C-346/93) [1995] ECR I 615; [1996] QB 57.

[21] The member States which argued that the case was one relating to a contract were Spain, France and the United Kingdom. I am very grateful to Mr Nicolas Lockhart of the Chamber of Judge David Edward in the Court of Justice of the European Communities, for kindly supplying me with copies of the Report for the Hearing in the case.

ways. Roch LJ derived support for his conclusion from earlier authority in the European Court of Justice that a matter relating to a contract included one where the parties' relationship was akin to a contract;[22] and took the view that, since English law would apply to the claim, giving jurisdiction to the English court meant that the territorially best-qualified court would decide the matter.

Much of this is plainly result-oriented rather than conceptual reasoning, and does not wholly convince. As Leggatt LJ points out, most European jurisdictions recognise contract, tort and restitution as three distinct branches of the law. A restitutionary claim is therefore not a contractual one, and there was no doubt that the present claim was restitutionary in nature. The view that English law was applicable appears to rest on Article 10(1)(e) of the Rome Convention on the Law Applicable to Contractual Obligations 1980 (made part of both Scots and English law by the Contracts (Applicable Law) Act 1990), which declares that the consequences of a null contract are governed by the law applicable to the contract. But this overlooks the express reservation against Article 10(1)(e) having the force of law in the United Kingdom made in section 2(2) of the 1990 Act precisely because this is a matter, not for the law of contract, but for the law of unjustified enrichment.[23] The omission of a provision in the Brussels Convention with regard to jurisdiction equivalent to that of the Rome Convention on applicable law could be taken as showing legislative intent in the former to exclude the consequences of nullity from the exceptions to the general rule that the appropriate jurisdiction to deal with the dispute is that of the defender's domicile. It is no objection that this means a Scottish court deciding a case according to English law; such is the very stuff of international private law. Most of Millett LJ's arguments also lack conviction: it seems counter-productive to regard a void contract as some sort of contract for at least some sorts of purposes, and there is no reason, in a pure question of law and interpretation, to give greater value to the views of a majority of those EC member States and institutions which had made observations on the subject to the European Court. The only argument of Millett LJ by which I find myself at all swayed is the strangeness of a court being able to determine that a contract is void (it is accepted that a claim that a contract is void is a matter relating to a contract for the purposes of the Brussels Convention[24]) but not the consequences of that voidness; and even that remains a result-oriented rather than a conceptual objection.

[22] *Martin Peters Bauntemehmung GmbH* v. *Zuid Nederlandse Aannemers Vereniging* (Case 34/82) [1983] ECR 987. This case is not on all fours with *Kleinwort Benson* v. *Glasgow*, since it involves what is clearly a valid consensual relationship (membership of a voluntary association) which happened not to be treated as contractual under either of the two potentially relevant laws (German and Dutch).

[23] *Hansard* (1990) 513 HL Deb, cols 1258–9. In its submissions to the European Court of Justice the German Government suggested that Art 10(1)(e) was of no value in interpreting the jurisdiction convention since two contracting states had entered a reservation in respect of it.

[24] *Effer* v. *Kantner* (Case 38/81) [1982] ECR 825.

The *Kleinwort* case is to go to the House of Lords, and it will be clear from what I have said that I believe reversal of the Court of Appeal would be correct. However, it is probably unlikely; the English courts have historically been avid for jurisdiction. Conversely, the Scottish courts have often been strangely happy to turn customers away, usually to England![25] Presumably, however, if a claim to restitution following a void contract is "a matter relating to a contract", then so will be those cases such as *Devos* and others to which I will refer later where enrichment or enrichment-based claims arise in situations where there is a valid contract; that is, on breach or frustration.

## *Choice of Law*

The *Kleinwort* case also indirectly raises choice of law issues at the interface of contract and unjustified enrichment. So far as the particular issue of void contracts is concerned, the matter is not settled for the United Kingdom as a result of its express reservation from Article 10(1)(e) of the Rome Convention. Also open is the situation where the void contract is one to which that Convention does not apply, or, again, where an enrichment claim arises in connection with a contract which is not void. Is this a matter of contract or enrichment law? The result could make a crucial difference to which system of law applies to the claims arising. Following some academic discussion, the Scottish courts have recently had a first opportunity to pronounce on choice of laws in enrichment cases, in *Baring Bros & Co Ltd* v. *Cunninghame DC*.[26] Do we look at the place of divestment or the place of enrichment? Do we take the law of the forum in which the issue is being settled? If a contract, void or otherwise, is lurking in the background, do we take the law applicable to the contract? In the *Barings* case, another litigation arising from an aborted "swaps" transaction, Lord Penrose was confronted with a void contract which had contained a choice of English law. The pursuer argued that therefore English law governed its restitutionary claim arising from the nullity of the contract. After an extensive review of academic writing, Scottish and foreign, the judge took the view that the choice of law in a void contract could not determine the law to be applied to consequential enrichment remedies. While recognising a degree of force in the argument that the ends of justice and consistency might be best served if the law determining the nullity and the consequences thereof were the same, he pointed out that capricious results might also follow where, for example, there was a wholly artificial choice of law with no objective reality in the context of the parties' relationship. The qualified enactment of the Rome Convention in the United Kingdom recognised the possibility of two systems being applicable at different points in the unravel-

[25] See for example *Bank of Scotland* v. *IMRO* 1989 SLT 432.

[26] 1996 GWD 25-1405; J. Blaikie, "Unjust Enrichment in the Conflict of Laws" 1984 *JR* 112; A.E. Anton, *Private International Law*, 2nd edn (1991), 309; Stewart, *The Law of Restitution in Scotland* (1992), 206–11; F.D. Rose (ed), *Restitution and the Conflict of Laws* (1995).

ling of a void contract. In the end Lord Penrose endorsed the preferred general view amongst Scottish academics, which is that the country with the closest and most real connection with the enrichment should provide the applicable law, even if that could mean an outcome different from that applying to the contract, whether void or valid. The parties' intention, expressed in the void contract, was one but not a decisive factor. In a cross-border "swaps" transaction the identity of enrichment creditor and debtor oscillated, and it was pure chance which party ended up as creditor and which as debtor; so the location of the final enrichment could not be a decisive factor either. Accordingly the matter was appropriate for full evidence of the parties' relationship before a final decision.

At one point in his opinion Lord Penrose comments that[27]:

> "it may be that in the majority of cases in which a remedy in restitution is required following failure of a contract, for whatever reason, the facts and circumstances are likely to point to the same system of law as appropriate for the resolution of the quasi-contractual issues between parties as would have been appropriate for the resolution of contractual issues had the contract stood."

The *Devos* case (in which choice of law issues were not in fact raised, presumably because there was an express choice of Scots law, or a deliberate tactical decision not to raise the matter) can be used to illustrate some of the potential hazards. Article 4 of the Rome Convention will presume in the absence of other factors that the law applicable to the contract is that of the country where the party rendering the contract's characteristic performance has its domicile or central administration. The contract was one for the sale of goods, and the characteristic performance of such a contract is the non-money obligation, namely the supply of goods. The law applicable to the contract is therefore that of the supplier's central administration, that is, Belgium. But when the supplier makes his claim for enrichment, Scots law may be applicable because the enrichment took place in Scotland.

## 2. TREATING ENRICHMENT AND CONTRACT TOGETHER

In 1985 Peter Birks expressed the view that, not only were contract and unjustified enrichment quite distinct areas of the law of obligations, but also that "these involuntary obligations [*of unjustified enrichment*] ought to be treated entirely separately from contract".[28] While this proposition seems reasonable for initial exposition of the two subjects, there are a number of qualifications which ought to be entered. It would be a poor lawyer who was not fully aware of the interaction between contract and unjustified enrichment, and it is

[27] *Supra* n 26; transcript, at 59. I am very grateful to my colleague David P. Sellar, advocate, for obtaining a copy of the opinion of Lord Penrose for me.

[28] Birks, *supra* n 1, 228.

absolutely necessary for these advanced purposes to treat the two together at some stage. For confirmation of this, one need only look at some of the recent attempts to produce "codes" embodying internationally acceptable principles of contract law (e.g. those produced by UNIDROIT,[29] the European Contract Commission led by Professor Ole Lando,[30] and Harvey McGregor QC for the English and Scottish Law Commissions[31]), all of which have to deal with enrichment or restitutionary issues at various points. Again, the Scottish Law Commission has recently published for discussion a draft code of enrichment law which is the personal work of Dr Eric Clive, one of the Commissioners, and it makes frequent reference to contract law.[32] Enrichment cannot ignore contract, any more than contract can enrichment.

### *Enrichment Lawyers Cannot Ignore Contract Law*

First, then, why can an enrichment lawyer not ignore contract law? In various ways Scots law limits the availability of enrichment remedies where there is a contract. It is obvious that a contractual arrangement of this performance for that price cannot be upset by a claim on either side that the other is enriched under the contract. Fair price doctrines long ago evaporated in Scots law, if they were ever part of it. The Clive code of unjustified enrichment follows the existing law when it provides that an enrichment is justified and irrecoverable if the enriched person is entitled to it by virtue of a contract.[33] It has recently been held in the Inner House that even "windfall" gains which can be traced to contractual entitlements do not constitute enrichment.[34] There is also a rule clearly articulated in the cases that where there is a valid subsisting contract there can be no claim in recompense.[35] *Connelly* v.

[29] *Principles of International Commercial Contracts* (1994) (henceforth "PICC"); reprinted in F.D. Rose (ed), *Blackstone's Statutes on Contract, Tort and Restitution*, 7th edn (1996) 383.

[30] O. Lando and H. Beale (eds), *Principles of European Contract Law* (henceforth "PECL"); reprinted in F.D. Rose (ed), *Blackstone's Statutes on Contract, Tort and Restitution*, 7th edn (1996) 374. A first volume of these *Principles* was published in 1995, but the full version will appear in 1997. The present writer is the Scottish representative on the Lando Commission.

[31] H. McGregor, *Contract Code Prepared for the English Law Commission* (1993) (henceforth "McGregor Code"). For the background to this work in a joint project of the Scottish and English Law Commissions in the late 1960s and early 1970s to produce a contract code for the whole of the UK, see also A.E. Anton, "Obstacles to codification" 1982 *JR* 15, 20–2; Lord Davidson, "Law reform—the Case for Caution in an Age of Revolution" (1990) 35 *Journal of the Law Society of Scotland* 219, 220–1.

[32] Dr Clive's code (henceforth "the Clive code") appears as a separately published Appendix to Scottish Law Commission, "Judicial Abolition of the Error of Law Rule and its Aftermath" (Discussion Paper No 99 1996). It represents Dr Clive's personal views rather than those of the Scottish Law Commission, and is not a restatement of the existing law.

[33] Clive code, r 5(1)(d).

[34] *Dollar Land (Cumbernauld) Ltd* v. *CIN Properties Ltd* 1997 SLT 260. I am again grateful to David P. Sellar for providing me with a transcript of the judicial opinions in this case.

[35] W.M. Gloag, *The Law of Contract*, 2nd edn (1929) 320; *NV Devos Gebroeder* v. *Sunderland Sportswear Ltd* 1990 SC 291; *Morgan Guaranty Trust Co of New York* v. *Lothian RC* 1995 SLT 299, 309J–K, per Lord President Hope; *Dollar Land (Cumbernauld) Ltd* v. *CIN Properties Ltd* 1997 SLT 260.

*Simpson*[36] is authority for the proposition that, apart from frustration, the *condictio causa data causa non secuta* is not available in cases where there is a contractual relationship between the parties; a view propounded vigorously and persuasively both before and after that case by Robin Evans-Jones.[37] In the great case of *Morgan Guaranty Trust Co* v. *Lothian Regional Council*[38] Lord President Hope stated that the orderly development of Scots enrichment law would be best served if in general there were not different rules to be applied in each of its remedies without clear justification;[39] and it seems highly likely that there is a general rule against using any of the enrichment remedies where there is a valid subsisting contract.

This view gathers support from Niall Whitty's masterly analysis of indirect enrichment claims in Scots law.[40] In general it is clear that recovery of indirect enrichment is extremely rare in Scotland. One of the major factors in the cases deciding against recovery has been the existence of contracts in the enrichment chain between the pursuer and the defender. Where a pursuer has contracted with a third party (T) and from that contract there ensues a benefit to the defender, the Scottish courts have tended to the view that the pursuer relied on the credit of T rather than the defender in performing the contract, and hence has no recovery against the latter. Sometimes this is expressed as a matter of the pursuer's having suffered no loss, or as the defender's benefit being incidental, or as being simply a matter of the contract's existence being an absolute bar to the enrichment claim.[41] The existence of a contract between T and the defender may also have an effect, inasmuch as, if T uses moneys obtained from the pursuer to perform his contract with the defender, the latter cannot be enriched by payment of what he was owed by T, nor should he be exposed to a second claim by the pursuer, having given value for what he has received, albeit to the middleman T rather than to the pursuer, nor should he unfairly lose the advantage of defences available against T but not the pursuer.[42]

### *Contract Lawyers Cannot Ignore Enrichment Law*

A contract lawyer cannot ignore enrichment law because that law may solve some of the problems left by the application of contract law in particular situations.

[36] 1993 SC 391.

[37] See his articles, "Contract, Unjust Enrichment and the Third Reception of Roman Law in Scotland" (1993) 109 *LQR* 663; and (with J.A. Dieckmann), "The Dark Side of *Connelly* v. *Simpson*", 1995 *JR* 90.

[38] 1995 SLT 29.

[39] *Ibid.* at 310B. The Lord President was thinking in particular of the error in law rule in repetition (the *condictio indebiti*).

[40] "Indirect Enrichment in Scots Law" 1994 *JR* 200, 239 (two parts).

[41] *Ibid.*, 211–17.

[42] *Ibid.*, 217–21.

**Contract rules hold that there is no contract**

Many of the rules of contract law concern whether or not there is a contract. As noted above, the result of applying these rules may be that there is no contract although the parties act as though there was one. Instances of such situations would be the rules on void and illegal contracts, and agreements which are not recorded in due form (for example, in writing). In such cases, enrichment rules are frequently used in Scotland as in South Africa, to do justice between the parties in respect of performances rendered despite the invalidity.[43] This is also the approach to be found in the UNIDROIT and Lando Commission principles and the McGregor code.[44] Of course, this does not offend against the principles outlined in the preceding paragraphs, because in these situations there is no contract and so no problem on those grounds about setting enrichment law to work.[45] Furthermore, and subject to the debates mentioned below about the appropriateness of particular actions in different situations, in Scotland there is generally no need to point to "unjust factors" requiring the enrichment to be reversed, as may be the position in parallel situations in England;[46] it is usually enough that a transfer was made under a contract which was void. The legal cause of the transaction does not exist and retention of the enrichment is *ipso facto* unjustified. This is also the approach to be found in the Clive code.[47]

There may be other problems: for example, applying enrichment law to contracts void or unenforceable on grounds of illegality may cut across the policy underpinning the illegality of the contract.[48] Moreover, in Scotland there are debates over which of the various remedies may be applicable in given situations. In the *Morgan* case, it was held that repetition (the *condic-*

[43] See generally Scottish Law Commission, "Recovery of Benefits Conferred Under Error of Law", vol 2 (Discussion Paper No 95, 1993), paras 2.204–2.225. There are difficulties arising from Scots law's recognition of the *Abstraktionsprinzip*: see K.G.C. Reid, "Unjustified Enrichment and Property Law" 1994 *JR* 167, 175–8. For South Africa see J.G. Lotz (revised A. de W. Horak), "Enrichment", 9 *LAWSA*, paras 79, 83.

[44] PICC, *supra* n 29, art 3.17; PECL, *supra* n 30, art 4.116; McGregor Code, paras 565–7, 573–4, 585–7.

[45] For civilian systems generally see Englard, *supra* n 4, paras 5.64–5.127; P. Gallo, "Unjust Enrichment: a Comparative Analysis" (1992) 40 *AJCL* 431, 445–8, and R. Zimmermann, "Unjustified Enrichment: the Modern Civilian Approach" (1995) 15 *OJLS* 403, 406–7.

[46] For the debate on this subject in England see *Westdeutsche Landesbank Girozentrale* v. *Islington LBC* [1994] 4 All ER 890 (Hobhouse J and CA), commented upon by A. Burrows, "Swaps and the Friction Between Common Law and Equity" (1995) 3 *RLR* 15–29. In the House of Lords the case was determined solely upon whether or not compound interest was recoverable, but see the comments of Lord Goff [1996] AC 669, 682–3.

[47] Rules 2(3), 5(3), 7(2)(a).

[48] See for civilian systems generally K. Zweigert and H. Kötz, *Introduction to Comparative Law*, 2nd revd edn, trans T. Weir (1992) 614–20; for Scotland, R. Evans-Jones, "Repetition of Payments in *sponsiones ludicrae*" (1993) 61 *Scottish Law Gazette* 11; for South Africa, Lotz revd Horak, *supra* n 43, paras 82–4. The McGregor Code, paras 515–18, provides for "exceptional cases" where restitution upon illegal contracts is allowed.

*tio indebiti*) was the appropriate remedy for void contracts, a view supported by Robin Evans-Jones, and the position of South African law.[49] Niall Whitty and the Scottish Law Commission have however made a powerful argument that, where the voidness arises from the incapacity of the enriched (as in the *Morgan* case), the appropriate remedy is recompense.[50] Again, where a contract is illegal, there is debate as to whether the remedy (if there is to be one) is the *condictio ob turpem vel injustam causam* (as in South African law[51]), the *condictio indebiti* (this having embraced the former) or perhaps recompense.[52] The leading case of *Cuthbertson* v. *Lowes*[53] does not make explicit the basis upon which the pursuer was able to recover the market value of goods supplied under an illegal contract and presumably consumed. It may be that this debate underlines the need for Scots law to move forward from its traditional distinctions between different forms of action and concentrate instead upon the identification and application of general principles of unjustified enrichment.

**Pre-contractual negotiations**

A recurring issue in the Scottish cases is that of pre-contractual negotiations which leave it uncertain as to whether or not the parties have concluded a contract, or which are broken off without a contract being concluded.[54] Here the question is not the invalidity of an apparent obligation but whether the parties have reached sufficient agreement for there to be a contract at all. If not, and if there have nonetheless been exchanges of value between the negotiating parties, there seems no reason in principle why enrichment law should not be invoked.[55] On the whole, however, the Scottish courts have been

[49] R. Evans-Jones, "Swaps, Error of Law and Unjustified Enrichment" (1995) 1 *Scottish Law and Practice Quarterly* 1; R. Evans-Jones "From 'undue transfer' to 'retention without a legal basis' (the *condictio indebiti* and *condictio ob turpem vel injustam causam*)" in R. Evans-Jones (ed), *The Civil Law Tradition in Scotland* (Stair Society supplementary series, 1995). For South African law see Lotz revd Horak, *supra* n 43, para 79.

[50] N.R. Whitty, "Ultra Vires Swap Contracts and Unjustified Enrichment", 1994 *SLT (News)* 337; Scottish Law Commission, *supra* n 43, para 2.216; Scottish Law Commission, *supra* n 32, paras 4.28–4.40.

[51] Lotz revd Horak, *supra* n 43, paras 82–3.

[52] See Scottish Law Commission, *supra* n 43, paras 2.220–2.223, 3.1–3.12; R. Evans-Jones and D. McKenzie, "Towards a Profile of the *condictio ob turpem vel injustam causam* in Scots law", 1994 *JR* 60; Evans-Jones, *supra* n 49; A.F. Rodger, in *Gloag and Henderson's Introduction to The Law of Scotland*, 10th edn (1995), paras 29.6, 29.15 (p 484); W.D.H. Sellar, "Unjust enrichment" in *The Laws of Scotland: Stair Memorial Encyclopedia*, vol 15 (1996), para 66.

[53] (1870) 8 M 1073. This case was followed in the leading South African decision *Jajbhay* v. *Cassim* 1939 AD 537.

[54] For the comparative position see Englard, *supra* n 4, paras 5.128–5.131.

[55] There is also the situation where one party incurs pre-contractual expenditure without conferring a direct benefit on the other negotiating party. Scots law has allowed the party suffering loss to claim what is usually known as "reimbursement" in such cases, but the remedy has not been granted much in modern cases. The authorities are reviewed in *Dawson International Plc* v. *Coats Paton Plc* 1988 SLT 854.

reluctant to grant enrichment remedies in modern times, perhaps on the basis that where one party anticipates a successful conclusion to the bargaining process by commencing performance, the risk that the contract will not be concluded falls on him.[56] Sometimes in order to avoid apparently unjust results the court has adopted a broad approach as to what constitutes a contract, thereby enabling it to grant contractual remedies. A recent example is *Avintair Ltd* v. *Ryder Airline Services Ltd*.[57] The claim was for payment of commission in respect of services rendered. The defender argued that, although the services had been rendered, the parties had also been negotiating over the price and, in the absence of agreement on this essential term, there could be no concluded contract, and so no basis for payment existed. The court held that there was a contract despite the existence of dissensus between the parties. Lord President Hope commented:[58]

> "There is no doubt that parties must achieve consensus in idem upon all the essential matters before there can be said to be a contract between them . . . But it does not always follow that there is no contract where something which affects the parties' contractual relationship has not yet been agreed . . . But there is an important difference between cases where nothing has been done by either party to implement the alleged contract and cases where a party to the alleged contract has already provided the goods or services for which he seeks payment. It is likely to be more difficult in the former case to enforce the contract if there is no agreement about the remuneration which is to be paid, because in the ordinary case the price is one of the essential matters upon which agreement is required. Where goods or services have been provided, however, the usual rule is that there is an obligation to pay for them unless they have been provided gratuitously. So it is easier in these case, if there is no agreement about the price or remuneration, for an obligation to pay a reasonable sum to be implied."

With respect, this reasoning seems either to conflate the question of whether there is a contract with that of the price, if any, to be paid if there is a contract, or to assume, highly debatably, that there was a contract which did not contain a provision about price. It also seems to suggest that the question of whether or not there is a contract depends upon whether or not the parties have commenced performance. Thus Lord President Hope comments that the "no contract" argument "does not take sufficient account of the fact that the pursuers' case is that they have already rendered the services for which they claim payment".[59] A preferable approach would be to determine first whether or not there is a contract, and then to consider what if any payments should be made in respect of any actual exchanges of value between the parties. Where parties are still negotiating over a major term, it cannot be right to say that that process can be short-circuited by rendering performance and asking

[56] McBryde, *Contract*, 35–8.
[57] 1994 SLT 613.
[58] *Ibid*. at 615H–616A.
[59] *Ibid*. at 617D.

the court to fix a reasonable price on the basis of implied contract. But that is not to say that, if negotiations are broken off after performance has been rendered in good faith, there can never be any recovery. Unjustified enrichment may well have taken place and, in the circumstances of the *Avintair* case, the remedy in Scotland appears to be recompense.[60]

The case also illustrates an uncertainty often encountered in Scots law between the enrichment remedy of recompense and an implied contract.[61] Thus Lord President Hope comments that ". . . goods or services were provided which ought to be paid for. In such circumstances a claim may be based either on recompense or implied contract".[62] Earlier in his opinion he quotes with approval the comment of the textbook writer Gloag that "it may often be unnecessary to decide whether a claim for payment should be rested on implied contract or on the principle of recompense".[63] It has been rightly observed, however, that "this approach tends to obscure the distinction between contract and unjust enrichment".[64] The principal distinction referred to in the textbooks lies in the measure of recovery: *quantum meruit* in implied contract, *quantum lucratus* in recompense; but there may well be others, such as the availability of defences in one and not the other. The uncertainty may also be observed in cases where A allows B to use his property in circumstances where there is no intention to confer a gratuitous benefit. It has been suggested that wherever the background to this is consensual the appropriate action is implied contract; otherwise the case is one for recompense on the grounds of interference with proprietary rights.[65]

### Enrichment claims on valid but no longer subsisting contracts

Where a contract—or, more accurately, a contractual obligation—has ceased to subsist in the sense that although the contract was valid it is no longer enforceable, enrichment remedies may be used in respect of performances rendered under the contract for which there cannot now be a contractual recovery. The performances rendered under subsequently frustrated contracts which contain no provision dealing with this eventuality may be restored or paid for by enrichment remedies.[66] Insofar as this has involved the use of the *condictio causa data causa non secuta*, the authorities have been the subject of academic criticism in recent times but are probably too well-entrenched to be

[60] For further comment on *Avintair* also favouring an enrichment rather than a contractual approach, see G.D.L. Cameron, "Consensus in Dissensus" 1995 *SLT (News)* 132.

[61] See e.g. *Shetland Islands Council* v. *BP Petroleum Development Ltd* 1990 SLT 82; *Hamilton DC* v. *Lennon* 1990 SLT 533; *Rochester Poster Services Ltd* v. *A G. Barr Plc* 1994 SLT (Sh Ct) 2; *GTW Holdings Ltd* v. *Toet* 1994 SLT (Sh Ct) 16.

[62] 1994 SLT 613, 617F.

[63] Gloag, *Contract*, 291.

[64] Cameron, *supra* n 60, 134.

[65] *Shetland Islands Council* v. *BP Petroleum Development Ltd* 1990 SLT 82. See further A.J.M. Steven, "Recompense for Interference in Scots Law" 1996 *JR* 51, 52–6.

[66] See Englard, *supra* n 4, paras 5.167–5.199; McGregor Code, paras 598–9.

uprooted.[67] And there seems no reason why Scots law should not follow the example of South African law, and use other condictiones in such situations (e.g. the *condictio ob causam finitam*[68]) or its native remedy of recompense in services cases such as the English *BP Exploration Co (Libya) Ltd* v. *Hunt (No 2)*.[69] Contractual obligations may also cease to subsist through prescription—the absence of a relevant claim under or acknowledgement of the existence of the obligation for a continuous period of five years—and, as we have seen, the Scottish courts have accepted in principle that there may be an enrichment claim in respect of performances made under the prescribed contract.[70]

Valid contracts may be discharged by performance or lapse of time according to their terms. If performance continues thereafter without a new contract, enrichment may have a role. There are Scots cases where a contract for the hire of moveables came to an end, but the hirer continued in possession and was found liable in recompense.[71]

**Subsisting contracts: the claims of contract-breakers**

There are also situations where enrichment remedies may arise in respect of performances rendered under a valid and subsisting contract. A simple example is overpayment by a debtor in a contractual relationship.[72] The same would presumably be true in a case where the supplier of goods (and services?) oversupplied. The Scottish courts have also indicated on numerous occasions that enrichment remedies may be available to a contract-breaker who is unable to recover for his performance under the contract in consequence of the doctrine of mutuality, which, like the South African doctrine of reciprocity, states that a party in breach may not claim performance of what is due to him under the contract.[73] It seems that before the enrichment remedy may be used the innocent party must have terminated the contract. The classic case is that of the builder who fails to complete or completes defectively; but a

[67] Evans-Jones, *supra* n 37; G. MacCormack, "The *condictio causa data causa non secuta*", in R. Evans-Jones (ed), *The Civil Law Tradition in Scotland* (Stair Society supplementary series, 1995).

[68] For the *condictio ob causam finitam* in Scots law see Stair, *Inst*, I, vii, 7. It is also mentioned in Craig, *Jus Feudale*, III, v, 23. For the interesting suggestion that this *condictio* was (unwittingly) applied in the leading Scottish case of *Cantiere San Rocco SA* v. *Clyde Shipbuilding and Engineering Co Ltd* 1923 SC (HL) 105, see *Parkin* v. *Smuts* 1978 3 SA 55 (T), 58, per Van Reenen J.

[69] [1979] 1 WLR 783; *affd* [1981] 1 WLR 232; *affd* [1982] 2 AC 352.

[70] *NV Devos Gebroeder* v. *Sunderland Sportswear* 1990 SC 291.

[71] *Chisholm* v. *Alexander* (1882) 19 SLR 835. See further Steven, *supra* n 65, 53–5.

[72] See e.g. *Strathaird Farms Ltd* v. *G A Chattaway & Co* 1993 SLT (Sh Ct) 36.

[73] See generally for this and what follows H. L. MacQueen, "Unjustified Enrichment and Breach of Contract" 1994 *JR* 137, 149–66; also Sellar, *supra* n 52, para 67. On mutuality, which clearly derives from the civilian *exceptio non adimpleti contractus*, see most recently W.W. McBryde, "Remedies for Breach of Contract" (1996) 1 *Edinburgh LR* 43–78; *idem*, "Mutuality Retained", *ibid.*, 135–9.

number of other situations are illustrated in the Scottish sources.[74] Very often the courts have managed to resolve the problems without invoking the law of unjustified enrichment. By holding that a contract-breaker is not in material breach, and thereby removing the innocent party's remedy of termination, they have allowed him to sue for the contract price with a deduction or set-off for the other party's claim to damages for breach. However, this approach is simply not possible in all cases. The best example in the Scottish case law is *Thomson* v. *Archibald*,[75] where a builder abandoned the contract with the work only 45 per cent done. It cannot be pretended that the builder here was in anything but material breach, and it would be extraordinary if the contractual price was the starting point for any claim he might have. Equally there can be no claim at all unless the employer uses the work done as the basis for completion by another builder, because otherwise there can be no question of his being enriched. Given that the contract provides no answer if the employer does use the first builder's work as a basis for completion, it seems that resort must be had to the law of unjustified enrichment. Finally, this claim by the builder can of course be met by the employer's claim for damages for breach of contract.

The position which results may be complex. Let us suppose a building contract under which the price is £10,000. The builder abandons, having done 45 per cent of the work; for simplicity's sake, suppose that work is worth £4,500. The employer completes through a second builder at a cost of £7,000. If he does not have to pay the first builder, the employer is in fact better off through the breach and can get no or only nominal damages from the first builder. If however the first builder has an enrichment claim, the picture begins to change. If he gets £4,500, then the building has cost the employer £1,500 more than the original contract price. He has a loss which he can set off against the builder's enrichment claim. Thus it is only if the builder's claim does not lead to the employer having to pay more than the contract price *in total* that it can be made good in full. It was in this sense that I observed in 1994 that the contract price limits the enrichment *recovery*, rather than making a suggestion that it provided a limit for the enrichment *claim*.[76]

Given the background of his own case law, the Scots lawyer reacts with interest to the South African position, under which the contract-breaker disabled from making a contractual claim by the doctrine of reciprocity may nonetheless have a claim if the innocent party accepts the defective work even

[74] The latest case, *Dollar Land (Cumbernauld) Ltd* v. *CIN Properties Ltd* 1997 SLT 260, concerned the landlord's justified termination of a commercial lease and a claim by the erstwhile tenant to a "windfall" gain thereby allegedly arising for the landlord. It was accepted that a contract-breaker might have an enrichment claim but held (Lord Rodger of Earlsferry dissenting) that on the facts the gain was an intended contractual entitlement and that the contract expressly excluded recovery in the circumstances.

[75] 1990 GWD 26-1438 (Edinburgh Sheriff Court).

[76] See MacQueen, *supra* n 73, 163, more accurately expressed than the sentence at *ibid.*, 166, criticised by Dieckmann and Evans-Jones, *supra* n 37, 100 n 29.

when the contract has not been terminated. There has been controversy as to whether or not this is a contractual or an enrichment claim.[77] Other civilian systems also allow the contract-breaker a claim, usually classified as contractual, if the innocent party "accepts" the performance, subject to cure of any outstanding defects at the contract-breaker's expense.[78] Professor Visser, drawing on readings from Voet and other civilians, has argued that the South African courts have been wrong to deny the possibility of a contract-breaker's claim being one for enrichment.[79] The key to this is that a contractual claim will tend to start, as in Scotland, with the contract price, which incorporates an element of profit for the contract-breaker; a more appropriate start-point for recovery is surely the extent to which, if at all, the innocent party has been enriched by the performance actually rendered.

### *Contract Rules which Prevent Unjustified Enrichment*

A third point is that prevention of unjustified enrichment is one of the roles of contract law. There are a number of rules in which this is clear. Three examples seem particularly significant: restitution upon termination for breach, so-called *quantum meruit* claims, and *restitutio in integrum* after the reduction of a voidable contract.

#### Restitution upon termination of contract for breach

Scots law allows a party who has terminated a contract for the other's breach to claim restitution of any performance rendered before the termination.[80] "Restitution" is here used neither in its Scots technical sense as one of the enrichment remedies nor in the English sense as a general term for unjustified enrichment, but simply to mean "restoration". The basis of this in Scotland seems to be that an anticipated counter-performance under the contract has not been received, and that accordingly the contract-breaker is enriched. But this does not mean necessarily that enrichment law is operating within contract law in this instance. After *Connelly* v. *Simpson*[81] it would seem to be correct both as a matter of authority and of principle to say that this right of restitution is not an instance of the *condictio causa data causa non secuta*.[82]

[77] *Hauman* v. *Nortje* 1914 AD 293; *BK Tooling (Edms) Bpk* v. *Scope Precision Engineering (Edms) Bpk* 1979 (1) SA 391 (A).

[78] G.H. Treitel, *Remedies for Breach of Contract: a Comparative Account* (1988), 289, 308–10; Englard, *supra* n 4, paras 5.153–5.155.

[79] D.P. Visser "Rethinking Unjustified Enrichment: a Perspective of the Competition between Contractual and Enrichment Remedies" 1992 *Acta Juridica* 203, at 231–6.

[80] MacQueen, *supra* n 73, 139–49; Dieckmann and Evans-Jones, *supra* n 37; Sellar, *supra* n 52, paras 38–43. For the equivalent rules in South Africa see van Rensburg, Lotz and van Rhijn revd Christie, "Contract" 5(1) *LAWSA*, para 256, and for a more general comparative picture see Treitel, *supra* n 78, 382–92, and Englard, *supra* n 4, paras 5.135–5.146.

[81] 1993 SC 391.

[82] Scottish Law Commission, *supra* n 32, 86 n 305 suggests that the views which I expressed in MacQueen, *supra* n 73, are in conflict with the views of Professor Evans-Jones about the role

However, this does not mean that enrichment considerations are irrelevant, and in Scotland it is undecided whether a full-blown enrichment analysis can be applied to the claim, taking account, for example, of change of position defences which might be offered. German law clearly holds that the claim is contractual, and so requiring full restoration of what has been performed,[83] while South African law also appears to reject an enrichment approach to the question.[84] However, Professor Visser has argued that restitution upon termination of contract in South Africa is based on unjustified enrichment.[85] The Clive enrichment code provides that a person is to be treated as enriched if he has acquired an economic benefit under a contract terminated by rescission for breach, even if the benefit was received for some consideration under the contract, and that the contract will not justify retention of the enrichment;[86] meaning that the action for recovery in his scheme would be one under the general law of enrichment.

A crucial point is the tension between the restitutionary claim and the general acceptance in Scotland of the theory that termination of a contract is generally prospective in effect rather than retrospective. The tension is resolved in Scots law through the concept of accrued rights, which points to the enrichment-preventing nature of the remedy. There can be no restitution in respect of such accrued rights. The courts have been reluctant to hold that rights have accrued merely because they fall due under the contract. The concern has been that this could mean something akin to forfeiture of performances tendered before termination of the contract. Instead there is a clear tendency to find accrual when a performance has been met by the anticipated counterpart performance on the other side,[87] underlining the point that the contract rules are here operating to prevent enrichment of one side at the expense of the other.

An interesting recent decision on accrued rights is *Lloyds Bank* v. *Bamberger*.[88] A seller of heritable property rescinded from the contract

of the *condictio causa data causa non secuta*. This is a misrepresentation of my views: the article emphasises the existence of a right of restitution after breach, and avoids any comment on whether it is to be explained by the *condictio*.

83 Treitel, *supra* n 78, 388.

84 *Baker* v. *Probert* 1985 3 SA 429 (A). The point was of importance here because the plaintiff was seeking recovery of money paid to the defendant's agent but not transmitted on to the defendant, and it was argued against recovery that the defendant was therefore not enriched. It was held that payment to the agent was payment to the principal and that contractually the principal was bound to repay. The enrichment liability of a principal when only his agent has been benefited is an unresolved question in Scotland but there seems no strong reason of principle or common sense why he should not be liable: see Scottish Law Commission, *supra* n 43, 182–3.

85 Visser, *supra* n 79, 225–31. Note also R.H. Christie, *The Law of Contract in South Africa*, 2nd edn (1991), 635: ". . . the object of cancellation . . . is . . . to terminate the contract there and then but not retrospectively. Restitution by either or both parties should therefore be ordered only to the extent necessary to avoid unjustified enrichment".

86 Rules 2(3), 7(2)(b).

87 MacQueen, *supra* n 73, 144–6.

88 1993 SC 570.

following the purchaser's failure- to pay the price on time. Under a clause in the contract, the seller then claimed interest on the price for the period from the contractual date of entry to the date of the rescission. The court refused the seller's claim, on the basis that by rescinding the contract he was intimating that he was no longer prepared to accept payment of the price due under the contract, and could not now enforce a claim for interest on a price which *ex hypothesi* was no longer payable. The sellers argued that the rights under the interest clause had accrued prior to rescission, making the interest payable even though the price was not. There was much reference to, but little analysis of, the controversial English case of *Hyundai Heavy Industries Co* v. *Papadopoulos*.[89] There the House of Lords held that buyers of a ship to be built remained liable for an instalment of the price due on 15 July even after the shipbuilders rescinded for non-payment on 6 September, on the basis that the shipbuilders' right to the instalment had accrued before the rescission. This result looks like a forfeiture for breach, and the decision was by the narrowest of majorities, with one of the dissenters being the Scottish judge Lord Keith. The other Scottish judge (Lord Fraser) was however in the majority. However, he reasoned on the basis that the instalments were not simply part of a purchase price for goods but were designed to meet the shipbuilder's need for cash flow as work proceeded. In his view it was only if contractual payments were of this nature that a right to payment arising but not fulfilled before termination was not destroyed by that event. In other words, the right to payment did not accrue simply because the contract said payment was due; accrual occurred because the creditor had in some sense earned it.

*Lloyds Bank* v. *Bamberger* supports this approach as to when a contractual right may be said to have accrued so that it remains enforceable after rescission, and to be a rejection of the extreme interpretation of *Hyundai*, which is that rights arising before rescission are unaffected because rescission is only prospective in its effects. It is part of the court's argument that rescission can have retrospective effects, including restitution of payments made in advance of the receipt of the other side's performance. Lord Justice Clerk Ross states[90]:

> Under our law, a seller who rescinds such a contract of sale [*of land or goods*] cannot retain advances or instalments of the price that he has received, but is required to repay these to the purchaser unless the payment falls to be regarded as a deposit.

The possibility of restitution means that rights cannot be held to have accrued simply because they have fallen due and or have given rise to performance, unless the contract clearly so provides.

The Clive enrichment code also gives effect to the principle that restitution does not affect rights which have accrued in the sense that the performance has been reciprocated:

[89] [1980] 1 WLR 1129, HL.
[90] 1993 SC at 573.

> 7(3) . . . a contract which provides for performance in severable parts or stages is presumed, unless the contract indicates the contrary, to exclude redress in so far as performance by one party under, and substantially in accordance with, the contract has been met by performance by the other party under, and substantially in accordance with, the contract.

Although the right of restitution upon termination thus depends upon non-reciprocation, there is not any requirement of "total failure of consideration" apparent in Scots law in this area.[91] So restitution may follow upon proper performance upon both sides of the contract giving each party accrued and irrecoverable rights, with the restitution being only in respect of that part of the contract which was improperly performed.[92] A difficult question which has not received much attention is the relationship between the concept of accrued rights and the possibility of mutual restitution, as may happen in sale of goods when the buyer rejects faulty goods, returning them to the seller while at the same time reclaiming any payment of or towards the price. Perhaps it may be said that no right has accrued until the performance on one side has been met by the correct and non-contract-breaking performance of the other side.

The crucial question to which the existence of this right of restitution gives rise is whether the claimant may use it to avoid a bad bargain; that is to say, whether the contractual expectation may be defeated by the restitutionary approach.[93] The best Scottish illustration of such a situation is *Connelly* v. *Simpson*.[94] C paid £16,000 to S for one-third of the shares in S's company, but did not take delivery because he wished to minimise the value of his estate during his divorce proceedings which were also under way at this time. Over the following two years, the company did badly; S first issued more shares to raise capital, thereby diluting the value of C's holding, and then put the company into voluntary liquidation. C's shares were now worth just £400, and he was offered this sum by the liquidator. C's bargain was evidently a bad one, and he sought restitution from S of his £16,000. There are a number of technical difficulties about the case, including an uncertainty as to whether S was truly in breach and, as already noted, a debate about the applicability to the case of the *condictio causa data causa non secuta*. Setting these to one side, however, the real issue was whether C could avoid the consequences of a bad bargain, and the decision of the court was that he could not. Johannes

[91] There is an incautious reference to "total failure of consideration" by Lord Ross in *Lloyds Bank* v. *Bamberger* at 573 but it is submitted that this should be regarded as *per incuriam*.

[92] *Graham* v. *United Turkey Red Co* 1922 SC 583 may provide an instance where an agent was held entitled to commission earned before he broke the contract with his principal, but not to commission earned thereafter. Had the principal paid in advance, or paid before discovering the breach, he presumably could not have recovered pre-breach commission but only post-breach commission.

[93] See Burrows, *supra* n 5, 112–14.

[94] 1993 SC 391.

Dieckmann and Robin Evans-Jones have persuasively argued the opposite point of view, on the grounds that S was indeed in repudiatory breach and that it was therefore inappropriate for C to bear the resultant loss. However, it was not pleaded that S was in breach, and it is debatable whether the commercial decisions that he made did in fact constitute breach or repudiation. Thus, had S not put his company into liquidation, the Insolvency Act 1986 might have entailed his incurring personal liability to the company's creditors for unwisely keeping the company going in bad times rather than winding it up. Earlier, issuing shares may have been the only option by which the value of C's acquisition had some chance of being preserved. There certainly seems to be a considerable difference between this situation and the rather unlikely one figured by Dieckmann and Evans-Jones, where F pays J in advance for goods on a falling market and J in breach then somehow manages to resell the goods to H at a higher price. It could be readily agreed that J should repay F in these circumstances without it being an inexorable conclusion that in the *Connelly* case S should repay C.

The case also points back to the concept of accrued rights. For what had C paid his £16,000? The answer may not be shares but rather a right to delivery of shares upon demand. On both sides of this bargain rights had therefore accrued and could not be reversed through the subsequent ill fortunes of S's company. Lord McCluskey's opinion also dwells on the long interval in time which elapsed after C had paid his £16,000 as a factor against restitution. One is reminded of the limited period which a buyer has in a sale of goods to reject the goods; there may be acceptance barring rejection and restitution of the price by lapse of a reasonable time, although the buyer does of course still have a right to damages for the breach of contract.

A further interesting issue about restitution, rescission for breach and contract arises from a decision of the House of Lords in an English appeal, *Pan Ocean Shipping Ltd* v. *Creditcorp Ltd (The Trident Beauty)*.[95] In this case, P entered a time charterparty with the owners of a vessel (T). Under the charterparty hire payments were made in advance for 15-day periods. T assigned its rights to C under a credit facility arrangement. P usually paid C direct. T was unable to provide the ship for a period in respect of which P had paid C. T was not worth suing, and P claimed restitution from C. The judge at first instance upheld the claim but was reversed in the Court of Appeal.[96] The latter ruling was upheld by the House of Lords.

The ratio seems to be that the charterparty provided a mechanism for restitution by T if the ship could not be provided after an advance payment had been made. Lord Goff said that "it is always recognised that serious difficulties arise if the law seeks to expand the law of restitution to redistribute risks for which provision has been made under an applicable contract".[97] It was

[95] [1994] 1 WLR 161.
[96] [1993] 1 Lloyds Rep 443.
[97] [1994] 1 WLR 161, 166.

argued that on ordinary principles of assignation C could be in no better position than T with regard to the money. But the answer to this is that assignation can only transfer rights, not liabilities. As Lord Woolf put it: "Why should Pan Ocean have two alternative parties to whom to look for a repayment merely because Trident, as part of their own financial arrangements, have assigned their right to receive payment to a third party, Creditcorp?"[98] The difficulty is that in fact P had paid C direct, and not through the intermediary, T, and C knew what the payments were for; but the sparse Scottish authority supports the outcome in *The Trident Beauty* and the reasoning which underlies it.[99] In particular, while the debtor may take against the assignee the *defences* which it has against the cedent, it cannot invoke against the assignee the *counter-claims* which arise against the cedent.

Finally in connection with restitution upon termination, it is worth considering the relevant provisions of the UNIDROIT, Lando Commission and McGregor codes of contract law. The effect of termination under both the Lando (Article 4.305) and UNIDROIT (Article 7.3.5) codes is to release parties from their obligations to effect and to receive future performance. The Lando code alone states that accrued rights and liabilities are unaffected. Termination is thus basically prospective rather than retroactive. Nonetheless, under the Lando code the terminating party may reject property previously received from the other party if its value to the former has been fundamentally reduced as a result of the latter's non-performance (Article 4.306).[100] Money which has been paid for a performance which has not been received, or has been properly rejected, may be recovered after termination (Article 4.307). Similarly with property supplied and capable of return for which payment or other counter-performance has not been received (Article 4.308). If a performance has been rendered and cannot be returned, but there has been no counter-payment or counter-performance, a reasonable amount can be recovered for the value of the performance to the other party (Article 4.309). It should be noted that these remedies are also available to the contract-breaker.

UNIDROIT also provides for rights of restitution on termination, which may be applied for by either party, and is subject to concurrent restitution on the other side (Article 7.3.6). Where restitution in kind is not possible or appropriate, allowance should be made in money wherever reasonable. However, restitution is not to affect accrued rights: "if performance of the contract has extended over a period of time and the contract is divisible, restitution can only be claimed for the period after termination has taken effect".

[98] *Ibid.* at 171–2.

[99] See *Binstock Miller & Co* v. *Coia & Co* (1957) 73 Sh Ct Rep 178; supported as correct by W.A. Wilson, *The Scottish Law of Debt*, 2nd edn (1991), para 27.2 n 94, but criticised by McBryde, *Contract*, para 17.86. McBryde's criticisms are answered by H.L. MacQueen, "Title to sue", *The Laws of Scotland: Stair Memorial Encyclopedia*, vol 15 (1996), para 864.

[100] PECL 182, *supra* n 30, provides illustrative examples: (1) supply of computer without software; (2) supply of computer system without essential component.

The McGregor code also makes quite elaborate provision for a right of restitution upon termination (Articles 461–71). Either party may claim; there must be failure of a counter-performance but there is no need for "total failure of consideration"; there is no restitution where neither party is in substantial breach; and the contract consideration provides a ceiling on recovery.[101]

**Quantum meruit claims**

In *ERDC Construction Ltd* v. *H M Love & Co*[102] the Second Division of the Court of Session held that an innocent party who has terminated a contract following the other party's material breach may make what is called a *quantum meruit* claim in respect of the performance rendered before termination; essentially payment at a reasonable rate (as distinct from the contract price or the enrichment of the recipient of the performance). In so ruling the court followed English and Canadian authority.[103] The practical benefit for the innocent party arises where the contract provides no mechanism for pricing the work done prior to termination (as, for example, in a lump sum building contract) while at the same time avoiding the alternative but necessarily speculative claim for damages. Possibly, it may also give a better return than would be provided by either damages or the original contract price.[104]

As James Wolffe has pointed out,[105] the terminology of *quantum meruit* has a contractual overtone for the Scots lawyer;[106] yet the claim is one under which there is departure from the terms of the contract. The aim is clearly to prevent the enrichment of the defender at the expense of the pursuer. It would seem more appropriate to regard it as an enrichment claim, arising because a contractual claim for the price of work done is unavailable to one who has not yet completed the contract work.[107]

**Voidable contracts and** restitutio in integrum

Another body of contract rules which seem to function to prevent enrichment is that concerned with the reduction of voidable contracts. Scots law has accepted the doctrine that before a voidable contract can be reduced there must be *restitutio in integrum*, that is, restoration to the position before the contract was made. It has been argued by Professor Visser that, where

[101] Note that the Uniform Law on International Sales, art 78(2), and the Vienna Convention on the International Sale of Goods, art 81(2), also provide for restitution upon termination.

[102] 1995 SLT 254.

[103] *Lodder* v. *Slowey* [1904] AC 442; *Morrison-Knudsen Co Inc* v. *British Columbia Hydro and Power Authority* 85 DLR (3d) 186 (1978).

[104] As for example in the famous Californian case of *Boomer* v. *Muir* (1933) 24 P d 570 (Cal App 2).

[105] "Contract and recompense: *ERDC Construction Ltd* v. *H M Love*" (1997) 1 *Edinburgh LR* (forthcoming).

[106] See also *supra*, p 213.

[107] However, it cannot be said that no contractual remedy is available, given that there may be an action for damages.

applied, this remedy reverses enrichment.[108] Both parties are under a duty to restore; the requirement that *restitutio* be possible may give what is in effect a non-enrichment or change of position defence. In Scots law a very literal approach has been taken to the requirement that *restitutio in integrum* be possible, which tends to mean that restitution does not take place. In the last major case, however, a decision of the House of Lords in 1939, this literal approach was discouraged in cases of fraud, and monetary restitution was allowed.[109] Were a provisional proposal of the Scottish Law Commission that the courts be generally empowered to grant a monetary surrogatum for *restitutio in integrum* to be introduced, it would clearly be possible for the award to be determined according to enrichment criteria not confined to pure restitution in the Scottish sense of restoration of full value.[110] The Commission figures a case in which the voidable contract is for the sale of a painting believed to be a modern copy of a Rubens, but in fact a genuine Rubens which is then sold on; the buyer, it suggests, should not be liable to pay back the full value of a genuine Rubens but simply for the profit he has made on the transaction.[111] This seems perfectly consistent with the general principles of recompense.[112] It may finally be noted that the Clive enrichment code includes voidable contracts within its scope.[113]

## 3. CONCLUSIONS

What conclusions may be drawn from this rather brief survey of the Scottish position on the relationship between contract and unjustified enrichment? Put very simply, it seems that although, like other civilian and mixed systems, the law draws a clear distinction between the two branches of the law of obligations, this does not preclude a functional linkage in that very often the consequence of applying contract rules will be to leave the field open to unjustified enrichment. This is not merely a matter of saying that enrichment steps in when, despite what parties may expect and intend, no contract ever exists, or when a contract ceases to exist or to be legally enforceable, although that is obviously one of the most important roles of enrichment law. Clearly, however, enrichment can also operate when there is a contract, providing the solution when that contract does not yield up the answer to a problem. The classic example is that of the contract-breaking part-performer who nonetheless does effect a transfer of value to his contractual partner. In many cases it

108 Visser, *supra* n 79, 210–25.

109 *Spence* v. *Crawford* 1939 SC 52; [1939] 3 All ER 271, HL.

110 Scottish Law Commission, "Defective Consent and Consequential Matters" (Memorandum No 42, 1978), vol 2, Part IV.

111 *Ibid.* at 155.

112 See Steven, *supra* n 65, especially at 59–61.

113 Rules 2(3), 5(3).

would either be wrong or impossible to provide an answer to this problem by way of the contract, and the appropriate way of looking at the matter seems to me to be through the law of enrichment. I do not think that this will lead to over-protection of contract-breakers, because what must always be kept in mind is the undoubted existence of a breach of contract claim in the other direction, which will almost certainly ensure that the contract-breaker does not do better out of the breach than he would have done by performing.

This leads on to the perception that there is a fundamental antithesis between enrichment law, which effects restoration of parties to their pre-exchange position, and contract law, which puts parties in the position they expected to be in as a result of the transaction. But the distinction is a fine one in many instances, notably the type of case in which the Scottish courts have fumbled rather uncertainly between implied contract and recompense; that is to say, those involving the supply of goods which are then consumed, the supply of services, and the use of someone else's property. The upshot of such cases, whether determined according to contract law or enrichment law, is usually that the recipient pays the market rate for what he has received, looking very much more like a fulfilment of the transaction than a restoration. Again, in contract law it is clear that there are rules which allow the restoration of parties to a former position: restitution upon termination for breach and *restitutio in integrum* following the reduction of voidable contracts. There are other rules which show that prevention of unjustified enrichment is one of the goals of contract law.

Is there then a value in retaining the traditional distinction of contract from the law of unjustified enrichment? I would argue that there is, for at least two very obvious reasons. We began with Peter Birks' fear that unjustified enrichment might become contaminated by contract law in that it might be thought that no enrichment could be reversed unless there was some sort of contract-like relationship between the parties. That remains an important point, if only because there are so many non-contractual situations in which the law of unjustified enrichment quite properly applies, and misunderstanding would threaten that position. Equally, however, we should take the converse fear, that contract law might become contaminated by enrichment law. If prevention of enrichment is a function of contract law, it is quite clearly not the dominant function of contract law. To allow concepts of unjustified enrichment an unbridled scope throughout contract law would be to undermine fatally the fundamental justification for enforcing contracts, which remains the legitimacy of the pursuit of improvement in one's position even at another's expense, provided that certain minimal rules are complied with.[114]

[114] This article first appeared in 1996 *Acta Juridica*.

# 15

# *Contract, Unjustified Enrichment and Concurrent Liability: A Scots Perspective—A Comment*

JOHN STEVENS

It is impossible for an English property lawyer to do justice to Professor MacQueen's clear and comprehensive analysis of the availability of enrichment and contractual claims in Scotland. I will confine myself to a number of observations from his chapter and to raising a significant conceptual question which remains unanswered.

## Maintaining a Conceptual Distinction Between Contractual Obligations and Enrichment

From the perspective of English law, where much effort has been devoted to achieving the conceptual independence of unjust enrichment from the historical straight-jacket of the implied contract theory of restitution, it might be thought that a legal system with civilian roots would be better placed to avoid the confusion between enrichment and contractual claims. Professor MacQueen makes clear that in general conceptual confusion has been avoided. For example, the remedy of recompense of the price of goods which had been supplied under a contract was held to be distinct from a contractual obligation to pay the contract price in *NV Devos Gebroeder* v. *Sunderland Sportswear Ltd*[1] since it was not founded on the basis of the parties' agreement and the assessment of the remedy was determined by the receivers' enrichment rather than the contract price of the goods supplied. The fact that the Scottish prescription period is identical for contractual and enrichment claims also removes any incentive to confuse contractual claims as enrichment for procedural advantage.[2] However, the distinction has sometimes seemed in danger of being blurred as a consequence of the inevitable contextual overlap

[1] 1990 SC 291.

[2] Prescription and Limitation (Scotland) Act 1973. Unlike the English Limitation Act 1980, the Scottish provisions make explicit reference to obligations "based on redress of unjustified enrichment".

of the situations in which enrichment and contractual remedies operate. For example, where the parties have engaged in negotiations and one has conferred a benefit to the other without an express agreement having been reached as to price, it seems unclear whether the remedy available to the party who has conferred the benefit is founded on enrichment or contract. The Scottish courts have been willing to found an obligation to pay a reasonable sum for the benefit conferred on the basis of an implied term of a contract concluded between the parties, and in *Avintair Ltd* v. *Ryder Airline Services Ltd*[3] Lord President Hope suggested that it was unnecessary to determine whether the right to recovery was founded on recompense or an implied contract. This reasoning encourages an artificial approach to the formation of contracts where incomplete negotiations are given full contractual force, and opens the door to conceptual contamination between the enrichment and contractual obligations.

In common with English law the relationship between contractual and enrichment claims has come under close scrutiny in matters of private international law. Since the Civil Jurisdiction and Judgements Act 1982 makes no explicit reference to enrichment claims but refers to "matters relating to a contract", the question has arisen whether enrichment claims are to be regarded as sufficiently contractual to fall within this terminology for the purposes of jurisdiction. In *Strathaird Farms Ltd* v. *GA Chattaway & Co*[4] the court held that the phrase "relating to a contract" meant "based on a contract" so that a claim to restitution of an overpayment made by a company domiciled in England did not entitle the payee to seek recovery in Scotland where he had been entitled to be paid. As Professor MacQueen indicates, this approach may need revision in the light of the English Court of Appeal decision in *Kleinwort Benson* v. *Glasgow District Council*,[5] where recovery of a payment made under a void contract was held to be a matter "relating" to a contract. The problem of confusion between contract and enrichment is also evident in questions of the appropriate choice of law rules for a claim. If there was a void contract, are all issues arising therefrom to be determined by the proper law of the contract? This was avoided in *Baring Brothers & Co Ltd* v. *Cunninghame DC*[6] when it was held that a claim to enrichment arising from the nullity of a contract should be governed by the jurisdiction with which the enrichment had the closest and most real connection, not by the proper law of the contract, which was English law. These cases demonstrate that in Scotland, as in England, difficulties occasioned by the inadequacy of the present conflict of laws principles relating to enrichment claims should not be permitted to distort the hard won conceptual distinctions within the domestic jurisdiction.[7]

[3] 1994 SLT 613.
[4] 1993 SLT (Sh Ct) 36.
[5] [1996] 2 WLR 655.
[6] 1995 GWD 25-1405.
[7] See Rose (ed), *Restitution and the Conflict of Laws* (Mansfield Press, 1995).

**Comparative Substance of Scottish and English Law**

Professor MacQueen's survey of the availability of enrichment remedies also raises a number of comparisons with the substantive content of English law, and suggests that in both jurisdictions a measure of reform is necessary of the circumstances in which an enrichment remedy should be available. In Scotland, when a contract is subsisting the doctrine of mutuality prevents a party in breach claiming what is due to him under the contract. An enrichment remedy will only be available if the contract is terminated. However, the courts have tended to force such cases into contract rather than enrichment by holding that any breach was not material and the innocent party had no right to terminate. Such reasoning may be artificial and cannot always be sustained.[8] In relation to claims where the contract has been terminated as a result of breach, the Scottish approach is to treat the termination as prospective rather than retrospective and as a result enrichment claims are avoided in relation to rights which are regarded as accrued under the contract. Where restitution is available of benefits which have been conferred in the absence of accrued rights there is no requirement of a total failure of consideration before restitution is available. In *Connelly* v. *Simpson*[9] the Scottish court seemed right to conclude that a restitutionary remedy could not be used as a means of avoiding a bad bargain by recovering the price paid of shares where a person had purchased shares which had fallen in value before they were delivered to him. Professor MacQueen also suggests that the same result would have been reached if the facts of *The Trident Beauty*[10] had called to be determined by Scottish law, since a debtor may not invoke against an assignee counter-claims which arise against the cedent. As with English law, in the context of voidable contracts the application of the requirement that the parties must make *restitutio in integrum* limits the availability of enrichment remedies.[11] The Scottish Law Commission has suggested a monetary surrogatum for *restitutio in integrum* which would widen the availability of the enrichment remedy. Such monetary re-adjustment of the parties' position to take account of an inability to make *restitutio in integrum* would also be a welcome reform in English law, since there is no insurmountable difficulty assessing the value of a benefit which cannot be returned at a reasonable rate. Where a contract has been repudiated for material breach the innocent party is entitled, as in English law, to a *quantum meruit* at a reasonable rate in respect of his performance.[12]

[8] For example in *Thomas* v. *Archibald* 1990 GWD 26-1438.
[9] 1993 SC 91.
[10] [1994] 1 WLR 161.
[11] See, e.g., *Pearce* v. *Bain* [1929] 2 KB 310; *Valentini* v. *Canali* (1889) 24 QBD 166.
[12] *ERDC Construction Ltd* v. *H M Love & Co* 1995 SLT 254.

**An Unanswered Question: Are Contractual and Enrichment Remedies Cumulative?**[13]

Having provided a thorough survey of the relationship between enrichment and contractual claims in Scottish law, the central remaining question is as to the principles governing the availability of contractual and enrichment remedies which may arise out of the same facts. If the facts of a case could justify both enrichment and contractual claims, is the claimant entitled to recover both, or is he limited to one claim, or is his right of overall recovery in some way capped? Professor MacQueen anticipates the possibility of rival claims arising out of the same facts when he suggests in the light of *NV Devos Gebroeder* v. *Sunderland Sportswear Ltd*[14] that "a party may frame a claim in terms of contract and enrichment as alternative juridical bases for the action". The implicit assumption is that the contractual and enrichment remedies are alternative and not concurrent in nature, which would prevent the claimant obtaining double recovery. The Privy Council decision in *Tang Man Sit (Personal Representatives)* v. *Capacious Investments Ltd*[15] makes clear that the remedies of compensation or restitution for a wrong are alternative and a plaintiff must elect between them and cannot seek both. However, there is no direct authority as to the relationship between contractual and enrichment remedies and whether they are to be regarded as alternative in this way. Professor MacQueen's chapter indicates a number of potential resolutions to the problems of cumulative liability. Scottish law restricts the availability of actions so that a contractual remedy and an enrichment claim cannot be sought at the same time. In *NV Devos Gebroeder* v. *Sunderland Sportswear Ltd*[16] recompense was held unavailable while there was a contract which could still be enforced and in *Connelly* v. *Simpson*[17] it was held that the *condictio causa data causa non secuta* was not available where there was a contractual relationship between the parties. This leads Professor MacQueen to conclude that "it seems highly likely that there is a general rule against using any of the enrichment remedies where there is a valid subsisting contract". However, this does not answer the conceptual problem whether where a contract has been terminated a party is entitled to claim both his expectation loss and restitution of any enrichment he has conferred. For example, if a builder has contracted to build a house and is unable to complete performance because of the other party's breach, is he entitled to recover only the contract price for his work, or can he claim restitution of the value of the enrichment he has conferred on the purchaser (namely the value of the uncompleted

[13] This section owes much to the comments of Professor Andrew Burrows at the discussion which followed the original presentation of Professor MacQueen's paper.

[14] 1990 SC 291.

[15] [1996] AC 514; Birks (1996) 112 *LQR* 375; J Stevens [1996] *RLR* 117.

[16] 1990 SC 291.

[17] 1993 SC 391.

house) and the measure of profit which he would have obtained under the contract if it had been fully performed? Where a claimant is seeking restitution of the value of work he has done Professor MacQueen suggests that the contract price that he agreed for the work should provide a cap to limit the amount of the enrichment conferred he can recover,[18] so that the other contracting party will never have to pay remedies in excess of the contract price *in total*. However, this is tantamount to suggesting that the restitutionary claim is not autonomous of the contractual claim since the measure of recovery is not the objective value of the benefit conferred but the contract price. This may raise no objection if the contract price was freely agreed, but why should the claimant of an enrichment be limited to the contract price of his work if the pricing is unduly low because of the lawful but intrinsically stronger bargaining position of the other party? Or, why should a contract price which was agreed under duress, whether traditional or economic, provide a limit to recovery in enrichment? If the right to restitution is genuinely "not *ex contractu*, by virtue of any promise or agreement . . . but *ex lege* because it would be unjust to allow the [recipient of the enrichment] to retain what he has received",[19] there is no theoretical justification why the contract price should determine the extent of recovery.

Similar difficulty arises where a contracting party seeks a *quantum meruit* of work done when he has breached his contract because he has made a bad bargain and wishes to recover the true market value of his work rather than the contract price.[20] Again there is an intuitive feeling that such a result would be incorrect, since it allows a party to escape a bad bargain and not take the consequences of his failure to negotiate a realistic price, but if the enrichment claim is distinct from the contractual claim there is no obvious legal reason why recovery should be so limited.[21] The argument that the contractual price should serve as the means of calculating restitution on a *pro rata* basis and form a "valuation ceiling"[22] of the enrichment may serve to avoid a result which is felt to be inappropriate, but suggests that any enrichment must simply be a sub-species of the expectation interest generated by the contract, a consequence which is inconsistent with the supposedly autonomous nature of the enrichment claim. It seems illogical to suggest that the cause of action is autonomous but that the assessment of the remedy flowing from it is not.

Despite the intuitive feeling that there should be no recovery of both restitution and compensation, there is as yet no developed theoretical justification why a claimant should be denied recovery of both. The most simple solution, namely that restitution and compensation are alternative remedies, cannot be

[18] See also H.L. MacQueen, "Unjustified enrichment and breach of contract" 1994 *JR* 137.

[19] *Strathaird Farms Ltd* v. *GA Chattaway & Co* 1993 SLT (Sh CT) 36, 37.

[20] As in *Boomer* v. *Muir* 24 Pd 570 (1933). See Burrows, "Solving the Problem of Concurrent Liability" [1995] *CLP* 103, 112–12.

[21] See Burrows, *The Law of Restitution* (Butterworths, 1995), 268–70.

[22] See Birks, "In Defence of Free Acceptance", Ch 5 of A. Burrows (ed), *Essays on the Law of Restitution* (Clarendon Press, Oxford, 1991), 105, 135–7.

sustained, as has been demonstrated by Professor Treitel.[23] The problem is that enrichment and contractual remedies derive from separate and distinct causes of action, in much the same way as tortious and contractual causes of action may arise from the same facts.[24] However, while both tortious and contractual causes of action seek to achieve the same objective of compensating the plaintiff for his loss, albeit that such loss may be differently assessed, enrichment and contractual causes of action serve fundamentally distinct purposes. Where it may be correct to prevent a plaintiff recovering his loss, which is singular, by two separate routes, is there a genuine difficulty of double recovery where enrichment and loss are claimed? Professor Treitel suggests that there is an inherent limitation on a claimants recovery in that "*full* damages and *complete* restitution . . . will not be given for the same breach of contract",[25] on grounds of the policy against double recovery, but recovery is only double if in some sense the restitutionary measure of recovery is subsumed within loss or *vice versa*. Even an award of *partial* restitution and *partial* compensation may exceed either *full* restitution or *full* compensation alone, and therefore give rise to the intuitive feeling that double recovery, or at the very least excessive recovery, must have taken place.

Professor MacQueen is surely right to conclude that there is a "fundamental antithesis between enrichment law, which effects restoration of the parties to their pre-exchange position, and contract law which puts parties in the position that they expected to be in as a result of the transaction" but in the light of the inevitable contextual overlap between them this very antithesis demands that the law analyse more closely the relationship between the contractual and enrichment causes of action and the restitutionary and compensatory remedies available to satisfy them. This relationship has yet to be clarified by either English or Scottish law, and it is imperative that a principled rather than purely intuitive solution be developed to solve the problems of cumulative liability between enrichment and contractual claims.

23 *Remedies for Breach of Contract* (1988), 98–100. See also Birks (1996) 112 *LQR* 375.

24 See Burrows, "Solving the Problem of Concurrent Liability" [1995] *CLP* 103.

25 Citing A.L. Corbin, *On Contracts* (1963); *Baltic Shipping Ltd* v. *Dillon* (1992) 176 CLR 344.

# 16

# *Contract and Restitution: A Few Comparative Remarks*

ELTJO SCHRAGE*

The Dutch Supreme Court (the Hoge Raad) recently gave judgment in a case which goes to the heart of my topic. The general background to these decision is not really complicated. In outline it is as follows. The sale and delivery of medicines and drugs in the Netherlands is mainly regulated by a statute of 1958, which has undergone several changes in the course of the years. The general principle is that the sale and delivery of drugs obtainable upon prescription is restricted to licensed pharmacists. There is, however, a problem which arises from the transition from a previous system: there survives a limited number of general practitioners in the countryside who still fulfil the role of a pharmacist. The statute tolerates this exception to a limited degree, in that the doctor is allowed to sell prescription drugs under licence but only to his own patients. There was a further restriction, limiting the doctor's right geographically, so that he could not sell within five kilometres of the nearest pharmacy. This geographical restriction, however, was recently replaced by another one: section 6.1 of the statute concerned states that the doctor is only allowed to sell and deliver drugs when his practice is established in a community if no pharmacist is established in either that or in one of the neighbouring communities.

There is no provision in the statute concerning the question whether the doctor is entitled to damages when he loses his right as a consequence of the establishment of a professional pharmacist in the neighbourhood. For that reason the professional organisations, the Royal Society for the Advancement of the Medical Science and its counterpart for Pharmacy, entered into a contract, containing model calculations for the compensation to be paid by the pharmacist to the doctor in cases in which the licence to sell drugs passed from the doctor to a pharmacist.

Both Royal Societies encouraged their members to conclude their contracts on the conditions and against the prices stipulated by the Societies. The model contract even included a calculation for variable conditions. If a doctor loses his licence as a consequence of the institution of a pharmacy and he refuses to transfer the goodwill of his drugs business immediately, the recommended

* I am grateful to Peter Birks for help in finalising the English text of this paper.

price declines to 75 per cent after one year, and 50 per cent after two years. At seven years the amount payable falls to nil.

The story begins in 1980. The plaintiff, Batelaan, was a general practitioner, licensed to practise and to have a pharmacy as part of his practice in a few communities in the countryside. In March 1980 a pharmacist, Van der Tuuk Adriani, settled in one of these communities, thus foreseeably causing the discontinuation of the drugs element of Batelaan's practice. Batelaan and Van der Tuuk Adriani entered into negotiations about the compensation the latter would pay for the goodwill, but Batelaan declined an offer of 125 per cent of the standard calculation scheme worked out by the two Royal Societies.

Subsequently Batelaan tried to avoid the termination of his licence by moving his pharmacy from one community to another in the region over which is practice extended. This stratagem proved to be in vain. After a struggle of more than three years the cessation of his licence turned out to be inevitable. Every appeal against the decision of the responsible committee to terminate the licence was dismissed. Thereupon Batelaan began to regret declining the original offer made by Van der Tuuk Adriani and he hoped still to be able to accept it. Van der Tuuk Adriani, however, was of the opinion that his offer had expired, first of all since it was initially declined, secondly since he had incurred great losses because of the lack of clients, who, being patients in Batelaan's practice, had generally preferred to stay with him over the three years of the dispute.

The High Court accepted Van der Tuuk Adriani's argument and dismissed Batelaan's claim. The Court of Appeal, however, reversed this judgment by stating that the High Court had wrongly omitted to discuss another (possible) legal foundation of the claim of the plaintiff. It should have considered the claim as one based on unjustified enrichment. The lengthy judgment of the Court of Appeal can be summarized as follows:

(1) There are several statutes in which the financial consequences of a change or a termination of a licence are regulated so as to produce the result that third parties who because of the elimination of competitors acquire a greater potentiality to make profits, and consequently are enriched, should pay compensating damages. Batelaan's claim thus fits into the Dutch legal system and appears to be on all fours with the explicitly regulated types of cases.

(2) The fact that the statute concerned leaves the question whether compensation should be paid or not undecided does not in itself derogate from the principle which the cases mentioned in (1) support.

(3) Some weight must be given to the fact that the professional organisations both of doctors and pharmacists drew up a model contract, which provided for a certain compensation in case of the transfer of the pharmacy business of the surgery to the newly established pharmacist.

(4) It is also of some importance that the fact of Van der Tuuk Adriani's

having himself made an offer to Batelaan was used as an argument in the decisions of the courts of administrative law as tending to justify the decision to dismiss the appeal against the termination of Batelaan's licence.

Consequently, the Court of Appeal decided that the appeal should be upheld. It considered that a remedy in restitution should lie in this case. The amount of money that should be paid, however, remained to be decided.

This brings us to the heart of our subject. The facts of the case definitely do not justify a contractual claim, since the offer was definitely declined and the plaintiff had refused to enter into a contract of sale. Under these circumstances can a claim nevertheless be maintained for restitution, based on unjustified enrichment? The case went up on a further appeal, and this was exactly the question that the Dutch Supreme Court had to answer.

One preliminary remark should be made. Although the case was decided by the Supreme Court on 15 March 1996, the applicable law was still the law of the previous Civil Code, the 1838 Civil Code, since the facts had taken place before the enactment of the New Civil Code of 1992. Although this might at first sight seem to be significant, it turns out not to be. The 1838 Civil Code was modelled after the French Code Civil. Consequently it contained a limited number of particular provisions which imposed on a person who had been enriched at the expense of another the duty to make good the other's loss. There was, however, no *general* provision imposing this liability on any person who was unjustifiably enriched at the expense of another. In the leading case in this field, analogous interpretation of the particular provisions was made possible by the Dutch Supreme Court. The court had ruled that a claim in restitution could be maintained in a case for which no remedy had been expressly provided, provided only that the new remedy fitted into the Code's framework and closely resembled the cases expressly covered.[1]

It is exactly for that reason that the greater part of the discussion before the Court of Appeal and the Supreme Court was devoted to the question whether there are other statutes to be found in which a principle is codified that the withdrawal by the government of a licence from one party and the subsequent granting of a similar licence to another party gives rise to an obligation in restitution so that the enriched party is obliged to compensate the impoverished side for the losses he suffered. It seems as if there is a certain parallel regulation to be found in the law of transport: if a licence for transport of persons (or of goods) is withdrawn in the public interest from one company and granted to another one, a certain compensation is due.

This part of the debate, however, is concentrated around specifically Dutch statutes and consequently it is from a comparative point of view of minor interest. More important is the general question whether an action for enrichment should be available even when the person impoverished could have

[1] *Quint* v. *Te Poel*, HR 30 January 1959, NJ 1959, 548.

contracted and could then have relied on a contractual action to obtain an indemnity for the loss he suffered. In other words, should the action for enrichment be of a subsidiary character, or not?

In the civil law tradition the requisites of a claim for unjustified enrichment are commonly discussed under a certain number of headings,[2] such as: (i) the enrichment of the defendant; (ii) the impoverishment of the plaintiff; (iii) the causal relation between these two; and (iv) the absence of a justification or a just cause for the enrichment. Already in the *Accursian Gloss*, which dates back to the first half of the thirteenth century, it is said that an enrichment is not unjustified if it emanates from a contract, a statutory provision or from prescription.[3] For example, if the parties, the seller and the buyer, agree upon a price which turns out to be either much too high or much too low, one party will be enriched and the other impoverished, but no remedy for unjustified enrichment will lie. It is another question whether a remedy can be brought, based on error or based on the doctrine of the just price; but in such a case there is certainly no remedy for unjustified enrichment available to the plaintiff. The same holds true in cases of acquisitive prescription. There is no reason why the enrichment should be undone, since it is not considered to be unjustified.

The fifth requisite is known under the name of subsidiarity: (v) in one way or another the remedy in restitution gives way to the remedy in contract or the remedy in tort.

Besides these five requisites, two others are sometimes discussed, in principle deriving from the *actio negotiorum gestorum*, the action for the plaintiff who claims compensation for his expenses (his impoverishment) should not have acted in his own interest and at his own risk and that he should not have been at fault.

The principle that there is no remedy for unjustified enrichment in case of a contract is also formulated as the rule of subsidiarity. The Italian Civil Code is the most overt in its codification of this principle. Article 2042 says that "the action for enrichment is not available when the person impoverished can bring another action to obtain an indemnity for the loss which he has suffered".[4]

The forensic importance of this principle becomes clear in the cases of partial performances, as Hector MacQueen has pointed out in his chapter,[5] but even clearer in three-party cases of a likewise familiar kind, e.g. the French

[2] It is not totally accidental that there is a certain resemblance between the structure Steve Hedley in his chapter claims to have found in Peter Birks' works and this enumeration of requisites of a claim for unjustified enrichment in the civil law traditions: see Hedley, *infra* Ch 18.

[3] e.g. the *Accursian Gloss* to D. 50,17,206: "*Haec regula fallit in usucapionem et praescriptionem quae auferunt praescribendi commodum cum alterius damno—de praedictis et similibus oppositionibus respondeas: quia licet fiat cum aliena iactura, tamen non fit cum aliena iniuria, cum fiat legum auctoritate*".

[4] Codice civile (Carattere sussidiario dell'azione), art. 2042: *l'Azione di arrichimento non è proponibile quando il dannegiato può esercitare un'altra azione per farsi indennizarre del pregiudizio subito*".

[5] *Supra*, Chap. 14.

*Boudier* case.[6] There the plaintiff had sold a quantity of manure to a tenant and had spread it over the land. The bill, however, was left unpaid. The tenant, running into financial problems, ceded the crop that was to be harvested to his landlord and dissolved the tenancy agreement. The plaintiff then brought an action for unjustified enrichment (the *actio de in rem verso*) against the landlord.

According to Italian law this enrichment action would be excluded on the ground of the subsidiarity principle: since there is in principle another remedy available (the action in contract against the tenant), the enrichment action is not open. Italian law seems to be most rigorous: even if it is unthinkable that, in the circumstances of the particular case, the plaintiff will derive any benefit from the action in contract (as in the *Boudier* case), the principle of subsidiarity bars the enrichment action.

Following Italian writers, Professor Nicholas calls this extreme interpretation of the subsidiarity principle the abstract version of it, and he correctly notes that this abstract version leaves little scope for the enrichment remedy.[7] It is, indeed, one of the paradoxes of the civil law of restitution that the Italians, who codified one general action for unjustified enrichment, severely limited its availability via the abstract use of the subsidiarity principle, whereas the French, who did not codify the general provision but stuck to an enumeration of the historically important particular provisions which imposed on a person who had been enriched at the expense of another the duty to make good the other's loss, eventually extended these specific remedies to the extent that the *actio de in rem verso* covers (almost) every case of unjustified enrichment.

This is already shown in the *Boudier* case: although there was a valid contract between him and the tenant, the plaintiff chose to bring the *actio de in rem verso* against the landlord, since in the given circumstances the contractual remedy against the tenant would have been fruitless because of the tenant's insolvency. According to French law the mere existence of the contractual remedy does not bar the enrichment action. Thus, the full rigour of the abstract meaning of the subsidiarity principle is rejected in French law. Does this imply that French law knows of a more concrete meaning?

One of the general problems of a dogmatic nature here is the overlap between the requisite of the absence of a justification or a just cause for the enrichment and the subsidiarity principle. If the enrichment results from a contract between the impoverished plaintiff and the enriched defendant, there is no doubt that the contractual rules, being of a more specific nature, should have priority: *lex specialis derogat legi generali*. Professor Birks uses other words but he comes to the same conclusion[8]:

6 *Patureau-Miran* v. *Boudier* [1893] SI 281; [1892] DI 596.
7 Nicholas, *infra* n. 11, p. 88.
8 Birks, *An Introduction to the Law of Restitution*, rev'd edn (1989), 46–7.

"When . . . alternative analyses disclose both a contract and an unjust enrichment in the same facts, the contract may have a content different from that of the restitutionary obligation. Consequently there has to be a rule to the effect that, at least unless and until the contract is prematurely discharged by frustration or in reaction to a repudiatory breach, the plaintiff can never put himself in a better position by suing in unjust enrichment rather than in contract.

The French Cour de Cassation had already stated the same principle in 1914, ruling that the plaintiff cannot claim a higher indemnification by way of the enrichment action than he could have claimed by bringing the action in contract.[9] The enrichment claim cannot serve: "*à déguiser une demande en supplément de prix prohibée par l'art. 1793 en cas de marché à forfait*".[10] There is, however, a more recent French case, to which Professor Nicholas has drawn attention.[11] Although it seems at first glance to point in the opposite direction, on closer inspection, the decision is nevertheless similar to the one in the *Boudier* case. In both cases the insolvency of the primary debtor let in an enrichment action against a third party.

After a divorce the wife married another man and some time later obtained a declaration that her second husband was the father of a child born to her when she was still married to the first husband. Since the first husband had until then been paying maintenance for this child, he brought an action against the wife for the restitution of those payments as money paid when it was not owing. This action was ineffective because the wife was insolvent, but the plaintiff successfully brought an enrichment action against the second husband as the legitimated father. The first husband was impoverished by his payments and the second husband was enriched by the discharge of his legal duty to support his legitimated child. The action against the mother, though it was available—and had indeed been brought—was ineffective because of her insolvency.

As far as French law is concerned, the full rigour of the abstract meaning of the subsidiarity principle is rejected. It turns out that the enrichment action can be brought if the other action, though in principle available, is made ineffective by the defendant's insolvency. The term coined for this phenomenon is the "*concrete*" version of the subsidiarity principle. Whereas Italian law maintains the abstract meaning, French law adheres to the concrete meaning. The difference between the two legal systems becomes clear from the decision

[9] C.d.C. 12 March 1914, S. 1918/1919, 1, 41. M.H. Bregstein, "Het nieuwe B.W. Ongegronde verrijking", in [1953] *Weekblad voor Privaatrecht, Notarisambt en Registratie* 4300; also published in his *Verzameld Werk I* (Zwolle, 1960), 299–311, at p. 306.

[10] C.d.C. 2 March 1915, D. 20.1.102. Cf. HR 24 February 1938, NJ 1938, 952: the enrichment of the tenant is not unjustified since the improvement of the house falls within the framework of the contractual relation between the parties.

[11] Civ. 1.2.1984, D. 1984.388; Mestre [1984] Rev.trim.dr.civ. 712. See B. Nicholas, "Modern developments in the French law of unjustified enrichment", in Paul W.L. Russell (ed.), *Unjustified Enrichment: A comparative study of the law of restitution* (Amsterdam, Juridische Reeks Vrije Universiteit 14, 1996), 77–95, at p. 88.

just mentioned (which is similar to the verdict in the *Boudier* case). It has been remarked already that an Italian judge would have decided the other way round, although Italian law codified a general action. I called that a paradox, but the civil law is even more complicated. The Italian judge would find his German colleague on his side, but for completely different reason.

It is a much disputed question whether German law codified a general action for unjustified enrichment in BGB § 812 or whether the action formulated there is bound to specific requisites which, if lacking, cannot be replaced by recourse to general principle, *bona fides* or equity. It is said that the European *Ius Commune* prior to the nineteenth century codifications knew of an *actio de in rem verso* which could be brought by the impoverished party against an enriched third party (as in the *Boudier* case). The German codifiers, however, intentionally did not codify this *actio de in rem verso*; they stuck to the specific remedies, which only lie between the parties themselves: *Leistungskondiktionen*, which are claims based on unjust enrichment following a performance (*Leistung*) made by the plaintiff that lacks consideration (*ohne rechtlichen Grund*), and *Nichtleistungskondiktionen*, which are claims to recover an enrichment obtained in another way, without any performance made by the plaintiff.

For German law it is therefore not possible, in our kind of situation, for a plaintiff to reach someone who is not immediately involved in the contractual relation between the parties. In a case similar to the *Boudier* case the seller can only sue the buyer, certainly not an outsider such as the owner of the land, although the latter turned out to be the enriched person. The reason for this restrictive position is twofold: a strict interpretation of the notion of privity and an uncompromising adherence to the *paritas creditorum*: everybody faces the risk of insolvency of his contractual partner, and, when that risk materialises, he cannot escape it by jumping over the inconveniently insolvent contracting party and claiming against a third person enriched by a receipt from the insolvent.

Consequently the subsidiarity principle in its German version has a meaning completely different from its counterpart in French or Italian law: since every action is bound to its own limits and can only be brought when its own requirements are satisfied, the subsidiarity principle has nothing to do with creating a hieriarchy of remedies in contract and in restitution. On the contrary, internally within the law of unjust enrichment, it merely orders the relationship *inter se* of the available claims. Thus, nobody may claim from another person by bringing a *Nichtleistungskondiktion* what the latter received on the basis of a performance (*Leistung*). Application of this principle to the fact pattern of the *Boudier* case leads to a dismissal of the claim: the owner of the ground received the manure on the basis of a performance by the tenant; consequently the seller cannot bring a *Nichtleistungskondiktion*.

The foundation of this interpretation of the subsidiarity principle is sometimes found in the text of §812 of the German Civil Code. It is said to be logically impossible for an enrichment to be acquired "in another way" (*in sonstiger Weise*) so as to justify a *Nichtleistungskondiktion* if in fact the enrichment originates in a performance by the plaintiff. This rather formalistic argument, however, is of less importance than the historical argument: the second committee that codified the German Civil Code intentionally suppressed the *action de in rem verso* of the *Ius Commune*. Not everybody who is impoverished in favour of another should be entitled to indemnification; the circle of the plaintiffs should be limited to the contractual partner or those who are otherwise enriched at the straightforward expense of the plaintiff. By the expulsion of the *actio de in rem verso* the German legislator aimed at limiting the remedies in restitution to certain specific requisites, thus avoiding giving the principle too vast an application. Exceeding the boundaries imposed by privity would be too vast an application of the remedies in restitution.

If, therefore, for an obvious and specific reason the contractual remedy will be ineffective (e.g. insolvency of the defendant, insufficient evidence of the terms of the contract, prescription, forfeiture, *res iudicata*) and the question arises whether the plaintiff should be allowed recourse to a remedy in restitution, the answer is not very simple, since it varies from one legal system to another and depends on the interpretation of the subsidiarity principle. This leads to the crucial question, whether there is a justification to be found for the requirement of subsidiarity. Why should the plaintiff not be entitled to choose freely between the enrichment action and another action?

Italian law (which adheres to the extreme and abstract version of the subsidiarity principle) and German law (which rejects it) concur in so far as both legal systems end by denying remedies for unjustified enrichment through a third party and do not accept the *actio de in rem verso* in the French sense. Maybe that is important in this context. The requirement of subsidiarity is a technique of limiting the applicability of the general remedy for unjustified enrichment. The same end can be reached by different means, as indeed the German law shows (by its elimination of the *actio de in rem verso*). The common law also pursues the same objective without once using the word "subsidiarity".

The common law allows a person upon whom a tort has been committed to elect to sue in restitution to recover the defendant's unjust benefit rather than to sue in tort to recover damages; he has a choice of alternative remedies. This is the so-called waiver of tort. Waiver can be used as a means of circumventing the limitation period appropriate to the tortious means. It is unthinkable that a plaintiff's claim in tort may be barred by lapse of time when a restitutionary claim may not.[12] The common law struggles with this problem. Goff and Jones are of the opinion that there is no reason to con-

[12] *Chesworth* v. *Farrar* [1967] 1 QB 407; *Universe Tankships Inc. of Monrovia* v. *International Transport Workers' Federation, The Universe Sentinel* [1983] 1 AC 366; Goff and Jones, *Law of Restitution*, 4th edn (1993), 728.

clude that, in principle, the actions in tort and in restitution should necessarily terminate at the same time, but they leave the solution to statutory provisions such as the Limitation Act 1980.[13]

French law knows of the same problem. There it has been decided in a number of cases[14] that, if the other action is barred by prescription, the enrichment action may not be brought; and the position is the same if the other action is excluded by the plaintiff's inability to produce the written evidence required by the Civil Code to support the other action. In short, the Cour de Cassation distinguished between cases in which the other action is excluded by an obstacle of law (e.g. prescription, forfeiture, foreclosure, *res iudicata*) or by an obstacle of fact (insolvency). Only when the other action is barred by an obstacle of law, is the remedy in restitution excluded as well.[15]

The requirement of subsidiarity is a technique of limiting the applicability of the general remedy for unjustified enrichment. Therefore its exact meaning is a matter of legal policy. The Dutch Civil Code of 1992 does not mention the word subsidiarity. Professor Meijers devoted some attention to it in his explanatory introduction. According to him, reversing an enrichment may be governed by the provision containing the general action for unjustified enrichment but also by other statutory regulations. The question whether the plaintiff can freely choose between the two regimes depends on the purport of the other provision. Meijers refers to the subsidiarity principle in Italian, French and Belgian law and the vast literature and case law, but he is of the opinion that a satisfying and principled system is not to be found. Consequently he states that if the requirements for liability in tort are fulfilled where an unjustified enrichment can be found as well, the claim for recompense (for damages) may be brought either in tort or in restitution. If, however, the statutory provision given for that factual state of affairs purports to regulate that situation exclusively, the claim for unjustified enrichment cannot be brought. An example is to be found in the regime for the nullification of legal acts such as contracts: after expiration of the prescribed period during which the plaintiff may seek to nullify the contract, both the claim in contract and the claim in restitution are barred.

Meijers was apparently of the opinion that the abstract (Italian) version of the subsidiarity principle should not be introduced in Dutch law, and he found the application of the concrete version confusing.

It is tempting to glance at the Dutch parallel to the Anglo-Saxon waiver of tort. In a case of concurrence between contract and tort, Dutch law does allow a person against whom a tort has been committed to elect to sue in contract for breach of contract (or the other way round) to recover damages; provided that the necessary requirements for either action are fulfilled, he has a choice of alternative remedies. This happens, for example, in cases of malicious

[13] *Ibid.*, Chap. 38.

[14] Beginning with Civ. 18/19.7.1910, DP 1911.1.355. See Nicholas, *supra* n 11, at n 89.

[15] Civ. 29.4.1971, Gaz.Pal. 1971.2.554; Nicholas, *supra* n 11, at nn 43–4.

damage to another person's property which the tortfeasor possesses pursuant to a contract. The choice has not very many repercussions since the main consequences of the alleged breach of duty, the obligation to pay damages, is the subject of uniform regulation.[16] But there still are a few differences: the limitation period appropriate to the tortious claim may differ from that of the contractual claim; the contractual liability may be limited by statute or international treaty, whereas the tortious liability may not be; different judges or magistrates may be competent; and so on.

It is definitely the purport of the regime provided by the legislator that it is the contractual relationship which decides whether there is room for the tortious claim instead of the contractual one. Thus, the legislator took the decision that in the case of a contract of transport only the contractual claim can be brought.[17] The same holds true for the contract concerning medical treatment, and the same approach determines the possible liability in tort of the employee towards the client of his employer.[18] There again it is the legislator who decided that only the contractual claim can be brought.[19]

This being said, coming back to our case, it should be noted that the Court of Appeal explicitly discussed the question whether the conduct of the parties during the period of negotiations between them necessarily leads to the conclusion that only the regime for contracts should be applicable. The court repudiated that position and decided that in this case the claim in restitution could be brought. The Supreme Court supported the view of the Court of Appeal. Van der Tuuk Adriani had argued that in this case there is no enrichment which should be seen as unjustified, since it is caused and sanctioned by law, and furthermore there is no actual shift of assets. This argument, however, is rejected. The sole circumstance that the transfer of the licence to sell drugs, which causes the loss of income to Batelaan and enhances the earning capacity of Van der Tuuk Adriani, is based on the statute does not entail the

[16] The New Dutch Civil Code of 1992 is arranged according to a layered structure: the general precepts precede the more specific ones. What is general need not be reiterated when the more specific items are dealt with. Among these general principles we find a section on reparation of damages (Book 6, Title 10, i.e. arts 95–110), which contains the regulations common to all types of liability in private law, whether of a contractual or an extra-contractual nature. Thus, the general part of the regulations concerning the obligations to pay damages caused by breach of contract (art 6:74 *et seq*), torts (art 6:162 *et seq*), product liability (art 6:185), *negotiorum gestio* (art 6:198) and unjustified enrichment (art 6:212) are brought together in Book 6, Title 10. The various specific obligations may find their special regulations at their individual place in the legislation, e.g. the obligations to give compensation for a performance which was not owed, but which cannot be made undone as such (art 6:210(2) ) or the obligations to repay an amount which is to be established by the judge in his discretion. See further E. Schrage, "Dutch Civil Code (1992), Book 6, Title 4)" [1994] *RLR* 202.

[17] Art 8.361 *et seq*, replacing art 4 *wet overeenkomst wegvervoer*, Asser Hartkamp, *Verbintenissenrecht*, vol. 4 III, "De verbintenis uit de wet" (Zwolle, 1994), p. 10.

[18] P.G. Invoeringswet Boek 6, p. 1371.

[19] This recourse to the legislator finds a striking parallel with how Goff and Jones, *supra* n 13, leave the solution of the problem what to do if the actions in tort and in restitution do not terminate at the same time, to statutory provisions such as the Limitation Act 1980.

consequence that Van der Tuuk Adriani may keep this enrichment totally for himself without paying a reasonable compensation to Batelaan.

It was relevant in the court's view that it was Van der Tuuk Adriani's own initiative to move into and to establish himself in Batelaan's area of operation and it was also Van der Tuuk Adriani who took active steps to terminate Batelaan's licence. In the professional circles to which the parties belonged there was a shared expectation that under these circumstances a certain compensation for the loss suffered by the doctor would be payable. The sole fact that Batelaan had refused the initial offer made by Van der Tuuk Adriani did not lead to the consequence that Van der Tuuk Adriani could take over the pharmacy without paying any compensation.

The Advocate General to the Supreme Court, Mr Koopmans, had strengthened his advice (which pointed in the same direction as the court would finally go) by sketching a general trend in Dutch law to acknowledge goodwill and customer portfolio as an asset. In lease contracts concerning business sites and related immoveables the preceding lessee may be entitled to compensation for the goodwill and the customer portfolio.[20] There is even a European directive that upon termination of an agency agreement the agent is entitled to an indemnification which is related to the growth of the customer circle of the principal which the agent had procured.[21]

As for the argument that the principle of subsidiarity required this matter to be treated as belonging to the law of contract and only to the law of contract, to the extent that the failure of negotiations should be taken to exclude recourse to any non-contractual regime, the answer is that the requirement of subsidiarity is no more than a technique for limiting the applicability of the general remedy for unjustified enrichment. It must not be given a dogmatic or doctrinaire life of its own. Its exact meaning is a matter of legal policy, and in Dutch law it will be developed on a case to case basis.

Batelaan was judged to be entitled to a certain indemnification. Compare the situation which arose recently when the Amsterdam Airport Schiphol enlarged the number of licences for ground services from two to three. As a result KLM and Nedlloyd (or, rather, its subsidiary Aero Goundservices) suffered substantial losses due to the intervention of the new competitor. It will be commonly accepted that it is the legitimate desire of the airport authorities to improve the quality of the services rendered to the public by enhancing competition. Under these circumstances there is no basis for obliging the newcomer to give compensation to the older competitors. The enrichment of the newcomer, and the corresponding impoverishment of those previously in the field, cannot be judged as unjustified. There is an obvious challenge to juristic science to specify with precision the exact nature of the difference between the case of Batelaan and that of KLM and Nedlloyd. That

[20] HR 25 juni 1993, NJ 1993 669, concerning goodwill of a camping site.

[21] See, e.g., in relation to Great Britain, Commercial Agents (Council Directive) Regulations 1993 (SI 1993 No 3053), art 8.

enrichment at the expense of KLM and Nedlloyd was not unjust or unjustified will, however, strike every reader as intuitively correct. In the end the plaintiff's claim can only succeed in the case in which it is possible for the court to conclude that the defendant was indeed unjustly enriched at the expense of the plaintiff.

# 17

# *Contract and Restitution: A Few Comparative Remarks—A Comment*

BRICE DICKSON

Professor Schrage[1] has performed a valuable service in reminding us that legal concepts and categories, however useful they might be for pedagogic purposes, can easily cloud our grasp of policy preferences. I take the nub of his argument to be his statement that: "The requirement of subsidiarity is a technique of limiting the applicability of the general remedy for unjustified enrichment". He ably demonstrates how this requirement of subsidiarity is interpreted in the legal systems of Italy, France and Germany, though curiously he is less specific about the relevant Dutch and English law. The *Batelaan* case which he discusses shows that the Dutch law is still in a formative phase. English law, I think, already has the principles to hand to deal with the situation arising there.

Professor Schrage says that in France the subsidiarity principle does not prevent an enrichment action being available if the reason for the main action being ineffective is the insolvency of the person being sued. He later states the more general proposition that the subsidiarity principle does not prevent a claim in unjust enrichment being available if there is a factual obstacle to the main action, only if there is a legal obstacle. In support of this he cites the case of *L* v. *V*, decided by the Cour de Cassation in 1984,[2] where a man succeeded in his claim for reimbursement of child maintenance expenses brought against his ex-wife's new husband, the father of the child. In that case, though, the Cour de Cassation did not itself make the law/fact distinction which Professor Schrage cites. We find it mentioned in the note on the case by Mme Huet-Weiller, who in turn cites a decision of the Cour d'appel de Toulouse in 1973,[3] but there too the distinction is not expressly drawn. In that case the widow of a lawyer successfully claimed reimbursement of FF 180,000 which her husband had paid to another lawyer whose practice he wanted to buy; because of the latter's bankruptcy the money had been used to pay off his

[1] *Supra*, p 000.

[2] D.1984.338 (note Massip); D.1984. IR.315 (note Huet-Weiller).

[3] D.1973.509 (note Aubert).

debts and the payer's widow therefore sought to claim from the regional bar association, which would otherwise have been liable to those creditors.

It seems to me that in that case, as well as in the 1984 case, the claim being made was not a subsidiary one at all but rather a main one against a defendant who was liable to the plaintiff quite independently of whether anyone else was liable too. The defendant may not have been liable as an alternative to someone else until the claim against that person became unavailable, but nevertheless it was a primary and not a secondary claim. In another note on the 1984 case this appears to have been conceded:

> "Ce n'est pas une action en responsabilité qu'exerce le premier mari mais une action en répétition de l'indû à l'encontre de la mère, une action fondée sur l'enrichissement sans cause a l'égard du second mari de celle-ci."[4]

It follows that a better way of formulating the subsidiarity principle in French law is to say that it prevents an action in unjust enrichment being brought against a person if another legal action against that same person has become unavailable. In other words, the subsidiarity principle should be seen as one which applies in two-party situations, not in three-party ones. I have never understood the French position to be that an unjust enrichment action cannot be brought against Y just because it (or some other action) has ceased to be available against X; I take the principle as saying that an unjust enrichment action cannot be brought against Y if a contractual or some other action has ceased to be available against Y. It has always seemed to me to be close cousin of the rule of *non-cumul* in the context of contract and delict claims.[5]

On my reading, even the *Boudier* decision[6] is not an exception to the subsidiarity principle, precisely because it involved three parties, not two, and the fact that the tenant-farmer had no money to pay for the fertiliser in that case was as much a reason for his not being sued in unjust enrichment as it was for his not being sued in contract. The cause of action against the landlord was an independent action. Indeed the fact that the subsidiarity principle was not adverted to in that case, but was constructed later by judges and academics dealing with other cases, helps to show that it is not appropriate in three-party situations. I venture to suggest that, if the facts of *Boudier* were to recur today, but the tenant-farmer were not bankrupt, the landlord would still be held liable if he in some way unjustly benefited from the enrichment at the plaintiff's expense.

Professor Schrage's portrayal of the German view of subsidiarity is also, I think, slightly misleading. The Germans, as far as I know, do not employ any such term as "subsidiary" when determining the availability of remedies for

[4] Jacques Massip, D.1984.388, 390.
[5] For criticism of this rule see the chapter by Professor Lapoyade-Deschamps, *supra* p 000.
[6] D.1892.1.596.

*ungerechtfertigte Bereicherung.* What they do employ, of course, is quite a strict doctrine against allowing recovery of *indirect* enrichments. This is their way of denying recovery in three-party situations and such denial occurs whether the ineffectual claim against the "first" defendant is in respect of a *Leistung* or not, which gives the lie to Professor Schrage's contention that the way in which the Germans categorise their unjust enrichment actions is an illustration of the subsidiarity principle at work. It is true that the Germans draw a fairly rigid distinction between claims for "performance" enrichment (*Leistungskondiktionen*) and claims for "interference" enrichment (*Eingriffskondiktionen*), but this operates just as much in two-party situations as it does in three-party ones.[7]

Whatever the real position in French and German law, it seems clear that the Italian interpretation of the subsidiarity requirement, as characterised by Professor Schrage, is completely untenable. In so far as the French have preferred a moderated Italian approach, they are to be congratulated.

The facts of Professor Schrage's Dutch case brought by one pharmacist against another cannot of course be divorced from the particular statutory provisions in question. As he himself admits, decisions based on statutory provisions are of minor interest to comparativists. Nevertheless, the process at work in such cases, where a court has to try to determine the purpose of the statute in question and seek to make its policy fit with the principles of existing law, is one that is common to all legal systems. The English law of restitution—still more so the English law of contract and tort—is full of instances where statutes have had to be interpreted, not least in the context of "illegal" transactions.[8] On many occasions the peculiarities of the statute have rendered the decision less than useful at the general level of principle.

In the Dutch case the claim basically related to loss suffered as a result of an anticipated contract that did not in the end materialise. In English law the equivalent case that springs to mind is *William Lacey (Hounslow) Ltd* v. *Davis*,[9] where further work had been done on a tender at the specific request of the other party. Professor Birks justifies recovery in this and similar cases on the principles that the services provided were "freely accepted" and that retention of the benefit would be unjust,[10] while Professor Burrows prefers the view that recovery is based on a failure of consideration and a gain to the defendant that has been "subtracted" from the plaintiff.[11] Whatever the justification, there are few who would deny the justice of granting recovery in such cases (provided there is evidence of at least some "request" on the part of the defendant). To deny recovery would be to let oneself be blinkered by the

[7] B. Dickson, "The Law of Restitution in the Federal Republic of Germany: A Comparison with English Law" (1987) 36 ICLQ 751.

[8] English law has not engaged the benefit of a general statutory provision dealing with this problem, unlike New Zealand's Illegal Contracts Act 1970.

[9] [1957] 1 WLR 932.

[10] Birks, *An Introduction to the Law of Restitution*, rev. ed. (1989), 270–6.

[11] Burrows, *The Law of Restitution* (1993) 293–9.

constraint of existing legal concepts such as contract and tort. It would be to let the causes of action dictate the course of justice in the way that stymied development of the law in centuries gone by.

And, just as legal categories should not be immutable or blind us to the justness of "novel" claims, so the attempts to create a structure for restitution law in England must not be taken too far. While catagories are commendable in so far as they help us to avoid inconsistencies and vagueness, they must not be allowed to mask policy choices which often have to be made in "new" cases. In the last 20 years or so English law has begun to realise that attempts to create sub-rules and pre-conditions in the law of negligence can prove counter-productive if they become either too constraining or too loose: if we are to avoid the mistakes made in that context, where judges have often arrived at the same conclusion by different routes through the conceptual maze attending the tort (duty of care, proximity, reasonable foreseeability, standard of care, etc), we must allow room for open discussion in court of the 'pros' and 'cons' of adopting one position rather than another.

It would therefore be retrogressive for English law to look to any of the systems analysed by Professor Schrage for guidance as to what form of subsidiarity principle to adopt. English law simply does not need such a principle. What it does need are reasonably fixed, yet flexible, principles on when something constitutes an enrichment and on when its retention by D rather than P would be unjust. It seems to me that the ideal vehicle for enunciating such principles is legislation. Provided an appropriate level of generality is adopted in the legislative wording, perhaps with guidelines and non-inclusive definitions appended, there is no reason why this should not be every bit as good an initial guide for businesses and their advisers in the future as the case law of judges.

# 18

# *Restitution: Contract's Twin?*

STEVE HEDLEY*

This chapter has several distinct themes, though I hope to argue that they are not as disparate as might at first be thought. As a modern legal historian, I see a close parallel between the development of textbook contract law a century ago and the law of restitution over the past 30 years. Yet, through a quirk of timing, the decay of contract coincides with the coming-together of restitution. The paradox involved in this is profound: as the disadvantages of such super-theories become more and more apparent in the context of contract, nonetheless those same disadvantages are ignored in the context of restitution. There is much insight to be gained, in my view, in both contract and restitution by comparing the two attempts at theorisation. But I am not arguing that we "ignore history at our peril". Legal theorists *necessarily* work within some historical conception of their subject, and the danger is not of "ignoring history"—I doubt if that is possible—but of doing history *badly*, of basing our modern law on premises which are not merely history, but are *bad* history. In particular, to view the enterprise modern restitution theorists are engaged in as a "rejection" of the implied contract doctrine seems to me an *historical* mistake, as well as a bad idea. We have forgotten how it can ever have been plausible to talk of "implied contracts", and reject the notion without realising what we are doing.

Of course, how acceptable my thesis is to any given individual will to a certain extent depend on the background of that individual. To those who have come to restitution through specialist areas—say, an interest in maritime salvage or subrogation—then probably what I am saying will be easy to accept. It's all too obvious that salvage makes perfect sense in its own right, and does not need to be "explained" in terms of something bigger such as unjust enrichment. Or again there will be those, like me, who learned their restitution when they were very young, and are now very old. To people like that, it is obvious that restitution can be learned and understood without a patina of high-level theory—we learned it that way—and it should simply be a pragmatic question, whether any proposed theory makes matters better or worse. We can drop the idea of an "implied contract" without rushing into accepting

* My thanks to all who commented on the paper on which this chapter is based before, during or after the SPTL Conference, and in particular to John Carter, Andrew Kull, Eoin O'Dell, Steve Smith and Robert Stevens.

some other over-arching notion in its place, at least until its superiority is proved. The hardest to convince will be those who have learned restitution in the last decade, and so who have never known restitution without an over-arching theory, or the promise of one. For those people, I think the point to bear in mind is that the four-part theory (enrichment, at the expense of the plaintiff, of which it is unjust not to make restitution, but subject to defences) was introduced and used because it seemed to provide the solution to certain problems. If, after a decade of use, it appears that it not only cannot solve those problems but throws up many more of its own, then it was, in retrospect, not a useful innovation, and needs to be abandoned.

But my arguments on the modern development of each in no way depend on acceptance of my historical thesis. Rather, I urge that we need to view doctrinal innovations such as the introduction of "unjust enrichment" ideas to promote structure in restitution on a strictly cost-benefit basis. Does the attempt to reduce restitution to the four-part formula seem likely to serve some useful goal? I argue not, and appeal both to the theory of the matter and to the actual execution of that reductionist plan.

## 1. RESTITUTION

Development of legal theoretical concepts is typically a slow process, and when it is fast it is almost invariably because of factors outside the legal academy: Parliament has changed the law, or new case developments have forced the academics to re-think their basic presuppositions. The recent history of restitutionary theory in the English jurisdiction is thus quite remarkable, and extremely unusual. The pace has been frenetic, and (so far as I can tell) driven almost entirely by work and discussions within the law schools.

Birks' *An Introduction to the Law of Restitution* was published only in 1985. Like many common law innovators before him, Birks insisted that he was no innovator at all, but was merely revealing a pre-existing order of things. He provided for the first time a rigid theoretical structure for the subject: "the simplest structure on which the material in *Goff and Jones* can hang".[1] This is the now-familiar division of restitutionary issues into the four questions: (1) was the defendant enriched? (2) was the enrichment unjust? (3) was the enrichment at the plaintiff's expense? and (4) is there any defence? This simple four-part structure was then immediately taken up and developed by others. To a legal historian, it is startling how quickly Birks was accused of misapplying the theory which he was himself primarily responsible for developing: how quickly, in other words, it was *forgotten* that the theory was an invention with an inventor, and was treated as the inevitable framework for

[1] P. Birks, *An Introduction to the Law of Restitution* (Oxford, 1985), 3.

discussion of restitutionary issues.[2] The years from 1987 onwards saw a flood of discussion of high-level theory, nearly all of which took Birks' basic ideas for granted, and which sought to tackle the main problems it had set itself but which remained unanswered in its own terms: principally concerned with the valuation of benefits, but also with the elaboration of the "unjust factors" Birks had introduced so very recently.

The capstone was set on these debates in 1993, with the publication of Burrows' *Law of Restitution*, written in triumphalist tone after the decision of the House of Lords in *Lipkin Gorman* v. *Karpnale Ltd*[3]—a case which seemed to guarantee the future of the subject, by explicitly recognising the principle of unjust enrichment as the basis of restitution. It is not entirely true to say that *nothing* has happened since then, but it has been at the level which is more usual in common law development: largely a matter of fitting new case law developments into the existing theoretical structure. And the theoretical debates of the late 1980s and early 1990s lie where they were at the end of that time: not in *consensus ad idem* but, on the contrary, in a failure to agree. There seems to be a high degree of unanimity on the basic structure of the subject: it is a structure in four parts, necessitating consideration of whether the defendant in any case was enriched, whether this enrichment was unjust, whether it was at the plaintiff's expense, and whether there is any defence. Yet the serious disagreements on what those terms mean, and how they apply to real situations, have not been resolved. Our teachers confidently teach their students that the law is best stated by reference to this four-part structure, and treat disagreements over what it means as relatively unimportant, if frequently absorbing, theoretical puzzles.

To argue that this entire theoretical turn since 1985 is a mistake is not, of course, the way to instant popularity. It suggests that rather a lot of people have been wasting their time, looking for solutions in the wrong place. Further, it risks confusion between the various different issues that need to be addressed. For example, the question whether restitution should be taught in universities at all is obviously quite distinct from the question whether restitution has any particular theoretical basis. This theoretical issue could be answered in various ways, by a variety of theorists, all of whom were however equally committed to teaching the subject in their various ways. Yet denials of the four-part classification seem to be treated as if they were denials that restitution can or should be taught at all. It is as if these thinkers have posed themselves a very simple question—Does restitution exist as a subject, or does it not?—and have interpreted all answers to this as either "Yes" or

[2] I have performed no thorough survey, but the earliest "post-Birks" articles I know, where Birks' theory is no longer perceived as such but is taken to be the law (Birks himself being relegated to the rôle of eminent but not-always-reliable commentator) are A. Burrows, "Free Acceptance and the Law of Restitution" (1988) 104 *LQR* 576 and S. Arrowsmith, "Ineffective Transactions and Unjust Enrichment; a Framework for Analysis" (1989) 9 *LS* 121.

[3] [1991] AC 548.

"No", despite the complexities they know to exist.[4] This perhaps explains why the current judiciary have been claimed as supporters for the four-part classification, even though they have said little or nothing, collectively or individually, to justify this: by agreeing that there is such a thing as restitution, they are taken to have committed themselves to the entire gamut of restitutionary theory, even though they have said nothing of the sort.[5]

Of course, there may be a *psychological* argument that the four-part classification is necessary if restitution is to survive. If one hopes to gather followers, it is perhaps helpful to have a banner for them to flock to. On this view, we can perhaps expect the attraction of the classification to fade as restitution becomes more established. Tort lawyers do not have to demonstrate that there is some hidden unity behind their discipline, and many believe that there isn't one—yet this in no way imperils the future of tort. Perhaps in time this will become true of restitution as well. But, true or not, that is psychology, not law. Here I will simply be arguing that the four-part structure for the subject is a hindrance to the rational study of restitution. And the most sensible place to start seems to be with the law of contract, on which a similarly rigid theoretical structure was imposed a century ago, a structure to which the later one owes a great deal, one way and another.

## 2. CONTRACT AND RESTITUTION

If we go back to the early years of the nineteenth century and ask where "contract" and "restitution" were, they turn out to be part of the same area of law, principally (in the common law courts) *assumpsit* and related notions. Relevant case law and statutes were highly particularistic and scattered. The underlying common law ideal was that of trial by jury, and so the system was far stronger on procedure than on clarity of legal principle. The seeds of more general doctrinal ideas were there if you looked for them; but neat formulae could not capture all or even most of the nuances of what the courts actually did, though they provided the substance of some eloquent and passionate rhetorical declarations.

Partial order was imposed by the rise of the general law of contract, the results of which we are all familiar with. This happened, one might say, at the earliest time it *could* have happened. A number of developments conspired to make such broad theories a possibility in the 1870s, and "contract" immediately took its chance. Broad theories which are theories of law, and not of procedure, could not really have existed while the law was still dominated by the forms of action. A theory of the way the *whole* law treated contracts would certainly have been awkward while different parts of the law were administered in different courts entirely. And while it is not *quite* impossible

[4] e.g. A. Burrows, *The Law of Restitution* (London, 1993), 6.

[5] On this point see S. Hedley, " 'Unjust Enrichment' " [1995] *CLJ* 578, 580–5.

to discuss how the law applies to the facts in a system where facts are still largely the province of juries, the decay of that system of civil justice removed a substantial obstacle to the new way of thinking. Finally, and perhaps most importantly (for theories do not build or maintain themselves), a regular corps of university law teachers would appear to be a necessity for any decent theory. The law of contract, as I say, took advantage of these interlinked developments as soon as they happened. Pollock's *Law of Contract* (1876) first reached the bookshops a mere five years after the Universities Tests Act, which permitted scholarship to assume something like its modern form[6]; and only a year after the Judicature Acts, which fused the principal central courts, sealed the doom of the forms of action, and took the decisive steps in weakening civil juries.[7]

Restitution has taken a little longer, even though the development of a rigid law of contract plainly pointed to its existence: if "contracts" were now to be based on a strict notion of agreement, then it was obviously no longer accurate to base restitution on contracts, "implied" or not.[8] A few faint voices from the 1930s onwards, inspired by the *Restatement of Restitution*, urged that a similar theoretical development should take place; yet the first major textbook waited until the 1960s. The world we now inhabit only started in 1985, with Birks' *An Introduction to Restitution*, with its rigorous distinctions between different types of liability, and the distinctive four-stage pattern of analysis. The major part of this paper is concerned with the merits and future prospects of this analysis, and some at least will not be vastly surprised to know that on the whole I am more against it than for it. My own view of the area is that it contains much that is useful and important, and deserves all the attention it has received in recent years, and more—but that attempts to find common threads or principles running through it all have failed, and seem likely to go on failing. Simply because 20 or more heads of liability are interesting and important, and collectively deserve a course to themselves, does not show that they have anything much in common with one another—and, for me, the case for a theory to unite restitution has not been made.

But it is important to start with the earlier story, of the rise and then the fall of the general theory of contract, which is tied up with the restitutionary story in so many ways. One prominent proponent of "unjust enrichment" ideas has chided those who feel this way for placing too much weight on the historical *derivation* of concepts: "[T]he days of legal scholarship based on a reinterpretation of history are gone".[9] And it is a vaguely amusing fact that

[6] This act permitted academics generally not to subscribe to the 39 articles of religion.

[7] I treat Pollock's treatise as the decisive innovation here, though that is not to ignore the claims of *Leake* (1867) or *Anson* (1879). See generally, A.W.B. Simpson, "Contract: The Twitching Corpse" (1981) 1 *OJLS* 265.

[8] This was obvious from the first. See especially W. Anson, *Principles of the English Law of Contract* (Oxford, 1879), Appendix.

[9] J.W. Carter, "Services Rendered Under Ineffective Contracts" [1990] *LMCLQ* 495, 497. When were those days here?

several of the common lawyers prominent in denying "unjust enrichment" a very great rôle in the common law—Holdsworth[10], Atiyah[11], Simpson[12], and very much last, myself—have done so from a historical perspective. But history dictates much of what we lawyers say regardless of whether we want it to, or are even aware that it does so. One of my major themes in what follows is the extent to which the "unjust enrichment" theorists have committed themselves to a really quite old-fashioned view of the law of contract: a view which modern contract theorists find embarrassingly simplistic, and which is certainly no secure foundation for the theory they seek to base on it.

## 3. "THE DEATH OF CONTRACT"

If we look at the model of contract proposed in the original Victorian textbooks, it is actually quite simple, at least to people like you or me who have been brought up on it, and do not find the whole thing very novel. We can summarise the main points in 7 propositions: (1) When parties contract, they do so at a clear moment in time, by a clearly identifiable process of offer and acceptance. (2) People are free to contract or not, as they please. (3) Contracting parties are absolutely bound by their agreements. (4) Their agreement affects only them and not others. (5) The courts will not add to the terms of the agreement. (6) The courts will not allow other bodies of law to interfere with the parties' agreement. (7) In summary, it is the parties' own will that governs their arrangement, and not the arbitrary will of parliament or judges.

It is the last point, which sums up the earlier ones, that sets contract aside from other heads of the law. Contract law is the law the parties set for themselves, whereas other heads of the law represent rules which are imposed on them. This is the famous "sanctity of contract": whatever one makes of judicial creativity in other fields, the law's rôle in contract cases should be limited to identifying the rules the parties have chosen for themselves, and enforcing those rules and not others. And of course a sharp division between contract and restitution follows necessarily from this: if it is a given that contracts are made by the parties, not the courts, then obviously the "implied contract" in restitution cases is an awkward fiction.

Nothing is wrong with this general scheme, of course, if the parties truly were free to make such terms as they wished, genuinely discussed which terms were to apply, and thoroughly considered all the implications of their decision—and there were no other significant bodies of law applicable to their deliberations. But life is not like that. Much of the so-called "death of contract" is the slow realisation that the fully negotiated contract between

[10] W.S. Holdsworth, "Unjustifiable Enrichment" (1939) 55 *LQR* 37.
[11] P.S. Atiyah, *The Rise and Fall of Freedom of Contract* (Oxford, 1979), 768.
[12] A.W.B. Simpson, *A History of the Common Law of Contract* (Oxford, 1975), 489.

parties free to bargain, so lightly taken by the Victorian academics as the paradigm of all contracts, is actually a rather rare bird. With the benefit of hindsight, there was a serious choice to be made—should "contract law" confine itself to cases of reasonably full negotiation, or should it aim to capture *all* significant commercial relationships?—but the Victorian academics fudged it, by pretending that most significant commercial arrangements *were* fully negotiated, and that the exceptions were sufficiently rare to be hived off to specialist subject areas.

That this was always a pretence, and not a mere matter of choice in legal analysis, should not be doubted. But it is *also* true that the reasons for its wrongness are more blatant today than they were a century ago. In material terms, we are incomparably richer than the Victorians, and so it is hardly surprising that our economy is more complicated as well. When we speak of the "death of contract",[13] what really died was the idea that this simple set of ideas could explain the law's reaction to a significant number of contracts; and what has taken its place is at least some recognition of the diversity of approach the law displays. As Reiter puts it, "[i]f a new legal theory of contracts is to emerge, we must come to notice all of the lattices of the snowflake and we must cease to devote our exclusive attention to their meeting point at the centre".[14] Perhaps a different metaphor is needed, and we should speak not of contract's "death", but of its middle-age spread: the slow transition from the sylph-like structure of the early textbooks to the ample if unwieldy range of theoretical concepts necessary for a full treatment of the modern law. A general sketch of this unravelling of the neat model of contract proposed in the late nineteenth century would go something like this:

(1) "When parties contract, they do so at a clear moment in time, by a clearly identifiable process of offer and acceptance". But:

(a) the effective moment of commitment may be postponed[15];
(b) pre-contractual negotiations may create substantial rights[16];
(c) a clear moment of commitment may be hard to discern at all[17] (especially in the case of "implied" agreements);

[13] The phrase "the death of contract" is usually traced to Grant Gilmore, *The Death of Contract* (Ohio, 1974), though it now stands for many things in addition to those intended by Gilmore. It is misleading to the extent that it implies that there are fewer contracts about nowadays, which (as I understand it) was never what was being argued. Gilmore's thesis has elicited both praise and damnation from a variety of critics: see especially "Symposium: Reconsidering Grant Gilmore's *The Death of Contract*" (1995) 90 *Northwestern ULR* 1-266.

[14] B.J. Reiter, "The Control of Contract Power" (1981) 1 *OJLS* 347, 374.

[15] By specific legislation (e.g. Consumer Credit Act 1974, Unsolicited Goods and Services Act 1971) or by denying substantial enforcement until the arrangement is relied on. See generally "Contracts, promises and the law of obligations" in P.S. Atiyah, *Essays on Contract* (Oxford, 1986), 10.

[16] Whether those rights are in tort (e.g. *Crossan* v. *Ward Bracewell* (1986) 136 NLJ 849), contract (e.g. *Harvela Investments Ltd* v. *Royal Trust Company of Canada* [1986] AC 207) or restitution (e.g. *British Steel* v. *Cleveland Bridge and Engineering Co Ltd* [1984] 1 All ER 504).

[17] As result of party inattention to the matter (see H. Beale and T. Dugdale, "Contracts Between Businessmen" (1975) 2 *BJLS* 45), or of a "battle of the forms" (e.g. *Butler Machine Tool*

(d) presence or absence of reliance is now a factor[18];
(e) "agreement" may be largely fictitious[19] or otherwise unsatisfactory.[20]

(2) "People are free to contract or not, as they please". But abuses of this power may be limited, by:

(a) competition law[21];
(b) anti-discrimination legislation.[22]

(3) "Contracting parties are absolutely bound by their agreements". But this principle will be modified in cases of:

(a) misrepresentation and non-disclosure[23];
(b) duress or undue influence[24];
(c) abuse of superior bargaining strength[25];
(d) lack of good faith[26];
(e) mistake[27];
(f) variation by the parties[28];
(g) frustration[29];
(h) relational contracts.[30]

(4) "Their agreement affects only them and not others". But agreements necessarily affect many, not just the parties, and this is recognised:

(a) through tort[31];

Co v. *Ex-Cell-O Corporation* [1979] 1 WLR 401) or the weakening of formal requirements (Law Reform (Enforcement of Contracts) Act 1954).

[18] See for example P.J. Cooke and D.W. Oughton, *The Common Law of Obligations*, 1st edn (London, 1989), 82–97; D. Nolan, "The Classical Legacy and Modern English Contract Law" (1996) 59 *MLR* 603, 606–9.

[19] e.g. "intention to create legal relations", on which see S. Hedley, "Keeping Contract in its Place" (1985) 5 *OJLS* 391.

[20] "English law, having committed itself to a rather technical and schematic doctrine of contract, in application takes a practical approach, often at the cost of forcing the facts to fit uneasily into the marked slots of offer, acceptance and consideration": *New Zealand Shipping* Co v. *AM Satterthwaite & Co, The Eurymedon* [1975] AC 154, 167, per Lord Wilberforce.

[21] e.g. Competition Act 1980.

[22] e.g. Race Relations Act 1976.

[23] e.g. Misrepresentation Act 1967.

[24] e.g. *Barclays Bank Plc* v. *O'Brien* [1994] 1 AC 180.

[25] e.g. *Schroeder Music Publishing* Co v. *Macaulay* [1974] 1 WLR 1308.

[26] "Good faith" has many meanings. See Unfair Terms in Consumer Contracts Regulations 1994 (SI 1994 N. 3159); J. Beatson and D. Friedmann (eds), *Good Faith and Fault in Contract Law* (Oxford, 1995).

[27] e.g. *Solle* v. *Butcher* [1950] 1 KB 671.

[28] See especially J. Beatson, *The Use and Abuse of Unjust Enrichment* (Oxford, 1991), 126–9.

[29] e.g. *BP Exploration Co (Libya) Ltd* v. *Hunt (No. 2)* [1979] 1 WLR 739; [1981] 1 WLR 232; [1983] 2 AC 352.

[30] e.g. I. Macneil, "Relational Contracts: What we Know and do not Know" [1985] *Wisconsin LR* 483; D. Campbell and D. Harris, "Flexibility in Long-Term Contractual Relationships: The Role of Co-operation" (1993) 20 *J L & Soc* 166.

[31] e.g. *White* v. *Jones* [1995] 2 AC 207. See generally S. Whittaker, "Privity of Contract and the Tort of Negligence: Future Directions" (1996) 16 *OJLS* 191.

(b) through "network contracts"[32];
(c) through taxes on contracts[33];
(d) through public law controls on terms.[34]

(5) "The courts will not add to the terms of the agreement". But the courts may effectively add terms:

(a) directly, at common law[35];
(b) via collateral contracts[36];
(c) as a consequence of statute.[37]

(6) "The courts will not allow other bodies of law to interfere with the parties' agreement". But many other bodies of law now intrude into contracts:

(a) negligence[38];
(b) "legitimate expectations"[39];
(c) "*pacta sunt servanda*"[40];
(d) estoppel[41];
(e) restitution.[42]

(7) "In summary, it is the parties' own promises and will that govern their arrangement, and not the arbitrary will of parliament or judges". But:

(a) the considerable freedom of choice the courts have is there whether or not the judges acknowledge it;
(b) identifying "the intentions of the parties" is not a neutral or mechanical process;
(c) differences between different types of contracts and different parties to them seem too important to ignore[43];
(d) it is not clear that enforcing promises is entirely distinct from the imposition of morality generally[44];
(e) the unitary court structure may not always be the best solution to the problems we want solved.

[32] See H. Collins, *The Law of Contract*, 2nd edn (London, 1993), 124–8; G. Teubner, "Piercing the Contractual Veil?" in T. Wilhelmsson (ed), *Perspectives of Critical Contract Law* (Aldershot, 1993), 211–38.
[33] e.g. Value Added Tax Act 1983.
[34] See G. Borrie, "The Regulation of Public and Private Power" [1989] *PL* 552; Unfair Terms in Consumer Contracts Regulations 1994 (SI 1994 N. 3159), reg 8.
[35] e.g. *Johnstone* v. *Bloomsbury AHA* [1992] QB 333.
[36] e.g. *City & Westminster Properties* v. *Mudd* [1959] Ch 129.
[37] e.g. Landlord and Tenant Act 1985.
[38] e.g. *Henderson* v. *Merrett Syndicates Ltd* [1995] 2 AC 145.
[39] See J. Beatson, "Public Law Influences in Contract Law", in J. Beatson and D. Friedmann (eds), *Good Faith and Fault in Contract Law* (Oxford, 1995), 263.
[40] See J.F. O'Connor, *Good Faith in English Law* (Aldershot, 1990).
[41] e.g. *Crabb* v. *Arun DC* [1976] Ch 179.
[42] D. Nolan, "The classical legacy and modern English contract law" (1996) 59 MLR 603, 610–12.
[43] *Ibid.* at 614–19.
[44] See P.S. Atiyah, *Promises Morals and Law* (Oxford, 1981), especially Ch 7.

## 4. CONTRACT LAW AND THEORY TODAY

So what we have, still quite recognisable, is a Victorian theory of contracts, which must nonetheless be supplemented in various ways if it is to make any kind of sense as a description of the modern law; and the Victorian confidence that "contract" can neatly be carved off from other types of liability seems over-optimistic. Few, I think, would defend the adequacy of the Victorian model as a statement of the modern law, but for a number of reasons it is not possible to do away with it just like that. It would be surprising if any theory of such general import were suddenly abandoned, whatever could be said against it.[45] And there are many social pressures tending to maintain the theory against all attacks: student lawyers are required to display knowledge of it, and its apparently general nature tends to ward off questions about usefulness.[46] Even if the "general" theory has, on a particular point, been found unsatisfactory, it nonetheless persists, with the "general" theory untouched, but corrected in each practical context by particular rulings or legislation.[47] Yet there is no unanimity on what would be better; or indeed even that something better should be looked for. The Victorian schema is, after all, by no means unfair when considered on the fairy-tale assumptions on which it was based: the assumptions that everyone knew the law, and had adequate opportunity to negotiate reasonable contract terms in the light of it. And while these assumptions are manifestly wrong, better ones (*workable* better ones, that is) are hard to come by.

The result is therefore that, while the weaknesses of the Victorian schema leap to the eye, it is by no means so obvious what to replace it with. Yet, rather than conflicting over our very different assumptions, we politely ignore what the others are up to—with only occasional exceptions.[48] We can roughly divide the different approaches into three: traditional approaches, modernist approaches and post-modernist approaches.

*Traditional approaches*. A traditional approach concentrates on notions of agreement, ruminating in general terms on the law as applicable in all situations. There is relatively little to say from this point of view, as the theoretical work has largely been done already; nor are there many new cases to spark controversy, as few areas spawn points germane to the general theory, and they tend to be very factual when they do. However, there is life in the

[45] D. Campbell, "The Undeath of Contract: A Study in the Degeneration of a Research Programme" (1992) 22 *HKLJ* 20.

[46] J. Wightman, *Contract: A Critical Commentary* (London, 1996), 13–15.

[47] This has been going on for a long time, almost as long as there has been a "general" theory at all. So *Derry* v. *Peek* (1889) 14 App Cas 337, which required actual dishonesty before certain misrepresentations were actionable, was on its own facts almost immediately reversed by statute (Directors' Liability Act 1890). Yet the case continued until the 1960s as the "general rule" relating to misrepresentation in contract generally.

[48] Of which an outstanding example is A.J. Weir's hostile review of Collins, *The Law of Contract*, 1st edn (London, 1986), at [1986] *CLJ* 503.

old dog yet.[49] Manifestly, the four-part model of restitution relies heavily on the traditional approach to contract. Insisting that contract is based on intent, and that restitution is not, is a good way of driving a wedge between them; recognition that matters are not so simple threatens the four-part model.

*Modernist approaches.* Modernist approaches, by contrast, argue that traditional theory is out-dated, and that there is a great deal of work to be done in bringing contract theory up to date, to reflect modern values. Naturally, there is a great deal to say from this angle, as the appropriate direction for changes is not obvious; modernist approaches today are now the main approach in the scholarship, and have a substantial hold over the textbook market as well.

It is now common for modernist writers to plead their cause by a particular way of characterising the change in the law of contract: it is now said that there was originally a neat and tidy "classical" approach to the law of contract, which may have fulfilled the needs of its time, but which over the course of a century has been slowly pushed out of the way by a new, rather mushier, modern law of contract. "Contract" has thus been transformed.[50] Yet in what direction does the wish for a modern contract law take the theorists? Manifestly, different types of contract are treated differently in case law and by statute. Manifestly, the insistence on a *general* theory is one of the prime defects of the "classical" vision. A sale of half a kilo of grapes is very different from a performance guarantee or partnership agreement; and to dissect out the few respects in which they resemble one another would lead, I suspect, to a rather whimsical list, of questionable utility in describing contract law. All this and more is accepted by most modernists. Yet to write a contract text on that premise is to write a text that cannot possibly be of much use to a student studying "contract law". Students need at least a working knowledge of the "classical" approach to satisfy professional requirements, and the most compelling theoretical arguments for the inadequacy of such an approach have not so far altered that.

Inevitably, therefore, modernist approaches are relatively timid in their suggestions as to what the new law should look like. They may, for example, suggest amendment to specific "classical" doctrines, such as privity.[51] But the scope for this is limited; effectively, it limits the modernists to an agenda set by the classical law, to the topics on which the classical law had something to say. More innovative are wholesale attempts to limit the classical view, by reference to new doctrines based on new values, incompatible with the values motivating classical law: notably fairness,[52] inequality of bargaining power,[53]

[49] e.g. the dispute over "objective agreement": materials referred to in S. Hedley, "Contracts as Promises" (1993) 44 *NILQ* 12, 25 n 47.

[50] e.g. H. Collins, *The Law of Contract*, 2nd edn (London, 1993).

[51] e.g. H. Beale, "Privity of Contract: Judicial and Legislative Reform" (1995) 9 *JCL* 103.

[52] e.g. S. A. Smith, "In Defence of Substantive Fairness" (1996) 112 *LQR* 138.

[53] e.g. H. Collins, *The Law of Contract*, 2nd edn (London, 1993).

good faith,[54] and welfarism.[55] These are vague notions. In the 1970s, there were attempts to dress them up as developments of classical law: in this the theorists were following the lead of Lord Denning MR in postulating a broad doctrine of "inequality of bargaining power" as a generalisation from classical doctrines such as duress and undue influence.[56] But (I think it is fair to say that) it is now widely recognised that this will not do. There is a distant similarity between the case of someone given no practical alternative but to sign a standard form, on the one hand, and someone forced to sign because the other party is holding a knife to their throat, on the other. But if the relevant doctrines are to be stated with any precision—and to have any real bite, they must be—the differences between the two situations far outweigh the similarities, and this is now reflected in the literature.[57] The new model of contract is quite different from the old, and cannot be regarded as a perfection of it.

At the moment, therefore, what students tend to get is exposition of the "classical" view, with various critiques added on to demonstrate its inadequacy, but without any very clear overall picture of where the new vision leads. "Reliance", "unjust enrichment", "good faith" and "welfarism" are firmly on the syllabus, but their relation to the concepts they are meant to supplant remains ambiguous. Whether it is possible to replace the "classical" law entirely is currently an open question. If it is actually true that a new vision demands separate consideration for each type of contract, then obviously it cannot; nothing very much can change without a radical change in attitude by the professional bodies, which does not seem to be in prospect. Still, some argue that a new, general law of contract "is not a lost cause",[58] though it is not entirely clear how it could be brought about—the diversity of values the new law would have to accommodate seems hopelessly broad. And certainly any such development would have to involve rehabilitation of the notions of "promise" and "agreement", perhaps along the lines suggested by King[59] or Collins.[60] It also needs to be recognised, I think, that the project is exciting analytically but not politically: for all that talk of "inequality of bargaining power" and "fairness" *sounds* like a challenge to the rule of the market, there

[54] e.g. J. Beatson and D. Friedmann (eds), *Good Faith and Fault in Contract Law* (Oxford, 1995).

[55] e.g. R. Brownsword, G. Howells and T. Wilhelmsson (eds), *Welfarism in Contract Law* (Aldershot, 1994).

[56] *Lloyds Bank Ltd* v. *Bundy* [1975] QB 326.

[57] See especially H. Beale, "Legislative Control of Fairness", in J. Beatson and D. Friedmann (eds), *Good Faith and Fault in Contract Law* (Oxford, 1995), 231.

[58] R. Brownsword in T. Wilhelmsson (ed), *Perspectives of Critical Contract Law* (Aldershot, 1993), 245.

[59] D. King, "Reshaping Contract Theory and Law: Death of Contract II: Part one: Generalised Consent with Lawmade Obligations" (1994) 7 *JCL* 245.

[60] H. Collins in T. Wilhelmsson (ed), *Perspectives of Critical Contract Law* (Aldershot, 1993), 303 *et seq.*

is nothing necessarily very radical about it.[61] It can be *combined* with such radicalism,[62] but that is another matter. To give a better description of current political practice is by no means necessarily to advocate change in it.

*Post-modern approaches.* A final school of thought here, whom I have tentatively labelled post-modernists, concentrate on contract doctrine *considered as rhetoric.* They start pretty much from the modernist view—opposing "classical" and "modern" tendencies in the law—but are primarily interested in that clash of ideas, rather than in ways it could fruitfully be resolved. The clash is the point, and the point is jurisprudential.[63] Approaches which attempt merely to state the law are, if not condemned outright, at least regarded as sorely inadequate "rule-books": "just as we would not think that someone who could recite British Rail timetables understood railways, we should not think that an ability to recite the rule-book indicates an understanding of contract".[64] "In our view, it is a mistake to think of contract as a train-load of doctrine chugging along in one direction. Rather, it is carried on several trains, some bound on collision courses with one another".[65] At present, the rhetoric is only analysed in two dimensions—a "market-individualism" v. "consumer welfarism" axis and a "Realist" v. "Formalist" axis—but no doubt the transition to further, possibly hyperspatial dimensions is only a matter of time. In my view, this approach is interesting, but ultimately sterile. We are all trapped in the prison-house of rhetoric, but there is plenty to occupy us while we are here, and it seems strange to make *this* the principal insight we try to pass on about contract.[66]

This then is the current state of contract law. A century ago, a neat theory was propounded to make sense of the cases, and rapidly gained acceptance. A century later, that model is not only deeply controversial but a deeply puzzling political and rhetorical phenomenon as well.

## 5. DEVELOPMENT OF RESTITUTION

What chance is there that restitution will follow a similar pattern of development? The enterprise attempted is obviously very similar in many ways. At several levels, there is a close parallel between the late-nineteenth century rise of contract theory and the late-twentieth century rise of restitutionary theory.

[61] T. Willhelmsson in T. Wilhelmsson (ed), *Perspectives of Critical Contract Law* (Aldershot, 1993) 45–8.

[62] e.g. J. Wightman, *Contract: A Critical Commentary* (London, 1996).

[63] Notably J. Adams and R. Brownsword, *Understanding Contract Law* (London, 1987); D. Oughton and M. Davies, *Sourcebook on Contract Law* (London, 1996).

[64] J. Adams and R. Brownsword, *Understanding Contract Law* (London, 1987), 16.

[65] J. Adams and R. Brownsword, *Understanding Contract Law* (London, 1987), 19.

[66] It may be that the writers I have described as "post-modernist" would not acknowledge that their approach differs fundamentally from those I have described as "modernist", merely providing an additional, rhetorical dimension to their modernism.

In both instances, a small group of academics determinedly pushed a particular analysis of the area, which (if accepted) united previously disparate areas of liability into a single theory. And both theories satisfy elementary pedagogical criteria: roughly, they are simple to explain to students without too many preliminaries. I stress, as Birks himself stresses,[67] that this is *not at all* the norm in the rise of new legal disciplines. We do not teach consumer law, company law or constitutional law in terms of such a rigid theory. Nor do we justify their teaching in terms of one: the reasons why these other topics are important do *not* depend on prior acceptance of a particular theory, and could in principle be explained to someone with no knowledge of theory at all. Consumer issues are important *whether or not* there is some homogeneity or regularity in the legal doctrines brought to bear on them; and so on. (For that matter, it would be perfectly possible to justify the teaching of contract law without appeal to any theory supposedly behind the law: in a capitalist economy, its importance would rapidly be conceded *whatever* the law's response consisted of.) It is a rarity indeed to find an area being sold to its potential audience *purely* on the strength of a theory said to lie behind its materials.

Is it likely that restitution will follow a similar course to contract, leading to its acceptance as a core discipline? The main burden of this chapter is that it *should* not, rather than that it *can*not—that it would be a mistake, rather than that it would be impossible. Nonetheless, there are reasons for doubting whether it is likely to do so, quite regardless of the question of desirability. We are not now working with a blank canvas, as were the academics of the 1870s. The territory of restitution avoids falling into other disciplines not because the common law is largely unmapped—the contrary is the case—but because other disciplines have not regarded its subject-matter as worth taking. And topics such as maritime salvage, which got by for centuries without bothering themselves too much about whether they are part of some wider whole, are unlikely to be revolutionised by the assertion that they are "really" examples of restitution for services rendered. The abolition of the forms of action took place some time ago, and the conceptual redrawing of boundaries that followed it is now well over.

As to my substantive case against the "unjust enrichment" theory, I have written on this general theme elsewhere,[68] and so will confine myself here to emphasising two parts of the case that have not yet received sufficient attention. First, the idea that there is a moral principle forbidding unjust enrichment at all seems to be confused and confusing, and I examine its credentials as a basis for the law. Secondly, the theory seems to me to be pitched at too high a level of generality: there is relatively little to say about "unjust enrichment" as such, and that little is perhaps best left unsaid. Restitution is import-

[67] P. Birks, *An Introduction to the Law of Restitution* (Oxford, 1985), 73–4.

[68] Most recently "Unjust Enrichment" [1995] *CLJ* 578. As there, I use "unjust enrichment theorists" to refer to writers who enthusiastically use the four-part scheme, and have done my best not to confuse the issue by including writers whose enthusiasm for it is limited or imperceptible.

ant and worthy of study because the individual topics within it are interesting and worth of study. The search for a broad theory to unite them is a distraction.

## 6. "UNJUST ENRICHMENT" AS A MORAL NOTION

First, morals. It is confidently asserted that there is a moral principle against unjust enrichment, and this has not really been controversial. No-one likes to be seen supporting the retention of unjust benefits. I argue, however, that, while the idea that there is a moral rule against "unjust enrichments" is far from meaningless, it has not yet been given any very coherent meaning when used in the way that "unjust enrichment" theorists have sought to use it. It does not denote a distinct area of liability. If the moral principle against unjust enrichment is to be identified with any particular feature of our legal system, then most obviously it denotes the rules on which assets and advantages one is entitled to secure for oneself and those which it would be "unjust" to acquire—in other words it refers to the institution of property (taken in a very broad sense), and every legal institution that could be said to protect property—of which "restitution" is a rather small part.

There is a preliminary difficulty in making sense of this moral principle at all. It does not feature in places one expects to find moral axioms, like ethical or religious codes. What sense, then, can we make of it?

The first sense would simply be that there is an "unjust enrichment" where one party has control of some asset or item of value that ought in justice to belong to another. If I ought to pay you £100, then I am "unjustly enriched" if I do not do so. This is a perfectly defensible usage, but of course there is then no very obvious difference between saying that I am "unjustly enriched" to the tune of £100, in this sense, and saying I owe £100. This sense, then, fits well into a general theory of debt where debts are sometimes created expressly and are sometimes "implied"; but that is precisely what the "unjust enrichment" theorists wish to escape.

The second idea is that of a specific moral injunction against enriching yourself in particular ways. But this is close to tautologous. No doubt one should not unjustly enrich oneself; one should not do anything at all unjustly. This is what "should" and "unjustly" *mean*. Moral and religious codes of course have much specifically to say on this; I note, for example, the Biblical injunction against usury. But that does not seem to be what modern theorists have in mind. Or again, there is the injunction in every practical legal code against taking things that are not yours: to avoid the wrath of God, or the tragedy of the commons, or a great decline in utility, or whatever, not everyone can have every asset they want. This again is not what the restitution theorists have in mind, and their major instances of liability—recovery of money paid over in certain dubious circumstances—frequently do not involve any moral wrongdoing on the part of the defendant at all. It simply will not do to postulate parallelism between tort and restitution here, to say that, just as someone who inflicts loss on another should compensate them, so someone who unjustly gains at another's expense should compensate them. Harms are obviously bad things anyway, regardless of the question of compensation, whereas the same is not true of gains.[69]

Thirdly, there is a general sense in which we might be said to view people in a more favourable moral light when they have bestowed benefits on others, rather than simply watching out for their own interests. Again, this is a perfectly defensible usage, but it does not do what the "unjust enrichment" theorists want. This moral principle appears everywhere, without regard for subject classifications—a prominent example being the "rescuer" principle in tort, where the plaintiff is viewed more favourably because s/he was trying to confer a benefit on the person requiring rescue.[70] The rôle played by "benefit" in law and morals is complex indeed, and does not seem reducible to any simple principle affecting a discrete class of cases.[71]

A final, and more fruitful, idea is that, if conduct is wrongful, then benefits gained from the wrongful course of action should be removed. This is distinct from sense (2), because the wrongfulness has no necessary connection with gain. It is wrong to kill your mother *whether or not* this makes you financially better off, but moral principle may require that you should then be deprived of any benefit under her will *as well as* suffering whatever punishment is imposed for the crime. As suggested moral principles go, this is on the plausible side. Obviously it becomes less plausible as we go down the scale of seriousness of crimes; but it sounds at first like a promising line of enquiry.

However, we are *not* at the start of this particular line of enquiry but several decades down it, and it has become clear that this moral principle bears little relation to the "unjust enrichment" model, and indeed is something of an embarrassment to it. It is irrelevant to restitution cases based on "subtraction", where the defendant's gain is precisely equivalent to the plaintiff's loss; these cases are not based on any idea of wrongdoing by the defendant. And these cases form, on any view, the bulk of the law of restitution. If the supposed moral principle of removing benefits gained through wrongdoing is relevant to restitution at all, it is only in the explanation of a rather small body of cases of "restitution for wrongs"—small and getting smaller, as

[69] C.T. Wonnell, "Replacing the Unitary Principle of Unjust Enrichment" (1996) 45 *Emory LJ* 153, 175.

[70] And for "unjust enrichment" in contract see S.M. Waddams, "Restitution as Part of Contract Law", in A. Burrows (ed), *Essays on the Law of Restitution* (Oxford, 1991) 197; J. Gordley, "Enforcing Promises" (1995) 82 *California LR* 547.

[71] C.T. Wonnell, "Replacing the Unitary Principle of Unjust Enrichment" (1996) 45 *Emory LJ* 153, 162–74; J.L. Coleman, "Corrective Justice and Wrongful Gain", in *Markets Morals and the Law* (Cambridge, 1988), 184; R.A. Epstein, "The Ubiquity of the Benefit Principle" (1994) 67 *South California LR* 1369. For *all* private law recovery as the correlation of gain and loss see E.J. Weinrib, *The Idea of Private Law* (Cambridge, 1995) especially Ch 5.

"unjust enrichment" theorists progressively try to explain these cases away on other grounds.

There are still a few writers who are openly indignant that the courts have not simply accepted the notion of recovery of profits for deliberate wrongdoing,[72] though there are an increasing number who recognise not merely that no adequate theory of recovery has so far been developed by the academics, but also that it is unreasonable to expect the courts to proceed without one.[73] Neither the courts[74] nor the Law Commission[75] show any sign of going down that road; and the financially-motivated murderer has long since been given up as a lost cause.[76] It is unreasonable to expect unanimity of view here, but it is fair to say that "restitution for wrongs" is currently under siege, from writers otherwise fully committed to "unjust enrichment" notions. The credentials of the notion look distinctly shaky.

The key to the matter is to see which instances of liability we are trying to explain here; there appear to be two. First, there are cases where the profit is removed from the wrong-doing defendant for some clear reason of policy—probably having something to do with discouraging this particular form of wrongdoing.[77] Secondly, there are cases which, properly seen, are subtractive after all.[78]

Taking the first category first, it is clear that it is not easy to find a single theory which explains all the diverse instances of liability, despite some rather frenzied searching. What is gratifying in the recent literature is the realisation that to look only at restitution cases is a mistake, even for those committed to the "unjust enrichment" theory. Once it is admitted that the restitutionary liability is a punitive or quasi-punitive response to a particular, sharply-defined situation, then it is no longer obvious that it has to consist of removing *precisely* the defendant's enrichment. As Jaffey notes, it is a poor form of punishment that can do nothing more than restore the punished person to the position they were in before they did the prohibited act.[79] Sometimes more

[72] e.g. R. O'Dair, "Remedies for Breach of Contract: A Wrong Turn" [1993] *RLR* 31, 41, criticising *Surrey CC* v. *Bredero Homes* [1993] 1 WLR 1361 as "deeply disappointing to those concerned with the rational and coherent development of the law".

[73] e.g. P. Birks, *Restitution—The Future* (Sydney, 1992), 25.

[74] *Stoke-on-Trent CC* v. *W & J Wass Ltd* [1988] 3 All ER 394 is typical.

[75] Rather, the suggestion has been to reiterate and strengthen the common law's emphasis on the proprietary torts: Law Commission, "Aggravated, Exemplary and Restitutionary Damages" (LCCP No 132, 1993), para. 7.20.

[76] For Burrows' reasons why this denial of title to murderers is not restitutionary, but rather a manifestation of property law, see A. Burrows, *Law of Restitution* (London, 1993), 380. Where restitution "ends" and property "begins" is a matter of some controversy. On the view presented here, there is a mere matter of pedagogy, unless (as occasionally happens) it is necessary to characterise it for conflict of laws purposes.

[77] This is Barker's "instrumentalism" (K. Barker, "Unjust Enrichment: Containing the Beast" (1995) 15 *OJLS* 457) and Jaffey's "quasi-punitive" liability (P. Jaffey, "Restitutionary Damages and Disgorgement" [1995] *RLR* 30).

[78] Barker's "individualism" and Jaffey's "true restitutionary damages" (*supra* n 77).

[79] Jaffey [1995] *RLR* 30, 37–8.

will be required, sometimes less, and perhaps only rarely the precise amount. Nor will it always be obvious that whatever is taken from the defendant must be given to the victim, as distinct from (say) being forfeited to the state.[80]

Yet writers who have seen this (and there are several) have to my mind acted curiously. Jaffey surveys the range of responses the law can take to profitable wrongdoing—including the imposition of criminal penalties or exemplary damages awards—and seems to conclude that we should retain flexibility, yet *call* the remedy "restitutionary" when it removes the defendant's enrichment and gives it to the plaintiff[81]! The function or utility of the label "restitutionary" is not explained. For Barker and for McBride and McGrath, the open-endedness of the notion is fatal: a theory which points in the direction of such a broad question must be wrong (per McBride and McGrath[82]) or at least dubious (per Barker[83]).

This drives them to the second analysis, that of treating as many of these cases as possible as examples of subtractive restitution. This might at first sight seem difficult; the distinguishing feature of these cases is precisely that the defendant's gain exceeds the plaintiff's loss, rather than exactly matching it, which is why the category was thought necessary in the first place. The trick is done by a subtle change of emphasis. If I acquire your £100, there is no difficulty in seeing this as subtractive: you lose £100, I gain it. If I acquire your car, it seems not to be so simple: perhaps I do not gain financially from this at all, and it may be hard to place a value on my use. The trick is to keep our eyes on the asset concerned, and for its value simply to refer to the market. You have lost your car, I have gained it: loss and gain are equal, and have a definite price in the market. Or if the loss is only temporary, analogous reasoning applies: you have lost the use of your car for a period, I have gained that very thing, and the market can say how much that forced loan is worth. The trick is not confined to personal property, either. Temporary use of real property, or indeed any right or privilege can be subjected to this analysis. All these cases—and they constitute nearly all of the ones needing explanation—can then be claimed for "subtractive" restitution.

How satisfactory is this? It can certainly be said against it that it takes a very particular, and somewhat artificial, view of "benefit": it refers to the market whether or not the parties are likely to have resorted to it, and regardless of whether their projected or actual use would have been more or less valu-

80 Barker (1995) 15 *OJLS* 457, 466–7.

81 Jaffey [1995] *RLR* 30, 37–42.

82 And so for them "[t]here is no concept known to English law as restitution for wrongs": N. McBride and P. McGrath, "The Nature of Restitution" (1995) 15 *OJLS* 33, 44.

83 Barker (1995) 15 *OJLS* 457, 466–7. Barker's thesis is aimed principally at distinguishing this "instrumentalist" approach from the "individualist" (subtractive) approach, though he drops numerous hints that he prefers the latter, despite the *descriptive* merits of (some versions of) instrumentalism (*ibid.*, 466). It is a pity that he did not consider more actual instances where the law openly allows instrumentalism, e.g. *Chief Constable of Kent* v. *V* [1983] QB 34; Proceeds of Crime Act 1995.

able. The remedy is for the market price of whatever is taken, regardless of whether the benefit measured in other ways would be less or more. (That is no novelty in the law of obligations, of course.) But if that disadvantage is swallowed, these cases have been classified out of the "restitution for wrongs" category and into the "subtractive restitution" category. The "wrong" takes on a new and a different significance. So, if I build in a way which you have the right to prohibit me by injunction, we do *not* reason that I have done a wrong against you, so that you may have the benefit I acquire. Rather, we say that you had a right to prevent me, and as I have taken this right for myself I can charge you the market value of that right—the amount I would have paid you in advance, had we bargained. On this view, the "wrong" fades from view; it provides a marker to show that defendant has taken an asset that is rightly the plaintiff's, but restitution is granted because the defendant has taken the asset, not because the manner of taking was "wrong".[84]

This does not seem implausible to me. I suspect it will prove less acceptable to many "unjust enrichment" supporters once its implications sink in. In particular, it undermines the idea that restitution is particularly about *benefits* as distinct from losses. If the "restitution for wrongs" category is effectively wiped out, we are left with the "subtractive" cases, where gain and loss are agreed to be co-extensive. Moreover, it is not obvious that either "gain" or "loss" describes the measure of recovery better. Indeed, the various writers who have made proposals along these lines have given very different accounts of what they are describing. Sharpe and Waddams call it a "loss": the plaintiff's loss through being deprived of the right to bargain with the defendant.[85] Birks, protesting against over-extension of ideas of loss, insists that what we are giving is (one measure of) the defendant's "gain".[86] McBride and McGrath deny this: the sum is not the measure of the defendant's gain, but rather the sum necessary to make the defendant's gain a just one, to square the defendant's gain with the plaintiff's rights.[87] Or, again, it can be seen (more convincingly in some cases than others) as the term the law implies in the contract between the plaintiff and the defendant.

Can we say that what the law is really doing is protecting property rights, pure and simple? This is the neatest idea; it reflects the point that one side has lost and the other has gained, without making too much of a song and dance

[84] Barker does not take his own reasoning far enough here. We are *not* giving a "flexible and open-textured" meaning to "wrong" ( (1995) 15 *OJLS* 457, 470–1), but forgetting the label altogether. It is not sensible to retain it when it has been drained of meaning, and surely the English language is rich enough to find a word that *does* fit.

[85] R.S. Sharpe and S.M. Waddams, "Damages for Lost Opportunity to Bargain" (1982) 2 *OJLS* 290.

[86] P. Birks, "Civil Wrongs: A New World", in *Butterworth Lectures 1990–91* (London, 1992), 74–7. His complaint against "loss", that we refer to the market whether or not the parties themselves are likely to have done, is of course equally a point against "gain".

[87] N. McBride and P. McGrath, "The Nature of Restitution" (1995) 15 *OJLS* 33, 47. Interestingly, they combine respect for "unjust enrichment" with considerable scepticism as to the concept of "benefit" itself.

over either.[88] Yet, for reasons which do not seem entirely logical, "property" is usually reserved for physical objects.[89] A wider conception is needed to cover everything I have mentioned; perhaps the best word is *assets*.[90] And of course, so defined, there is no substantial difference between the "unjust enrichment" conception of restitution and Stoljar's "proprietary" conception[91]; and the moral basis of the area is (presumably) Thou Shalt Not Steal, or something remarkably similar.

## 7. TOO HIGH A LEVEL OF GENERALITY

One of the hall-marks of the new "unjust enrichment" theory is to insist that it applies quite generally, so that what can be said of one type of unjust enrichment can be said of others. Indeed, quite extravagant phrases are used on the point.[92] Yet matters are not so simple. As I have argued elsewhere, money is special: and the argument to the contrary assumes that an answer has been found to a clutch of problems about "enrichment" which have resisted solution for quite a while now.[93] I would like to argue here that services, too, cannot be fitted into a unitary model, for it is quite unclear what it means to be "enriched" by the receipt of services.

[88] This appears to me to be the kernel of truth in the notion that restitution for wrongs is available mainly for "proprietary" wrongs. The point is that the proprietary torts are themselves conceptually awkward, requiring us to say that the plaintiff is "injured" by losing her property, the "harm" being assessed as the value of the property. Much of the difficulty goes if we acknowledge that it is not the plaintiff who is injured, but the plaintiff's property interest.

[89] This is a complex issue. See generally K. Gray, "Property in thin Air" [1991] *CLJ* 252; and Beatson on "wealth", in "Benefit, Reliance and the Structure of Unjust Enrichment" [1987] *CLP* 71, 74–6.

[90] Following McBride and McGrath ( (1995) 15 *OJLS* 33, 39–40). Opinions would then differ as to whether "pure" services can be incorporated into that model or require separate treatment.

[91] As Fitzgerald points out (B.F. Fitzgerald, "Ownership as the Proximity or Privity Principle in Unjust Enrichment Law" (1995) 18 *UQLJ* 166, 173–8), most criticism of Stoljar rests on misconceptions about what Stoljar meant by "property", and he can claim considerable support in the authorities (e.g. P. Birks, "The English Recognition of Unjust Enrichment" [1991] *LMCLQ* 473, 482).

[92] So Birks describes the contrary view as an "illusion" and "plainly nonsense": P. Birks, *Restitution—The Future* (Sydney, 1992), 86. He blames this "illusion" on the historical development of the common law (*ibid.*, 90). It does not seem to me that the common law can so easily be separated from its history, but in any event there are ample analytical reasons for different treatment.

[93] S. Hedley, " 'Unjust Enrichment' " [1995] *CLJ* 578, 596 *et seq*. I entirely agree with Dawson's comment that "[t]he ideal expressed—that one should not become richer (*locupletior*) through another's loss—has been gathering new meanings for more than 1800 years and we could not, if we would, discard it" (J.P. Dawson, "Restitution without Enrichment" (1981) 61 *Boston ULR* 563, 577). There is only a problem when this view is combined with a conceptual approach that tries to *deduce* the law from certain of those meanings—a course Dawson for one manifestly would not advocate.

### *The Problem of Services*

If the problem of the valuation of services has not yet been solved, it is not for want for trying.[94] The following suggestions have been made: that services are valuable (a) if acquiesced in, or at least freely accepted, by the recipient[95]; (b) if they saved the recipient an otherwise inevitable expense[96]; (c) if the recipient has disentitled himself from denying their objective worth[97]; (d) if the benefit is "incontrovertible"[98]; (e) if the benefit has been bargained for[99]; (f) if the transfer of property in like circumstances would have been enriching, one's right to the fruit of one's own services being a sort of "self-ownership".[100] In each instance there is significant doubt as to when the measure is meant to apply.[101] It is not merely that each writer has a different theory; each writer has a *bundle* of theories, and it is rarely made clear when each writer would apply each theory. And there seems no surer way of starting an argument between "unjust enrichment" theorists than to assert that particular hypothetical facts constitute an uncontroversial example of enriching services.[102]

All this will be familiar to those in the area. Equally well known, but rarely remarked upon, is the poverty of the case law support for any coherent idea of restitutionary recovery for services. There has been much discussion of individual cases, of course; much gnashing of teeth at individual rulings, and at how uncongenial their reasoning is for theorists. What is not so often

[94] The first major article is P. Birks, "*Negotiorum Gestio* and the Common Law" (1971) 24 *CLP* 110, and there have been a good number since then.

[95] e.g. G. Jones, "Restitutionary Claims for Services Rendered" (1977) 93 *LQR* 273.

[96] P. Birks, "*Negotiorum Gestio* and the Common Law" (1971) 24 *CLP* 110.

[97] e.g. A. Burrows, *Law of Restitution* (London, 1993), 16. Note that this involves a tacit fiction: D may not have been benefited, but we prevent him from pointing this out. The great advantage of the "implied contract" theory was that we *knew* it was a fiction. With "enrichment", we are never sure.

[98] It appears that an "incontrovertible" benefit is a distinct beast from an "objective" benefit: see P. Cooke and D. Oughton, *The Common Law of Obligations*, 1st edn (London, 1989) 103.

[99] See generally A. Burrows, "Free Acceptance and the Law of Restitution" (1988) 104 *LQR* 575.

[100] e.g. N. McBride and P. McGrath, "The Nature of Restitution" (1995) 15 *OJLS* 33, 37: "it can reasonably be said that I 'own' my capacity for work". But see *ibid.*, 47–8.

[101] For a general and sceptical review see J.W. Carter, "Services Rendered under Ineffective Contracts" [1990] *LMCLQ* 495.

[102] It will be remembered that the spark for one of the major conflagrations of academic disputation here was Birks' adoption of the window-cleaner as the archetypal sympathetic plaintiff. (Birks' example supposed that the house-holder knew the cleaner was there, and deliberately held back from an acknowledgement of the services until they were conferred: see P. Birks, *An Introduction to the Law of Restitution* (Oxford, 1985), 265.) This put the wind up at least two writers, neither of whom were prepared to take such a thing for granted: see A. Burrows, "Free Acceptance and the Law of Restitution" (1988) 104 *LQR* 576; G. Mead, "Free Acceptance: Some Further Considerations" (1989) 105 *LQR* 460. This is all quite apart from those who have argued that services are not, as such, enriching at all: e.g. J. Beatson, "Benefit, Reliance and the Structure of Unjust Enrichment" [1987] *CLP* 71. In Watts' theory (P. Watts, "Restitution: A Property Principle and a Services Principle" [1995] *RLR* 49), services are treated as a distinct division within restitution, and there is no axiom that services are enriching: 72–3.

pointed out is that these "unsatisfactory" cases are all there is. There is not one single instance of a restitutionary recovery in England which is universally regarded as a paradigm case, as a good example of what we have in mind when we talk of recovery for beneficially enriching services.

I realise that my last statement needs the odd footnote to back it up, so I have surveyed the cases with that in mind. (To avoid irrelevant controversy, I have confined myself to cases in the current century.)[103] There would appear to be some 85 cases which could, on a broad view, be regarded as examples of restitutionary recovery for valuable services.[104] However, we can immediately shrink this number considerably by excluding those where leading "unjust enrichment" theorists have their doubts whether the case is truly an example of restitutionary recovery. Several of them seem fairly universally agreed to be examples of contractual[105] or tortious[106] recovery. Estoppel or constructive trust cases are more controversial, but the more "commercial" examples are generally agreed not to be restitutionary,[107] and there is certainly no unanimity for including the more "domestic" cases: so Burrows argues that efforts to include these cases as part of unjust enrichment "[f]ar from furthering the cause of the law of restitution . . . cloud analysis and add fuel to the argument that reference to the principle of unjust enrichment is nothing more than an excuse for sloppy palm tree justice".[108] He also has his doubts about cases involving remuneration of trustees.[109]

Similarly controversial are cases of maritime salvage, which are manifestly examples of recovery of benefits conferred, yet proceed by their own rules and

[103] The most often-cited pre-1900 services case is *Planché* v. *Colburn* (1831) 8 Bing 14. Some seem to take the result as axiomatic. But of course the case was argued before modern ideas of anticipatory breach were accepted; the restitutionary point would not arise today in that form. Views differ on whether *Planché* is restitutionary: compare A. Burrows, *Law of Restitution* (London, 1993), 267, with P.J. Cooke and D.W. Oughton, *The Common Law of Obligations*, 1st edn (London, 1989), 103.

[104] I mention each of them at least once in the notes following. There are also quite a few instances where the court refuses liability, but indicates other circumstances where it might have been available; their reasoning has not impressed the "unjust enrichment" school either. See for example E. McKendrick, "Negotiations 'Subject to Contract' and the Law of Restitution" [1995] *RLR* 100, 103–4, criticising *Regalian Properties Plc* v. *London Docklands Development Corp* [1995] 1 WLR 212.

[105] *H. Dakin & Co Ltd* v. *Lee* [1916] 1 KB 566; *James* v. *Kent* [1951] 1 KB 551; *Stevens* v. *Bromley* [1919] 2 KB 722. It is not entirely clear to me whether cases such as *Hoenig* v. *Isaacs* [1952] 2 All ER 176 are claimed as being restitutionary or not: compare P. Birks, *An Introduction to the Law of Restitution* (Oxford, 1985), 239, with A. Burrows, *Law of Restitution* (London, 1993), 277.

[106] *Cunningham* v. *Harrison* [1973] QB 942; *Donnelly* v. *Joyce* [1974] QB 454; *Haggar* v. *De Placido* [1972] 1 WLR 726; *Roach* v. *Yates* [1937] 3 All ER 442.

[107] *Crabb* v. *Arun* [1976] Ch 179; *Taylor Fashions* v. *Liverpool Victoria* [1981] 1 All ER 897; *Watson* v. *Goldbrough* (1986) 1 EGLR 265.

[108] A. Burrows, *Law of Restitution* (London, 1993), 38. The cases in issue are: *Chalmers* v. *Pardoe* [1963] 1 WLR 677; *Eves* v. *Eves* [1975] 1 WLR 1338; *Hussey* v. *Palmer* [1972] 1 WLR 1286; *Pascoe* v. *Turner* [1979] 1 WLR 431.

[109] A. Burrows, *Law of Restitution* (London, 1993), 240 n 11, commenting on *Re Duke of Norfolk* [1982] Ch 61. Presumably he has similar doubts over *Foster* v. *Spencer* [1996] 2 All ER 672.

with no attempt to justify themselves by reference to some more general theory.[110] This is a prime example of the weakness of the general theory of restitution now being so eagerly pursued: where material does not fit into the model, it is either given very short treatment, or is made subject to elaborate doubts as to whether it is "truly" restitutionary:

> Although the restitutionary measure is not overtly appealed to and may possibly not apply, it is not clear that the factors which are taken into account are not the very factors defining the value of the salvor's services. Much depends on the theory of value which is ultimately applied in this field. Only when that is more clearly settled will it be possible to see whether maritime salvage can properly be regarded as an example of restitution.[111]

So, even though the main lines of maritime salvage have been settled for many, many years, nonetheless the question of its proper characterisation must await the clarification of the theory of "enrichment": potentially a very long wait indeed.

Of the remaining cases, a significant number are obscure and little-discussed today,[112] usually for good reason, such as supervening statutory changes,[113] or the brevity of the court's discussion of the issue.[114] If a principle of "restitution for services" were accepted in English law, some of these cases could constitute minor examples of its application; but they cannot in themselves justify such a principle.

[110] These claims constitute the bulk of successful reported restitutionary claims for services: *Beaverford* v. *The Kafiristan* [1938] AC 136, *Elliott Steam Tug* v. *Admiralty Commissioners* [1921] 1 AC 137, *Industrie Chimiche* v. *Tsavliris* [1990] 1 Lloyd's Rep 516, *The Amity* [1959] 1 Lloyd's Rep 329, *The Boston Lincoln* [1980] 1 Lloyd's Rep 481, *The Bosworth* [1959] 2 Lloyd's Rep 511, [1960] 1 Lloyd's Rep 163, *The Cargo ex Port Victor* [1901] P 243, *The Corcrest* (1946) 80 Lloyd's Rep 78, *The Driade* [1959] 2 Lloyd's Rep 311, *The Emelie Galline* [1903] P 106, *The Evaine* [1966] 2 Lloyd's Rep 413, *The Frisia* [1960] 1 Lloyd's Rep 90, *The Harold Brown* [1959] 2 Lloyd's Rep 187, *The Hassel* [1959] 2 Lloyd's Rep 82, *The Helenus and Montagua* [1982] 2 Lloyd's Rep 261, *The Ilo* [1982] 1 Lloyd's Rep 39, *The Kangaroo* [1918] P 327, *The Kedah* (1948) 81 Lloyd's Rep 217, *The Lyrma* [1978] 2 Lloyd's Rep 30, *The M Vatan* [1990] 1 Lloyd's Rep 336, *The Macgregor Laird* [1953] 2 Lloyd's Rep 259, *The Makedonia* [1958] 1 QB 365, *The Nagasaki Spirit* [1996] 1 Lloyd's Rep 449, *The New Australia* [1958] 2 Lloyd's Rep 35, *The Orelia* [1958] 1 Lloyd's Rep 441, *The Port Caldeonia and The Anna* [1903] P 184, *The Powstaniec Wielkopolski* [1989] QB 279, *The Queen Elizabeth* (1949) 82 Lloyd's Rep 803, *The Rilland* [1979] 1 Lloyd's Rep 455, *The Sandefjord* [1953] 2 Lloyd's Rep 557, *The Southwark* [1962] 2 Lloyd's Rep 62, *The St Alicia and The Gorm* [1961] 2 Lloyd's Rep 20 (salvage/towage), *The Susan V Luckenbach* v. *Admiralty Commrs* [1951] P 197, *The Teh Hu* [1970] P 106, *The Telemachus* [1957] P 47, *The Tojo Maru* [1972] AC 242, *The Winson* [1982] AC 939, *Troilus* v. *Glenogle* [1951] AC 820.

[111] P. Birks, *An Introduction to the Law of Restitution* (Oxford, 1985), 307–308.

[112] *Gross Fine* v. *Clifton* (1974) 232 EG 837; *Holder* v. *Holder* [1968] Ch 353, 373–4 (the counter-restitution point); *Lawford* v. *Billericay RDC* [1903] KB 772; *Lee-Parker* v. *Izett* [1971] 1 WLR 1688, [1972] 1 WLR 775; *Re Allison* [1904] 2 KB 327; *Re English and Colonial Produce* [1906] 2 Ch 435; *Re Jarvis* [1958] 1 WLR 815; *Société Franco-Tunisienne* v. *Sidermar* [1961] 2 QB 278; *Tappenden* v. *Artus* [1964] 2 QB 185; *The Iolo* [1916] P 206; *Turriff Construction* v. *Regalian Knitting* (1971) 222 EG 169.

[113] *Munro* v. *Wilmott* [1949] 1 KB 295; *Scott* v. *Pattison* [1923] 2 KB 723.

[114] *Cotronic* v. *Dezonie* [1991] BCLC 721; *Faraday* v. *Tamworth Union* (1917) 86 LJ Ch 436; *Peter Lind* v. *Mersey Docks* [1972] 2 Lloyd's Rep 234; *Proctor* v. *Islington* (1903) 67 JP 164.

This leaves a hard core of 13 cases, which seem pretty universally agreed to be examples of restitutionary recovery for services. If there is a principle of restitution for enriching services in English law, it will surely be in those cases. Yet for each and every one of them, there is controversy over how, if at all, they can be fitted into the general theory of "unjust enrichment".[115] Sometimes it is the "enrichment" aspect that is wrong: that the court used "somewhat artificial reasoning",[116] or took a view which is "troublesome" and leads to a "real problem",[117] or took a "false step" in its reasoning,[118] or gave a remedy where it is "doubtful . . . whether any remedy should have been awarded",[19] or simply seems "wrong".[120] Sometimes "enrichment" is agreed to exist, but its basis is disputed.[121] Sometimes the court did not explain how the enrichment was calculated: "there was no discussion of the need for free acceptance or some other answer to subjective devaluation",[122] or "[h]ow the

[115] As I have noted elsewhere, discussions of "enrichment" in the cases have an artificial air: the commentators proceed as if the four-part theory were accepted by the courts, and that the worst that can be said of a judge is that s/he had *misapplied* the theory. This frequently involves writers in ludicrous anachronism, as (for example) where McKendrick criticises a judgment of Lord Denning MR's as "rather cavalier" in its disregard for the theory—in a case over a decade before the theory was first enunciated ("Restitution and the Misuse of Chattels—The Need for a Principled Approach", in N. Palmer and E. McKendrick, *Interests in Goods* (London, 1993) 599, 602)!

[116] P. Birks, *Restitution—The Future* (Sydney, 1992), 95, and similarly A. Burrows, *Law of Restitution* (London, 1993), 255, 260, 309, criticising *Rover International Ltd* v. *Cannon Film Sales Ltd* [1989] 1 WLR 912.

[117] A. Burrows, *Law of Restitution* (London, 1993), 297, criticising *Brewer Street Investments Ltd* v. *Barclays Woollen Co Ltd* [1954] 1 QB 428.

[118] See A. Burrows, *Law of Restitution* (London, 1993) 291, criticising *BP* v. *Hunt (No 2)* [1979] 1 WLR 783. Of course, the heaviest criticism was reserved not for Robert Goff J's judgment, but rather for the Court of Appeal, who reminded the "unjust enrichment" theorists that, given the discretionary nature of the 1943 Act, Robert Goff's answer was *one* right answer, not *the* right answer: [1981] 1 WLR 232, 238, criticised by P. Birks, *An Introduction to the Law of Restitution* (Oxford, 1985), 254 ("disappointing lack of interest in settling the principles on which the discretion should be exercised").

[119] A. Burrows, *Law of Restitution* (London, 1993), 125, criticising *Upton-on-Severn RDC* v. *Powell* [1942] 1 All ER 220; for a different criticism see G. McMeel, *Casebook on Restitution* (London, 1996), 85.

[120] A. Burrows, *Law of Restitution* (London, 1993), 270, criticising *Lodder* v. *Slowey* [1904] AC 442. Burrows suggests that the case might be salvaged if it were established that the enrichment in the case represented necessary expenses saved by the defendant ("Free Acceptance and the Law of Restitution" (1988) 104 *LQR* 576, 587).

[121] See competing explanations for *Craven-Ellis* v. *Canons Ltd* [1936] 2 KB 403, in A. Burrows, *Law of Restitution* (London, 1993), 307. After protracted argument in academic journals, the latest edition of Goff and Jones is happy to assert that the existence of a benefit there is "incontrovertible" (p. 24)—and so (presumably) the extensive articles in learned journals controverting that very point need not have been written. Would that all technical legal issues could be solved so simply and unequivocally! See also disputes over the nature of the enrichment in *Way* v. *Latilla* [1937] 3 All ER 759 and *William Lacey (Hounslow) Ltd* v. *Davis* [1957] 1 WLR 932: P. Birks, *An Introduction to the Law of Restitution* (Oxford, 1985), 270–4; A. Burrows, *Law of Restitution* (London, 1993), 295.

[122] P. Birks, *An Introduction to the Law of Restitution* (Oxford, 1985) 125, criticising *Boardman* v. *Phipps* [1967] 2 AC 46 (the counter-restitution point).

'enrichment' issue . . . was settled is something of a mystery".[123] Or sometimes the problem lies elsewhere: some of the reasoning "can be criticised",[124] or provides only "shadowy signposts" to liability,[125] or the judge in the case "did not analyse with any care" what he was doing[126]; or the question whether one can "realistically" see matters the judge's way is "debatable".[127]

Let it be said that I have no objection at all to criticism of the judiciary, and I am assured that it works wonders in appropriate cases. And the point is not that all of this criticism is particularly damning. It varies considerably in strength. The point is rather the *absence* of any agreed instance of liability: any one case that all who believe in "unjust enrichment" in respect of services can point to and say "this is the sort of thing we mean". This goes beyond the margin of appreciation that must be allowed in academic theories, and points to a lack of agreement on basic ideas. We have a theory whose own proponents cannot agree on how it should be applied, who cannot agree on a single unequivocal instance of its application, and who spend an unreasonable amount of their time complaining that the judges have not solved these problems either.

### *The "Terminological Minefield"*

So that is "restitution for services". Plenty of single instances in the law. But it is another question whether we need to build up a general theory to knit them all together. Restitution does not have to be studied at that level. Yet modern theorists seem reluctant to explore other possibilities, or even to acknowledge their existence. They openly claim that there is no real alternative, giving dark warnings of the collapse of legal science if their approach is not adopted,[128] or equating interest in "unjust enrichment" with interest in "restitution", so that to neglect the one is to neglect the other,[129] or talking of the "time-wasting semantic nonsense" which must follow if "unjust enrichment" concepts are not used.[130]

This refusal to treat other possibilities as meaningful has thus resulted in a particularly futile form of legal commentary, where the author pretends that the judiciary as a whole subscribes to the "unjust enrichment" theory, and

123 P. Birks, *An Introduction to the Law of Restitution* (Oxford, 1985) 124, criticising *Greenwood* v. *Bennett* [1973] QB 195; at p. 279, he refers to "the routine difficulties" of explaining what the enrichment in the case was.

124 A. Burrows, *Law of Restitution* (London, 1993), 192, criticising *O'Sullivan* v. *Management Agency & Music Ltd* [1985] QB 428 (counter-restitution point).

125 R. Goff and G. Jones, *Law of Restitution*, 4th edn (1993), 558, criticising *British Steel* v. *Cleveland Bridge* [1984] 1 All ER 504 and other cases.

126 E. McKendrick, "Rejection of Goods, Restitution for Services and Incontrovertible Benefit" [1989] *LMCLQ* 397, 402 n 3, criticising *Marston Construction* v. *Kigass* (1989) 46 *Build LR* 109.

127 A. Burrows, *Law of Restitution* (London, 1993), 239–40, criticising *Re Berkeley Applegate* [1989] Ch 32.

128 D. Stevens, "Restitution, Property, and the Cause of action in Unjust Enrichment: Getting by with Fewer Things: Part I" (1989) 39 *UTLJ* 258, 277–8.

129 A. Kull, "Rationalising Restitution" (1995) 83 *California LR* 1191, 1241.

130 P. Birks, "The English Recognition of Unjust Enrichment" [1991] *LMCLQ* 473.

then berates individual judges for supposed errors or sloppiness in applying it. Indeed, some scholars do not scruple to say openly that restitution cases which cannot be squared with "unjust enrichment" notions must be wrong.[131] The truth is of course that, while many judges are happy to talk of "unjust enrichment", it is hard to find a single one prepared to accept the theoretical baggage theorists wish to attach to the phrase. Academic writings on "unjust enrichment" are read by the judges, and utilised where they seem useful in the instant case—but the broader merits claimed for the theory pass the judges by. Perillo's comment on the American cases two decades ago seems apt for the English cases today:

> Court decisions which pay lip service to the [unjust enrichment] theory but which in fact do not carry it out have, as always, an unsettling effect on the law, giving the sensitive a feeling of lawlessness, the logician a feeling of irrationality and the average lawyer a feeling of confusion.[132]

Yet the use of such a high-level theory seems to be increasing, rather than diminishing, the level of uncertainty in the subject. The terminology of "unjust enrichment" grows more and more. Even one of its supporters has been driven to describe the subject as a "terminological minefield",[133] and another has acknowledged that closer attention has not resulted in greater clarity.[134] And a further consequence is the shrinkage of the subject, as rules and doctrines that do not fit increasingly precise theoretical notions are excluded from restitution. "Unjust enrichment" theorists have now effectively said good-bye to any case involving real property rights, salvage or benefits accruing from crime; it is an open question how long they will hang on to unconscionability, title to personal property, or subrogation.[135] There is also a growing movement to exclude restitution in any case of contract or near-contract: if the parties could easily have contracted over the conferment of the benefit or (*a fortiori*) if they did in fact contract over it, then restitution should not be allowed to intrude. Contract is said to be the best mechanism for regulating the exchange of benefits, and restitution's role should be strictly subordinate to it.[136] It follows

[131] "Rights and remedies not referable to unjust enrichment either find a better explanation elsewhere, or they signal restitution cases wrongly decided": A. Kull, "Rationalising Restitution" (1995) 83 *California LR* 1191, 1241.

[132] J.M. Perillo, "Restitution in a Contractual Context" (1973) 73 *Col. L.R.* 1208, 1223, omitting footnotes.

[133] G. McMeel, *Casebook on Restitution* (London, 1996), vii.

[134] P. Birks (ed), *Laundering and Tracing* (Oxford, 1995), xi.

[135] The most interesting recent development here is C. Mitchell, *The Law of Subrogation* (Oxford, 1994), which attempts to bring subrogation within the four-part model and to rebut the doubts of Burrows (*Law of Restitution* (London, 1993), 92). For criticism see M. Quinn, "Subrogation, Restitution, and Indemnity" (1996) 74 *Texas LR* 1361, 1396–8.

[136] See especially A. Kull, "Restitution and the Noncontractual Transfer" (1997) 11 *JCL* 93. A. Kull, "Restitution as a Remedy for Breach of Contract" (1994) 67 *Southern California LR* 1465; and compare R. Long, "A Theory of Hypothetical Contract" (1984) 94 *Yale LJ* 415. No doubt there is considerable scope for argument over *which* issues any one contract is to be taken to have settled.

that the court should only act where one of the parties now realises that it would have been better to form a contract at an earlier stage, *and* the court thinks this sloth pardonable. It would be ironic if this view were accepted in England, for it would mean that the proposition which the "unjust enrichment" school have so energetically attacked—that restitution concerns the circumstances in which the courts may legitimately imply a contract between parties—would turn out not merely to be right all along, but to be the key to understanding the area.[137]

It is an obvious point, that every topic surrendered in this way is one more blow to the prestige of the subject as the theorists would like it to be: that this "purification" of theory does not enhance the status of the subject (after all, most legal subjects get away without any such theory) but rather diminishes it. Yet still the status of the subject is trumpeted out by supporters of "unjust enrichment": one has even opined that "[i]t cannot now seriously be denied that the subject is as important and central as, say, contract and tort".[138] Statements of that sort are, I feel, too confused to be described as "wrong". Important to whom? If to judges, law students, practitioners or lecturers, then it is all too easy to deny. By any of the normal criteria—number of cases, number of specialists in academia or practice, general recognisability by the average lawyer—it is nowhere near as important as either. Central to what? Not legal education. Perhaps the learned writer meant merely that the topic should receive greater attention than it does—which is true, but it is breathtaking to assert that restitution is in any special case here. Many topics deserve more attention. Few will receive it. Restitution does not stand out in any obvious respect, or at least I have seen no reasoned case that it does.

This has emerged most strongly in recent months with the injection of European ideas. After long years of common law indifference, it seems to have been assumed that civilian systems, which recognise "unjust enrichment", will be in tune with the new approach to restitution. Seeing the choice as being between ignoring restitution and granting it full status as an important discipline, they assumed the continentals would take the latter option. Yet from the drafting of the Brussels Convention, a third possibility emerged: that it might be recognised, yet not regarded as particularly important, or deemed worthy of mentioning in the same breath as contract or tort.[139]

137 To repeat a point made by Ball in a much-neglected article ("Work Carried out in Pursuance of Letters of Intent—Contract or Restitution?" (1983) 99 *LQR* 572, 578), the solution to over-rigidity in contractual matters is *not* the adoption of an equally rigid restitution to supplement it, but a more flexible attitude in contract.

138 A. Burrows, *Law of Restitution* (London, 1993), vii.

139 See J. Riley, "Void Contracts, Restitution and Jurisdiction" [1996] *LMCLQ* 182; G. Virgo, review of F.D. Rose (ed), *Restitution and the Conflict of Laws* (1995) [1996] *CLJ* 170; R. Stevens, "Restitution and the Brussels Convention" (1996) 112 *LQR* 391. For general reviews of "unjust enrichment" in continental systems see R. Zimmermann and J. du Plessis, "Basic Features of the German Law of Unjustified Enrichment" [1994] *RLR* 14; R. Zimmermann, "Unjust Enrichment: The Modern Civilian Approach" (1995) 15 *OJLS* 403.

## 8. A POSITIVE VISION FOR RESTITUTION

It is important to end on a high note. Nearly all legal subjects get by without a theory as all-embracing as the four-part model proposed for restitution. To attack that theory is therefore not to attack restitution itself, or theories themselves. Rather, the decision whether to adopt the theory must be based on solid grounds, and not on any notion that the heavens will fall if we do not. Restitution is highly miscellaneous, and can safely remain so until some intrinsic order is demonstrated; it need not be forced.

# 19

# *Restitution: Contract's Twin?—A Comment*

ROBERT STEVENS

## Introduction

In resolving the majority of legal disputes most lawyers can get by without needing to think about the particular classification of the legal issue with which they are dealing. The classification may be obvious or make no practical difference. Chancery lawyers, for example, do not often have to concern themselves with the question whether resulting or constructive trusts arise in order to reverse unjustified enrichment. The process of legal taxonomy is not easy and most of us are happy to avoid resolution of such difficult questions.

There is more than one possible method of legal categorisation. Consumer law, labour law and computer law do not require a theory to explain their separate existence.[1] They are each unified by their particular context: consumers, employees or computers respectively.[2] Further, legal categories can arise wholly or partially by reason of the history of a legal system. Tort law, for example, can be seen as the common law's category of civil wrongs[3] which are not breaches of contract, trust or other equitable obligation. That this category does not include the equitable wrong of dishonest assistance in a breach of trust appears to be solely, or at least largely, a result of history, arising from the English legal system's division into law and equity.[4] Why should this wrong be seen as different in kind from the torts of deceit or inducing breach of a contract? Equity employs rules, techniques and remedies unknown to the common law but the reason for the division between law and equity is an historical one. Consequently "equity can be described but not defined".[5]

[1] See Birks, *An Introduction to the Law of Restitution*, revised edn (1989), 73–4.

[2] Although a theory is necessary to tell us who is an employee or a consumer.

[3] "Wrong" is here used in the sense "breach of duty".

[4] Sir L. Hoffmann, "The Redundancy of Knowing Assistance", in Birks (ed), *The Frontiers of Liability*, vol 1 (1994), 27; Birks, "Civil Wrongs—A New World" in *Butterworths Lectures 1990–1991*, 73, at pp. 98–109; *Salmond & Heuston on Torts*, 21st edn (1996), 12; cf. Davies, "Restitution and Equitable Wrongs", in Rose (ed) *Consensus ad Idem (Essays on the Law of Contract in Honour of Guenter Treitel)* (1996), 156 at 176.

[5] Meagher, Cummow and Lehane, *Equity Doctrines and Remedies*, 3rd edn, 3.

Categories can also overlap without our being overly concerned. If part of the law of property forms part of the law of restitution and *vice versa* this should be no more alarming than the fact that the category of "mammals" overlaps, but is not co-extensive, with the category "animals that live in the sea".

Restitution's claim to exist as a separate category[6] in English law cannot be based on its historical provenance, encompassing as it purports to do areas traditionally seen as distinct: e.g. the action for money had and received and some constructive trusts. Its sole justification to exist as a separate legal classification is that it is a conceptually unified and distinct area. If restitution really is made up of "20 or more heads of liability . . . [without] much in common with one another",[7] this does not affect the individual importance of each head of liability, but it does destroy the claim that they should be treated together.

English law can, and does, adopt different characterisations of legal issues for different purposes. For example, English private international law does not divide the law of property along the (historical) lines of personalty and realty which English domestic law employs, but rather adopts the (conceptual) categories of movable and immovable property. That restitution should be seen as a separate legal category for one purpose does not mean, therefore, that it should necessarily be seen as a distinct category for all purposes. However, without some means of telling when liability is restitutionary and when it is not, it could not sensibly be treated as a separate category for any purpose at all.[8]

The tort of negligence can be divided into a series of questions: Was there a duty of care? Was the duty breached? Did the breach cause the defendant loss? Was the loss too remote? Is there any defence? No one could pretend, however, that this simple structure provides answers to all the questions that can arise: it merely provides a framework for thought. Similarly too much should not be claimed for the division of the law of restitution into a four-stage enquiry: Was the defendant enriched? Was the enrichment unjustified? Was the enrichment at the plaintiff's expense? Is there any defence? The adoption of a different theoretical framework, or indeed no framework at all, may not lead to different results in all or even the majority of cases. Some disparate examples, by no means exhaustive, of the practical significance of concluding

[6] Several commentators have argued that restitutionary liability may arise for two distinct reasons: Birks, *An Introduction to the Law of Restitution*, revised edn (1989), 40–4, 313–15; Burrows, *The Law of Restitution* (1993), 16–21; cf. Beatson "The Nature of Waiver of Tort", in *The Use and Abuse of Unjust Enrichment* (1991), 206–43. A defendant may be under an obligation to disgorge a gain made due to his wrongdoing. Alternatively, a defendant's obligation to return a gain received from the plaintiff may arise independently of any wrongdoing on his part. Only in the latter case is it appropriate to talk of unjustified enrichment as an independent source of obligations. Whilst potentially extremely important, this distinction will not be discussed further.

[7] Hedley, *supra*, p 251.

[8] Atiyah, *The Rise and Fall of Freedom of Contract* (1979), 768–70.

that there is no method for determining when liability is restitutionary may, however, be given.

## Change of Position

The defence of contributory negligence is generally thought not currently to apply to purely contractual actions.[9] This is one reason why it is important to be able to distinguish between purely contractual claims and those which could be based upon a tort. A similar problem arises in relation to defences which are specific to claims based upon unjustified enrichment.

The fourth element of the unjustified enrichment enquiry is, perhaps, the least thoroughly examined. Some defences are common to all causes of action. For example, all claims are susceptible to the defences of estoppel[10] or *res judicata*. If there are or should be defences which are specific to claims based upon unjustified enrichment, it is necessary to have some method for identifying which claims these are. The most important defence which is specific to such claims is that of change of position.[11] It is no coincidence that the recognition in England of the defence of change of position in *Lipkin Gorman* v. *Karpnale Ltd*[12] coincided with the clearest judicial recognition so far of a coherent body of law concerned with the reversal of unjustified enrichment at the expense of another. The rationale for the defence of change of position is to protect the defendant's security of receipt. The defendant asserts that he is no longer enriched and should therefore no longer be required to make restitution. Frequently, whether a claim is based upon unjustified enrichment will be obvious. The recovery of money paid under a mistake of fact, for example, is often seen as a paradigm instance of restitution. The position is not always that easy however. Should proprietary claims contingent upon a tracing exercise be characterised as restitutionary?[13] Are all constructive trusts, some of them, or

[9] *Forsikringsaktieselskapet Vesta* v. *Butcher* [1989] AC 852; *Barclays Bank Plc* v. *Fairclough Building Ltd* [1995] QB 214; Treitel, *The Law of Contract*, 9th edn (1995), 887; cf. Burrows, *Remedies for Torts and Breach of Contract*, 2nd edn (1994), 85–7.

[10] Although it has been suggested that claims based upon unjustified enrichment should not be subject to the defence of estoppel: *R.B.C. Dominion Securities* v. *Dawson* (1994) 111 DLR (4th) 230; Burrows, *The Law of Restitution* (1993), 438. If this suggestion were to be adopted it would provide another reason why it is necessary to be able to ascertain whether a claim is so based or not.

[11] Other potential defences which may be peculiar to unjustified enrichment include passing on, ministerial receipt and counter restitution impossible. The existence of each has been doubted: see *Kleinwort Benson Ltd* v. *South Tyneside BC* [1994] 4 All ER 972, 984–6; *Kleinwort Benson Ltd* v. *Birmingham City Council* [1996] 3 WLR 1139 (passing on); Birks, "Overview Tracing, Claiming and Defences" in Birks (ed), *Laundering and Tracing* (1995) 341–7 (ministerial receipt); Burrows, *The Law of Restitution* (1993), 132–6, 313–15 (counter-restitution impossible).

[12] [1991] 2 AC 549.

[13] cf. Matthews, "The Legal and Moral Limits of Common Law Tracing" and Birks, "Overview Tracing, Claiming and Defences", both in Birks (ed) *Laundering and Tracing* (1995), 23–71, 317–19.

none of them based upon unjustified enrichment?[14] Similarly is rescission of a contract always, sometimes or never restitutionary?[15]

It might be argued that the common law managed for a considerable time without a generalised defence of change of position and that its recognition is a mistake.[16] This may or may not be true but it is an inescapable conclusion if there is no method for distinguishing between claims based upon unjustified enrichment and other species of action.

## Limitation Periods

Broadly speaking, an action founded on a tort or a contract must be brought within six years of the accrual of the cause of action.[17] There are of course exceptions to these rules, in the context of defamation or latent damage, for example. As the time of accrual of a cause of action in tort or contract are not necessarily the same, it is important to know whether a claim should be characterised as contractual, tortious or both concurrently.[18]

There is no statutory limitation period specifically applicable to all claims based upon unjustified enrichment. Unsurprisingly the courts have not reached the conclusion that no limitation period applies to such claims. One technique has been to interpret the Limitation Act 1980 in a "somewhat cavalier fashion"[19] so that, for example, the action for money had and received is within the category of actions "founded on a simple contract" within section 5 of the Limitation Act 1980.[20] This might be taken as some evidence that it is not currently necessary to differentiate restitutionary liability from other species of liability for purposes of limitation. However, this is probably incorrect. Different limitation periods currently apply to contractual damages, tortious damages and liability to make restitution due to the differences between when the causes of action accrue: generally at the times of breach, damage and unjustified enrichment respectively. The different times for accrual are due to the different underlying rationales for the existence of liability.[21]

[14] cf. *Hussey* v. *Palmer* [1972] 1 WLR 1286, 1289–90; *Carl Zeiss Stiftung* v. *Herbert Smith (No 2)* [1969] 2 Ch 276, 301; *Muschinskiu* v. *Dodds* (1984) 160 CLR 583; *Baumgartner* v. *Baumgartner* (1987) 164 CLR 137; A.W. Scott, "Constructive Trusts" (1955) 71 *LQR* 39, 41; W.F. Fratcher (ed), *Scott on Trusts*, 4th edn (1989), vol V, §462–1; Burrows, *The Law of Restitution* (1993), 39; Birks, *An Introduction to the Law of Restitution* (revised edn (1989), 88–9; Elias, *Explaining Constructive Trusts* (1990), esp 1–7, 48–85; Hayton, "Constructive Trusts: Is the Remedying of Unjust Enrichment a Satisfactory Approach?" in Youden (ed), *Equity, Fiduciaries and Trusts* (1989), 105 at p. 210; Martin, *Hanbury & Martin's Modern Equity*, 14th edn (1993), 286.

[15] Burrows, *The Law of Restitution* (1993), 31–5; Birks, "Overview Tracing, Claiming and Defences", in Birks (ed) *Laundering and Tracing*, 327.

[16] Hedley "Unjust Enrichment" [1995] *CLJ* 578, 585.

[17] Limitation Act 1980, ss 2 and 5.

[18] *Henderson* v. *Merrett Syndicates Ltd* [1995] 2 AC 145.

[19] Goff and Jones, *The Law of Restitution*, 4th edn (1993), 765.

[20] *Westdeutsche Landesbank* v. *Islington LBC* [1994] 4 All ER 890, 940.

[21] The point at which a cause of action arises also determines from when interest may be awarded under the Supreme Court Act 1981, s 35A.

Furthermore, it is not unarguable that restitutionary liability should be subject to its own rules. Should, for example, limitation periods run from the time of the receipt of the benefit or the accrual of the cause of action, where different? That rescission may be barred by lapse of time provides one instance where a potentially restitutionary liability is barred by a passage of time commencing prior to the accrual of the obligation to make restitution. Should time run against a plaintiff who is not or could not be aware of his claim for restitution? Does the defence of change of position justify a longer limitation period than the six years applicable to other claims? It may well be that Professor Burrows is correct to suggest that: "The law on limitation as a defence to restitution is ripe for statutory reform. It cannot be sensible for there to be no provision in the 1980 Act expressly dealing with restitutionary claims."[22]

**The Conflict of Laws**

The rules which have been developed to determine whether a court has jurisdiction to hear a particular claim and which law is to be applied if it has jurisdiction, are expressed in terms of legal categories.[23] Some issues of characterisation are only relevant in the context of the conflict of laws. Should, for example, the court adopt the characterisation of the domestic law of the forum or of the applicable foreign law? The answers to these questions are beyond the scope of this comment.

Since the sixth edition published in 1949, Dicey's *The Conflict of Laws*[24] has had a separate rule for determining the law applicable to restitutionary obligations. The judicial authority for a unified choice of law rule applicable to all restitutionary obligations is usually considered to be scanty.[25] It could be that several different rules apply to such obligations, and some support for this might be gathered from the fact that *Dicey and Morris*[26] treats restitutionary obligations arising in connection with a contract as governed by the law applicable to the contract. Indeed in *Macmillan* v. *Bishopsgate Investment Trust*[27] Auld LJ expressed the view that "the concept of a 'receipt based' restitutionary claim would not . . . provide a firm basis in the circumstances of this case for identifying [the law governing the dispute]". The Court of Appeal's conclusion that it is necessary to characterise the issue in dispute and that more than one system of law may determine the outcome of a claim which may or may not be characterised as restitutionary, might be used in

22 Burrows, *The Law of Restitution* (1993), 450.

23 L. Collins (ed), *Dicey & Morris on The Conflict of Laws*, 12th edn (1993), 34.

24 The first edition edited by John Morris. Kurt Lipstein edited the chapter on "quasi-contract".

25 *Arab Monetary Fund* v. *Hashim* [1993] 1 Lloyd's Rep 543, 566 (Evans J); *affirmed* [1996] 1 Lloyd's Rep. 543; *Baring Bros & Co Ltd* v. *Cunninghame District Council* 1996 GWD 25–1045.

26 L. Collins (ed), *Dicey & Morris on The Conflict of Laws*, 12th edn (1993), Rule 201.

27 [1996] 1 WLR 387, 396.

support of the argument that the search for a generalised choice of law rule applicable to all claims based upon unjustified enrichment is a mistake.[28] Without any method for distinguishing restitution from other categories, it is certainly a fool's errand.

In civil and commercial matters, the Civil Jurisdiction and Judgments Act 1982, which enacts the Brussels Convention on Jurisdiction and the Enforcement of Judgments in Civil and Commercial Matters 1968, provides a scheme for allocating jurisdiction between the courts of the contracting states when the defendant is domiciled within one of them. The primary[29] rule is that jurisdiction is vested in the courts of the state where the defendant is domiciled.[30] In matters relating to contract, tort, delict and quasi-delict there are rules whereby a court may have special jurisdiction despite not being the court of the state where the defendant is domiciled. No specific rules apply to claims based upon unjustified enrichment. It may be doubted whether this actually reflects the relative importance attached to claims based upon unjustified enrichment by the domestic legal systems of those who drafted the Convention. Rather, it may simply demonstrate that there is no compelling reason why special jurisdictional rules are required for such claims.[31]

Outside the Brussels Convention, the High Court has a discretion to entertain an action under Order 11 of the Rules of the Supreme Court against a defendant who is not in England at the time for the service of the writ. The discretion is only exercisable if the plaintiff's action falls within one of the heads of jurisdiction contained in Order 11. Whilst specific heads of jurisdiction exist for contract and tort, no such all-embracing rule exists for claims based upon unjustified enrichment. Some such claims are clearly covered (e.g. money had and received and constructive trusts under RSC Ord 11 r1(1)(t)) whilst others have to be included by a "liberal" interpretation of the statutory language (e.g. contract interpreted to include quasi-contract[32]). Some instances of claims based upon unjustified enrichment are probably incapable of being shoe-horned into one of the specific rules that exist, leading to the potentially unfortunate result that service out of the jurisdiction can never be obtained in relation to that type of claim. Whether a specific rule for restitution is possible depends upon whether it is possible to identify which obligations are restitutionary and which are not. Whether it is actually desirable may be more difficult to answer. Are claims based upon unjustified enrichment potentially so diverse that a single rule which purports to be applicable to all of them would, inevitably, be inappropriate?

[28] Cf. Rose (ed), *Restitution and the Conflict of Laws* (1995), Ch 3 (Bird) and Ch 5 (Stevens).

[29] *Kalfelis* v. *Schroder* [1988] ECR 5565, para. 19.

[30] Article 2.

[31] cf. Briggs [1992] *LMCLQ* 283; Peel, in Rose (ed), *Restitution and the Conflict of Laws* (1995), Ch 1, at p. 20.

[32] *Bowling* v. *Cox* [1926] AC 75; *Rousou's (A Bankrupt) Trustee* v. *Rousou* [1955] 1 WLR 545, application to set aside dismissed; *Trustee of Rousou (A Bankrupt)* v. *Rousou* [1955] 3 All ER 486; *Re Jogia* [1988] 1 WLR 484.

**Remedial Responses**

The conceptual basis of a claim inevitably affects the most appropriate remedial response the court should adopt. If the reason that contracts are enforced is that promises which have been paid for ought to be kept, then the court's most appropriate or usual remedial response to a refusal to perform is, presumably, to enforce the promise or, if this is impossible or inappropriate, a monetary remedy which is the nearest approximation to enforcement of the promise. If, by contrast, restitutionary obligations are concerned with the unjustified enrichment of the defendant at the plaintiff's expense, one would expect the court's remedial response to be to reverse the gain made by the defendant and not, say, to compensate the plaintiff for any expenses he may have incurred. It is probably true that a remedial response may be adopted as a surrogate for another one, as a "next best", perhaps because of the difficulty of proof of the preferred measure: a point most famously made by Fuller and Perdue.[33] In general, however, the remedial response adopted should seek to reflect the underlying reason(s) for the imposition of the obligation.

Liability may arise for more than one reason. If this were not true there would never be concurrent liability. It may also be argued that obligations never arise for one reason alone. The ideas of unjustified enrichment, injurious reliance and promise-keeping, for example, may all have some role to play throughout the law of obligations. If this is correct, one would tend to expect the courts to adopt a fluid remedial response and not, for example, to treat expectation damages as the normal measure of loss in the law of contract.

There are instances where the courts have not consistently adopted one remedial response in preference to another. In the context of proprietary estoppel, where the plaintiff has done some work on the defendant's land due to the expectations induced by the defendant, the plaintiff has, at various times, been awarded his reliance expenditure,[34] his proprietary expectation[35] and the disgorgement of the enhancement in value of the defendant's property.[36] One view would be that this flexibility is to be welcomed as demonstrating the courts adopting a pragmatic approach to a difficult situation. Alternatively, it could be argued that the uncertainty leads to inconsistency and litigation.

**Pedagogy**

If unjustified enrichment could not be differentiated from other sources of liability we might expect this to influence the courses taught and the books

[33] Fuller and Perdue, "The Reliance Interest in Contact Damages" [1936] 52 YLJ 52, 66–71.
[34] *Dodsworth* v. *Dodsworth* [1973] EG 1115.
[35] *Re Basham* [1986] 1 WLR 1498.
[36] *Van den Berg* v. *Giles* [1979] 2 NZLR 111.

written. That the English and Commonwealth markets for writings on the law of restitution is "approaching saturation point"[37] is partially a result of the attraction to academics of the relatively straightforward conceptual structure proposed by Professor Birks. The conceptual categories we adopt are not, however, co-extensive with those we use for pedagogical purposes. Indeed they are usually not particularly significant. This is obviously true of contextual subjects such as labour law, consumer law or computer law. Even in relation to subjects traditionally justified by their conceptual coherence, no topic can properly be understood without a grasp of the surrounding area: "an enormous hole would exist in a student's grasp of contract law if he knew nothing about restitutionary remedies arising from breach or frustration or part performance".[38]

## The Western Legal Tradition

The conceptual classifications we adopt are not inevitable and immutable, although one method of classification may be better than another. Professor Zimmerman has argued that "England in reality was never completely cut off from continental legal culture"[39] and that the English and civilian "way of thinking about law has been decisively moulded by the Roman lawyers".[40] In particular Roman law is our common source for "the contract-delict dichotomy; unjustified enrichment as an independent source of liability; the concept of a consensual contract; [and] even the basic notion of an obligation".[41] Whether meaningful comparative legal lessons can be learnt from other European legal systems turns, to an extent, upon whether we adopt the same or similar legal classifications. Indeed, our common inheritance from Roman law also "provides the intellectual and doctrinal framework within which a new European legal unity may one day emerge".[42] Sensible people may disagree as to whether or not such a goal is desirable, but whether it is possible turns upon whether we share a common legal taxonomy.

## Conclusion

If we are to treat like cases alike and different cases differently the legal categories we adopt are, inevitably, of practical significance. No lawyer can get by all the time without needing to think about the particular classification of

[37] McKendrick (1996) 112 *LQR* 689.
[38] Atiyah, *Essays on Contract* (1986), 50.
[39] Zimmerman, *The Law of Obligations: Roman Foundations of the Civilian Tradition* (1990), xi.
[40] *Ibid.*, viii.
[41] *Ibid.*, viii.
[42] *Ibid.*, x.

the legal issue they are dealing with. If the "all-embracing four part model proposed for restitution" is not to be adopted, different better classifications must be used.[43]

[43] Consider Hedley "Contract, Tort and Restitution; or On Cutting the Legal System Down to Size" [1988] *LS* 147, 150–71.

# *The Publications of Sir Guenter Treitel 1951–1996*

BOOKS

| | |
|---|---|
| 1961 | *The Law of Contract* (Stevens & Sons, London, 1962), lvii and 641 pp. |
| 1966 | *The Law of Contract*, 2nd ed. (Stevens & Sons, London, 1966), lxi and 708 pp. |
| 1970 | *The Law of Contract*, 3rd ed. (Stevens & Sons, London, 1970), lxxi and 864 pp. |
| 1975 | *The Law of Contract*, 4th ed. (Stevens & Sons, London, 1975), lix and 706 pp. |
| | *An Outline of the Law of Contract* (Butterworths, London, 1975), xxiv and 368 pp. |
| 1979 | *An Outline of the Law of Contract*, 2nd ed. (Butterworths, London, 1979), xlv and 370 pp. |
| | *The Law of Contract*, 5th ed. (Stevens & Sons, London, 1979), lxii and 782 pp. |
| 1983 | *The Law of Contract*, 6th ed. (Stevens & Sons, London, 1983), lxii and 794 pp. |
| 1984 | *An Outline of the Law of Contract*, 3rd ed. (Butterworths, London, 1984), xlix and 350 pp. |
| 1987 | *The Law of Contract*, 7th ed. (Stevens & Sons, London, 1987), lxxxvii and 815 pp. |
| 1988 | *Remedies for Breach of Contract: A Comparative Account* (Clarendon Press, Oxford) (1988); paperback (1991), 409 and lvi pp. |
| 1989 | *An Outline of the Law of Contract*, 4th ed. (Butterworths, London, 1989), lx and 364 pp. |
| 1991 | *Unmöglichkeit, "Impracticability" und "Frustration" im anglo-amerikanischen Recht* [Schriften der Ernst von Caemmerer-Gedächtnisstiftung, Band 1] (1991), x and 151 pp. |
| | *The Law of Contract*, 8th ed. (Sweet & Maxwell/Stevens & Sons, London, 1991), cix and 937 pp. |
| 1994 | *Frustration and Force Majeure* (Sweet & Maxwell Ltd, London, 1994), lxxxi and 584 pp. |
| 1995 | *An Outline of the Law of Contract*, 5th ed. (Butterworths, London, 1995), xli and 404 pp. |
| | *The Law of Contract*, 9th ed. (Sweet & Maxwell Ltd, London, 1995), cxiv and 954 pp. |

CONTRIBUTIONS TO BOOKS

1958 (Ed.) Ch. 6 "Domicile" (pp. 85–126), Ch. 14 "Lunatics" (pp. 409–417), Ch. 32 "Substance and Procedure" (pp. 1087–1106), Ch. 33 "Proof of Foreign Law" (pp. 1107–1116), of J.H.C. Morris (Gen. Ed.), *Dicey's Conflict of Laws*, 7th ed. (Stevens & Sons Ltd, London, 1958).

1959 "Les Infractions Sexuelles", Ch. IV of M. Ancel and L. Radzinowicz, *Introduction au Droit Criminel de l'Angleterre* (Les Editions de L'Epargne, Paris, 1959), 135–156.

1966 "Contract". Ch. 6 of H.W.R. Wade (ed.), *Annual Survey of Commonwealth Law 1965* (Butterworths, London, 1966), 240–284.

1967 "Contract". Ch. 6 of H.W.R. Wade (ed.), *Annual Survey of Commonwealth Law 1966* (Butterworths, London, 1967), 261–312.

(Ed.) Ch. 6 "Domicile" (pp. 78–120), Ch. 16 "Lunatics" (pp. 409–414), Ch. 34 "Substance and Procedure" (pp. 1089–1109), Ch. 35 "Proof of Foreign Law" (pp. 1110–1119), of J.H.C. Morris (Gen. Ed.), *Dicey & Morris on the Conflict of Laws*, 8th ed. (Stevens & Sons Ltd, London, 1967) (with Supplement 1968).

1968 (Ed.) Vol. I: Ch. 2 "The Agreement" (pp. 21–49), Ch. 3 "Consideration" (pp. 50–76), Ch. 4 "Form" (pp. 77–92), Ch. 10 "The Crown and Public Authorities" (pp. 246–258), Ch. 17 "Privity" (pp. 453–468), Ch. 27 "Specific Performance and Injunction" (pp. 709–729); Vol. II: Ch. 6 "Gaming and Wagering" (pp. 393–409) of A.G. Guest (Gen. Ed.), *Chitty on Contracts*, 23rd edn. (Sweet & Maxwell, London, 1968) (with 6 Supplements 1970–1975)

1969 "Contract". Ch. 6 of H.W.R. Wade (ed.), *Annual Survey of Commonwealth Law 1968* (Butterworths, London, 1969), 321–374.

1971 "Contract". Ch. 17 of H.W.R. Wade (ed.), *Annual Survey of Commonwealth Law 1970* (Butterworths, London, 1971), 537–576.

1974 Ch. 18 "Overseas Sales in General" (pp. 687–765), Ch. 19 "C.i.f. Contracts" (pp. 766–849), Ch. 20 "F.o.b. Contracts" (pp. 850–911), Ch. 21 "Other Special Terms and Provisions in International Sales" (pp. 912–957) of A.G. Guest (Gen. Ed.), *Benjamin's Sale of Goods* (Sweet & Maxwell, London, 1974).

1976 "Remedies for Breach of Contract (Courses of Action Open to a Party Aggrieved)". Ch. 16 of Arthur von Mehren (chief ed.), *International Encyclopedia of Comparative Law*: Vol. VII: *Contracts in General* (J.C.B. Mohr (Paul Siebeck), Tübingen, and Mouton, The Hague, 1976), 185 pp.

1977 (Ed.) Vol. I: Ch. 2 "The Agreement" (pp. 21–62), Ch. 3 "Consideration" (pp. 63–108), Ch. 18 "Privity" (pp. 512–536), Ch. 27 "Specific Performance and Injunction" (pp. 774–801); Vol. II: Ch. 8 "Gaming and Wagering" (pp. 662–685) of A.G. Guest (Gen. Ed.), *Chitty on Contracts*, 24th ed. (Sweet & Maxwell, London, 1977), (with Supplement 1979).

1981 "Contract and Crime". Ch. 5 of C.F.H. Tapper (ed.), *Crime, Proof and Punishment (Essays in Memory of Sir Rupert Cross)* (Butterworths, London, 1981), pp. 81–108.

Ch. 18 "Overseas Sales in General" (pp. 759–854), Ch. 19 "C.i.f.

Contracts" (pp. 855–954), Ch. 20 "F.o.b. Contracts" (pp. 95–1021), Ch. 21 "Other Special Terms and Provisions in International Sales" (pp. 1022–1076) of A.G. Guest (Gen. Ed.), *Benjamin's Sale of Goods*, 2nd ed. (Sweet & Maxwell, London, 1981).

1983 (Ed.) Vol. I: Ch. 2 "The Agreement" (pp. 25–78), Ch. 3 "Consideration" (pp. 79–156), Ch. 18 "Privity" (pp. 662–691), Ch. 27 "Specific Performance and Injunction" (pp. 977–1011); Vol. II: Ch. 8 "Gaming and Wagering" (pp. 781–806) of A.G. Guest (Gen. Ed.), *Chitty on Contracts*, 25th ed. (Sweet & Maxwell, London, 1983) (with Supplement 1986).

1986 "Barry Nicholas". In Peter Birks (ed.), *New Perspectives in the Roman Law of Property (Essays for Barry Nicholas)* (Clarendon Press, Oxford, 1986), pp. 1–3.

1987 "Fault in the Common Law of Contract". Ch. 11 of Marten Bos and Ian Brownlie (eds), *Liber Amicorum for the Rt. Hon. Lord Wilberforce, PC, CMG, OBE, QC* (Clarendon Press, Oxford, 1987), pp. 185–210.

Ch. 18 "Overseas Sales in General" (pp. 889–1020), Ch. 19 "C.i.f. Contracts" (pp. 1021–1156), Ch. 20 "F.o.b. Contracts" (pp. 1157–1234), Ch. 21 "Other Special Terms and Provisions in International Sales" (pp. 1235–1297) of A.G. Guest (Gen. Ed.), *Benjamin's Sale of Goods*, 3rd ed. (Sweet & Maxwell, London, 1987).

1989 (Ed.) Vol. I: Ch. 2 "The Agreement" (pp. 33–103), Ch. 3 "Consideration" (pp. 105–199), Ch. 18 "Privity" (pp. 817–861), Ch. 27 "Specific Performance and Injunction" (pp. 1201–1241); Vol. II: Ch. 8 "Gaming and Wagering" (pp. 885–916) of A.G. Guest (Gen. Ed.), *Chitty on Contracts*, 26th ed. (Sweet & Maxwell, London, 1989).

1992 Ch. 18 "Overseas Sales in General" (pp. 917–1071), Ch. 19 "C.i.f. Contracts" (pp. 1072–1222), Ch. 20 "F.o.b. Contracts" (pp. 1223–1309), Ch. 21 "Other Special Terms and Provisions in International Sales" (pp. 1310–1374) of A.G. Guest (ed.), *Benjamin's Sale of Goods*, 4th ed. (Sweet & Maxwell, London, 1992).

1994 Vol. I: Ch. 2 "The Agreement" (pp. 89–163), Ch. 3 "Consideration" (pp. 165–262), Ch. 18 "Privity" (pp. 901–952), Ch. 27 "Specific Performance and Injunction" (pp. 1281–1321); Vol. II: Ch. 38 "Gaming and Wagering" (pp. 851–883) of A.G. Guest (Gen. Ed.), *Chitty on Contracts*, 27th ed. (Sweet & Maxwell, London, 1994).

1995 "Alternatives and Frustration". Ch. 15 of J. Beatson and D. Friedmann (eds), *Good Faith and Fault in Contract Law* (Clarendon Press, Oxford, 1995), pp. 377–296.

## PAMPHLET

1981 "Doctrine and Discretion in the Law of Contract" (An Inaugural Lecture delivered before the University of Oxford on 7 March 1980) (Clarendon Press, Oxford, 1981), 31 pp.

PAPERS

| | |
|---|---|
| 1951 | "The Standard of Proof of Adultery and Cruelty in Divorce Proceedings" (1951) 14 M.L.R. 225–230. |
| | "Two Highway Accidents" (1951) 14 M.L.R. 347–352. |
| 1952 | "The Nature of Trespass" (1952) 15 M.L.R. 84–85. |
| | "Covenants in Restraint of Trade and the Health Service" (1952) 15 M.L.R. 364–367. |
| 1953 | "The Straffen Case" (1953) 16 M.L.R. 74–79. |
| | "The Doctrine of Ultra Vires in English Company Law" [1953 April] *Journal of the British Chamber of Commerce in Belgium* 41–42. |
| | "The Coronation Cases" [1953 May] *Journal of the British Chamber of Commerce in Belgium* 26–27. |
| | "Contracts by Unformed Companies" [1953 June] *Journal of the British Chamber of Commerce in Belgium* 24–25. |
| | "Foreign Confiscatory Decrees" [1953 July] *Journal of the British Chamber of Commerce in Belgium* 21–22. |
| | "The Proper Law of a Contract" [1953 August] *Journal of the British Chamber of Commerce in Belgium* 21–22. |
| | "The Formation of Contracts" [1953 September] *Journal of the British Chamber of Commerce in Belgium* 21–22. |
| | "The Deserted Wife's Right to Pledge Her Husband's Credit for Necessaries" (1953) 16 M.L.R. 221–225. |
| | "Liability for the Acts of an Agent" (1953) 16 M.L.R. 378–379. |
| 1954 | "Agency of Necessity" (1954) 3 U.W.A.L.R. 1–12. |
| | "Nervous Shock and Homicide" (1954) 70 L.Q.R. 168–169. |
| | "The Liability of Requisitioning Authorities for Defective Premises" (1954) 17 M.L.R. 464–467. |
| | "The Presumption of Death" (1954) 17 M.L.R. 530–546. |
| 1955 | "Exemption Clauses and Third Parties" (1955) 18 M.L.R. 172–177. |
| 1957 | "The Infants Relief Act, 1874" (1957) 73 L.Q.R. 194–211. |
| | "Crown Proceedings: Some Recent Developments" [1957] *Public Law* 321–339. |
| 1958 | "The Infants Relief Act, 1874—A Short Rebutter" (1958) 74 L.Q.R. 104–107. |
| | "Limited Interests in Chattels" (1958) 21 M.L.R. 433–438. |
| | "The Law and Restraint of Trade" (1958) 60 *The Listener* 823–825. |
| 1960 | "Exemption Clauses and Third Parties" (1960) 64 *The Listener* 510–511. |
| 1961 | "Mutuality in Contract" (1961) 77 L.Q.R. 83–97. |
| 1965 | (with F. M. B. Reynolds) "Consideration for the Modification of Contracts" (1965) 7 Malaya L.R. 1–23. |
| | "Is Malice Infectious?" (1965) 73 *The Listener* 589–591. |
| | "An English Visitor's View of The Law School" (1965 Winter) 13(l) *The University of Chicago: The Law School Record* 27–28. |
| 1966 | "Specific Performance in the Sale of Goods" [1966] J.B.L. 211–231. |
| | "Memoirs of an Infant" (1966) 76 *The Listener* 344–346. |
| | "Fundamental Breach" (1966) 29 M.L.R. 546–556. |

"Law Reform in the Court of Appeal" (1966) 29 M.L.R. 657–665.
1967 "Exclusion Clauses: Possible Reforms" [1967] J.B.L. 200–209, 334–345.
"Some Problems of Breach of Contract" (1967) 30 M.L.R. 139–155.
(with P.S. Atiyah) "Misrepresentation Act 1967" (1967) 30 M.L.R. 369–388.
"Specific Performance and Third Parties" (1967) 30 M.L.R. 687–693.
1968 "Trade Descriptions Act 1968" (1968) 31 M.L.R. 662–668.
1969 "Damages for Deceit" (1969) 32 M.L.R. 556–563.
1976 "Consideration: A Critical Analysis of Professor Atiyah's Fundamental Restatement" (1976) 50 A.L.J.R. 439–449.
1978 "The English Law Commission: Its Work in the Law of Contract" (1978) II(1) *Albertus Magnus* 4–7.
1984 "Jane Austen and the Law" (1984) 100 L.Q.R. 549–586.
"Rights of Rejection under C.I.F. Sales" [1984] L.M.C.L.Q. 565–577.
1986 "Bills of Lading and Third Parties" [1986] L.M.C.L.Q. 294–305.
1986–87 "Legal Puzzles in Jane Austen's Works"
[1986] *Jane Austen Society Annual Report* 45–57
and [1987] *Magdalen College Record* 52–64.
1987 "Damages on Rescission for Breach of Contract" [1987] L.M.C.L.Q. 143–146.
1988 "Mistake in Contract" (1988) 104 L.Q.R. 501–507.
"Damages for Breach of a C.I.F. Contract" [1988] L.M.C.L.Q. 457–465.
1989 "Bills of Lading and Implied Contracts" [1989] L.M.C.L.Q. 162–173.
1990 "Passing of Property under C.I.F. Contracts and the Bills of Lading Act 1855" [1990] L.M.C.L.Q. 1–4.
" 'Conditions' and 'Conditions Precedent' " (1990) 106 L.Q.R. 185–192.
1991 "Time of Shipment in F.O.B. Contracts" [1991] L.M.C.L.Q. 147–154.
"Damages for Non-Delivery" (1991) 107 L.Q.R. 364–366.
1992 "Damages for Breach of Contract in the High Court of Australia" (1992) 108 L.Q.R. 226–235.

## ANNOTATIONS OF STATUTES

1967 "Misrepresentation Act 1967" [1967] *Current Law Statutes* c.7 (6 pp.).
1968 "Trade Descriptions Act 1968" [1968] *Current Law* Statutes c.29 (38 pp.).

## BOOK REVIEWS

1954 I. S. Pawate, *Contract and the Freedom of the Debtor in the Common Law* [1953] (1954) 70 L.Q.R. 575–577.
1956 B. Chedlow (ed.), *Chitty's Mercantile Contracts* [1955] (1956) 72 L.Q.R. 299.
H.R. Gray, *The Law of Civil Injuries* [1955] (1956) 19 M.L.R. 326–327.
1958 O. Hood Phillips, *Constitutional Law*, 2nd ed. (1957) and *Leading Cases in Constitutional Law*, 3rd ed. (1957) [1958] P.L. 315–316.

| | |
|---|---|
| | J.F. Wilson, *Principles of the Law of Contract* [1957] (1958) 74 L.Q.R. 594–597. |
| | J.C. Smith and J.A.C. Thomas, *A Casebook on Contract* [1957] (1958) 74 L.Q.R. 597–599. |
| 1960 | *Dicey's Introduction to the Study of the Law of the Constitution*, 10th ed. with Introduction by E.C.S. Wade [1959] (1960) 76 L.Q.R. 595–598. |
| 1962 | E.C.S. Wade (ed.), E.C.S. Wade and G. Godfrey Phillips, *Constitutional Law*, 6th ed. [1960] (1962) L.Q.R. 123–124. |
| 1963 | I. Zamir, *The Declaratory Judgment* [1962] (1963) 79 L.Q.R. 270–272. |
| | O. Hood Phillips, *Constitutional and Administrative Law*, 3rd ed. (1962) [1963] P.L. 267–268. |
| 1964 | B. Coote, *Exception Clauses* [1964] (1965) 8 J.S.P.T.L. 121–123. |
| 1966 | L.M. Friedman, *Contract Law in America: A Social and Economic Case Study* [1965] (1966) 33 U of Chicago L.R. 418–425. |
| 1968 | G.H.L. Fridman, *The Law of Agency*, 2nd ed. (1966) [1968] C.L.J. 156–158. |
| 1969 | J.F. Garner, *Administrative Law*, 2nd ed. (1967) [1969] P.L. 185–188. |

## PERSONALIA

| | |
|---|---|
| 1981 | "Obituary—Sir Rupert Cross" (1981) 1 L.S. 115–116. |
| 1984 | "In Memoriam: Dr J.H.C. Morris" (1984) 55 B.Y.I.L. ix–xiv. |
| | "Master John Morris, Q.C., F.B.A., D.C.L. (1984) 88 *Graya* 41–42. |
| 1985 | "John Humphrey Carlisle Morris" [1985] *Magdalen College Record* 34–41. |

# Index

www.ingramcontent.com/pod-product-compliance
Ingram Content Group UK Ltd.
Pitfield, Milton Keynes, MK11 3LW, UK
UKHW020202290926
15471UKWH00005B/1024

9 781901 362046